RACE AND RACISM

RACE AND RACISM

CANADA'S CHALLENGE

Edited by

Leo Driedger and Shiva S. Halli

PUBLISHED FOR CARLETON UNIVERSITY
BY McGILL/QUEEN'S UNIVERSITY PRESS,
MONTREAL & KINGSTON/LONDON/ITHACA

ISBN 0-88629-365-0 (paper)

Printed and bound in Canada

Canadian Cataloguing in Publication Data

Main entry under title:

    Race and racism : Canada's challenge

Essays originally presented at a conference held in Winnipeg,
    Nov. 25-27, 1996.
Includes bibliographical references and index.
ISBN 0-88629-362-6 (bound) ISBN 0-88629-365-0 (pbk.)

    1. Canada—Race relations. 2. Racism—Canada.
I. Driedger, Leo, 1928- II. Halli, Shivalingappa S., 1952-

FC104.R311 2000   305.8'00971   C99-901509-5
F1035.A1R322 2000

Interior: Lynn's Desktop Publishing.

McGill-Queen's University Press acknowledges the financial support of the Government of Canada through the Book Publishing Industry Development Program (BPIDP) for our publishing activities. We also acknowledge the support of the Canada Council for the Arts for our publishing program.

CONTENTS

TABLES

FIGURES

PREFACE

TEN YEARS AGO, Halli, Trovato and Driedger invited the top demographers and ethnic scholars in Canada to a study conference in Winnipeg. The participants presented their papers, and many of these appeared in *Ethnic Demography*, published by Carleton University Press in 1990. As the editors stated in the preface, it was a first "volume combining the two fields of demography and ethnicity." The purpose was "to make available to students and policy-makers the latest data ... from the 1981 and 1986 censuses and recent surveys." This work has been widely used, and it went into a second printing.

In October of 1996 two of the same editors invited many of the same scholars, and others who have entered the field since, to again present 40 papers at a second study conference in Winnipeg. Fourteen of the forty papers have been edited, and are made available here in *Race and Racism*, using the latest census data, and especially the more qualitative research on race which has emerged in the last ten years. Most scholars who attended the conference agreed that discussions, the intellectual ferment, and excitement, spurred them on to greater research efforts in the future. The quality of the papers was high, so that fourteen more papers were edited, and have appeared in another book entitled *Immigrant Canada*, published by the University of Toronto Press.

American social science scholars have researched race and racism since the beginning of the century. This has not been the case in Canada, because the Canadian population, even as late as 1971, was 95 percent white. Since then, however, other more visible minorities, including aboriginals, have doubled their proportionate weight to 10 percent as of 1991. Estimates are that peoples of colour will again double to 20 percent of Canada's population by 2016, especially because of more open immigration laws. Thus, it is essential that we present the fourteen papers read at our study conference, which focused on race and racism.

Many have made this publication possible, including Heritage and Multiculturalism Canada; the Metropolis Project; James Gardner, Vice-President (Academic), Joanne Keselman, Vice-President (Research), and Raymond Currie, Dean of Arts, and Emoke Szathmary, President, all of the University of Manitoba; and the Prairie Centre of Excellence for Research on Immigration and Integration.

Several scholars who are working for federal agencies are concerned that we make it clear that the opinion expressed in their papers are not those of the government but their own. This proviso refers to work done by Sylvia Wargon, Monica Boyd, Gustave Goldman, Pamela White, Ravi B.P. Verma, Kwak Chang, T. John Samuel, and Aly Karam.

Darlene Driedger and Abdolmohammad Kazemipur have both contributed much to the processing of this work, for which we sincerely thank them.

Leo Driedger and Shiva S. Halli

CONTRIBUTORS

JOHN BERRY, Department of Psychology, Queen's University, Kingston, Ontario

MONICA BOYD, Center for Study of Population, Florida State University, Tallahassee, Florida

KWOK BUN CHAN, Department of Sociology, National University of Singapore, Singapore

LEO DRIEDGER, Department of Sociology, University of Manitoba, Winnipeg, Manitoba

GUSTAVE GOLDMAN, Demography Division, Statistics Canada, Ottawa, Ontario

SHIVA S. HALLI, Department of Sociology, University of Manitoba, Winnipeg, Manitoba

NANCY HIGGITT, Department of Family Studies, University of Manitoba, Winnipeg, Manitoba

RUDOLF KALIN, Department of Psychology, Queen's University, Kingston, Ontario

ALY KARAM, Carleton University, Ottawa, Ontario

HELEN RALSTON, Department of Sociology, Saint Mary's University, Halifax, Nova Scotia

ANGUS REID, Angus Reid Group, Vancouver, British Columbia

KAREN M. RUGGIERO, Harvard University, Cambridge, Massachusetts

T. JOHN SAMUEL, Ottawa, Ontario

JOSEPH O'SHEA, Montreal, Quebec

DONALD W. TAYLOR, Department of Psychology, McGill University, Montreal, Quebec

GUANG TIAN, Joint Centre for Asia-Pacific Studies, Toronto-York Universities, Toronto, Ontario

RAVI B.P. VERMA, Demographic Division Statistics Branch, Ottawa, Ontario

SYLVIA WARGON, Census and Demographic Statistics Branch, Ottawa, Ontario

PAMELA WHITE, Demography Division, Statistics Canada, Ottawa, Ontario

SIU KWONG WONG, Department of Sociology, Brandon University, Brandon, Manitoba

STEPHEN WRIGHT, University of California, Santa Cruz, California

I

THE RACE CHALLENGE 2000

LEO DRIEDGER AND SHIVA S. HALLI

THE TERRITORY NOW CALLED CANADA was originally occupied by diverse, plural groups of aboriginals. By 1867, the time of the confederation of four provinces, Ontario, Quebec, Nova Scotia and New Brunswick, Canadian censuses show that the British comprised almost two-thirds of the population of the federated territory and the French one-third, and that the Germans (who likewise were north Europeans), were the third largest group. The aboriginals were not counted in the vast stretches of space north and west of this tiny new nation, known as the Northwest Territories. The confederation of provinces called Canada remained largely north European and white for a century. By 1991, however, Canadians of non-European origin had doubled to ten percent, so that they were very visible in the European sea of white faces. Among Canadian cities Toronto and Vancouver, especially, began to see that "visible minority" numbers would double in a generation or two. Estimates are that "people of colour" will make up twenty percent of Canada by 2016. Immigration laws which had favored north Europeans were changed in the 1960s, when more equitable laws were passed which, especially for Asians, increased the chances of coming to Canada.

RACISM IN HISTORIAL PERSPECTIVE

Stratification by race is a fairly recent phenomenon, maintained in existence especially during the last several hundred years by white Europeans and their ancestors. It has been particularly severe in the United States, where slavery lasted for centuries, but it is also present in Canada and will likely become more important as increasing numbers of immigrants from the Third World enter the country.

The view of ethnicity and "race" does clash with the two dominant ideologies of industrial societies — liberalism and socialism. Ethnicity and "race," I will argue, are extensions of kinship, and, therefore, the feelings of ethnocentrism and racism associated with group membership are extensions of nepotism between kinsmen.... If my argument is correct, then it follows that ethnocentrism and racism, too, are deeply rooted in our biology and can be expected to persist.... In liberal ideology ethnocentrism and racism are archaic, irrational residues of preindustrial societies, which can be expected to yield to universalism under conditions of "modernization." In socialist tradition, these phenomena are seen as the product of the capitalist mode of production and as misguided forms of "false consciousness" designed to wither away after the advent of socialism. Both ideological traditions have been equally at a loss to explain the persistence, indeed, the resurgence, of ethnic and racial sentiments (van den Berghe, 1981:xi).

Van den Berghe (1981:1-3) argues that in the second half of the nineteenth century social Darwinists such as Herbert Spencer and William Sumner tended to uphold genetic determinism, which influenced sociology until the 1920s. However, the pendulum began to swing toward environmentalism when Franz Boas and Robert Park emphasized the opposite view of cultural relativism that was expounded by liberals like Adorno, Myrdal, Warner, Allport, Frazier, Klineberg, and Dollard, and which held sway until the 1960s. The liberals played down racial distinctions, an attitude closely linked with the assimilationist ideology and the optimistic notion of a melting pot. Robert Park and many of the Chicago School tended to see little difference between race and ethnicity and used the terms interchangeably. They expected both to disappear through assimilation.

Since the sixties, however, heritage roots, ethnic identity, and 'Black is Beautiful' sent scholars looking for black culture, black soul, and black roots clearly based on the physical and biological differences of the 12 percent of Americans who were black. Thus Pierre van den Berghe (1981) began to develop a theory of socio-biology that takes both the social environment and the biological inheritance seriously. He sees race as a special marker of ethnicity, upon which 'dominance orders,' 'hierarchies,' and 'pecking orders' are based. Racism thus becomes a cultural invention, and ethnicity and class (including race) become two alternative and competing principles of sociality (van den Berghe, 1981:58, 257).

Race, and its meaning, has evolved and changed over time. Explorers and traders were finding people who looked and behaved somewhat differently from themselves, so they became interested in common and distinctive features and invariably began to wonder about the origin of these differences in colour and physical characteristics. At first "the race of mankind" had been used, generally distinguishing *Homo sapiens* from other animals, but now, increasingly, people were faced with the task of classifying the varieties of human beings into categories or races. So "race" today is defined as an arbitrary biological grouping of people on the basis of physical traits.

Banton (1967:19) has defined the concept of "racism" as the doctrine that behaviour is determined by stable inherited characteristics deriving from separate racial stocks, which have distinctive attributes and are usually considered to stand to one another in relations of superiority and inferiority. As white Europeans came more and more into contact with peoples around the world, and as the theory of evolution developed, there were many attempts at arranging the varieties of *Homo sapiens* into distinctive groupings. There was often the tendency to identify Europeans as superior and others as inferior, especially because white Europeans at the time had a relatively well-developed technology. Racists today believe that some people are inferior or superior biologically; as a result, they often treat people of other races negatively.

While "racism" is a negative concept, based on the belief that some races are inferior to others, the concept of inequality is an attempt at ranking people more objectively on the basis of opportunities to compete in the social, economic, and political spheres of our society. It is assumed that humans have roughly the same abilities, but for many reasons they do not all have the same opportunity to fulfil their potential. In this sense inequality is a part of the social structure of a society, rather than a form of biological determinism. While biological features are difficult to change, social structures can be changed, although not easily.

The concept of race is difficult to define, and it is difficult to classify, so why do we continue to try? Because humans need to simplify and order the universe to be able to comprehend it. But, more importantly, whites of European Caucasian origin have judged — and continue to judge — others on the basis of skin colour. Racial attitudes and behaviour based on physical characteristics are a fact in North America, and we are forced to deal with the phenomenon of racism. Many North Americans display attitudes that conform to Bantan's definition of racism, cited above. This is racism.

Aboriginals in North American were slaughtered or placed on reserves. Blacks in America were forced to become slaves; the Japanese in Canada and the United States, during the Second World War were forcibly transferred, into the interior. Blacks and coloureds in South Africa lived in ghettos and needed passes to enter white territories. These are but a few examples of racism. Let us explore how such thinking developed over time.

White European Dominance

White Europeans represented only one-sixth of the total world population prior to the sixteenth century. However, when the Protestant Reformation began in the 1500s — the time at which European explorers began to discover the rest of the world — ideas, inventions, and technology developed to enhance European world power and dominance (van den Berghe, 1981). As European industry flourished, Europe's population exploded and new settlements were established; soon Europeans became one-third of the world's population (Driedger, 1996:238).

In earlier centuries, Europeans had traded with the Chinese, South Asians, and others, their contacts being facilitated by Arab and other middle entrepreneurs who brought spices and goods across the lands and deserts. After Columbus, however, Europeans soon established links with the East via the sea. Asians looked physically different; their features were very different. Europeans now had direct contact with these "different" peoples. As they sought to find a direct passage to the East going west, the Spaniards and Portuguese discovered South and Central American aboriginals; the British, French, and Dutch found more aboriginals in North America. Some, such as the Maya, Aztec, and Inca, had developed great civilizations, but others were in the food-gathering stages. These people, too, looked different physically. The same was true of the darker peoples on the coasts of Africa. One dominant impression these new experiences left was that other peoples of the world are not white. Skin colour became an easy way of differentiating between white Europeans and others (van den Berghe, 1981).

White invaders from Europe were both awed by some of the great and old civilizations that they had found and hard pressed to seek ways of justifying their presence there. Since European technology permitted extensive sea travel, technological advances, white physical appearance, and a sense of a superior 'white image' soon became present around the world. It was only a matter of time before 'white is more beautiful' became popular with the Europeans, first no doubt as an unconscious attitude, and later justified by various ideologies.

Colonialism

In some parts of the world, trading relationships developed, in others exploitation was extensive, and in still other areas pioneer settlers came to possess the land. The patterns of contact varied. Since the Asians had highly developed civilizations, the Europeans desired their finely crafted cloth, their spices, and many other articles of trade. Europeans created small port enclaves on the coastlines of China, India, Indonesia, and elsewhere to establish trading communities. Raw materials such as furs were also desired, so forts were established across North America where the fur trade flourished. In all of these trading relationships Europeans were a small minority, but they possessed sufficient technological superiority to protect themselves and maintain their white bases amidst peoples of many varieties of colour (Driedger, 1996:239).

The great Mayan, Aztec, and Inca civilizations of Latin America provided special opportunities for exploitation (van den Berghe, 1981:85-90). In the 1530s gold was found by the Spanish among the Inca in what is now Peru. Small groups of powerful Spanish and Portuguese subjugated and often exploited aboriginals, and sometimes enslaved them to work in mines. Many European men, away from their families, exploited native women, and many married them and created families.

Pioneer settlement was a third form of white European contact, taking shape when North Europeans settled in North America. The French and British created communities on the American and Canadian east coasts and soon began to differentiate between white Europeans and aboriginals. Most of the latter were food gatherers, less technologically advanced, and skin colour or differentiation by physical features became an important means of social differentiation.

Immigration Policies

Aboriginals, the first immigrants to the americas, came at least 12,000 years ago. These early groups of *Homo sapiens* possessed the land now called Canada, the United States of America, Mexico, and Central America for a period twenty-five times as long as the time in which any Europeans have lived here. In Canada most of the aboriginals were food gatherers, although food producing had begun among the Hurons and Iroquois in southern Ontario, and large-scale fishing, chiefdoms, and a distinctive art had developed on the northwest coast. In Mexico, Central America, and Peru some of the civilizations of the Aztec and Inca were still flourishing when Europeans invaded and exploited their land.

After 1600 British, French, Spanish, and Dutch colonies were established in what is now Canada and the United States. Most of these were peopled by families settling permanently, and they needed the land that the aboriginals used for hunting. At first their needs were limited, but slowly white agriculturalists began to crowd out native food gatherers. As the latter were increasingly pushed westward, the number of whites and their dominance and power increased, leading to conflicts, in what is now Canada, with the Iroquois, the Hurons, and later the Metis, with whom battles took place in 1870 and 1885 at Fort Garry and Batoche (Stanley, 1969). Treaties were signed, and Riel was hanged. The last stand of Indians and Metis had taken place; the white traders and agriculturalists had triumphed.

White European industrial dominance over coloured Africans and Asians as preindustrial suppliers and servants was a common pattern which emerged around the world (van den Berghe, 1981:111-36). Most countries of Europe created colonies that supplied raw materials for the European industrial revolution. These colonial arrangements usually benefited the whites, and in some places took such brutal forms as slavery, especially in colonial America where blacks were brought mainly from Africa to work in the cotton fields of the Deep South. White dominance had taken the most blatantly inhumane course — the buying and selling of humans as commodities. Ideologies such as the Christian religion of love, professed by many, had to be adjusted in order to present a sense of consistency (van den Berghe, 1981:111-15). The doctrine that blacks were less than human, or subhumans, followed. Others argued that God had created some to be dominant and others to be subservient. Still others exploited their fellow humans at will, without thought of morality or justice for all. Usually, European whites were the masters, and coloured phenotypes were the servants. We propose that these are some of the historical reasons for the white preoccupation with race.

Barely one hundred years ago, the two charter groups laid the foundations of the Canadian confederation, so that white Europeans became the legal and dominant force in the shaping of the dominion.

For the most part, Canadian immigration policy preferred north European immigrants and allowed very few non-Europeans to enter. There were exceptions, however, as when Chinese were brought in to build the railroad in British Columbia in the 1880s, or when labourers were needed in mines in the North or the factories in southern Ontario. An informal agreement was made with Japan so that few Japanese entered after the initial ones came during the turn of the century. Often head taxes were imposed to discourage "the yellow hordes of Asia" from entering (Driedger, 1996:241).

The new point system introduced in the early 1970s was important in Canadian immigration policy. Immigration became possible in three ways: citizens of Canada willing to take responsibility for the care and maintenance of their parents, brothers, or sisters could sponsor them and have them enter Canada under the category "Sponsored Dependants" (Richmond, 1991:1210). Since most Canadians are of northern European ancestry this opportunity heavily favoured further white European immigration. However, a category for Independent applicants permitted entrance for those who could score fifty out of a possible one hundred points. This category allowed anyone in the world to compete to enter Canada, especially those in possession of sufficient educational, occupational, and language skills (Richmond, 1994:117-30).

The change in the leading source countries of immigrants after the introduction of the point system is quite evident. In 1951 the ten countries that contributed the largest number of immigrants to Canada were all European except for the United States. By 1995, most of the ten top contributors were in Asia and the Caribbean. A large proportion of the new immigrants was highly visible; many brought with them different religions and cultures as well as racial differences. Since Canada is large and has a relatively sparse population, and since the world pressures for living space are increasing, many people expect Canada to take in more refugees and immigrants who have been left homeless. We can expect that in the future more non-whites will enter Canada and that the proportion of Asians, Africans, and other visible minorities will increase. It is interesting to note that during economic downturns there are usually pressures from labour unions and others to restrict immigration, based on the argument that there are not enough jobs for everyone. This conflict of interest can lead to changes in laws to restrict immigrants. Such changes, some of them very recent, have been part of the fluctuating dynamics of Canada's immigration history.

While the proportion of Canadians of Asian and African racial origin was only about three percent in 1971, by 1991 it had increased to nearly 10 percent. This increase in visible minorities, nearly 2.5 million of the total Canadian population in 1991, was largely due to a change in immigration policy. Current Canadian immigration policy clearly gives immigrants from the Third World a better chance to compete. Many more visible minorities have arrived in the past decade.

Racism and Japanese Internment

The literature is full of the documentation of enslavement of blacks. Lest some think that such mistreatment happened long ago, the evacuation of Japanese from the Pacific coast to the Canadian interior during the Second World War is an objective, documented illustration of racism in Canada as well.

A small number of Japanese began to settle in Canada around 1884, and by 1894 about 1,000 had entered Canada. They had been good fishermen in Japan and found it relatively natural to continue their trade on the Canadian west coast. Indeed, they were able to compete so well that other Canadian fishermen soon saw them as a threat. Cries to stop Japanese immigration increased until, in 1908, Japan and Canada signed a "gentlemen's agreement" which effectively limited Japanese immigration to less than 1,000 per year. In 1908 alone, 7,985 Japanese entered Canada (Nakamura, 1975:301). Citizens in British Columbia had previously pressured governments to restrict immigration of Asians in general, and especially the Chinese. Political and labour leaders marched into Chinatown in 1907, causing a riot and thousands of dollars worth of damage. They were stopped by the Japanese from entering the Japanese quarter on Powell Street. Even prior to 1941, discrimination against Asians was commonplace, with many legal restrictions and injustices (Driedger, 1996:254).

Chinese and Japanese Canadians established segregated areas where they did their business and where they lived and built their social institutions (Sugiman and Nisheo, 1983; Kobayashi, 1987). The largest Chinatown in Canada is still in Vancouver. Prior to the bombing of Pearl Harbor, many of Canada's Japanese lived in two large communities: 2,151 in Steveston, a fishing community on the coast south of Vancouver, and 8,427 in Vancouver (Nakamura, 1975;309). In Steveston, the Japanese were the majority. They owned a fleet of fishing boats, and their various organizations processed and marketed their catch. They had a thriving segregated community where they used their own language and supported their schools, clubs, and religious and social organizations. The same was true on Powell Street in the heart of Vancouver, where Japantown was a growing bustling enclave, like many of the Chinatowns we know today (Broadfoot, 1977).

In 1941, 21,175 of the 23,149 Japanese in Canada were located on the British Columbia coast. A small minority, less than 8 percent was scattered throughout the rest of Canada. Ten years later, in 1952, only 12 percent remained on the West coast and the majority had been sent inland, 4,527 to the eastern Canadian provinces (Nakamura, 1975: 330). Three-fourths of the Japanese Canadians in 1941 were Canadian-born. Many families had lived in Canada for several generations (Sunahara, 1980:93-120).

The evacuation and relocation caused significant changes; it wiped out many of the hard-won economic gains that the Japanese had built up over the years. Most had to start all over again, because few of the 200 different Japanese organizations remained after the war. Kin associations, a traditional Japanese heritage, ceased to function; fathers were separated from families, and families were disbanded; Japanese-language schools and newspapers were closed down. The life, culture, customs, and traditions that were symbolized by Vancouver's Powell Street were over (Nakamura, 1975:33). The evacuation took nine months; the Japanese were sent to camp projects and old mining towns such as Tashme, Slocan and New Denver in British Columbia, and to sugarbeet projects in the prairies. Some were deported to Japan. The property of the Japanese, such as fishing boats, houses, businesses, and public buildings, was confiscated and often sold for a fraction of its value. Some Japanese have returned to the coast, but many have not. Only one block of Japanese businesses and shops remains on Vancouver's Powell Street today, a remnant of the former thriving Japantown (Petrie, 1982:11-46).

The destruction of the Japanese communities of the west coast through evacuation and deportation during the Second World War was possible because of racial hatred and pressures exerted by West Coast Canadians and politicians, who themselves were ready to condone and/or vote for discriminatory legislation (Kobayashi, 1992). Sunahara (1980:94) lists four major reasons. (1) Mackenzie King and the federal government often sympathized with or yielded to the American government, which may have influenced other Canadian politicians. (2) West Coast labour unions were threatened by the

Japanese and pressured politicians to eliminate the Japanese fishermen from the industry: evacuation accomplished this. (3) In general, the anti-Asian bias was so strong that very few people objected to the injustices which escalated into evacuation, confiscation, internment, and deportation (Broadfoot, 1977). (4) War hysteria added to the problem. Minority communities were destroyed, social institutions were wiped out, and the Japanese culture in Canada was greatly weakened.

Ujimoto (1983:141) suggests that the Japanese experience can be understood in terms of Daniels and Kitano's (1970:5) minority-majority model, which involves two categories:

By the 'two category' system, they mean 'a system of stratification that is divided into two broad categories: the white and the non-white.' In this system of analysis, it is assumed that the white group is superior to the other group. Although it is recognized that there are other systems of stratification, our analysis of Japanese Canadian historical data indicates that the prejudice, discrimination and concomitant segregation in internment camps inflicted on the Japanese Canadians can be adequately assessed in terms of the simple two category system.... It becomes evident how the social and political structures were manipulated, often by legislative means, in order to perpetuate the two category system of stratification. (Ujimoto, 1983:141)

In Table 1-1, we present Daniels and Kitano's (1970:11) four basic stages of racial separation, which begin as three ordinary solutions, and continue into a fourth drastic extraordinary solution. Research (Berger, 1981; Ujimoto and Hirabayashi, 1980; Ujimoto, 1983) shows that the first stage of prejudice — avoidance and stereotyping — was common in British Columbia before the First World War. There was fertile ground for more serious actions against minorities such as the Japanese, Chinese, and East Indians. Japanese successes in fishing, farming, and lumbering became a serious threat to many who found it hard to compete. "The anti-Japanese feelings and the eventual culmination of these feelings in the Vancouver Race Riots of 1907 probably best characterize the first stage of the two category system of stratification" (Ujimoto, 1983:144).

The second stage of discrimination — overt action — would be characterized by moves toward deprivation and more formal rules and laws aimed at limiting the economic threat. Many believed that the Japanese would deprive them of the majority of jobs and take away their employment opportunities, so that the political power of the

TABLE I-I

THE FOUR STAGES OF MAINTAINING THE TWO-CATEGORY
SYSTEM OF STRATIFICATION

	Stage	Belief	Action Effect	Primary Mechanisms
	1	Prejudice	Avoidance	Stereotyping, informally patterned rules governing interaction
Ordinary Solutions	2	Discrimination	Deprivation	More formal rules, norms, agreements, laws
	3	Segregation	Insulation	If the out-group is perceived as stepping over the line, there may be lynchings and other warnings
		A. Apartheid Concentration	Isolation	A major trigger such as war is necessary — out-group is perceived as a real threat or danger
Extraordinary Solutions	4	B. Expulsion Exile	Exclusion	to the existence of the host culture. Ordinary mechanisms (e.g., Stages
		C. Extermination	Genocide	1, 2, and 3) have failed.

Source: Roger Daniels and Harry H.I. Kitano, *American Racism: Exploration of the Nature of Prejudice* (Englewood Cliffs, NJ, 1970). By permisssion of Roger Daniels and Harry H.I. Kitano, copyright assignees.

majority must be used to stem the Japanese tide. "The Japanese were believed to constitute a threat to the economic and cultural supremacy of British Protestants and thus a significant threat to the distribution of power" (Baar, 1978:336). After 1908 the gentlemen's agreement with Japan had limited Japanese immigration to a trickle. In the second stage of discrimination, laws had been put into effect to restrict the Japanese minority influence.

Daniels and Kitano (1970:11) suggest that there would be a sequential escalation through the four stages, and indeed, this did happen in British Columbia. Stage three was the segregation and insulation effected through mass evacuation of Japanese Canadians from "protected areas" of British Columbia into interior camps and work projects; it effectively removed an economic threat presented under the guise of a political threat. "Former mining towns or 'ghost towns' in the province were renovated to house the evacuees: Greenwood (1,177 evacuees), Kaslo (964), Sandon (933), New Denver (1,505), and Slocan (4,814)" (Ujimoto, 1983:138). Complete insulation from the rest of society was accomplished by confiscating radios, cameras and automobiles; freedom of movement was restricted, and letters were censored. During the internment, higher education was not available, so that social mobility was restricted; institutionalized discrimination had taken place.

Daniels and Kitano's (1970) fourth extraordinary stage followed. Subtypes A (concentration and apartheid through isolation) and B (exclusion through expulsion and exile) both took place. In the case of Japanese Canadians, Canada called this exile "repatriation." The Second World War was the trigger for this extraordinary action. Through an Order-in-Council in December, 1945 (after the war was ended), Canada was still trying to deport Japanese Canadians (Ujimoto, 1983:140). Arrangements were made to deport 800 in January of 1946, but because many prominent Canadians opposed the measure it was not carried out. Some Japanese, however, had been deported earlier. In 1988 Canada and its Japanese agreed to a redress settlement as partial compensation for injustices suffered (Kobayashi, 1992:1-19). Canadians are often not aware of the lengths to which we have gone in the past to stratify ethnic minorities. We find it hard to believe that analogies to the Indian caste systems and apartheid in South Africa could be found here.

SKETCHING PATTERNS OF RACE AND RACISM

To explore the extent to which racial groups thrive in Canada, to document whether economic, political and social racism exists; and to identify the difficulties of coping with racism in urban settings, we present the work of contributors in fourteen chapters, which deal with these issues under four major headings. Let us introduce what the reader can expect.

Dealing With the Concept of Race

Since "official" Canada was largely north European, white, and Christian for a century, it should not be surprising that Canadians have had a great deal of ambivalence about others who are different. Sylvia Wargon, in Chapter 2, shows how much of the Canadian census-taking centered around sorting white Europeans. In fact, in the beginning the term "race" was used to distinguish Europeans. However, in 1946 after the horrors of Hitler and the Holocaust, the "racial origin" concept became a subject of discussion. Wargon compares American and Canadian differences: the Americans, because of black slavery, fought a civil war and never could pretend that race did not exist;

twelve percent of their population is Afro-American. In Canada, what is politically correct terminology has recently become an issue, because Canada too now has a population of visible minorities representing ten percent of the whole.

Boyd, Goldmann and White, in Chapter 3, document the variations in the Canadian Census methods of enumerating race, and they show that such variations co-vary with changing conceptualization of race and race relations. They point out that in the seventeen and eighteen hundreds origins were emphasized, by the turn of the last century, in 1901, racial origins were prominent, and after World War II, ethnic origins became popular. Use of "visible minority" is a recent phenomenon. The post-World War II period clearly displayed the trend "out with race and in with culture." Since the 1970s, things have changed again; increased diversity, following the change in the immigration laws, has brought with it the "Challenge of the next century." The 1996 census tries to wrestle with the negative public reactions to terminology which differentiates Canadians. "Racial" discourse is increasingly becoming a political football.

To gain a much broader macro-perspective on diversity, Driedger and Halli, in Chapter 4, discuss six theories of change gleaned from the sociological literature. Assimilation and acculturation theories assume that all minorities will eventually disappear into the major culture, which would be British (French in Quebec). At the opposite end are conflict and pluralist theories which assume that minorities either wish to remain separate and maintain their identities, or are forced to remain segregated or separated because of race, non-whites being devalued. They end with a model showing a number of distinct forces at work, where 1) the majority group ideally would like to see minorities conform to the Anglo way; 2) many religious minorities like Jews, Hutterites and others want to retain their separate identities; and 3) coloured visible minorities are separated involuntarily, and find it hard to compete in the work arena, where prejudice and discrimination are common.

Does all this apply also to Canadians living in Quebec, which was originally dominated and is still dominated by the French, who trace their origins from one of the earlier north European superpowers? Joseph O'Shea explores individual versus collective rights in Chapter 5. If Quebec separated and became a new nation, would it like the rest of Canada, also follow the north European tendency to dominate its minorities? French Quebecers have strongly insisted on a separate identity, which has aided other minorities to claim, in their turn, a right to their identities in a multi-ethnic Canada. O'Shea outlines the struggle French Quebecers face as their birthrates decline, and as new immigrants become more diverse culturally and racially. It is difficult to support a politics of the common good while respecting other individual and collective goals. The French communitarian model comes into conflict with a liberal tradition that emphasizes the rights of the individual and a diversity of ends.

Changing Economic and Social Issues

While in Part I we have wrestled with use of the concept of race, in Part II we turn to the Canadian economic and social context in which minorities must compete. As immigrants increasingly come from Asia, where cultures, religion and race are very different, adjustments become more difficult. Nancy Higgitt presents a model of refugee resettlement in Chapter 6, where she tries to better understand how refugees themselves define successful resettlement. The Higgitt model deals with economic, political and psycho-social well-being. Economic well-being includes finding employment, job satisfaction, security, income, housing and fair treatment; political well-being involves a sense of control, knowledge about society, acceptance by others and confidence in one's ability to participate; psycho-social well-being involves happiness, a sense of belonging and of self-worth, satisfaction and acceptance by others.

Verma and Chan focus on the economic adaptation of Asian immigrants, and find that they have lower incomes than the Canadian-born. The largest numbers of immigrants to Canada in the 1990s came from Asia. However, Asia is very large, and there are enormous differences between West Asian, East Asian, Southeast Asian and South Asian immigrants. East and South East Asians are of higher occupational status than West and South Asian immigrants. Verma and Chan sort the income, educational and occupational differences by country to show the wide range of variation. Special data indicate that immigrants from Hong Kong are pouring tens of millions of dollars into Ontario, followed by business people coming from Taiwan and South Korea. These are among the higher status Pacific Rim immigrants, and this fact raises interesting questions, such as how much racism is related to levels of income and occupational status.

The studies by Higgitt, Verma and Chan suggest that there is much potential for employment inequity among recent immigrants who are visible minorities. John Samuel and Aly Karam, in Chapter 8, examine the progress of employment equity for visible minorities in the federal workforce. They find that women were still underrepresented in 1994, although the gap has nearly closed since then. They observe that visible minorities were poorly represented in hiring, retention and promotion in the federal workforce. The private sector did much better, led especially by the national banks. Barriers which prevent more hiring of other racial minorities need to be explored more, and this is done in Part III.

Finding Race and Racism in Canada

In Part III, four chapters are devoted to racism and discrimination. Driedger and Reid trace the heightened "visibility" of new immigrants into a previously largely white population. Research on race was minimal in Canada prior to the 1960s, but as a result of the Bilingualism and Biculturalism Commission and changes in immigration policy, such research has increased. The authors use three major national surveys, collected by Berry, Reid and Bibby, to explore the attitudes of Canadians toward visible minorities. The 1976 survey by John Berry and associates clearly shows that north Europeans are rated most favorably, followed by other Europeans and visible minorities. The Angus Reid survey of 1991 displays the same trend, with Canadians feeling most comfortable around north Europeans, and least comfortable with Sikhs, Indo-Pakistanis, Muslims and Arabs. Reid suggests that about ten percent of Canadians are antagonists who have negative attitudes toward people of other races. Reginald Bibby, comparing his 1975 and 1995 national surveys, found that uneasiness with visible minorities was in decline over time. However, in 1995 more respondents felt that discrimination in Canada was on the rise.

Many of the chapters listed so far have been written by sociologists and demographers, but the next two are presented by social psychologists. Berry and Kalin explore more deeply the general findings of social surveys by measuring racism from a psychological perspective. They pursue the multicultural ideology which explores self and group identities anchored in values and communities. Many Canadians feel threatened by diversity, so that some feel the need to stereotype, and to distance themselves from other religions, races and status groups by means of prejudice and discrimination. Berry and Kalin found that the charter groups (British and French) usually rank on top with higher prestige, while visible minorities fall to the bottom.

Social psychologists Taylor, Wright and Ruggiero, in Chapter 11 pull no punches and call such prejudice and discrimination "an invisible evil." It is what people say at Thanksgiving dinner, or riding the commuter train, or at sports events, that is most telling. These results find that discrimination is subtle, and that social scientists often ask the wrong questions. Tokenism is one subtle form of discrimination, a strategy whereby a few capable members of a disadvantaged group are accepted into positions, while no further obligation is felt by majority members to enlarge the opportunities and circles. By using laboratory settings they were able to uncover more deeply held attitudes and disguised forms of unfair treatment. People who were confronted with discrimination tended to minimize its occurrence, an attitude which serves the interests of the advantaged group. Unfortunately, tokenism is highly effective for advantaged groups, because victims find it difficult to challenge discriminatory outcomes.

Coping in Difficult Urban Settings

It is in urban centres like Toronto and Vancouver that recent visible minority immigrants have tended to congregate heavily during the past two decades. One fourth to one third of the population of these two cities are coloured visible minorities, living in what used to be white European heritage settings. The three chapters in Part IV illustrate some of the difficult problems related to coping with existence in such metropolises. Helen Ralston illustrates the kinds of changes South Asian women have to go through, using the interconnections of gender, race and class. Comparing samples in Atlantic Canada and British Columbia, she found that 60-65 percent of these women were from India, and the remaining one-third from thirteen other counties. Punjabi and Hindi languages were spoken by a majority, but thirteen other languages were also in use. Two thirds of the subjects belonged to Hindu and Sikh groups, but five other religions were also represented. Problems that these women faced were learning English fluently, getting jobs outside the home, and lack of recognition of education and work experience obtained in their source country.

Siu Kwong Wong focuses on acculturation and Chinese delinquency in Winnipeg. Research showed that the Canadian-born are more prone to delinquency, and this correlates with acculturation. As acculturation of the Canadian-born Chinese increases, delinquency also increases. Chinese parental supervision and control played an important part in slowing acculturation and also delinquent behavior. Thus, Chinese immigrants are faced with trying to retain their Chinese identity, while at the same time trying to integrate sufficiently with the larger society to survive comfortably and to compete. The payoff for a successful balancing act seems to be lower rates of delinquency.

There are few studies which describe in depth how refugees, who have already seen much stress back at home, find themselves in many more stressful situations when they arrive in Canada. In Chapter 14 Guang Tian shares what it is like for Chinese refugees to cope with stress in Toronto. Many mainland Chinese are in Canada illegally. Stress shatters dreams in the course of the process of conflict between expectations (often unrealistic), and realities (hard to learn in a short time). Using in-depth interviews Tian points out the uncertainty of legal status. Separation from family supports, nostalgia for what home was like, perceived discrimination, loss of status and achievements in China, and lack of living skills in a strange land, all contribute to intense stress. Some are able to appraise and face the odds better than others, having more educational, linguistic, occupational and cultural resources. Tian shows that the degree to which Chinese refugees were able to cope with stress was closely related to their legal status, educational background, and length of stay in Canada.

When the speedometer on a car turns over and a long row of new numbers appear, there is excitement and anticipation as to what the next 100,000 kilometers will bring. So also we anticipate a major change when a new millenium begins in the year 2000. In the title of this first chapter we suggest that the challenge for Canadians in the year 2000, and in the century which follows, will be Race and Racism. We have dared to put it bluntly. Visible minorities in Canada have doubled in the last generation, and will most likely double again to twenty percent of the total population by 2016. One out of five Canadians will soon be coloured. How will majority white Canadians react, and will they be up to the demands of the situation? Will they continue to mould a pluralist, multiethnic and multiracial society?

The challenges of the 21st century are many. Canadian governmental policy changed in the 1960s, when a Bilingualism and Biculturalism Commission was formed to face the Quiet Revolution in

Quebec. Canada got a new flag and was declared officially bilingual. In 1971 Pierre Trudeau declared Canada bilingual and multicultural, followed by changes in immigration laws favouring acceptance of more immigrants from the Third World, including many refugees. Now that one in ten Canadians are members of visible minorities, can we accept them as equals? The challenges are especially great in urban centres such as Toronto and Vancouver, where visible minorities represent a third and a fourth of their populations, and will double in a generation. In the chapters which follow we describe more of the challenges of the coming millenium.

I

CONCEPTS AND THE THEORIES

2

HISTORICAL AND POLITICAL REFLECTIONS ON RACE

SYLVIA T. WARGON[1]

IN THIS, THE LAST DECADE of the twentieth century, there has been considerable discussion in the media and in the academic press about *race* in North America.[2] To determine what this discussion really signifies it is helpful to review some historical and political dimensions of the issue of race in Canada.

CANADIAN CENSUS CONCEPTS

Following Confederation, a question on *origin* appeared on the Canadian Census questionnaire in 1871 and in 1881, but not in 1891. In the twentieth century the 1901 questionnaire included a question on *racial origin*. An important aspect rarely, if ever, noted today is the fact that the English term "origin "was translated in the late nineteenth century for the French language versions of the Canadian Census publications as *nationalité* (Canada, 1872, 1876; Ryder, 1955). In any case, the English term "racial origin," used in the Canadian Census from 1901 to 1941, was rendered into French as *origine raciale*. The use of this concept is now seen as having played a certain role in early nation-building efforts, and in attempts to maintain the power of politically dominant groups (Beaud et Prévost, 1993; Boyd et al., 1993). From the point of view of the bodies of knowledge that began to emerge in the late nineteenth century and that blossomed in the early twentieth century, such as anthropology, sociology, human genetics and related fields, it is clear, in retrospect, that the concept was misapplied in Canada and elsewhere.

In early Canadian Census usage, the concepts race and racial origin were applied not only to Canada's aboriginal peoples, to the small number of blacks, and to the Chinese and Japanese, but also to all those immigrants and their descendants who had come first from France,

Britain and other North European countries, and, in the late nineteenth and early twentieth centuries, from eastern and southern
Europe. Hurd discussed the problems this created in the introductory
sections of his 1929 and 1937 monographs. In the early 1940s, the
problematical aspects of the concept of "race" were also eminently
obvious to Enid Charles, who, as Census Research Specialist at the
Dominion Bureau of Statistics in the 1940s, authored a Census monograph on fertility and family. In it she included explanatory materials
on the difficulties associated with the Canadian Census "racial origin "
concept (Charles, 1948:52-56, Appendix B, "Biological significance
of racial classifications," 293-94). Citing international experts, Charles
argued that "the biological basis of the major so-called races is obscure."
In this manner she took a position in the "nature and nurture" controversy, that is, the debate about the degree to which certain human characteristics are determined biologically and genetically, or socially and
culturally. Although she is reported to have played an important role in
the removal of the "racial origin" concept from the Canadian Census,
Charles simply explained, unobtrusively in a footnote, that it had been
changed to "ethnic origin" (Charles, 1948, 103). In Canada, as in the
rest of the world, the disastrous effects of the melding of early twentieth century eugenics and Nazi policies during the 1930s and 1940s led
to the virtual abandonment during the 1940s of the concepts race and
racial origin as applied to human population groups. In the mid-1940s
two distinguished scientists, who helped shed light on the destructive
fallacies of racial doctrines, pointed out that:

The misuse of "race" for political and military purposes ... has brought
the term ... into such disrepute that many people, including some scientists,
propose to abandon the term altogether as applied to human groups ... and
yet there are human entities for which the term race, if properly used, could
stand (Dunn and Dobzhansky, 1946:94).

The last statement is pertinent to developments in terminology
since the early 1970s in Canada. From the 1940s, it had become quite
unacceptable to use the word "race" to refer to any group whose
members differed ethnically, culturally and visibly from "mainstream"
Canadians. In empirical social science this posed certain conundrums,
and led to the coining of terms designed to avoid using "race." Yet in
the 1990s, in Canada, words like "race, racial, and multiracial," are
again being used in social science discourse.

The racial origin concept was officially discarded in 1946 (Ryder, 1955; Charles, 1956), and was replaced in the 1946 quinquennial Census of Manitoba, Saskatchewan and Alberta, and in the 1951 decennial Census, by the concept ethnic origin. Although the latter was more "neutral-sounding" and therefore acceptable, it was as problematic to operationalize as what it replaced. Furthermore, the definition of the concept and wording of the question, as well as the treatment of the resulting data, changed from one Census to the next. Therefore the inclusion of the origin question in the Canadian Census continued to arouse discussion and debate, with some "for" and others "against." French-speaking Canadians favoured retention, since it meant that they would continue to be identified in terms of their French ethnic and linguistic roots. However, as described by two social scientists (Vallee and de Vries, 1978:71), a favourite strategy used in the work on ethnic origin in Canada, even by those critical of the concept, was to cite Ryder's seminal 1955 article as "a caveat," and then to proceed to use the census ethnic origin data anyway! Interested social scientists made a case for the continued collection of information based on this question, notably Kalbach (1970:5, 6). A question on ethnic origin continued to appear on Canadian Census questionnaires, including those for the 1991 decennial and the 1996 quinquennial Censuses. Discussion in detail of the racial origin and ethnic origin concepts, and of the problems associated with changing definitions and data collection, compilation and publication procedures are not treated here; they are available in a number of historical and recent sources (Ryder, 1955; Canada, 1990; Kralt, 1990; Canada, 1992; White et al., 1993). At a joint American-Canadian conference on the challenges of measuring ethnicity it was generally agreed that however differently defined the concept may be among nations, however changing or "malleable" because of the nature of international migration in the modern world, and however ambiguous (see especially Lieberson, 1993), national statistical programs should continue to collect data on ethnicity. It was also generally agreed at this conference that the Census in most cases is a particularly appropriate vehicle for so doing (United States/Canada, 1993).

American and Canadian demographers and social scientists have produced bodies of work in the specialty currently called "ethnic demography," or, as preferred by Canadian French-speaking experts who consider it important to include language, "the demography of ethnic and linguistic groups." This is logically in accord with the prevailing view that since race is "socially constructed," it is appropriately included in the label "ethnic demography." Unfortunately, the latter brings to mind the current pejorative use of the words "ethnic/ethnics," which has inclined some historians and sociologists to favour the term "peoples" over "ethnic groups," and "cultural" over "ethnic." The term "ethnocultural demography" has recently gained a certain popularity in Canada (Federation of Canadian Demographers, 1995) and may provide a suitable alternative. Nevertheless, it appears impossible to avoid the term *race*. While some U.S. social scientists have no problem with the terms "ethnic" and "ethnicity" as labels for *all* dimensions of ethnocultural and immigrant experience, others prefer to speak of "race and ethnic groups," rather than classifying race as a special case of ethnic differentiation. In Canada, although reference to race continued to be carefully avoided after 1941, the term and its derivatives surfaced again in the 1980s and (to cite only one example) appeared in the volume *Ethnic Demography*, in the subtitle "Canadian immigrant, racial and cultural variations," and in some of the contributed papers (Halli et al., 1990). In 1996, the Canadian Census added a new question, the *visible minority* question, which some experts, critics and members of the media referred to as a "race question."

SOME AMERICAN/CANADIAN COMPARISONS

A comparison of the early American and Canadian approaches to the collection of information on the origins of their subpopulations shows how census practices and research in the two countries were influenced by differences in the composition of their respective early populations (see Bowles, 1982:133). The American census was always obliged to enumerate the white/non-white as well as other groups. Features of Canada's early history, especially the regional concentration of the English-speaking and French-speaking peoples, and the importance in the Canadian Census of various questions on language and related cultural variables, contrast with the situation in the United States. In view, moreover, of the ongoing political debate regarding Quebec's present status and future destiny in this country, it is understandable why Canadian novelist Barry Callaghan (1990) was reported to have said that Canada is obsessed with language in the same way that the United States is obsessed with race. This perception resonates in a recent article that refers to the contemporary white and non-white groups in the United States as "two nations" (Glazer, 1995:66), in much the same way that Canadians often refer to Quebec and the rest of Canada as two nations.

In the late eighteenth century, when a national program of census statistics was being developed in the United States, one of the many imposing challenges faced by data collectors was that of tracking and enumerating a white/non-white population (Beaud et Prévost, 1993). For simplicity, only those who were brought in as slaves to work the southern plantations are considered here. This population subgroup had to be reckoned with in the official American data collection and compilation procedures. In 1790 therefore, and in every American Census since that date, a question on *race* has appeared (Butz and Goldmann, 1993:15). Over the years other concepts have been added to enumerate a variety of ethnic groups (McKenney and Cresce, 1993). Recommendations for the American Census in the year 2000 propose continuation of these practices (National Academy Press, 1995). In Canada, early on, the aboriginal peoples (Indians and Inuit) and the relatively small numbers of blacks (mainly from the United States) and Asians (Chinese and Japanese who had come as labourers in the late 1800s and early 1900s), were enumerated and reported in a number of eighteenth and ninteenth century Censuses in terms of various labels denoting race (Canada, 1876), and in the decennial Censuses from 1901 to 1941 inclusive according to the *racial origin* concept (White et al., 1993). Subsequently, they were simply reported according to the special instructions that always accompanied the Canadian Census *ethnic origin* concept, so that enumerators (before self-enumeration was introduced) and, later, respondents themselves would reply in ways that permitted data compilers to distinguish those who were "white" from those who were "non-white" (Boyd et al., 1993). Moreover, in contrast to the American situation, one of the more imposing challenges facing the early collectors and compilers of official statistics in Canada was that of enumerating the wide variety of cultural and linguistic groups living in what was politically and geographically a biculturally and bilingually structured community.

In the years immediately prior to the Second World War, and then in the exuberant postwar period, there were frequent references in the sociological literature to the United States as a "melting pot" and to Canada as a "cultural mosaic," terms implying that there were great differences in the way in which the two societies integrated their various ethnocultural groups. Many social scientists maintained that these differences were exaggerated (see in particular Porter, 1987). In reality, in the United States the "melting pot" myth covered over the problematical white/non-white distinction. No melting pot there, but a seething cauldron that eventually boiled over, as Gunnar Myrdal had predicted it would some twenty years before (Myrdal, 1944).[3] In Canada, the "cultural mosaic," lauded by politicians and the media, was not as successful as they liked to imply. In 1963, the Royal Commission on Bilingualism and Biculturalism was established precisely to address the problems of political and social unity in Canada, including the open, public discussion of French-English relations (Canada, 1967) and the role of the "other" cultural groups (Canada, 1970).

After the Second World War, changing immigration streams gradually altered the cultural and ethnic composition of the two countries, although in different ways. The results in the United States have been cogently described (Massey, 1995). In Canada in the late 1960s, particularly with the change in regulations in 1962 and 1967 regarding groups permitted to enter this country, the composition of immigration flows included growing numbers of "new wave" immigrants from "non-traditional," non-European source countries in Asia, Africa, the Caribbean, Central and South America, etc. (Simmons, 1990). Inevitable changes in the ethnocultural composition of the nation's population seemed to open the door to the use of terms like "*race*," "*racial*" and "*multiracial*" for descriptive purposes. Increasingly, Canada was described as a multicultural and multiracial society, although John Samuel maintains that our country has always been *multiracial* (Samuel, 1990:388).[4] Raymond Breton notes that Canada's diverse peoples and cultures have always been recognized socially, with publicity freely given to aboriginal and other ethnic costumes, folk dances, food, dialects, languages, and similar colourful expressions of our population mix. In the political context, however, the recognition of Canada's multicultural and multiracial character came only with the promulgation in 1971 of Canada's multiculturalism policy. Breton emphasizes the significance of this policy for previously marginal groups, like the native peoples, who can now make use of political status in managing their affairs in this country (Breton, 1986:48). Burnet describes the various external and internal factors that led to the new multiculturalism policy, and explores its viability within Canada's bilingual framework (Burnet, 1978:206). Others explain that the policy was intended and designed to unify a widely disparate constituency, and to appease ethnic discontent with bilingualism and biculturalism by giving recognition and protection to the non-charter groups in Canadian society (Buchignani, 1982).

POLITICALLY CORRECT TERMINOLOGY

In the attempt to avoid the word "race," new expressions evolved in both the United States and Canada to refer to their non-white populations. American terminology referring to the descendants of slaves has evolved in this century from "coloured" (1940s, 1950s), to "Afro-American" (1950s), "negro" (1960s), and then to "black." In 1964, in the first issue of the American journal Demography, Donald Bogue published an article entitled "A new estimate of the Negro population and Negro vital rates in the United States, 1930-1960" (Bogue, 1964). "Afro-American" still has some advocates today, although the currently politically correct and apparently preferred term is "people of colour." Canada, in its usual conservative fashion, was slower to adopt a new vocabulary to refer to persons who could be identified according to physical features such as skin colour, but use of the term "race" was steadfastly avoided. In 1941, the instructions for responding to the racial origin question still referred to "halfbreed" to designate a person of mixed white and Indian blood (Kralt, 1990:Appendix A). But when Hurd's 1941 Census monograph was completed, it was shelved, and only released in 1965 in a limited edition, after sensitive terms like "race" and "racial origin" had been removed and the text thoroughly "sanitized." Subsequently, when the 1971 Multiculturalism policy (later revised) and 1986 Employment Equity legislation make it necessary to obtain information on the numbers whom such policies and programs were specifically designed to help, a new term began to be used: the made-in-Canada expression "visible minority" which surfaced in 1971 (Pendakur, 1993). Responses from a number of Census questions were used to compile information on visible minorities from the 1981, 1986, and 1991 Census data (for detail see Canada, 1995; Kelly, 1995). In the 1996 Census a new question was introduced to enumerate the visible minority population. The word race was not used in the actual question, but it appeared in the instructions for respondents, where the 1986 Employment Equity Act is quoted, with this definition of members of visible minorities: "persons, other than peoples, who are *non-Caucasian in race or non-white in colour*" (Canada 1996).

Critics of the concept and the data it provides point out that visibility is in the eye of the beholder, that some members of visible minorities are not visible, and that the term generates problems for social scientists and data collectors through imposition of arbitrary, imprecise and changing rules. In spite of such criticism, it is clear that the initiative to obtain the numbers of those in "visible minorities," in order to improve their chances and status in Canadian society, was well-intentioned. But even if many could be convinced of this, and the "proper" use of the terms *race* and *visible minority* was agreed upon and achieved, certain events and pronouncements that occurred at about the time at which the new Census question was being planned and put in place may have made the situation rather more murky than it should have been.

WHAT IS THE REAL ISSUE?

The controversy in Canada over the reappearance of the race issue in connection with the 1996 Census evokes a certain sentiment of "déjà vu." After all, to those acquainted with the relevant historical details the whole matter appeared to have been resolved in the mid-1940s, half a century ago, when the term *"racial origin"* disappeared from the Census questionnaire. The problem is that the recent discussion was not fuelled solely by the initiatives of officials addressing the obligations imposed by Canada's altered population composition, multicultural-ism policy and employment equity legislation. Another dimension was added: the public appearances and utterances, since the 1980s, of a University of Western Ontario academic, J.P. Rushton, and the release of his book *Race, Evolution and Behaviour* (1995), which followed the publication of "The Bell Curve" (Herrnstein and Murray, 1994). Both volumes summarize the previous research and published articles of their authors; both propose superiority/inferiority ratings for members of the human groups usually referred to as caucasians, orientals and blacks in respect of abilities, characteristics, and behaviour (Rushton), and intelligence (Herrnstein and Murray), which the authors claim are physically inherited, and therefore not amenable to change by govern-ment policies and programs. In other words, these authors have brought us right back to the early twentieth century focus of the debate: the presumed biologically inherited and unalterable character-istics of members of three broad human groups identified as races.

This is precisely why Enid Charles's pronouncements in the 1940s, and in a 1956 World Health Organization (WHO) report, have such a contemporary ring. Charles wished to see the terms "race" and "racial origin" eliminated from official statistics because in her day they implied the existence of groups whose members had certain inherited and immutable characteristics, with no account taken of the role and

importance of the social transmission of culture and cultural characteristics. Her views were based on conclusions drawn from pioneering
research by the foremost scientists of the day, in genetics, biology,
psychology, sociology and anthropology, and she continued to express
them in the 1950s. In a 1956 WHO report on a visit to Burma (now
Myanmar) she said:

When a country has been peopled by immigrants from a number of different
sources, and for this or other reasons groups of people differ according to
mother tongue, marriage customs, food habits, etc., it is a legitimate concern
of Government to ascertain their numbers and location, since their different
ways of life affect national planning. The word "race" has, however, a definite biological significance implying physical inheritance. There is only one
race to which human beings belong, and that is the human race (Charles,
1956, 9).

In an appendix to this report, she explained that she preferred the
term *ethnic group* because it was "neutral," had "little meaning" and
would therefore stimulate the search for a precise definition. This is
somewhat similar to Stanley Lieberson's advice, 35 years later, to collectors of official data from all over the world. Lieberson proposed that
it was necessary to "live with ambiguity" in the concept and in the census data on ethnicity, and added that, if necessary, data collectors
should respond to rapidly changing conditions in society by devising
new response categories. In defense of this position, he quoted a
philosopher of science who cautioned that "closure" and "closed
systems" are undesirable in science (Lieberson 1993, 32). In light of the
conclusions drawn in the Herrnstein and Murray and the Rushton
volumes, Charles's views bear re-examination, since they are vindicated
by the considerable research evidence that has piled up for many years
regarding the role of inheritance and the role of the environment in
determining behaviour, abilities, intelligence, etc. But given her position on the term *"race,"* what about its use in the new 1996 Census
question instructions? It can be shown that the new question was
considered necessary because of the accumulated changes in the ethnocultural composition of Canada's population, and the policies proposed to help improve the chances and status of members of certain
minority groups perceived to be at a disadvantage. These were circumstances that could not have been, or at any rate were not, foreseen by
Charles in the 1940s, and initiatives that would not have appeared

illogical to her, given her interest in accommodating practical concerns. It is obvious that the use of the term *race* created problems in the 1990s because it carries with it anachronistic meanings and implications, unfortunately revived by the appearance of the pseudo-scientific claims of Rushton and of Herrnstein and Murray.

The 1994 volume by Herrnstein and Murray has spawned a veritable industry of publication that includes extended review articles in some of the most prestigious American literary and scientific magazines and scholarly journals, as well as, to date, two edited collections of essays.[5] And all are uniformly critical, some extremely so, of the research methods used and the conclusions drawn by the authors. A review of Rushton's book (not the only one) written by a scientist who "specializes in the genetics of brain development and behaviour" is pertinent (Wahlsten, 1996:129-33). After noting that "today, the concept of race is more a social than a genetic category,"[6] this author concludes that Rushton's "low standards of scholarship" render his work irrelevant for modern science, and raises the question: "Why is so much attention devoted in the mass media to a work of this quality?" (A second question can be posed. Why did the work of Herrnstein and Murray lead to such a deluge of critical reviews in the academic press?)

The answer to both questions is clear. Although the debate on race has been reignited more than 50 years after the earlier discussions its focus in Canada in the 1990s has not shifted one iota: it still revolves about the issue of "nature and nurture" with opposing sides to the debate more polarized and politicized than ever. Furthermore, the reappearance of the issue of race in this unaltered form in the last decade of the twentieth century makes all thinking and well-intentioned citizens justifiably concerned about the future of fundamental democratic values in North America.

The demographic literature in twentieth century North America on the subject of the origins and characteristics of immigrants reflects enormous social changes that resulted in what appeared to be the triumph of the principles of freedom and equality for all peoples, whatever their race, creed or colour. An early edited collection on population problems in the United States and Canada included materials showing how first-generation immigrants to North America, even those from Europe, were perceived as "foreigners" having certain "innate" characteristics, so that concern was expressed about the degree to which they could "fit in" or become "assimilated" (Dublin, 1926). Corresponding Canadian materials for the same period on immigrants from abroad, particularly on eastern and southern Europeans (e.g., Jewish, Polish, and Italian), and on Chinese, Japanese and other visibly different groups, were often couched in language that clearly reflected the outlook, attitudes and values of the politically dominant groups, mind-sets that we now refer to as "prejudices." Similar language and treatment are not considered acceptable today, when terms like "*race,*" "*racial*" and "*multiracial*" are used in informed social science discourse for descriptive rather than evaluative or pejorative reasons.

Furthermore, it remains an open question whether contemporary "politically correct" social scientific language reflects a true decline in prejudice against aboriginal peoples, and those originally or visibly from other continents and cultures. Some see it as a superficial switch to the use of less value-laden terms and language, dictated by current norms in contemporary North American society, which only appear to endorse principles of equality, freedom from prejudice, and justice for all. Recent events on the international scene, in Germany, in (former) Yugoslavia, in Africa, in the Near East, indeed everywhere in the world, challenge us to maintain, uphold and foster those hard-won democratic principles and ideals of equality for all peoples that were such important achievements in twentieth century North American society.

NOTES

1. Statistics Canada provided space, library and manuscript-preparation services, which are gratefully acknowledged. Thanks also to the World Health Organization for permitting citation of materials from Enid Charles's 1956 report on Burma (now Myanmar). Dr. Jean Burnet offered comments on an original version which added information and clarity to the text. Ravi Pendakur provided useful historical detail. The author is solely responsible for any errors or misleading interpretations.
2. Based on Appendix II, "Notes on the issue of 'race' in Canadian Census Statistics. Historical, conceptual and political dimensions," from "History of demography in Canada" (Wargon, 1997). This paper is dedicated to Dr. Warren Kalbach for his considerable efforts in promoting and using Canadian Census data, particularly those on ethnic origin and immigration.

3. In the late 1930s this eminent Swedish economist and social sci-
    entist was brought to the United States specifically to direct and
    oversee one of the largest and most comprehensive social science
    projects of the day, the study of the Negro in the United States.
    According to social science belief and practice in the 1940s, it
    was felt that an "outsider" to North American society would
    bring greater objectivity to the examination of this problem
    than one who belonged and was involved on a daily basis. The
    research results of this project were documented in numerous
    publications released in the United States in the 1940s. Myrdal
    drew his final conclusions in the summary volume *An American
    Dilemma* in Chapter 10, entitled "America at the Crossroads"
    (Myrdal, 1944). He warned that if Americans did not change
    their ways, they would pay dearly for their undemocratic treat-
    ment of the non-white minority. Myrdal's prediction came true
    in the 1960s. Although important changes have occurred since
    then, there are those who say that the issues he discussed are still
    very much alive today, and may even be more acute now than
    they were when the Carnegie Corporation commissioned the
    inquiry in the summer of 1937 (*Daedalus*, 1995). For a
    thought-provoking commentary on this subject by a political
    activist see Glazer, 1995.

4. This raises two important questions. What is the definition
    of "a multiracial society"? When can a society be considered
    "multiracial"? John Samuel's (1990:388) statement obviously
    refers to the inclusion of people of colour, that is, "non-white"
    groups. Samuel quotes other sociologists, like Jean Burnet, who
    describe Canada as a multiracial society. But a well-known
    Canadian demographer noted, some years before Samuel's 1990
    statement, that: "Since 1976, the majority of immigrants have
    come from the Third World. Already multi-ethnic, Canada
    could become a multi-racial society during the next century"
    (Lachapelle, 1988). Is it *numbers* that determine when a society
    is "multiracial"? And if so, what are the crucial numbers?

5. I have read four extensive review articles and one edited volume
    of essays, all of which cite additional reviews, sources, articles,
    even a second edited collection of articles. These references are
    simply too numerous to include in the context of this brief
    paper. Besides, it is certain that since it was written more
    reviews will have appeared.

6. There appears to be a perceptible shift away from the purely sociological or "social construction" explanation to the "evolutionary psychological" explanation. The latter holds that classifying people according to race is not simply cultural, it is also a direct consequence of how the human mind develops and works.

3

RACE IN THE CANADIAN CENSUS

MONICA BOYD, GUSTAVE GOLDMANN, AND PAMELA WHITE

UNLIKE HER NEIGHBOUR to the south, Canada has an erratic history of enumerating the racial composition of her population. This enumeration history is characterized by three components: 1) temporal variation in the presence, or absence, of a census question relevant to the collection of racial data; 2) variation in question wording such that at times "race" is explicit and at other subsumed by the "origin" concept; and 3) variation in the larger societal ideologies of race relations that motivate data collection.

At the moment, Canada is at a crossroad. Considerable demand for data on "visible minorities" currently exists as a result of changing models of social inequality and related public policies of multiculturalism and employment equity. Public discourse on "racism" and racial discrimination has also fuelled such data demands. However, the 1991 Census failed to include a question that explicitly asks for "race," despite formal consultation by Statistics Canada and considerable public attention to the issue. The 1996 Census asked a question on the country's visible minority population for the first time. Yet, during the 1996 Census collection, diverse blocks of public opinion threatened to perpetuate societal and statistical ambivalence about asking the question at all.

The purpose of this paper is twofold: 1) to document the variations in the Canadian Census with regard to enumerating race; and 2) to show that such variations covary with changing conceptualizations of race and race relations. Pursuit of these objectives serves to confirm both common sense and expert assessments of ethnic and racial origin questions. How and when ancestry and/or phenotypical or somatic characteristics are collected by the Census is determined not only by the principles of social survey research but also by laws, politics, and broader societal representations of ethnicity and race (Goldmann and McKenney, 1993).

In order to provide background information on the Census as a measuring instrument, we present a brief overview of census-taking in Canada. We then discuss the changing history of enumerating race in Canadian censuses. Temporal variations exist in approaches to the enumeration of race. These variations reflect prevailing models of racial discourse and nation-building. In a subsequent section, we examine the specific issues that associated with attempts to devise a question on race for the 1991 Census. We conclude with a brief assessment of the issues which must be confronted in renewing attempts to field a race question in the 1996 census.

TAKING STOCK

As Priest (1990:1) observes, "[i]t is difficult to discuss the collection and use of ethnicity [and, we add, race] in the Canadian Census without recounting ... the struggle of the French and the British for control of the North American continent and to consider the history of census-taking itself." Priest's review enriches the context of early census-taking, beginning in 1665 with Jean Talon's enumeration of the population in the French territory which is now part of Quebec. Motivated by questions of political and economic domination through the mechanism of European settlement, these early Censuses focused on age, sex, marital status, professions and trades. Race, religion and origins were new dimensions added to the 1767 British-instigated Censuses in Nova Scotia, and race and origins reappeared in the 1824 census in New Brunswick (Priest, 1990).

To the extent that race, religion and origins were found in other earlier Censuses, much of the emphasis was on collecting data by religion and/or birthplace. Such information was central to broader issues of nation-building and sovereignty in a land whose colonization had been so much contested in the preceding two centuries. However, the demographic and economic expansion of Canada's western regions during the late 1800s brought with it increasing awareness of, and conflict with, the Aboriginal populations resident there. Following the uprising of Louis Riel and his Métis force, an 1885 Census of Assiniboia, Saskatchewan and Alberta included a count of wigwams and introduced the concept of "half-breeds" through a modification of the origin question.

The British North America Act, 1867, formalized nation-building endeavours. To meet the administrative needs of the Canadian govern-

ment it provided the legal mechanism for the continuation of decennial Censuses undertaken in 1851 and 1861. Since then the government
of Canada has been required to conduct a census of population in the
first full year of every decade. More recently the decennial Census has
been conducted under the authority of the Constitution Act, 1982.
National quinquennial Censuses began in 1956 and since this time
Canada has held a census every five years (Statistics Act, 1985).

Immigration was a major component of Canada's growth and
national development in the centuries following the travels of the early
European explorers. As Miles (1992) notes, how racially and ethnically
diverse newcomers are to be incorporated is a major question facing such
countries both then and now. Similar concerns and administrative needs
appear to underlie the continued interest in enumerating the origins of
Canada's population during the 1800s. Nevertheless, race as an explicit
term did not then enter into the census-taking. Table 3.1 shows the temporal variations in the focus on origins, race and visible minority group.

TABLE 3.1

HISTORICAL OVERVIEW OF CANADA'S COLLECTION OF ETHNIC
AND RACIAL ORIGIN DATA BY CENSUS YEAR, 1767 TO 1996

Census Year	Origins	Racial Origins	Ethnic Origins	Visible Minority Group
1767	X	X		
1824		X		
1851	X			
1861	X			
1871	X			
1881	X			
1891	NA	NA	NA	NA
1901		X		
1911		X		
1921		X		
1931		X		
1941		X		
1951			X	
1961			X	
1971			X	
1981			X	
1986			X	X*
1991			X	X*
1996			X	X*

X* Derived counts of visible minority population based on employment equity definitions.
NA= Not asked.
Source: White, Badets and Renaud, 1993. Modified to reflect 1996 Census.

Between 1851 and 1881, the primary focus was on the origins of the Canadian population. However, a discernible shift occurred following the 1891 Census, in which no question on origins or race was present, though information on persons of French Canadian background was collected. Between 1901 and 1941, racial origins were an explicit part of the wording of Census questions. Enumerators were provided with rules of enumeration that emphasized categorization according to lineage or descent. In 1951, however, explicit references to "race" were abruptly dropped. Between 1951 and 1991, data collection efforts relied on an ethnic origin question. In 1996, questions on ethnic origin, Aboriginal identity and visible minority group were asked.

If the explicit formulations of race questions vary, so too do the underlying conceptualizations of race. Given Canada's European settlement and attachments it is not surprising to find that images of, and discussion about, race parallel northern European changes in conceptualizing it. Miles (1989:31) argues that the idea of "race" emerged in the English language in the early sixteenth century, as part of nation-building and it largely referred to populations of emergent nation states. In its early usage in Europe the term "race" meant lineage or common descent and identified a population with a common origin and history, but not a population with a fixed biological character. However, the idea of race took on a new meaning with the development of science, its application to the natural world, and its extension to a social world (Miles, 1989). By the late 1800s, social Darwinism had permeated public and academic discourse.

Between 1901 and 1941, Canadian Censuses not only explicitly used the terms "race" and "racial origin," but also they contained elaborate instructions to enumerators on how to properly categorize respondents on the basis of race. The categories changed somewhat over time, but the emphasis was on demarcating a "white" population from groups which today are considered African, Asian or Aboriginal. As Table 3.2 shows, paternal ancestry was used to classify the European "white" groups. Indians [sic] were to be classified by the origin of the mother and all offspring of children of mixed marriages between white and other "races" were classified as belonging to the non-white "race."

In the Canadian Census questions on "race," the descent rules which were *de rigueur* up to 1941 are highly consistent with evolutionary theory. According to the nineteenth century evolutionary schemes, societies were classified on a scale that, based on Lewis Henry Morgan's

TABLE 3.2

DESCENT RULES, BY CENSUS YEAR AND BY
ETHNIC/RACIAL/TRIBAL ORIGIN

Census	White/ European	Indian	Métis	Inuit/ Eskimo	Other Non- White	Other Mixed
1871	Not specified	Not specified	Not specified	Not specified	Not specified	Not specified
1881	Not specified	Not specified	Not specified	Not specified	Not specified	Not specified
1891	N/A	N/A	N/A	N/A	N/A	N/A
1901	Patrilineal	Tribal	Complex	Not specified	Not specified	Not specified
1911	Patrilineal	Matrilineal	Not specified	Not specified	Not specified	Non-white
1921	Patrilineal	Matrilineal	Not specified	Not specified	Not specified	Non-white
1931	Patrilineal	Matrilineal	Not specified	Not specified	Coloured	Non-white
1941	Patrilineal	Indian	Half-breed	Eskimo	Coloured	Non-white
1951	Patrilineal	Patrilineal	Place of residence	Not specified	Patrilineal	Patrilineal
1961	Patrilineal	Patrilineal	Place of residence	Not specified	Patrilineal	Patrilineal
1971	Patrilineal	Patrilineal	Patrilineal	Patrilineal	Patrilineal	Patrilineal
1981	Ambilineal	Ambilineal	Ambilineal	Ambilineal	Ambilineal	Ambilineal
1986	Ambilineal	Ambilineal	Ambilineal	Ambilineal	Ambilineal	Ambilineal
1991	Ambilineal	Ambilineal	Ambilineal	Ambilineal	Ambilineal	Ambilineal
1996	Ambilineal	Ambilineal	Ambilineal	Ambilineal	Ambilineal	Ambilineal

Note: In the 1996 Census, the Aboriginal Identity question asks respondents to self-identify as being
North American, Indian, Metis or Inuit. Respondents can mark more than one group. Aboriginal
respondents are not asked to respond to the question identifying visible minorities as the Employment
Equity legislation defines visible minorities as persons who are other than Aboriginal persons.

interpretation, spanned a continuum from "savagery" to "barbarism"
to "civilization" (Zeitlin,1990). Evolutionists commonly believed that
in "civilized" societies descent was determined along patrilineal lines.
They also believed that among "barbaric" societies descent was matri-
lineally based and that among "savages" it was based on, "tribal" affiliation. With regard to Canada's Census, it is interesting to note that
according to this logic the Aboriginal population "evolved" from savagery to barbarism during the period 1901 and 1911. This contrasted
with the specification of rights in the Indian Act which designated
lineage according to patrilineal descent until changes were made by
Bill C-31 (1985).

However, if one focuses on the descent rules in the 1901-1941
Canadian Censuses as reflecting the then existing conceptualizations of
race one risks missing the broader motivating forces behind the adop-
tion of such conceptualization and measurement. Migration involves
contact with new societies, and in Canada's history it certainly con-

cerned the twofold activities of dominating the indigenous populations and creating a nation out of diverse peoples. Miles (1989:11) argues that such migration generates and reshapes imagery, beliefs and evaluations about the "Other" in order to formulate a strategy for interaction. In Canada, prior to the mid-1900s, the representations of the "Other" in "racial" terms emphasized biological properties associated with blood lineage. These representations, as embodied in descent rules, took different forms depending on the twin projects of colonialism and nationhood.

Colonialism is often defined as the military, political and/or economic dominance of one nation over a subordinate country. Internal colonialism exists where Europeans have settled in new lands, established European institutions and subjugated both indigenous and non-indigenous peoples (Satzewich and Wotherspoon, 1992). There are a number of dimensions to this internal colonialism, but one aspect of the colonization process is the creation of racism and a colour line to regulate social interaction between groups.

The settlement of the Prairies carried with it an agenda for the agricultural development of the region and the wresting away of control from the indigenous peoples. The establishment of a permanent Canadian presence in the West also diminished American influences. Evolutionary theory made it possible to develop a discourse of race that represented Aboriginals as the "Other," with capacities and achievements fixed by biological, natural and unalterable conditions (Miles, 1989). As observed by Satzewich and Wotherspoon (1992: 8), "ideologies of biological superiority and inferiority emerge[d] to justify the exploitation of Aboriginal people and their resources, to break down their resistance and to deter them from becoming full members of Canadian society." The Indian Act was a significant legislative instrument of policy, used by the Canadian government to maintain control over indigenous groups and to instill the notion of "Other."

However, non-European groups from abroad were not immune to social characterization. Late nineteenth-century reactions against the immigration of Chinese existed, with a head tax being imposed in 1886 and increased in 1900 and 1903. Indeed, the rules of descent as operationalized in the Census for the years 1901 to 1941 approximated the notion of the "one drop rule." This form of categorization had been in existence in the United States and prevented successive generations of mixed marriage offspring from ever being classified "white" (Davis, 1991).

As well, reputed biological properties were the basis of many admonitions against admitting European groups of dubious "suitability." As Porter (1965:64-65) notes British immigrants were never considered foreigners, but changing immigration patterns, reducing the proportion of Northern European and British settlers in favour of Eastern and Southern Europeans provoked debate about the desirability of other groups. Central to this debate was a focus on certain traits as biological, although there was much variation in opinion as to whether these traits were to be considered as cultural in origin, or as genetic, inherited and thus unalterable.

The 1908 book *Strangers at Our Gate*, written by J. S. Woodsworth, epitomized many of the beliefs and tensions regarding the relative desirability of various white "races." However, Woodsworth was not alone in his views. Such attitudes lasted well into the 1940s and served to exclude many groups from entry into Canada. For example, Abella and Tropper (1982) document the tragic consequences of Canadian immigration policies which prevented admission of Jews to Canada both before and after the Second World War.

The resulting schema of ranking clearly acknowledged the dominance of the British-origin group in Canada's economic, political and social life. For almost two centuries following the battle between British and French forces on the Plains of Abraham, international migration reinforced British domination. The Immigration Acts of 1910, 1927 and 1952 continued the exclusion of groups deemed undesirable according to ethnic/racial criteria and continued to favour the migration of people from the British Isles, Northern Europe and — if all else failed — other European areas (Harney, 1988). In actual fact, during the late 1800s and through the 1900s, migration from Europe ensured substantial ethnic diversification, yet the prevailing model remained that of assimilation to a British ethnic prototype (Breton, 1988; Harney, 1988). The creation of a common "Anglo" ideology and set of institutions and the pressing agenda of developing the western interior of Canada provided important contexts for debates on the characteristics of South and East European migrants. These debates accorded much attention to the ability of such groups to be assimilated and to strengthen Canada's nation-building endeavours.

To summarize: between 1901 and 1941 the context surrounding the "race" questions generated two models of incorporation into the Canadian mainstream. Both emphasized lineage and invoked distinctions between "we" and "they." In one model, firm unalterable boundaries existed around non-white groups. In the context of the Canadian Census, the instructions to census enumerators specified that the off-spring of mixed marriages (white/non-white) were to be assigned the non-white "race." These boundaries both derived from and reaffirmed prevailing ideologies in which white was superior and dominant in relation to other non-white groups.

The second model permitted boundary crossing for the white pop-ulation. Although various "white" immigrant groups were considered races, categorization in the Census was traced through the father's side. As a result, intermarriage for the white population could, and did, change the categorization of offspring. Such fluidity is consistent with the early twentieth century model of Anglo assimilation and with the transformation of the white "other" into the "self."

POST-SECOND WORLD WAR VIEW: OUT WITH RACE, IN WITH CULTURE

The period between 1941 and 1951 was in many respects a watershed. World War II sensitized the Western world to the genocidal policies that could — and did — accompany the conceptualization of race as biological and unalterable. This most certainly had an impact on the way in which the population was counted and classified in Canadian Censuses from that point on. The 1951 Census origins question con-tained no mention of "race" either in the instructions to enumerators or in the question description and wording. Instead, the emphasis was on ancestry or cultural origins on the father's side. Aboriginal peoples, Africans and persons of colour or with distinctive features continued to be enumerated as such, but the vocabulary of labelling and categoriza-tion officially changed to that of origin instead of race. With minor alterations, the approach adopted in the 1951 Census was repeated in 1961 and 1971. From 1981 onward, instructions to link origins to the paternal side were dropped and multiple responses were permitted.

While an important factor in the move away from an explicit "race" question, horror at Nazi termination policies does not adequately ac-count for the protracted postwar history of Census questions on ethnic origins as opposed to race. Nation-building was again an important fac-tor although the earlier ideologies of Anglo-conformity and colonialism were to be replaced by issues of multiculturalism and sovereignty.

In addition to Anglo-French relations (Breton,1988), demograph-ic change in the form of large postwar immigration provided an important impetus to development of the concept of nationhood and its legislative and institutional representations. During and after World War I the large numbers of migrants to Canada slowed considerably and became a trickle during the Depression years of the 1930s. After World War II, however, not only was Europe on the move, with the migration of displaced persons, but also there was an awareness in the Canadian government, due to the war, of the dangers of a sparsely settled country. In his 1947 statement to Parliament on immigration Prime Minister Mackenzie King explicitly noted that immigration would shore up Canada's small population. Europe was clearly the source for such reinforcements, given King's announcement that Canada did not wish there to be, as a result of mass immigration, any fundamental alteration in the character of the Canadian population. However, in 1962 and in 1967 changes in Canadian immigration regulations opened the doors to non-European groups. These changes, later embodied in the Immigration Act, 1976, replaced the national origins criteria for admission with those emphasizing family reunification and labour market contribution. Groups which previously could not immigrate to Canada because they were not from designated European countries were now admitted if they met family reunification, labour market or humanitarian criteria.

These policy changes altered the composition of Canada's migration flows and diversified the Canadian population. Of immigrants arriving before 1961 over 90 percent were born in the United States and Europe, while between one to two percent were Asian-born. In contrast, of those immigrating in the late 1980s, a little over 30 percent were from the United States and Europe, compared with over 40 percent from Asia. Today, close to three quarters of immigrants come from regions other than Europe and the United States.

Harney (1988) argues that the resultant ethnic diversity belied the old images of Canadian society and thus fuelled the search for a principle of collective national identity in the 1980s. However, the need to unify a country with major regional and linguistic/ethnic cleavages had been recognized by politicians much earlier. Starting in the late 1950s under Diefenbaker, and continuing under the Liberal governments of the 1960s and 1970s, a series of policies and actions were initiated which deliberately and directly appealed to Canada's inhabitants as Canadian regardless of where they lived or what language they spoke (Smith, 1989).

The development of Canada's multiculturalism policy can be interpreted as part of the efforts of the Canadian state to given recognition to the role that ethnic diversity plays in the forging of a Canadian identity. The original impetus for such a policy came from the Royal Commission on Bilingualism and Biculturalism, which was intended to review the status of the British and the French "founding peoples." However, non-British and French groups stressed in public hearings that their status too must be recognized (Sheridan and Saouab, 1992). As Stasiulius (1991) observes, various groups sought a policy of multiculturalism as a strategy for affirming their place in the nations's ethnocultural symbolic order.

Established in 1971, Canada's multiculturalism policy has gone through several evolutions (Sheridan and Saouab, 1992). In respect of data demands, the most significant events have been legislative. During the 1980s and early 1990s additional significant legislative developments included the creation of the Department of Multiculturalism and Citizenship. Major programs managed by this federal department, currently known as Heritage Canada, include: Race Relations and Cross-Cultural Understanding; Heritage Cultures and Languages; and Community Support and Participation. The data requirements of these programs were reinforced by two additional documents. The first was the Canadian Charter of Rights and Freedoms, 1982, which guaranteed rights regardless of origin, race, gender, age or disability. The second was the Employment Equity Act, 1986, which established a monitoring of hiring and promotion practices affecting visible minorities, women, Aboriginal peoples and persons with disabilities in federally regulated businesses.

Together, the creation of a federal department, the Charter and the Employment Equity Act created the policy rationales for collecting and disseminating information on various ethnocultural groups in Canada. Such matters as how the ethnic origin question is worded, whether ancestral origins, identity or visible minority status is captured or derived and whether or not multiple responses are permitted have become contested terrain for a large body of potential users including researchers, government agencies and ethnocultural groups. The debate in the public arena, discussed elsewhere (Boyd, 1993a, 1993b), derives as much from the politics of numbers as from the application of principles of sound survey design.

THE CHALLENGE OF THE 1990S

From 1971 onward, the collection of Census data through enumerators has been replaced by a methodology that primarily relies on self-reporting by respondents. As a result, Canadian Census planning now includes extensive pretesting of census questions and nation-wide public consultation. Ethnocultural questions are an integral subset of such pretests and consultations. After a hiatus of nearly 50 years, the need to collect data on race was actively discussed and explicitly tested as part of the 1991 and the 1996 Census consultation and testing.

In a contrast to earlier practices the question on race was now motivated by reformulated concepts of equality and a growing concern with discrimination and racism in Canadian society. As in the United States (Blauner, 1991) structural models of inequality emphasizing institutionalized barriers and discrimination had come, by the 1980s, to replace earlier individualist models of inequality, in which the central concern was lack of opportunity for individual achievement (Agocs and Boyd, 1993). In addition to academic research and public discourse, this paradigmatic shift also characterized legislation and policy. For example, section 15(2) of the Canadian Charter of Rights and Freedoms, 1982, removed obstacles to the subsequent passage of the Employment Equity Act, 1986. This Act and accompanying regulations were reviewed and strengthened in 1996.

The foundation document of Canadian employment equity policy was the 1984 report of the Royal Commission on Equality in Employment (Abella, 1984). This report corroborated the changed approaches to stratification, in which issues of difference were replaced in the 1960s by preoccupations with equality of opportunity. More recently, analysts have begun to emphasize the covert sources of disadvantage, produced as a result of traditional hiring and promotional practices (Agocs and Boyd, 1993).

Seeking to redress the effects of systemic discrimination, the Report of the Royal Commission on Equality in Employment recommended that the government of Canada pass legislation making employment equity mandatory for employers in the public and private sectors, and that there be effective arrangements to monitor compliance and impose sanctions for failure to demonstrate good faith efforts to attain employment equity goals. In response, the Conservative government of the day introduced two initiatives in 1986: the Employment Equity Act and the Federal Contractors Program.

Within the context of the Act, visible minorities are defined as "persons other than Aboriginal persons, who are non-Caucasian in race or non-white in colour and who so identify themselves to an employer or agree to be so identified by an employer for the purpose of the

Employment Equality Act" (Employment and Immigration Canada, 1989:25). The underlying concept of this definition is race. In the terminology the choice of "visible minority" is itself noteworthy. The term came into usage in the early 1980s. Given alternatives such as race (United States) and "ethnic minorities" (United Kingdom, Germany, Netherlands) an interesting question is what was the reason for constructing of a new nuance. While the answer may be partly found in the identity politics already practiced by Aboriginal people, another part of it may lie in the studied avoidance of the term "race" since the 1950s. Critics charge that this avoidance, and the accompanied nuances of "visible minorities," is also avoidance of the issue of racism (Stasiulius, 1991).

Under the Employment Equity Act, 1986 (and as reaffirmed in the 1996 legislation) federally regulated businesses are required to submit annual reports indicating their employment profiles in regard to the four target groups. These target populations are visible minorities, Aboriginal peoples, women and persons with disabilities. Self-identification categories for visible minority groups are Black, Chinese, Japanese, Korean, Filipino, Indo-Pakistani, West Asian and Arab, Southeast Asian, Latin American, Indonesian and Pacific Islander (Employment and Immigration Canada, 1986). Compliance with the Act involves comparisons with a reference population, usually that of the local labour market. Given this methodology and the implied requirements for geographically defined information, Census data represent a potentially important source.

These legislative demands have obliged Statistics Canada to provide data on a new construct. The methodology developed for the 1981, 1986, and 1991 Census data derives visible minority status from responses to Census questions on birthplace, ethnic origins, mother tongue and religion (the latter was not collected in the 1986 Census). These procedures were developed in collaboration with the federal departments responsible for the Employment Equity Act. The reliance on existing Census questions means that self-identification plays no role in defining "visible minority," unlike the methodology used to collect data at the business firm level.

It is important to note that Statistics Canada has experienced considerable difficulty in measuring ethnic and cultural self-identification. In 1986, for example, a question asking persons of Aboriginal background whether they "considered themselves to be an aboriginal or native person of Canada" produced a high level of "false positive response" on the part of respondents who did not understand such terms as Aboriginal and Inuit. At this time, Statistics Canada concluded that an identity question should not be edited for consistency with other responses, since the response provided was one based on respondent opinion and self-identity rather than fact. Data from this 1986 Census question were not published.

Similarly, testing after the 1986 Census revealed that the Federal Public Service question, which asked respondents to identify the visible minority group to which they considered themselves to belong, produced poor quality data when used in the 1986 Census Overcoverage Survey (White,1988). In this instance, respondents reported "immigrant," "Québécois" and "senior" as being the visible minority groups to which they belonged.

For the 1991 Census, questions were developed which asked respondents to report their ethnic origin while a certain subset of the population who completed the Aboriginal Peoples Survey responded to a question on Aboriginal identity. In 1996, however, the range of questions was expanded to include visible minority status, ethnic origin and Aboriginal identity.

Conscious of the need for data on the new concept of visible minority, Statistics Canada sought to determine if a direct question on race or visible minority status should be asked in the 1991 and the 1996 Censuses. During the Census content consultations, data users, ethnocultural groups and advisory bodies to Statistics Canada were asked to ponder the inclusion of a question on race, and its wording. In preparation for the 1991 and the 1996 Censuses, respondents to various surveys and pretests were asked a question on race, and qualitative assessments by focus groups on these questions were also undertaken (Breedon, 1988; White, 1988; Statistics Canada, 1994b).

The inquiry into racial differentiation of the Canadian population marked a fundamental turning point for the agency. Statistics Canada has been criticized in the past for being slow to measure social phenomena. To discuss the concepts of race, and to consider the measurement of race in a country which has frequently overlooked its racialized history (Abele and Stasiulius, 1989; Walker, 1985) is remarkable. The shift occurred in the aftermath of the 1980s, which was a turbulent period in the history of Canadian nation-building. Issues of Canadian identity, multiculturalism and the place of Quebec in a renewed federalism (Spicer, 1991) captured public attention, influenced Census consultations and generated discussions of the collection of visible

TABLE 3.3

1991 AND 1996 CENSUS: TEST AND CENSUS QUESTIONS

Survey	Question Asked	Response Categories	Comments
1986 Census Overcoverage Survey	Do you consider yourself to belong to Canada's visible or racial minority population?	No Yes: Specify Black Chinese South East Asian South Asian Pacific Islands Arab West Asian Indigenous Central/ South American Other (specify)	In the specified space entries included: immigrant Québécois, senior.
1987 Modular Test 2	Which of the following best describes your race or colour?	Black Korean Filipino Japanese Chinese Native/Aboriginal Peoples of North America South Asian South East Asian White Other (specify)	Small sample survey test used to test census questions. High non-response.
1988 National Census Test 1 (NCT1)	Which of the following best describes this person's race or colour?	White Asian Black Other (specify)	First 1991 NCT. Low non-response. Few backlash or nonsense responses. Persons of Arab and Latin American background reported White.
1988 National Census Test 2 (NCT2)	Which of the following best describes this person's race or colour?	White Asian North American Indian Métis Eskimo/Inuit Black Other (specify)	Second 1991 NCT. Low non-response. Few backlash or nonsense responses. Persons of Arab, West Asian and Latin American background reported White.

Survey	Question Asked	Response Categories	Comments
1991 Census	To which ethnic or cultural group did this person's ancestors belong?	French English German Scottish Italian Irish Ukrainian Chinese Dutch Jewish Polish Black North American Indian Métis Inuit/Eskimo Other (specify)	No race question was asked. Visible minority data were derived (based on employment equity specifications).
1993 National Census Test (NCT 1993)	Is this person?	White Chinese South Asian Black Arab/West Asian Filipino South East Asian Latin American Japanese Korean Indonesian/Pacific Islander Other (specify)	1996 NCT. Low non-response. Few backlash responses. Some reporting of White by respondents having as ethnic origin Arab, West Asian and Latin American.
1996 Census	Ethnic origin To which ethnic or cultural group did this person's ancestors belong?	Four (4) write-in spaces.	List of ethnic groups included in the list of examples shown on the questionnaire: French, English, German, Scottish, Canadian, Italian, Irish, Chinese, Cree, Micmac, Métis, Inuit (Eskimo), Ukrainian, Dutch, East Indian, Polish, Portuguese, Jewish, Haitian, Jamaican, Vietnamese, Lebanese, Chilean, Somali, etc. Groups shown in order of incidence in the last census with Aboriginal group lists as well as same groups from all area world areas.

(Table 3.3 *cont'd*)

Survey	Question Asked	Response Categories	Comments
1996 Census	Population Group	White	Some of the mark-in
		Chinese	entries contained
	Is this person:	South Asian	examples. For example
		Black	Black (e.g., African,
		Arab/West Asian	Haitian, Jamaican,
		Filipino	Somali)
		South East Asian	
		Latin American	
		Japanese	
		Korean	
		Other (specify)	

minority and "Canadian" ethnic origin data (Boyd, 1993a, 1996; Pryor et al., 1992).

Four 1991 Census pretest instruments explored various approaches to measuring ethnic origin and visible minority status (Table 3.3). The 1986 Census Overcoverage Survey (fielded six weeks after the 1986 Census) asked respondents, "do you consider yourself to belong to Canada's visible or racial minority population." This question was similar to the one developed by Treasury Board in that the term "visible minority" was used. Analysis of responses indicated a number of difficulties, including underidentification and considerable confusion as to what was meant by the term "visible minority," even thought the term "racial" minority was also part of the question (White, 1988). There was also a strong tendency on the part of members of linguistic groups to define themselves as members of visible minority groups when, in fact, cross-tabulations with other ethnocultural questions indicated that these members were not members of the designated groups defined for Employment Equity Purposes. Focus group testing in Toronto, Montreal, Halifax, Winnipeg and Vancouver supported the findings of the Overcoverage Survey question. The term "visible minority" was not well understood by the general public; and there was no widespread awareness of the federal Employment Equity program. Together, the results of the Overcoverage Survey and the focus group tests formed the bases for the decision not to use the terms "visible minority" or "employment equity" in the 1991 Census.

The Modular Test-2, undertaken in 1988 in preparation for the National Census Test, departed from the perceptual wording of the Overcoverage Survey and asked respondents to indicate which category(ies) (largely precoded) best described their race or colour. There was a high level of non-response to this question (over 10 percent) and substantial discrepancy between responses to questions on race and on ethnicity, ancestry and ethnic identity (White, 1988). Factors which contributed to this high rate of non-response included the poor placement of the "white" circle. This mark-in entry was located well down the list of possible choices. In addition, the examples used to define the groups were confusing to respondents, as the question displayed a mixture of ethnic, race, and colour examples to explain the content of the employment equity designated groups.

A reformatted and simpler question on race was repeated in the two National Census Tests held prior to the 1991 Census. The National Census Test-2 was modified to improve responses by the Aboriginal respondents but otherwise retained the limited set of categories to be marked. Both of the National Census Test (NCT-1, NCT-2) race questions experienced relatively low rates of non-response. The non-response rate of five percent in the NCT-1 was comparable to rates obtained in other NCT ethnocultural questions and the non-response rate for the NCT-2 was four percent. Both questions experienced few crank, nonsense or backlash responses. As well, within the bounds of sampling variance, the two National Census Test questions on race reproduced population estimates of the visible minority population.

Nonetheless, difficulties remained. In both National Census Test questions on race there was a tendency for respondents reporting West Asian, Arab, or Latin/Central/South American origins to mark "White" as their race or colour. While such self-assignment may be understood within the context of phenotypical self-description, these groups are considered part of the designated visible minority groups for Employment Equity purposes. Thus, the responses posed potential problems, since the purpose of the race question was to generate information relevant for Employment Equity programs.

Alongside pretests of alternative questions on race the public debate continued on whether to collect such data at all. Focus tests revealed considerable concerns about the intent of the question on race and many participants found it offensive (Breedon, 1988). Moreover, the Ethnocultural Council of Canada (ECC), an umbrella group representing nearly 40 national organizations, also felt that a question on race could be perceived as offensive.

As an aside, it is important to note the ECC found the notion of race to be problematic. Their major concern was focused on the view that strong "Canadian" responses to an ancestry question had the potential to reduce counts for many of the long-standing member groups such as

Ukrainian, German and Dutch. Political lobbying, which led to a response by Statistics Canada to the Parliamentary Committee on Multiculturalism and Citizenship (Petrie, 1989) focused on the dilemma of "Canadian" origin, identity and citizenship and not on issues of race, colour or equity legislation.

In the end, however, there was no question on race or colour in the 1991 Census. Visible minority information continued to be derived using several ethnocultural and linguistic census questions. Factors contributing to this decision included limited space on the questionnaire and the need to reduce response burden.

As Boxhill (1990) notes the Employment Equity data requirement was not solely founded on a narrow definition of race but rather on an amalgam of race, ethnicity and cultural group. For example, Chileans are not part of the visible minority group, while Mexicans are. There are requirements for data on various Asian groups: Korean, Japanese, Chinese and Filipino. African origin groups are classified as Black and no distinction was made between Afro-Canadian, Caribbean and African-born groups. Thus, for the 1991 Census, it was concluded that the demands of the employment equity program would best be met by the ethnic origin question, since in combination with questions on religion, mother tongue and birthplace it would permit the construction of "visible minority" groups (Boyd, 1993a; White, Badets, and Renaud, 1993).

1996 CENSUS: DIRECT QUESTION ON VISIBLE MINORITIES

Given legislative requirements and a public that is increasingly aware of Employment Equity issues, race relations and racism, the issue of including a question on race in Canada's census did not fade away. Instead, it resurfaced with the 1996 Census-taking efforts. In these the past activities with respect to the 1991 Census have informed the ongoing debate.

The 1991 Census ethnic origin question, as previously discussed, was designed to collect information required for Employment Equity and Multiculturalism programs. Negative public reactions to the mark-in entry "Black" by Afro-Canadian groups, who viewed it as a "racial" term, rather than an ethnic category (White, 1992), as well as increasing support for the specification of the ethnic origin "Canadian," resulted in continued consultation and testing prior to the 1996 Census.

The issue of "Canadian" further complicated the issue of meeting visible minority data needs. "Canadian" was the fifth largest single response ethnic group in the 1991 Census. The practice in past Censuses has been to list the ethnic groups in numerical order. If this practice were continued, the category "Canadian" would have to be included among the list of examples of ethnic groups shown for the ethnic origin question in 1996. For example, if a mark-in question were to be developed, "Canadian" would have been shown as the fifth mark-in entry. Or, if only write-in entries were permitted, then "Canadian" would be the fifth group shown in the list of examples of ethnic entries.

In addition to public reaction and the potential consequences of "Canadian" responses, another ground for change was the derivation of visible minority groups from ethnocultural questions. The decision to continue with the derivation of visible minority counts from the ethnic origin, place of birth, religion and language questions was not without its critics. During the 1996 Census consultation, the majority of data users voiced support for the testing and inclusion in the 1996 Census of a direct question designed to count the country's visible minority population (Statistics Canada, 1994a). The ethnic origin question, in particular, came under criticism from Canadian Black groups, who expressed a strong preference for reporting their ethnic background as, for example, Haitian, Jamaican or African-Canadian. Aboriginal peoples indicated that they too wished to report a tribal or First Nation origin rather than mark the entry "North American Indian" which had appeared in earlier censuses.

In sum, three forces underlay the decision to test a different set of ethnocultural questions in the 1996 National Census Test, fielded in November 1993: 1) the renewed interest and support for a direct question on visible minorities; 2) the need to change prespecified categories; and 3) the requirement to include "Canadian" in the listing of examples of ethnic groups shown on the questionnaire. The November 1993 NCT asked a series of questions on ethnic origin, Aboriginal identity, visible minority group, Status/Treaty Indian, and Band/First Nation. Various language questions were also asked (first language learned, home language, official and non-official language knowledge, language used at work and language of schooling). Prior to the inclusion of these questions in the National Census Test extensive qualitative testing was undertaken on such topics as respondent reactions to terms, response to direct questions and the understanding of why questions were asked.

The results of the 1993 National Census Test indicated that about 30 percent of respondents would report "Canadian" to the ethnic origin question (Statistics Canada, 1994b). Discrepancies also existed between responses to the ethnic origin question and responses to direct questions on Aboriginal identity and visible minority group. Inspection of responses to the latter direct questions revealed that some Aboriginal and visible minority respondents provided responses that appeared to be inconsistent. That is, they reported their ethnic origin as being Canadian, English, French or Spanish. As well, there was some reporting of "White" by members of some designated visible minority groups.

The results of the testing undertaken prior to the 1996 Census led Statistics Canada to conclude that a direct visible minority question would yield estimates of improved data quality, as compared with those the ethnic origin approach (Statistics Canada, 1994a). The primary rationales for including a direct visible minority question in the 1996 Census were threefold: 1) the overall high quality of responses to the visible minority question; 2) a low level of non-response and few nonsense or backlash responses (Renaud, 1994a,b); and 3) the legislated requirement to provide data on visible minorities.

During the interval between the testing of the 1996 Census question in 1993 and the date of the Census (May 14, 1996), several factors intervened which brought the issue of Employment Equity and the 1996 Census question under close scrutiny. One was the election in Ontario of a government which adopted as one of its major election issues the elimination of *provincial* Employment Equity legislation. Another was a concern regarding the continuation of high immigration levels during a time of poor economic performance and the concentration of certain groups in major urban centres.

The public media reaction was swift once the 1996 Census questions were published in *Canada Gazette* on August 22, 1995 (Mitchell, 1995). Criticism of the question focused on the usefulness of the federal Employment Equity legislation. Certain commentators felt such a Census question was based on outmoded ideas of race and had the potential to be socially divisive (Gardner, 1995; Loney, 1995). It should also be noted that during this period social tensions were heightened by such issues as a need for social cohesion and the apparent lack of common vision for the country as it faced the outcome of the October 30, 1995 referendum in Quebec.

Media reaction therefore focused on three topics: 1) the need for data showing various ethnic and visible minority groups; 2) the aims of

Employment Equity and Multiculturalism legislation; and 3) the perception of some Canadians that identification of groups as being other than "Canadian" contributed to a lack of social cohesion and national identity. In addition, certain commentators questioned the premise of economically based racial discrimination (Greenfield, 1996), though this point of view was questioned by Pendakur and Pendakur (1996). In addition to these themes, reaction also focused on question content. Some commentators disagreed with the categories and examples shown on the questionnaire. The inclusion of some groups and not others was criticized (Gwyn, 1996). The category "White" was also seen by some as being unacceptable (Gunter, 1996).

In response, members of the visible minority community (Cardozo, 1996), the ethnic media (Editorial, *Share*, 1996), as well as journalists writing for the major daily papers (Editorial, *Edmonton Journal*, 1995) provided support for the questions, for Employment Equity legislation, and subsequent collection of data by the 1996 Census. Thus the debate on the appropriateness of the Census question, the usefulness of the legislation and the deeper question of the divisions — real or apparent — in Canadian society, had become intense well before the May 14, 1996 Census Day.

In the year following the 1996 Census, media and public concern and confusion regarding the potential impacts of a direct question on race has not abated. A private member's motion (M-277) introduced by the Reform Party member for Beaver River, Debra Grey, was discussed in Parliament on November 26, 1996. This motion proposed that the government return to the word "Canadian" in questions of ethnic origin in the Canadian Census (*Hansard*, November 26, 1996). In fact, the "Canadian" category was included in the list of examples of ethnic groups shown on the 1996 Census form. Comments accompanying the motion indicate that it was the omission of "Canadian" from the visible minority question that was of concern. Grey's comments, as well as those made by other Members of Parliament in subsequent discussions on Motion 277, indicate considerable confusion between the two questions (ethnic origin and visible minority). Legislative rationales for asking a question on the visible minority population appear either to have been poorly understood or judged to be offensive. Moreover, the topic of Canadian unity and the importance of being able to classify oneself as Canadian were themes addressed both by Grey and by others speaking to the motion.

SUMMARY: RACIAL DISCOURSE

Motion M-277 continues the themes found throughout the late 1980s and early 1990s in the larger public arena. What is clear is the considerable lack of consensus regarding the Canadian racialized identities in a public increasingly concerned about what Canada is and what it, as a nation, will become. In fact, general dismay regarding the future of the Canadian state, following the 1995 Quebec referendum, the pressures of social adaptation required by high levels of immigration, and a troubling economic situation in the early 1990s, combined to focus attention on the means of achieving a sense of pan-Canadian identity in a context of policies, viewed as competing, with Multiculturalism, Employment Equity, and Aboriginal Rights. To see Canadian society as being racially constructed was antithetical to the attributes of many people. To have the racialized and ethnic character of the country measured in a national census reinforces stereotypes for some while for others this procedure confirms the structure of the Canadian social fabric.

Thus, in the 130 years since Confederation (1867) the use of the term "race" and the collection of "race" data have been erratic and changing. Asking a question on race in the Canadian Census is an exercise that goes beyond measurement issues. The questions asked between 1901 and 1941 rested on prevailing race relations and models of nation-building and incorporation. Recent initiatives to return to a question on "race" also incorporate models of nation-building, integration and race relations although all the parameters of all three have greatly changed since the first half of the century.

4

RACIAL INTEGRATION: THEORETICAL OPTIONS

LEO DRIEDGER AND SHIVA S. HALLI

WHEN THE VIETNAMESE IMMIGRANT FAMILY of five lands in Winnipeg, the parents, the two children under ten and the grandmother will face very different processes of change. The parents who find jobs face the workplace, the two children must survive in a new school and find new friends, and the grandmother away from her extended family will face a lonely empty household all day. They will all face internal family, cultural, social, economic and political change at three generational levels. We predict that the grandparent will change the least and the children the most, but this observation will not apply equally to all groups.

As they contact their worlds outside their family they also face a process of integration which will require adjustments on the part of both the new immigrant family and the host society and institutions they will become a part of. The challenge of integration is the incorporation as equals of this new family into the host society and its institutions. The extent to which the new family may wish to integrate, and the extent to which those who surround them are willing to let them become a part of the Canadian society, will vary. Let us examine six options that are available, in order to gain some sense of the degrees of integration and the forces which influence these complex processes.

Many theories have been developed to explain what will happen to ethnic groups in an industrial-technological society. The first two theories to be discussed, assimilation and amalgamation, assume that the urban industrial forces of technology and majority power will cause loss of ethnic identity. The third and fourth theories, modified assimilation and modified pluralism, admit that the technological forces will change ethnic minorities, but predict that minorities will retain ethnic characteristics partially or in changed forms. The remaining two theories, ethnic pluralism and ethnic conflict, emphasize that ethnic solidarity and identity can be maintained, despite industrialization, in both rural and urban environments. A discussion of the six theories follows, after which we present a model of ethnic integration.

SORTING THEORIES OF ETHNIC CHANGE

While the classical social theorists were relatively unconcerned with ethnicity in Europe, early sociologists in America and Canada have been greatly interested in ethnic change because most residents of North America are the descendants of immigrants who came fairly recently. They have faced enormous ethnic changes in this relatively short period. Fortunately, early sociologists of the Chicago School like Robert Park, Louis Wirth, W.I. Thomas, Florian Znaniecki, Robert Redfield and others did considerable research on immigrants during the industrial boom in Chicago (Persons, 1987). The logical question was, what will happen to these newcomers, and how will they change as a result?

These Chicago scholars of the 1920s and 1930s, influenced by writings of European sociologists, sought to systematize the European insights and thus establish a more rigorous investigation of their own contemporary urban community (Persons, 1987). Studies of race and ethnicity were at the centre of their interests. Since slavery and relations with blacks were such an important part of the American experience the focus of research centred more on race relations than on the study of European immigrant research. Many Chicago sociologists assumed that there would be assimilation, but they were not sure of what these European minorities would assimilate into. The melting pot and Anglo-conformity are two potential outcomes that we shall discuss first.

Assimilation: The Melting Pot

Weber, Durkheim, and Marx all agreed that the pervasive force of industrialization tends to attract workers and capitalists alike into the economic work arena, where making a living becomes a primary goal. All three agreed that industry was a major force of change, but they proposed different solutions as to what should be done about it.

Assimilation theory suggests that immigrant groups will be synthesized into a new group. This evolutionary process results in a melting pot different from any of the groups involved and different from the original melting pot.

A chief advocate of this view was Robert Park. He suggested that immigrants came into contact with the new society and either took the route of least resistance (contact, accommodation, and fusion) or a more circuitous route (contact, conflict, competition, accommodation, and fusion) (Shore, 1987). Whereas the latter route could take longer and could entail considerable resistance on the part of the immigrant, the end result would be the same — the loss of a distinctive ethnic identity. The new culture and values would emerge.

There were a sufficient number of minorities who did assimilate in the way Park predicted to keep American researchers preoccupied with documenting the progress of their assimilation. For fifty years, these scholars tended to ignore groups which retained a separate identity and to regard their separateness as a relatively insignificant factor in the total pattern of minority-majority relations. The assimilational theory was so influential, when combined with the evolutionary thinking of the day, that it was forgotten that such well-known pluralist studies as Thomas and Znaniecki's *The Polish Peasant in Europe and America* (1918), Louis Wirth's *The Ghetto* (1928), and Harvey Zarbaugh's *The Gold Coast and the Slum* (1929) illustrated considerable resistance to assimilation.

Herberg (1955) contends that in the United States the Protestants, Catholics and Jews have never "melted." Nor have they in Canada. Certainly the French in Quebec are a bulwark against assimilation, whose prophesied synthesis is not happening in Canada. The racial component, well represented in Canada by our Aboriginal peoples and in America by Blacks, Aboriginals, and Asians is not melting very noticeably either. To what extent other ethnic groups such as the Chinese and Italians are melting is the subject of much research, and it is as yet incomplete. Even in the United States, where the melting pot theory is often applied, more and more scholars are having doubts about its application to all ethnic groups (Kallen, 1924; Nagel, 1984; Reitz and Breton, 1994).

Canada's relatively open immigration policy has provided the opportunity for many peoples to contribute to a melting pot. At the time of Confederation, however, the two founding groups represented most of the population (90 percent); their historical influence has been much stronger than that of any of the other groups that followed. Early British and French influences have tended to dominate early Canadian history and the lives of more recent immigrants. The two charter groups have fought hard not to assimilate either culturally or linguistically; from the beginning, the Canadian melting pot has contained ingredients that do not melt easily.

The synthesis of British, French, Germans, Ukrainians, Italians, Canadian Aboriginals, and others into a recognizable national character has been slow. Some scholars think it is this melting process, more than any other, which is needed to develop a spirited Canadian nationalism. The Americans, on the other hand, have stressed assimilation more than the Canadians, and have evolved a stronger feeling of nationalism than Canadians have been able to achieve.

Amalgamation: Conformity to a Dominant Group

A second possibility in the change process is for minorities to join with or amalgamate with a dominant group. In Canada, the British represent the largest group, so we could call this process Anglo-conformity. In Quebec it would be Franco-conformity. While industrialization has escalated during the past several centuries, nationalism has greatly influenced North American ethnic development as well. McNeill (1986) shows that nationalism rose in western Europe between 1750 and 1920, especially in the most successful capitalist countries of Britain and France which were also the most influential European players in the development of Canada and America. In Canada, the French (largely in Acadia and Quebec) and the British (especially after the war of 1759) considered Canada in colonial terms (Breton, 1984). The influence of British nationalism and colonialism was greatly strengthened with the coming of the British Empire Loyalists to Canada.

McNeill (1986) suggests that the triumph of nationalism in Europe introduced the ideal of ethnic homogeneity within a geographic boundary; the rising emphasis on national sovereignty was accompanied by efforts to bring about monoethnicity within natural boundaries. The British and French, driven by the capitalist need for profits and colonization, greatly influenced North America. They fought many wars in an attempt to gain world dominance over resources. These wars had strong repercussions on Canada, especially in 1759, when the British finally conquered the French in that territory. While monoethnic nationalism may be the most efficient way to foster economic capitalism, with its motives of individual enterprise, competition, and profit, it is often directly contradictory to philosophies of political democracy and to the Christian religion, which are also important in western civilization. Democracy emphasizes universal suffrage and cooperation, not the competition of individuals for profit, and Christianity, the dominant religion in Canada, emphasizes brotherhood and sisterhood, human equality and the welfare of all.

There is a great deal of evidence in Canadian history supporting the view that many British leaders had an Anglo-conformity model in mind when they thought of the Aboriginal people, the French, and other immigrants (Breton, 1984). Lord Durham assumed that others would assimilate to a British legal, political, economic, and cultural system (Stanley, 1960). Leaders like Durham seem to have hoped that somehow even the French would finally amalgamate into the dominant culture, although not without conflict and competition. For them, the core of nationalism must remain English while French institutions, language and history would have to take a lesser role (McNeill, 1986). Canada did not sever its ties with the British as the Americans did, so the British colonial influence lasted longer and helped mould Anglo-conformity to a much greater extent than it did in the United States.

Modified Assimilation

The two theories of ethnic adjustment discussed so far are essentially ideal types of assimilation in which ethnic groups give up their identity. Weber liked to work with ideal types because they allowed him to delineate and distinguish complexes of social action, so that research could proceed in an orderly way. As we all know, however, ideal types rarely exist in real life because social behaviour is usually more difficult to classify in practice than in the ideal state. Thus, two modified versions (Modified Assimilation and Modified Pluralism) have been developed by Milton Gordon, in *Assimilation in American Life* (1964), and by Nathan Glazer and Daniel P. Moynihan, in *Beyond the Melting Pot* (1963). These versions lean to the assimilationist and pluralist sides respectively, but take numerous modifications into account. The modified theories can be applied very usefully to real ethnic group studies in North America.

Gordon suggests that assimilation is not a single social process, but a number of subprocesses, which he classifies under the headings "cultural" and "structural." Cultural assimilation includes the incoming group's acceptance of the modes of dress, language, and other cultural characteristics of the host society. Structural assimilation concerns the degree to which immigrants enter the social institutions of the society (e.g., political leadership) and the degree to which they are accepted into these institutions by the majority. Gordon suggests that assimilation may occur more readily in the economic, political, and educational institutions than in the areas of religion, family, structure and recreation. However, as Newman (1973:85) points out, "Gordon contends (that) once structural assimilation is far advanced, all other types of assimilation will naturally follow."

Gordon's multivariate approach forced scholars out of their unilinear rut. Each of the seven stages or types of assimilation he established tended, however, to be oriented toward either an assimilationist or an amalgamationist target. He saw seven distinctive forms of assimilation for ethnic groups in the process of decline: cultural, structural, marital, identificational, civic, attitudinal, and behavioural-receptional.

TABLE 4.1

THE ASSIMILATION VARIABLES DEVELOPED BY GORDON

Subprocess or Condition	Type of Assimilation
Change of cultural patterns to those of host society	Cultural or behavioral assimilation
Large-scale entrance into primary group level of cliques, clubs and institutions of host society	Structural assimilation
Large-scale intermarriage with host society	Marital assimilation
Development of sense of peoplehood based exclusively on host society	Identificational assimilation
Absence of prejudice in host society	Attitudinal assimilation
Absence of discrimination on the part of host society	Behavioral receptional assimilation
Absence of value and power conflict	Civic assimilation

Adapted from Milton M. Gordon, *Assimilation in American Life: The Role of Race, Religion and National Origins* (New York: Oxford University Press, 1964), 71.

Gordon's major contribution is his complex multilinear, multidimensional view of the assimilation process. It has been seen as a considerable improvement on Park's assimilation cycle. Although Gordon was primarily concerned with assimilation as such and did not dwell on pluralism, he did not deny the existence of pluralist expressions in religion, the family, and recreation.

Application of the seven assimilation variables to such ethnic groups as blacks, Aboriginals, French Canadians and Scandinavians results in varied patterns that are most interesting. Most blacks in Toronto and Halifax and most blacks in the U.S., for example, have undergone complete cultural assimilation: their former African languages, customs, and religion have been lost. They have not, however, assimilated with respect to the last five variables: intermarriage with whites is limited; they are identifiable racially; there is considerable prejudice and discrimination against them; and they have limited access to civic power (Henry et al., 1995). Aboriginals in northern Canada have hardly assimilated with respect to any of the seven variables, but this situation changes somewhat when they migrate into southern cities (Frideres, 1993).

One group, the Icelanders in Manitoba, has assimilated a great deal. Few Icelandic cultural and ethnic institutions remain; they intermarry freely; they attract little prejudice and discrimination; and some are entering positions of civic influence (Driedger, 1975). Most French Canadians in Quebec, in contrast, have not assimilated according to Gordon's criteria. They retain their language, culture, and French institutions. Most marry within the group. They have even achieved considerable civic power. Gordon's variables are useful, because they show that individuals of some groups assimilate more than others. The degree of variation depends on the ethnic group and its location and varies considerably (Guindon, 1988; Gagnon, 1993). We see that the process is complex, varied, and multilinear; it adds interest to multiethnic comparative research, such as Weber advocated.

Modified Pluralism

Glazer and Moynihan (1963) distinguish four major events in New York's history that they think structured a series of ethnic patterns reflecting modified pluralism rather than modified assimilation in that city. The first was the shaping of the Jewish community under the impact of the Nazi persecution of Jews in Europe and the establishment of the State of Israel. The second was a parallel, if less marked, shaping of a Catholic community through the re-emergence of the Catholic school controversy. The third was the migration of southern Blacks to New York following World War I and continuing after the fifties. The fourth was the influx of Puerto Ricans following World War II. These two latter migrations introduced the element of race.

Glazer and Moynihan suggest that the blacks are often discriminated against, and that their assimilation is not tolerated by the majority. The Jews, with their distinct religion, do not wish to assimilate
because they are proud of their distinct identity. The Puerto Ricans and
Irish Catholics represent combinations of these voluntary and involuntary pluralist variations. Over time they change, but they remain
distinct ethnic groups. Modified pluralism takes account of this process
of change, as do the assimilationist and amalgamation theories, but it
also provides for degrees of pluralism often demonstrated in North
American groups such as Aboriginals, Italians, French Québécois, Jews,
Asiatics, and many others.

Our fourth theoretical summary focuses on Glazer and Moynihan's
theory that, while all groups change, those that are able to shift from
traditional cultural identities to new interest foci may be able to maintain their distinctive identities. This formulation recognizes change and
maintains that identification can be shifted. It also suggests that some
groups may change more than others and implies that the outcome
may be a pluralist mixture differing from the Anglo-conformist target.
Indeed, Glazer and Moynihan contend that traumatic experiences such
as conflict encourage the development of a sense of identity among
minorities, and such a view may form the basis of a viable Canadian
pluralist theory.

The French in Quebec are an example of selected change, a form
of Glazer and Moynihan's modified pluralism. They are being transformed from a dominantly rural, religion-oriented population into an
increasingly urban, industrial people (Guindon, 1988). Nevertheless,
this enormous shift in value orientations does not seem to have affected their determination to survive culturally and structurally in North
America.

The Ethnic Mosaic: Multicultural Pluralism

Whereas proponents of the melting pot and Anglo-conformity assume
that minorities will assimilate and lose their separate identities, scholars
of pluralism and conflict focus on cultural, religious and racial differences (Berry and Laponce, 1994:3-16). Advocates of these theories
assume that there are alternatives to losing oneself in the industrial
arena, and that many individuals and groups have the creativity and
resources to fight modern alienation by maintaining their ethnic distinctiveness.

Ideal cultural pluralism may represent different ethnic groups that over time maintain their own unique identities. Cultural pluralism is often viewed as an arrangement in which distinct groups live side by side in relatively harmonious coexistence. The author of this view of pluralism was a Harvard educated philosopher of Jewish immigrant stock named Horace Kallen, who espoused pluralism for three main reasons (Newman, 1973:67). He argued that there are many kinds of social relationships and identities that can be chosen voluntarily, but that no one can choose his ancestry. He further stated that each of the minority groups has something of value to contribute to a country, and that the American Constitution carried with it an implicit assumption that all people were created equal, even though there might be many distinct differences. Kallen wished to refute the ideas of assimilation and the melting pot which had come to exercise considerable contemporary influence. Since then numerous sociologists have proposed plural theories of ethnic and religious identity (Dashefsky, 1975; Mol, 1985).

Dashefsky (1975) developed a fourfold model of ethnic identity that included two sociological perspectives — the sociocultural and interactionist — and two psychological approaches — group dynamicist and psychoanalytic — in the study of ethnic identity. The sociocultural perspective is especially important in the study of recent immigrants, Indian and Inuit Aboriginals, northern Europeans on the prairies, French Québécois in Quebec, and smaller groups like the Hutterites. The symbolic interactionist focus is more useful in exploring the identity of urbanites such as the Chinese and South Asians, racial and visible minorities who have come to Canada more recently.

Hans Mol (1985) has suggested that the role of religion and the process of sacralization are ideological and symbolic interactionist forms of identity. The Sacred, as introduced by Durkheim, and expanded by Peter Berger (1967) in his book entitled *The Sacred Canopy* shows potential for sacred identity. Here we have the opportunity to compare Canadian Aboriginals, Hutterites, and Jews. Whereas the preceding discussion of assimilation tends to emphasize the overwhelming influence of technology and urbanization as the master trend which sweeps away all forms of ethnic differentiation before it, cultural pluralism tends to focus on countervailing forces such as democracy and human justice which presuppose that all people are of equal worth and all should have the freedom to choose their distinct quality of life. Assimilation theories envision the disappearance of immigrant and racial groups; identity theories, in contrast, suggest that there may be greater resistance to assimilation and amalgamation than had formerly been thought. In fact, the trend toward permissive differentiation seems to be set. In North America we have accepted pluralist religious expressions, which were hardly tolerated in Reformation Europe. The same is now true of the political scene, where a diversity of political parties and ideologies exists and is accepted by society. Moreover, multiculturalism in Canada is now recognized federally, although not without some resistance.

Conflict: The Dialectic of Incompatibles

Assimilation and amalgamation theories perceive society as moving toward melting-pot or Anglo-conformist goals. They view group conflict as a temporary phenomenon which will improve after minorities have had sufficient time to adjust to the new situation and the new order. Both theories treat social change and conflict as a temporary dislocation in the normal ordered state of a uniform nation-state (Driedger, 1996). The theories of modified assimilation and modified pluralism allow for a greater measure of inherent conflict in the social system. The counterculture in pluralism becomes a subcultural antithesis to the larger society. Simmel (1955) contended that both conflict and consensus are ever present in society, and Coser (1956) and Dahrendorf (1959) tended to follow this view. It was the general assumption of these theorists that all social phenomena reflect a combination of opposed tendencies. In Western countries race is certainly such a factor. Theories of ethnic and racial conflict also have many dimensions and components related to change which need to be explored. The conflict approach, although concerned with structure and institutions, focuses a great deal on the processes of ethnic group relations. Since conflict suggests the meeting of people with dissimilar or opposite values, norms, and mobility, it includes the processes of competition and confrontation and a dialectic of opposites. Dahrendorf defines social conflict as consisting of "all relations between sets of individuals that involve an incompatible difference of objectives with regard to positions, resources or values" (1959:135).

The various theories of conflict are too many, and too complex, to discuss here in detail. However, we wish to touch on at least three aspects that are useful in our discussion of ethnic conflict. First, John Jackson (1975) suggests that, contrary to Park's assumption that minorities tend to move through his race relations cycle, some might remain very much in a state of conflict without advancing to competition, accommodation, and eventual fusion. Jackson tried to show in his study of French-English relations in an Ontario community that conflict was a normal and natural outcome of structural processes — of the interplay of power and position, and of boundary maintenance activity. It was not, for him, a pathological phenomenon. Other examples suggest that the separatist revolution in Quebec, the Aboriginal quest for land rights, and the racial relations between whites and visible minorities all demonstrate a constant potential for conflict. Examples of such ethnic countercultural conflicts include Hutterite expansion into Alberta farmlands and the province's subsequent restrictive legislation, the conflict of French and other ethnic groups over language rights and education during the Manitoba School question (Clark, 1968), Bill 22 and the conflicts of Italians and recent immigrants with the Quebec government over English education in Montreal, and conflict between blacks, Asians and people of European ancestry.

A second way is to view conflict as Marx did in *The Communist Manifesto* (1848), in which he saw "the history of all hitherto existing society as the history of class struggles." Marx saw the struggle for control over the economic and political institutions of a society as a pervasive conflict that could involve revolution and the overthrow of existing structures, so that those who were powerless might gain greater participation in their destiny. Most ethnic groups in Canada do not aspire to such an extensive power struggle, although the separatist movement led by Lucien Bouchard is a more recent form of institutional conflict, aimed at gaining sovereign control of Quebec's economic, political, and social institutions, and structure by means of a referendum on secession. Well-to-do Chinese from Hong Kong also have financial power which they will naturally use to attain their ends.

A third approach is that of Edna Bonacich (1972), who has expanded the Marxian argument and has applied it directly to ethnic relations and the "cultural division of labour" approach. She claims that ethnic solidarity is a derivative of the dual labour market exploitation that arises when immigrants enter lower paying jobs that others are reluctant to accept and, as a result, have little opportunity for advancement. Hechter (1978) suggests that minorities tend to be at the periphery of the industrial power centre and exploited by those in power; thus class distinctions emerge, and polarities for potential conflict develop. Norbert Wiley (1967) attempts to separate the structural, cultural, and social-psychological dimensions of the social class issues and suggests that minorities who remain within the ethnic sub-culture will have limited opportunities to achieve socioeconomic mobility (Isajiw, Sev'er, and Driedger, 1993). Most of these scholars see ethnic identity in stratification terms and expect that these class and ethnic strata will inevitably be in conflict. The situation of Blacks who have come recently as immigrants from Caribbean countries to Toronto would be a good example of racial conflict. South Asian Sikhs in Vancouver also represent visible minorities who may be in conflict with western values.

FINDING A CONCEPTUAL MODEL

Our discussion of the six theories of ethnic change and persistence needs integration if it is to guide the reader. Our focus is on ethnic identities, inequalities, and on varieties of modification in the process of integration. Let us begin by developing opposite tendencies on a continuum, and then develop a more complex model using more dimensions and variations as pattern variables. We shall use two continua, each with opposite polarities. In this model we will combine a conformity-pluralism continuum with a voluntary-involuntary continuum (Driedger, 1996).

The assimilation and amalgamation theories are located at the conformity end of the first continuum, where ethnic groups lose their distinctive identity and become part of a melting pot by conforming to a dominant group. The pluralism theory is at the opposite end of the continuum, where ethnic groups voluntarily retain their separate identity or are forced to remain separate. Modified assimilation and modified pluralism theories both fall in the middle; the first representing modification of assimilation; and the second, modifications of pluralism due to change.

In many respects a continuum with two polarities is simplistic and unidimensional because it does not take into account numerous other dimensions that should be added. Furthermore, it is difficult to include conflict theories unless additional dimensions are added to provide more contrast. Talcott Parsons is well known for his elaboration of numerous continua and his development of them into pattern variables or cells. Such elaborate patterns can become too rigid, locking us into social structures which do not include enough change and conflict. Nevertheless, we shall use a second voluntary-involuntary continuum, which does illustrate interesting pattern variables when contrasted with

FIGURE 4.1

A CONFORMITY-PLURALIST CONCEPTUAL MODEL

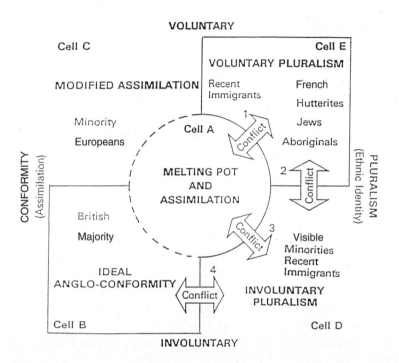

the conformity-identity continuum. The resulting four-cell model is shown in Figure 4.1. Other axes could also be added, but handling two at a time is complex enough, and the model does permit us to include conflict points as a third dimension, making it much more dynamic and interesting.

Conformity-Pluralist Model

Wsevolod Isajiw (1978:30) has suggested that the centre of Canadian society is the marketplace where all groups, including the various ethnic groups, must meet to make a living. The existing population cannot always supply the whole working force in any industrial society, so immigrants are usually brought in to augment the labour pool. In the industrial process, the many peoples in a country mix with each other. Some, however, will be closer to the centre of power and have more influence than others, while these others will find themselves in layers or concentric zones of less power and influence and farther removed from the centre (Driedger, 1989). In the centre of Figure 4.1 we have placed the melting pot as Cell A, the place where Park's assimilation is most influential. Various ethnic groups try to influence control over the industrial cell while others seek to separate themselves from it. Still others try to enter the industrial fray, but are often repelled or rebuffed. Let us discuss each of the five cells represented, after which we shall discuss the conflict at the various junctures. Of the six theories discussed earlier, at least one fits into each part of the model.

Weber, Durkheim, and Marx were all concerned with the pervasive influence of industrialization in western society, which we have plotted as the central Cell A in the middle of Figure 4.1. We agree with the classical theorists and the assimilationists that the capitalist political economy tends to draw all citizens into the middle of the economic arena because they need to earn a living in a common economic "watering hole." This sphere attracts the majorities and minorities alike, a new goal or target of assimilation with a melting pot as the outcome. The many groups will become not British, French, and Chinese, etc., but Canadians: a new entity different from any one of the ethnic contributors. Industry provides the crucible in which the many peoples meet to forge a living.

Thus, industrial changes to both societal structures and values tend to create a free-for-all in which new needs for *gemeinschaft*, or intimate relations, are created. The four cells (B,C,D,E) created by the intersection of our conformity-pluralism and voluntary-involuntary axes show that various means are used by different groups to preserve values important to them within new structures (Driedger, 1996). Let us think of the four corners of the model (B,C,D, and E) as four ways in which different groups attempt to create new means of dealing with industrial alienation.

As illustrated in Cell B, the largest (British) or most powerful group will try to shape society by leavening the whole (Cell A) so that its own language, culture, morality, and institutions are dominant and may often force conformity upon other minorities. Thus, the line between its goals (Cell B) and national economic and political values (Cell A) tends to be blurred (perforated line between Cells A and B). It is a nationalistic attempt at getting others to conform or assimilate or skew into the dominant form (Cell B of the model). Like all ethnic groups, the dominant majority wants to preserve and perpetuate its own cultural ethos; as the majority, it has the power to dominate. The French were in such a position in early Acadia, but with their defeat in 1759 the British became both the numerically and politically dominant group in Canada, although French separatists would like to gain the same status in Quebec. At the turn of the century, the British represented almost two-thirds of the population of Canada, but by 1995 they had declined to 28 percent of the total population, so that they remain the largest group, but not a majority numerically. Politically, however, they are more dominant than these figures suggest.

In Cell C are located the older, mostly northern European, groups such as the Scandinavians, Dutch, and Germans who have lived in Canada for a number of generations. Most of them have adopted the English language and are now beginning to conform and accommodate themselves voluntarily to an assimilationist goal in the centre (Cell A) where they compete quite well economically. Using Gordon's seven indicators, it may be said that northern Europeans are losing some of their cultural and structural accommodation to the forces in Cell A. Being Caucasian like the two largest groups, the British and French, they are subject to little prejudice and discrimination, and some are beginning to enter civic positions of power. With some exceptions, these Canadians follow the line of least resistance, as assimilationists would predict. They are modified assimilators because Gordon's seven factors of assimilation are hard at work. Depending on the group, some ethnic features are more in the process of assimilation into Cell A or amalgamation with the British in Cell B than others. Studies show that the Scandinavians in particular are assimilating into Cell A and amalgamating into Cell B quickly (Driedger, 1975; Isajiw, 1981).

Voluntary and Involuntary Pluralism

The minorities in Cells D and E are examples of voluntary and involuntary forms of pluralist identity (Driedger, 1996). Whereas Cell C represents intermediary forms of modified assimilation achieved by conforming voluntarily, Cell D is an intermediary process closer to the pluralism pole. In this cell, individuals and groups, forced to remain isolated because of race, remain pluralist involuntarily. Many visible minorities like Asians, South Asians, and blacks would like to participate more in the centre of the industrialization process but are often prevented from doing so fully because of racial prejudice and discrimination. They are likewise kept in their place by the majority groups of

Cell B and by other Caucasian pluralists of Cell E. It is this group that faces the greatest potential for conflict because Canadian and American charters grant them equal rights ideologically, but in real life this is often not the case. Democracy and Christianity say they are equal, yet visible minorities find themselves discriminated against in the market-place for reasons which are contradictory to such creeds of equality. Social and economic reality does not necessarily match national ideals. However, we shall enlarge on these three points of conflict below, in the section entitled "Race as a New Immigrant Factor."

Cell E represents Ideal Pluralism, in which individuals and groups voluntarily withdraw into their pluralist corner, seeking to remain sep-arate from industrial amalgamation into the national melting pot, and the French Québécois "nation" is the best example. In many ways these people are traditionalists, but their traditionalism takes a number of pluralist forms. We shall discuss four distinct forms of pluralist groups: rural French habitants, religious minorities like Hutterites and Jews, first-generation immigrants like the Italians and Greeks, and non-urban Aboriginals.

First, the large French population (25 percent), highly concentrat-ed in Quebec, has always made up a very substantial sociocultural tile in the mosaic; it has not melted, nor has it assimilated into the larger industrial pot (Cell A). Second, religious minorities such as the Hut-terites and the Jews are also placed in Cell E. The Hutterites on the prairies are a rural example of traditional pluralism, focused clearly on a separate Protestant religious ideology.

The orthodox Lubavitcher Chassidim Jews in Montreal are an excellent example of urban pluralism (Shaffir, 1993). Jews in general represent a distinct religious tradition different from that of the large Christian majority in North America. Religion is an important second factor for the maintenance of ethnic identity and solidarity in the plu-ralist Cell E. Recent first-generation immigrants are a third example of a pluralist group. Portuguese and Greeks have come to urban centres recently. Southern and Eastern Europeans such as Italians and Ukrainians, with their distinct languages and cultures, use cultural res-idential segregation as a spatial means of boundary separation in both rural and urban areas.

Fourth, rural Indian reserves also demonstrate ethnic territorial seg-regation. Many Aboriginals live in the Canadian northlands, isolated from other Canadians. Some of them are still in a food-gathering econ-omy and wish to retain a sacred way of life. We have placed these

Aboriginals in Cell E, but near Cell D, because they are also, to some extent, a visible minority. Rural and reserve Indians, however, usually wish to retain their distinct ethnic identity by staying close to the land. Increasingly, Aboriginals enter southern Canadian cities, and many of these could be placed in Cell D, where their visible distinctiveness keeps them from entering the industrial workplace in Cell A as freely as they would like.

Racial and Ethnic Conflict

Our model clearly demonstrates at least four points of conflict (1, 2, 3 and 4). One major point of conflict is between those in Cell E and Cell A; three points of conflict also involve Cell D as visible racial minorities in this cell come into contact with those in Cells A, B, and E (Driedger, 1996).

When ideal pluralists such as the French, Hutterites, Jews, recent immigrants, and Aboriginals (Cell E) seek to retain their culture and ethnic institutions, while earning a living in the melting pot economy (Cell A), there is bound to be a variety of conflict which we have labelled as our first point of stress. Now that the Constitution has declared Canada a bilingual country, French language rights are guaranteed. While such rights are easier to maintain in the province of Quebec, where French Québécois are segregated as a majority and have control over their provincial government, these language rights raise much conflict elsewhere, in localities where the French represent only a small portion of the population. The Hutterites and Jews seek to retain their distinctive religious traditions amid increased secularization in the larger society. First-generation immigrants often have severe conflict with the mainstream, and their children are seduced away from their language, culture, and traditions. As for Aboriginals their land claims represent but one point of conflict with the rest of Canada; constitutional guarantees are slow in coming, and untreated land is increasingly being invaded without legal settlement. There is a dialectic between those in Cell E, who voluntarily wish to retain a separate ethnic identity, and the assimilatory influences of the melting pot in Cell A.

In Cell D, visible minorities such as Asians, South Asians, and blacks, who also represent a large portion of recent immigrants, as well as urban Aboriginals, are in conflict at three different points (2, 3 and 4). With some exceptions, these visible minorities would likely be in closer contact and integration with those in Cells E, A, and B, but they are often unable to achieve this goal because of prejudice and discrimination. Such minorites in Cell D often see integration into Canadian society as a top priority, so their goals, in relation to the melting pot, are very different than those in Cell E. Many of the groups in Cell D want to get rid of special identity barriers and often see the protectiveness of ideal pluralists as racist. Whereas voluntary pluralists do not want to melt, visible minorities often do (although there are always exceptions). Thus, minorities in Cell D have quite different priorities and agendas, providing potential for conflict.

One of the greatest points of conflict is at point 3, between visible minorities in Cell D and the assimilated visible minorities in Cell A of the melting pot. Most Marxists and neo-Marxists see access to the labour market as the major locus of conflict in society in general and consider the plight of visible and racial minorities who are unable to compete for jobs in the melting pot to be just one version of this class conflict. There is always a potential for racial prejudice and discrimination as visible minorities try to enter the industrial melting pot and earn a living in a market of scarce resources and positions. This is especially the case for recent Asian immigrants. As Bonacich (1972) suggests these visible minorities are part of a cultural division of labour; they are in a dual labour market that exploits those who have to take lesser jobs because of their visibility and provides them with less opportunity for advancement. Since blacks represent a relatively large part of the American population, such racial conflicts have been common with them. In Canada, however, visible minorities represent only about 5-10 percent of all Canadians, so conflict of this type has been more dormant. However, to an increasing extent recent immigrants are visible minorities and this circumstance is already leading, and will increasingly lead, to more frequent conflict, especially in cities. We have placed these visible minorities in Cell D because they are, involuntarily, in situations preventing them from assimilating or integrating as quickly as many of them would like. They are on the pluralist end of the continuum because of their racial visibility; others keep them from integrating.

The fourth point of conflict is between visible minorities in Cell D and the largest, most powerful ethnic group in Cell B, which generally tries to persuade others to amalgamate with its British culture, institutions, and values. The point of conflict between these two cells is clearly a locus of class conflict. Hechter (1978) suggests that minorities are generally at the periphery of the industrial power centre and tend to be exploited by those in power. Visible minorities, therefore, will tend to see their relations with the British as a class struggle with the largest, most influential group in power. They view themselves as an exploited minority that finds it hard to enter civic, political, and economic arenas where it can have more influence. Recent visible minority immigrants cannot compete for such status and power for several generations, unless they are recent Hong Kong capitalists with superior skills and financial resources. Norbert Wiley (1967) suggests that such minorities are forced into ethnic and racial subcultures with limited opportunities to escape the socioeconomic mobility trap. Racial stereotypes remain with us, making these forms of stratification difficult to combat (Henry, et al, 1995). However, recent visible Asian and Caribbean immigrants can also be greatly differentiated and stratified.

The conceptual model we have just discussed is one way of trying to order some of the dimensions into a logical whole so that various relationships can be compared and observed. It is not without its limitations, because we can never include all of the factors which operate. In this model we have dealt with only two axes, leaving out others which also play a part. We do try to include conflict as a third dimension to make the model more dynamic. Such devices can be useful, but they can also become restrictive, and for some purposes they are too static.

Race as a New Immigrant Factor

Until 1967, Canadian immigration policies were considered discriminatory and favoured Europeans and Americans only. On October 1, 1967, a new immigration policy was introduced to abolish discrimination and serve the manpower needs of the Canadian economy. This policy was based on the use of a point system for independent immigrants to assess the education, occupational skill, age, personal qualities, employment arrangements, knowledge of English and/or French, and place of destination of potential immigrants. The new policy opened the door to Asian immigration. In the span of four years, beginning in 1967, the proportion of Asian immigrants into Canada almost doubled: from less than 2 percent before 1961 it rose to 6.7 percent in 1966 and to 13.6 percent in 1971 (Richmond and Kalbach, 1980). By 1981 European immigration had dropped below 30 percent of the total, while nearly 44 percent came from Asia. During the decade 1971-81 the total foreign-born population living in Canada increased by 17 percent, while the number who were born in Asia increased by 23 percent (Pryor and Norris, 1983).

Most of the Asian immigrants came from East Asia, Southeast Asia, and South Asia. In the early 1980s, when Asian immigration was dominated by refugees, they came predominantly from Indo-China. Immigrants from the Caribbean rose to 13 percent of total immigrants by 1974. By 1993, the seven top ten immigrant source countries were Asian (Driedger, 1993:61).

These immigrants mostly represent visible minorities. They are in a disadvantaged position with respect to distribution of power, prestige and resources. Numerous studies in Canada have shown that visible minority groups experience complex problems (Richmond, 1980; Kalbach, 1980) especially in their first five years. Important factors are high rates of unemployment, low levels of income, non-recognition of qualifications, lack of Western experience, language problems and discrimination. Hence, Neuwirth (1987) argues that many traditional theories fall short of explaining the process of adaptation of these visible minorities because such theories are based on European immigration to North America. Visible minorities are not only different from their hosts culturally but also tend to arrive during times of economic constraint. Consequently, new theoretical approaches are needed to account for characteristics of the new environment that facilitate or inhibit the process of integration of the visible minorities. A new approach should include the analysis of social and psychological characteristics of integration. Such an investigation would result in a thorough understanding of the differences between the cultures, their social and reproductive behavior and their institutions. This would help to promote a better relationship between immigrants and established Canadian residents and make possible more effective intergroup relations and cooperation. What is more important, such studies would help to prepare the receiving society to accept immigrants on better terms, because it would know how and why their cultures are different; in this way existing prejudice would be minimized.

In our model in Figure 4.1, we have used two assimilation-identity and voluntary-involuntary continuums as basic dimensions for the discussion of some of the major concerns of the mainly European immigrants who came to Canada in the past. With the large immigration of visible minorities, Canada is becoming more diverse racially. As already indicated in our discussion of Cell D in Figure 4.1, these minorities often have agendas of their own. An extended, or new, model could include dimensions such as social class — which would represent socioeconomic and political power (Isajiw, Sev'er, Driedger, 1993; Sev'er, Isajiw, and Driedger, 1993) — and residential segregation as commonly found in the United States and now increasingly in Canada (Balakrishnan and Hou, 1995). If we add these two dimensions to Figure 4.1, it becomes very complex, but they would enhance its relevance to the study of increasing inflows of Third World immigrants to Canada. At this time, we do not wish to take up the task of reformulating Figure 4.1, and will confine ourselves to a brief discussion of majority-minority power relations.

Minority-Majority Power Relations

Minority status has often been operationalized at the aggregate level, involving superordinate and subordinate ethnic or racial groups. The vagueness of the concept of subordination has caused some doubt as to whether it should be conceived of as numerical subordination or economic and political power subordination. The literature has emphasized the latter, that is, the socioeconomic position of ethnic or racial groups has been used as the factor determining minority group status.

A problem arises when we move from the aggregate categorization of minority group status to the individual level. As income, education, and occupation become similar to those of the dominant group in the society, cultural values tend to become similar.

Minority status may also reflect subcultural normative effects and these effects are mediated through intervening variables. Such variables can be studied through the ethnocultural perspective, which allows us to identify differences in beliefs, values, and norms regarding family size and pattern of living. These differences depend upon disadvantaged status associated with the psychological insecurities and the effects of prejudice and discrimination (evidenced by such trends as social distance and occupational segregation) which directly influence minority behavior (Li, 1982). Minorities seem to experience social and cultural changes at different points in their history. Therefore, the interpretations of minority status must be made within a dynamic framework of sociocultural and historical conditions.

A crucial question is whether or not being in a minority places one in a marginal position within the society, thereby producing a feeling of insecurity. A pattern of persistent homogamy provides adequate facilities for participation in ingroup life and effectively precludes assimilation in the dominant culture (Halli, 1987). Members of a minority group face the problem of adjusting to the values and behaviour patterns (i.e., cultural marginality) or of gaining entrance to some structural organizations (i.e., structural marginality). Hence, minority members may assimilate on some dimensions (e.g., education or occupation) but not on others (e.g., primary group attachments or intermarriage). The extent to which this discrepancy occurs produces insecurities with respect to the socioeconomic achievement.

SUMMARY

We have addressed the extent to which ethnic groups persist and maintain their solidarity, and the changes which occur in the process of integration. We discussed six theories of change, developed a conceptual model aimed at integrating some of the ideas.

Proponents of two of the six theories of change (assimilation and amalgamation) assume that the industrial magnet is irresistible, requiring minorities either to assimilate with others into a melting pot, or to amalgamate into Anglo-conformity. Proponents of two other theories (pluralism and conflict), however, suggest that minorities can retain their identity through a variety of traditional and ideological means and build a pluralist society in which they remain in conflict either voluntarily or involuntarily. Racially visible minorities often wish to become more integrated but the larger white population restricts their mobility.

To illustrate the complexity of the processes and the diversity of factors in operation, we showed what could be done when just two of the axes — conformity-pluralism and voluntary-involuntary — were plotted together in one diagram. Five cells were created, each representing one of five theories discussed, and a sixth theory — conflict — was also accommodated at the boundaries of each. Furthermore, we found that the many ethnic groups could be placed in each of the cells, to illustrate the point that Canadian ethnic groups fit all of the theories and cells. This fact demonstrates that the extent of integration of immigrants into Canada varies, depending on numerous factors related both to the new family's desire to integrate and to the host society's acceptance of new and different immigrants. Visible minorities who are of Asian and African origin often find themselves, involuntarily, restricted from participation because of prejudice, discrimination and racism.

5

INDIVIDUAL VERSUS COLLECTIVE RIGHTS IN QUEBEC

JOSEPH O'SHEA

A PERSISTENT ISSUE FOR CULTURALLY, linguistically or racially het-
erogenous societies is providing an appropriate environment for a collective commitment in which all groups feel they participate equally.
The ability of visible and ethnic minorities to achieve a more level playing field has been hampered by both individuals and institutions. The
hindrances are deeply embedded in the history, policies, and practices
of almost every major system in Canada, including employment, the
media, the justice system, law enforcement and the government itself.
Inequality results from the failure of these institutions to adapt their
modes of behaviour and procedure to the changing needs of a pluralistic, multiracial and multiethnic society. Policies and practices are being
institutionalized which ignore, or at best tolerate, the accommodation
of differences, whether they be those of language, customs or political
outlook.

A significant reflection of a homogeneous political culture which
continues to have difficulty in incorporating a variety of visions is the
set of political attitudes of the current government of the province of
Quebec. Since the election of the Parti Québécois in 1976 on a plat-
form of political sovereignty the overwhelming majority of Quebec's
multiracial and multiethnic citizens have rejected this option by supporting the federalist alternative in the 1980 and 1995 referendums.

This rejection was expressed in the outcome of the fractious debate
that occurred in the runup to the 1995 Quebec referendum and underlined some poignant and clear differences between the ways in which
many Canadians and many Quebecers view their national identity and
their respective collective goals. Moreover, it reflects the changes in the
Canadian and Quebec communities since the 1980 referendum in
Quebec. Since this referendum and several other failed constitutional
undertakings, a new generation of leaders within Quebec, in both the

political and the economic sphere, has emerged and forged a new collective consensus on the province's future. Old fears are replaced by new possibilities. Constitutional debates are now considered obsolete. The next step is a debate among equals and between nations.

The current political leadership of Quebec has convinced an increasing number of its citizens that this present drive for nationhood is not based on the old defensive (ethnic) nationalism of the past (based on language, religion etc.). Quebec is in the forefront of something new. The aim is to build a modern Quebec society on the North American continent. All are welcome, not just those who are Québécois "de souche" (old stock). However, the October 30th referendum recalled to many that tolerance of a variety of communities with varying collective goals may not be as close at hand as was so widely believed. The speech by former Quebec Premier Jacques Parizeau, which blamed the defeat of the sovereignist project on ethnics and money, left many with a feeling of disappointment. Non-Francophones have come to accept that various laws and regulations are necessary to protect an endangered Francophone community on the continent. Despite their best efforts to become full members of this global community, its definition seems to fall short of full inclusion. It has become apparent to the historic communities (Anglophones and First Nations), and to recent immigrants, that the collective good of the Francophone majority is in conflict with their own conceptions of what is good.

Charles Taylor, professor and political philosopher from McGill University, argues that a politics of the common good is necessary for Quebec, to ensure its ability to protect its distinct society status within Canada and North America. This model is in opposition to the predominant model, found within most liberal-democratic states, which promotes a politics of neutral concern (the idea that people are entitled to equal concern whatever their conception of the good may be). The emphasis in such states is on the individual, not on the community.

Is there room for other definitions of community within Quebec's liberal-democratic tradition? To what extent must they be subsumed in order to assure social cohesion? Quebec, concerned as it is with preserving a specific community, tends to depart from the individualist liberal-democratic tradition. There is some justification for the protection of an endangered community, but not if it involves the use of measures impinging on the individual and collective rights of its other citizens. This raises questions about how to fairly balance competing values.

Furthermore, if such protection includes the use of collective rights by the national majority, those outside the dominant group are left in a less advantageous position vis-à-vis the state. This therefore poses a question: how can all citizens be empowered?

To come to some understanding on these issues, specifically the accommodation and integration of multiethnic and multiracial communities in Quebec society, the discussion will focus on the following areas: 1) Charles Taylor's communitarian vision; 2) Minority communities within Quebec; 3) Possible room for other visions; 4) Recent challenges to minority inclusion, and 5) A future Quebec society: is there room for inclusion?

CHARLES TAYLOR'S COMMUNITARIAN VISION

The theoretical model providing the basis for this debate is the one predominant in most liberal-democratic states. It is the model which promotes a politics of neutral concern; the idea that people are entitled to equal concern regardless of their conception of the good. This therefore poses a question: how can all citizens be empowered?

The idea that liberalism cannot incorporate this relationship, this understanding of a shared cultural context, is the underlying theme for communitarians like Charles Taylor (1979:157-59). Liberalism is also to be rejected for its excessive "atomistic" individualism and its disregard of the manifest ways in which we are situated in various social roles and communal relationships. This, we think, is misleading. Communal tasks and projects are important but they should not be considered as "authoritative horizons" which set goals for us. In the view of adherents of liberalism, there should be nothing self-defeating for communitarians in acknowledging that these projects should be subject to individual evaluation and possible rejection.

Within the last two decades, liberal political thought flourished and John Rawls's *A Theory of Justice*, Robert Nozick's *Anarchy, State and Utopia*, and Ronald Dworkin's *Taking Rights Seriously*, gave it renewed vigour. The focus of these works was on individual liberty, rights and distributive justice. However, they were seen by communitarians as ignoring the social nature of the person and the value of community. Alasdair MacIntyre's *After Virtue: A Study in Moral Philosophy*, Michael Sandel's *Liberalism and the Limits of Justice*, Michael Walzer's *Spheres of Justice: A Defense of Pluralism and Equality* and Charles Taylor's *"Atomism" in Philosophical Papers* (volume 2), have become the seminal critiques of liberalism's elevation of the individual, which seems to be an impoverished conception of the self and fosters antisocial egoistic behaviour.

The core of this debate will be a communitarian descriptive claim about the nature and essence of persons, commonly known as Charles Taylor's social thesis. According to Taylor, people

only develop their characteristically human capacities in society. The claim is that living in society is a necessary condition of the development of rationality, in some sense of this property, or of becoming a fully responsible, autonomous being (Taylor, 1985:190-91).

This thesis is contrasted with the atomistic view that rationality and autonomous decision-making powers are given asocially, and thereby draws our attention to the cultural preconditions of autonomy. Against atomism Taylor argues that the free individual or autonomous moral agent can only achieve his identity in a certain type of culture (Taylor, 1985:205). It is, therefore, not possible for liberals to argue that individuals are self-sufficient outside society and not in need of the cultural context of choice in order to examine or choose their conception of the good life.

Taylor's charge is that liberalism is atomistic and fails to recognize the full implications of a complex range of options on communitarianism and individualism. He is correct in emphasizing the importance of the social thesis, and therefore the value of a secure cultural context. They are indeed relevant. However, liberal political philosophers like Rawls are on record as supportive of a social thesis. Rawls, for example, has made it quite clear that he recognizes the cultural preconditions of autonomy. In *A Theory of Justice* he states that

social life is a condition for our developing the ability to think ... and to take part in the common activities of society and culture ... and that persons need one another since it is only in active cooperation with others that one's powers reach fruition. Only in the social union is the individual complete (Rawls, 1971:522-25).

The specific premise of Taylor's social thesis, that liberals do not recognize, or, more specifically, neglect the social preconditions for the effective fulfilment of their interests, does not represent a central tenet of liberalism. Most, if not all, liberal political philosophers endorse

Taylor's social thesis that our moral capacity is only actualized through the habits, practices, institutions and laws in virtue of which individuals form a society.

Taylor also argues that liberals, because of their inadequate attention to the social thesis, overemphasize particular kinds of rights. According to Will Kymlicka, "Taylor thinks that a full acceptance of the social thesis would require abandoning a central tenet of liberalism, which he calls 'primacy of rights' (Kymlicka, 1989:75)." He is referring to the moral view that individual rights have primacy over moral notions like individual duties, virtue or collective good. Taylor's concern is that one of the features of liberalism is its insistence on the exclusion of ideals or, in other words, a neutral political concern: the idea that people are entitled to equal concern regardless of their conception of the good. This entitlement would allow me a veto on the collective pursuit of the ends shared by the majority where that pursuit violates my claim to equal neutral concern. However, Taylor insists that such a politics of neutral concern should be abandoned for what he calls a politics of the common good.

In *Struggles for Recognition in the Democratic Constitutional State,* Jurgen Habermas states that

Taylor proceeds on the assumption that the protection of collective identities comes into competition with the right to equal individual liberties so that in the case of conflict a decision must be made about which takes precedence over the other (Habermas, 1995:110).

According to Taylor, Quebec and its claim to a distinct society status within Canada is an example of this type of conflict between a politics of the common good and that of a politics of neutral concern. For him, a theory of rights that echoes the right of the individual to pursue his or her own conception of the good would be closed to collective goods of the following kind:

A society with collective goals like Quebec's violates this model.... On this model, there is a dangerous overlooking of an essential boundary in speaking of fundamental rights to things like commercial signage in the language of one's own choice. One has to distinguish the fundamental liberties, those that should never be infringed and therefore ought to be entrenched, on the one hand, from privileges and immunities that are important, but that can be revoked or restricted for reasons of public policy — although one would need a strong reason to do this — on the other (Taylor, 1995:58-59).

This alternative model, under certain conditions, would permit basic rights to be restricted by guarantees of status aimed at promoting the survival of endangered communities or cultural forms of life. Communitarians, like Taylor, dispute the ethical neutrality of the state, and would leave open, if need be, avenues to actively advance specific conceptions of the good life. Liberals, in contrast, call for an ethically neutral legal order that would hopefully assure everyone equal opportunity to pursue their own conception of the good.

Taylor proceeds on the assumption that the protection of collective identities comes into competition with the right to equal individual liberties, so that in the case of conflict a decision must be made about which takes precedence over the other. The argument runs as follows. Since the second claim requires consideration of precisely those particularities from which the first claim seems to abstract, the principle of equal rights has to be put into effect in two kinds of politics that run counter to one another — a politics of consideration of cultural differences on the one hand and a politics of universalization on the other. The one is supposed to compensate for the price the other exacts with its equalizing universalism. According to Habermas

Taylor spells out his opposition using the concepts of the good and the just, drawn from moral theory. He stands in an anti-theoretical position to liberals like Rawls and Dworkin who call for an ethically neutral legal order that is supposed to assure everyone equal opportunity to pursue his or her own conception of the good. He disputes the ethical neutrality of the law and supports the constitutional state, if need be, to actively advance specific conceptions of the good life (Habermas, 1995:111).

Within a society that supports state intervention in defence of collective rights for its national majority (Quebec), there is the possibility of subordination of other individual and collective goals. The common good, as defined by the majority, does not adjust itself to the pattern of people preferences and values. Instead, the majority decides the standards by which all other preferences are evaluated. The community's way of life forms the basis for a public ranking of conceptions of the good, and weight given to an individual's preferences depends on how much she conforms or contributes to the common good.

The public pursuit of the shared ends that define the community's way of life is not, therefore, constrained by the requirement of neutral concern. It takes precedence over the claim of individuals to the liberties and resources needed to choose and pursue their own ends. As a result, shared values, or a common good, carry greater weight among communitarians than liberals, and the possible existence of dissent from these ends is treated as less of a constraint on state action. This has certainly been the case in the aftermath of Quebec's recent referendum. As we will discuss later, an overwhelmingly high percentage of Allophones and Anglophones voted against the sovereignty option. This, however, has not slowed down the movement of the governing party along the road to the next consultative phase. The pursuit of this goal indicates to many outside the majority that, despite their disavowal of the sovereignty option, the state feels no responsibility to acknowledge their dissent.

The next phase of our discussion will examine the role of immigration and integration within Quebec society. It will speak to the unique role of immigration within Quebec and the way in which its integration process has been perceived. The former Premier, Jacques Parizeau, expressed for many his frustration at not being able to bring multiethnic and multiracial minorities into his vision for an independent Quebec. It is a realization that a pluralistic society has many competing visions and respect for such dissent is the cornerstone of a truly liberal-democratic society.

Is there Room for Other Minority Visions?

Quebec stands in a unique position with regard to immigration into Canada. It has been able, through a series of agreements beginning in 1971 (Fontaine, 1993:49-53; Vincent, 1994:103-07) to select, to an ever increasing degree, new immigrants. The consistently low birth rate within the last twenty years has underlined the necessity for more provincial government control within the immigration portfolio. As Figure 5.1 illustrates, the birth rate has fallen from a high of 4.1 births per family in 1931 to a low of approximately 1.6 births in 1991, a rate below the number (2.1) that is required for population replacement. This troubling decline of fertility has been accompanied by an increase in the number of immigrants that arrive in the province. As Figure 5.2 suggests quite convincingly, the number of immigrants within Quebec

FIGURE 5.1

BIRTH RATE IN QUEBEC, 1931-91

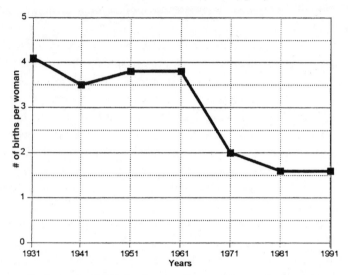

Sources: Duchesne, L. (1993) *La situation démographique au Québec* and Bureau de la statistique du Québec.

has risen from the immediate postwar low of 10,000 to a high of 41,000 in 1990. Except for the period between 1975 to 1985 the number of immigrants, both from other provinces and abroad, has steadily increased.

Another important reason for a more provincially oriented immigration selection process has been the realization on the part of Quebec elites that Anglophone institutions in Montreal had been able to maintain and even expand their power base by absorbing several waves of immigrants. The aim of the new legislative changes was to allow Francophone institutions to take over the immigrant integration process, a role in keeping with, and essential to, the goal of building a French language society in which mere ethnic differences would eventually be transcended. This aspect of Quebec's normalization process — that of having the institutions of the demographic majority finally fulfil their natural majority role — would also, according to Pierre Vincent,

FIGURE 5.2

IMMIGRANTS TO QUEBEC, 1945-90

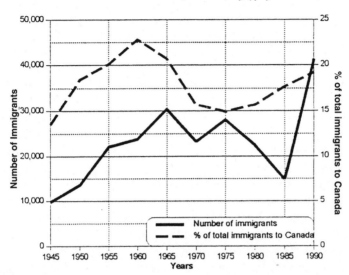

Sources: Emploi et Immigration Canada, *Statistiques sur l'immigration* (1993),
and Ministère des communautés culturelles et de l'immigration.

have the effect of cutting Anglophone institutions back to more reasonable
and modest dimensions and leave them with a much narrower demographic
base. The new measures were aimed at correcting the harmful overdevelop-
ment that Anglophone institutions had been allowed to undergo in the past,
and simultaneously at building Francophone institutions to the point of
permitting them to assume their rightful dominant role (Vincent, 1994:104-
translation).

The perception is that immigration has been harmful to the
Francophone community precisely because it has historically been
disproportionately absorbed by the Anglophone community. Francophones have been reluctant to accept immigration and the federal multiculturalism policy, and this attitude is no doubt linked to their
overriding concern to protect their institutions. It is also quite likely
that immigration has not been viewed as favourably as in the rest of
Canada because Quebec has historically benefited from it much less
than the rest of Canada. According to Leslie Laczko,

the majority of immigrants to Canada, and even to Quebec, have in the past tended to become more integrated into the Anglophone community than into the Francophone community, the lower proportion of relatively recent immigrants and their descendants in the Francophone community has in itself been a direct and important reason for the less than favourable view of immigration that the Francophone community displays (Laczko, 1995:165).

It seems, therefore, natural that Francophones display a healthy scepticism toward immigration, since it has been used to strengthen and buttress Anglophone institutions within Quebec and across Canada.

HISTORICAL PERSPECTIVE ON MULTICULTURALISM

Prior to the changes in Quebec described above and in Canadian immigration policy in the 1970s — i.e., the Multiculturalism Act of 1971 — immigrants to Canada were expected to shed their distinctive heritage and assimilate entirely to existing cultural norms. This was known as the Anglo-conformity model of immigration. Assimilation was seen as essential for political stability, and was further rationalized through ethnocentric denigration of other cultures. This commitment to Anglo-conformity is obscured by the popular but misleading contrast between the American "melting pot" and the Canadian "ethnic mosaic." While "ethnic mosaic" carries the connotation of respect for the integrity of immigrant cultures, in practice it simply meant

that immigrants to Canada had a choice of two dominant cultures to assimilate to. While Canada is binational, the uneasy tolerance which French and English were to show toward each other was not extended to foreigners who resisted assimilation or were believed to be unassimilable (Kymlicka, 1995:14).

According to Frances Henry and Carol Tator the removal of the overt provisions to the Multiculturalism Act did not necessarily change perceptions. The growing need for immigrants with managerial, professional, and technical skills from countries such as Pakistan, India and Uganda threatened many "white" Canadians. Thus, paradoxically,

although these new immigrants were far more skilled, secularized, and urbanized than previous immigrants (who were almost all unskilled and from rural areas), they were still perceived to be inferior and unsuited to the Canadian way of life (Henry and Tator, 1985:323).

These changes accentuated, at least on paper, a more tolerant and pluralistic policy which allowed and indeed encouraged immigrants to maintain various aspects of their ethnic heritage. However, while immigrant groups have increasingly asserted their right to express their ethnic diversity, they have done so within the public institutions of a bilingual and binational culture. Immigrants arriving in Quebec feel a dual pull. Integration into the common culture and language is a basic requirement for meeting daily needs and, in the long run, to be considered a Quebecer. Immigrants are also aware of the influential English minority and desire the opportunity to have the territorial and linguistic advantage after their prescribed years of residence within Quebec are completed.

A Troubling Phenomenon

The desire to utilize this territorial advantage remains a troubling phenomenon, particularly in the interprovincial context, among those Quebec immigrants who receive their citizenship. Figure 5.3 clearly indicates that Quebec, beginning in the 1960s and until the present, has continually lost a significant number of its immigrants to other Canadian provinces. According to a study completed by the *Ministère des communautés culturelles et de l'immigration* (MCCI) in 1986, they stated that

immigrants seem to only pass through Quebec. The history of migration among the Quebec population shows that Quebec, since the middle of the nineteenth century, has become a land of emigration, the net migration total being negative for this whole period (MCCI, 1986-translation).

In a follow-up study in 1989, the Ministry estimates that 28 percent of immigrants leave the province five years after their arrival in Quebec (MCCI, 1989-translation). Besides the economic and personal reasons that can be assigned to the outflow of these immigrants there is the question of the type of society that is being built in Quebec. This will be discussed in further detail later in this chapter. Another reason for uncertainty, according to many political and social commentators in Quebec, is the schizophrenic character of federal-provincial agreements which allow immigrants to be caught between two dominant cultures. If Quebec is seen as a semi-sovereign entity, then movement into Quebec is immigration, and newcomers need to be integrated into

FIGURE 5.3

INTER-PROVINCIAL MIGRATION, 1961-92

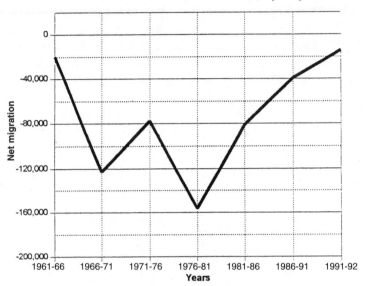

Source: Duchesne, L. (1993) *La situation démographique au Québec.*

Quebec. In Figure 5.3, we present immigration from Quebec to the other provinces.

The Definition of a Quebecer

So what do immigrants to Quebec integrate into? Who is a Quebecer? According to social and political commentator Henri Comte, in a column appearing in *Le Devoir,* Quebec's leading intellectual and nationalist newspaper,

Quebecers are suffering from a profound identity crisis. Commentators and politicians do not know what to call immigrants, do not know who a Quebecer is. A review of articles allow us to identify the following expressions to designate an immigrant: "Those who are not old stock" (Bernard Landry-Quebec's present vice-premier); "Quebecers of new stock," "Linguistic communities," "Non-francophone minorities" (Lysiane Gagnon-journalist, social commentator); "Those people" (Jacques Parizeau-former Quebec premier) (*Le Devoir*, March 10, 1993-translation).

For others, however, there is no problem or doubt about what type of society immigrants must integrate into. In a document commissioned by the Quebec School Commission, its authors define this society as

Quebec Francophones from old stock, from families arriving before 1760, who make up the majority of the Québécois and whose culture gives the central axis to Quebec culture. To renounce this principle would open the door wide to multiculturalism. This model does not apply to the situation in Quebec. It compromises the long term development and consolidation of Quebec francophones because it would lead to the multiplication of veritable socio-ethnic ghettoes (Vincent, 1994:111-translation).

This vision is not wholly accepted by most opinion-makers and social commentators. However, many remain silent. There is certainly no consensus about the type of society in which immigrants are welcomed. It does not take them long to realize, however, that they are placing themselves in a province with ambiguous views on their future status. This confusion is not altogether surprising, considering the positions held by many who shape opinion and implement policy on immigration.

That being said, however, many other Quebec nationalists and professionals take a strong stance against immigration itself. For Quebec demographer, Jacques Henripin, the real risk of a low birth rate is not that, one day, the population of Quebec would fall to zero. It is that

today's generation of Quebecers and their descendants would be progressively replaced by *others* [my emphasis], that is to say, by immigrants from Asia, Africa, Central America and other Canadian provinces. Even though massive waves of immigration would compensate for the low birth rate and maintain Quebec's population at seven million, it could, at its extreme limit, constitute the potential for a civil war (*La Presse*, June 20, 1987-translation).

This view is also echoed in his book *Naître ou ne pas être,* where he philosophizes on the consequences of replacing empty cribs by immigrants. Henripin believes that, "if the cribs remain as empty as they are at present, this strategy could lead us, between 2030 and 2080, to a Quebec population that is strangely constituted [my emphasis], four persons in ten being born outside the province" (Henripin, 1989:110-translation).

This alarmist tone is echoed by several other interlocutors in the debate on immigration. Michel Pallascio, president of the Montreal Catholic School Commission, says that Quebec "could not survive under an avalanche of non-Francophone immigrants and other non-Judeo-Christian religions" (Vincent 1994, 120). Sylvain Simard, president of the National Movement of Quebecers, says that "with one of the lowest rates of childbirth in the world, our original, distinct society is threatened, if not in danger of disappearing" (121). This exaggerated rhetoric is explained, in some degree, from Quebecers' lukewarm attitude toward immigration and ethnic diversity in general. The integration of immigrants as individuals into the Anglophone community constitutes, in a sense, an acceptance by immigrants of the Anglophone offer of individual incorporation that has long been collectively resisted by Francophones. Furthermore, multiculturalism is viewed as granting immigrant ethnic groups some sort of collective rights, which have heretofore been accorded, however grudgingly, to First Nation communities, Francophones, and Anglophones. Granting collective rights to immigrant ethnic groups would be seen as a reduction of the distinctive legal status enjoyed by the Francophone community (Rocher 1992).

Minority Communities and the Sovereignty Option

A significant reflection of the ability of ethnic communities to aspire to other individual and collective goals of their own has been the almost wholesale rejection of the nationalist and sovereignist option pursued by the Parti Québécois since 1976. In every subsequent election, non-Francophone Quebecers have voted massively and consistently against this government and its project of national sovereignty. The 1980 Quebec referendum exemplified the extent of Allophone and Anglophone rejection of the OUI side. In an analysis carried out by Quebec sociologist Pierre Drouilly, "an average of 4 percent of the vote of new Quebecers went to the OUI side" (*Le Devoir*, September 18, 1980-translation). In the 1992 vote on the Charlottetown constitutional accord, an analysis carried out by Drouilly within ridings with a large concentration of non-Francophone voters concluded that the vote against the federal sponsored initiative "was equal to or less than 10 percent, whereas the vote in predominantly Francophone ridings was two thirds against this accord" (*La Presse*, October 31, 1992-translation*).

This voting pattern is like a block of cement, according to Pierre Drouilly. He believes that the non-Francophone electorate confounds all sociological distinctions by consistently voting, in the last eight elections, against the Parti Québécois and its nationalist option, whether the option be sovereignty or an associationist model. He considers this behaviour to be exceptional and concludes that, whether we speak of one of the historic communities or a newly arrived immigrant, the Quebecer will always remain an indigenous being, with which these people, in every case, cannot identify.

Leaving aside the stridently political nature of this analysis, one finds in it a response that is very much in keeping with the attitude of a political and nationalist elite which has dropped any pretence of truly modern nationalism. Successful integration into the Québécois society does not require acceptance of one specific vision or good which is promoted by the majority. A more important question is why this society undervalues other individual and collective visions for the state. The protection of the common language and culture is not synonymous with a specific political agenda. Respect for the Francophone community and its unique history is a value that is willingly upheld by new immigrants. This view was echoed in a brief presented by the South Asian Women's Community Centre of Montreal to the Montreal Catholic School Commission in 1990. The Commission held public hearings concerning proposed regulations on the use of non-French languages between students when they were outside classrooms. The Community Centre assured the Commission that

it has always supported the concept that people who live and work in Quebec should make every attempt to learn and speak French. The Centre has held French classes for recent arrivals because we see the importance of being able to communicate in the language of the majority of Quebec.... Many measures can be taken to encourage the use of French and improve race relations in schools (South Asian Community Centre, 1992:169-70).

The willingness by new Quebecers to contribute to the common language and culture is an ongoing reality and reflects the readiness of most members of minority communities to integrate into Quebec society. This is accomplished without necessarily acceding to a specific political agenda, like sovereignty. The presence of these communities will certainly change the homogenous character of the province and with it the definitions of who a real Quebecer is.

As this section has attempted to illustrate, integration into a culture is a difficult process. The dual nature of immigration in Quebec makes it particularly difficult for new immigrants, since the predominant concern is to maintain protection for an endangered community. Even though political elites profess a desire to build a more modern nationalism, old remnants remain. Forging a more pluralistic vision for a modern Quebec is a challenging task. Inviting new citizens to join this endeavour will also necessitate accepting new visions, new common goals and the tolerance and respect to accept everything that a pluralistic society implies.

RECENT CHALLENGES TO MINORITY INCLUSION

It is axiomatic for Quebec governments that the survival and flourishing of French culture in Quebec is a good. Accordingly, political society cannot be neutral between those who value remaining true to the culture and those who might want to cherish some individual good of self-development. It could be argued that one could after all capture a goal like *survivance* for a proceduralist liberal society. One could consider the French language as a collective resource that individuals would wish to preserve. Adherents of this collective good, however, go one step further. It is not just a matter of having the French language available for those who might choose to use it. The end result is to ensure a community of people who will avail itself of the opportunity to use the language.

Quebecers tend to opt for a rather different model of a liberal society. In their view, a society can and should be organized around a definition of the good life, without this being seen as a depreciation of those who do not share this definition. According to this conception, a liberal society singles itself out as such by the way in which it treats its minorities, including those who do not share public definitions of the good, and above all by the rights it accords to all its members.

The ability of a society to accentuate a certain collective vision means, I believe, that it tolerates the exclusion of other legitimate individual and collective goals. At the outset I would like to insist that a society with strong collective horizons can be liberal, provided it is capable of respecting diversity and provided it can offer adequate safeguards for fundamental rights. However, some recent events in the last year have shown how tenuous tolerance can be toward those outside the vision put forward by the representatives of the national majority.

Language

In the most recent flare-up of the "language" question, specifically the issue of commercial signage, respect and tolerance for other legitimate visions has been in short supply. Bill 86, passed by the previous Liberal government to redress the issue of laws on the language of signs, has become the latest centre of attention. According to this bill, English words are allowed on commercial signs as long as French is also displayed and twice as prominently, or as long as there are twice as many French signs.

A number of English-rights activists and citizens have led boycotts in predominantly English-speaking neighbourhoods of Montreal, demanding that businesses apply the letter of the law. A number of institutions have complied, fearing economic hardship. The reaction on behalf of the government has been the threat to further restrict any appearance of English on commercial signs. The following are a few statements issued by the government in reaction to the citizens who expect the full implementation of Bill 86:

Premier Lucien Bouchard: "We will not allow the bilingualization of Montreal."
Vice-Premier Bernard Landry: "If we are going to have a more and more bilingual Montreal, you can be sure in one year from now we will have to react in the opposite direction."
Culture Minister Louise Beaudoin: "We won't let Montreal be bilingualized." (*Globe and Mail*, August 24, 1996)

Meanwhile, the protest against French-only store signs is being widely condemned by both French- and English-speaking commentators as petty and counterproductive. That, I believe, is too simplistic an observation. It is not an issue of shopping or language, but the misuse of state power. Quebec sign laws bring the full weight of the state to bear in an attempt to erase from view the pluralism that is part of the reality of life in Montreal. These laws are, in effect, about the marginalizing of non-Francophones in the public arena. While the presence of a strong non-Francophone population is a reality, visual evidence of their existence is not always appealing or welcome.

If the reaction of the government had been to acknowledge the protests as an attempt on behalf of these English-language groups to have a legitimate concern recognized, a feeling of inclusion would have been established. It would also have demonstrated that a society with a strong notion of collective rights could accommodate the differences, either individual or collective, that a pluralistic society will ask of its government.

Participatory Democracy

In the aftermath of the last referendum, hearings were conducted to establish whether there had been a systematic destruction of NO ballots in heavily populated immigrant ridings. The Chief Electoral Officer of Quebec, Pierre F. Côté, issued a report which established that an unnecessary amount of spoiled ballots had been found in these ridings. Before a parliamentary commission, Côté was asked to answer questions about his report and the functioning of his department. David Payne, Quebec cabinet minister and special advisor to the premier on the Anglophone community, wondered why it was necessary to have ballots in nineteen different languages, since French was the only legal language of the province. Mr. Côté's response was to advise him that it was necessary, in order to enable all Quebec's citizens to have the knowledge required for participation in elections, one of the cornerstones of a functioning democracy. If successful integration of the non-Francophone population into the Francophone collectivity is to happen, a more tolerant and respectful view of differences will have to be elicited from all their leaders in Quebec.

The challenge of immigrant integration implies such respect, which should not be the pretext for isolation and exclusion. Besides showing respect, Francophones must redefine the terms of their cultural identity and the function of the presence of non-Francophone communities who contribute to the formation of a pluralist state. Quebec society is centred on the predominance of French culture, but its composition also includes elements who do not share this heritage. An acknowledgement of other common goods will be an important instrument for ensuring the success of an integration process that currently does not always have an inclusive tone.

A Future Quebec Society: Is There Room for Inclusion?

Many Quebec Francophones wonder with anxiety about the future of their society. Is it condemned to disappear because of a low birthrate? Is its character to be drowned by a wave of immigrants? For some the answer is a pro-natalist position. For others, the solution is to adapt a positive attitude toward immigrants: they must learn French and adapt to our way of living — in other words, renounce who they are to become like us. The problem with this attitude is that the discussion is carried on only among Francophones, and the others are present only to be regulated by the majority.

The movement of populations into Quebec within the last decades has increased the sociocultural heterogeneity of the province. These waves of immigration have called into question the social fabric of a nation, its founding myths and its cultural identity. It challenges the dominant values and its physical and racial composition. The fear of many Quebec nationalists is that the combination of a low birthrate and increased immigration will weaken the distinctive character of their sociocultural and linguistic heritage.

Who then is the distinctive Quebecer? The definition has been changing ever since the arrival of Quebec's first francophone immigrants in the early sixteenth century. With each wave of immigration, the culture, language and religion has taken on new dimensions. The ability to move ahead, to adapt and to integrate aspects of the pluralistic cultures is, hopefully, what will move Quebec society away from an ethnic nationalism. However, perceptions of what it means to be a Quebecer seem to remain centred on a monolingual, monocultural vision which does not always seem to leave room for differences. Ability to utilize the pluralistic dimensions of this society would go a long way toward creating an adequate vision of the new Quebec of the twenty-first century.

We have shown the difficulty of supporting a politics of the common good while respecting and concretely acknowledging other individual and collective goals. There seems to be little doubt that a communitarian model comes into conflict with a liberal tradition that accentuates the individual and a diversity of ends. Is there room for other individual or community ends? A politics of the common good seems to negate that possibility. Liberal individualism does not undermine the necessary conditions of a shared cultural context. It allows various groups of people and individuals to fully pursue and advance their specific communal and cultural ends, without penalizing or marginalizing those groups or individuals who have differing conceptions of the good life. These are, hopefully, the best conditions under which all citizens, both as individuals and in community with others, can form and successfully pursue their understandings of the good.

II

ECONOMIC AND SOCIAL FACTORS

6

A MODEL OF REFUGEE RESETTLEMENT

NANCY HIGGITT

MIGRATION HAS PLAYED an important role in Canada's development. However, immigrants have not always been well accepted and public opinion linking economic and social problems with acceptance of foreigners has frequently influenced immigration policy (Dirks, 1977; Malarek, 1988). For instance, the Chinese who came to build our national railroad experienced discrimination in the form of head taxes and barriers to family reunification (Driedger, 1989). Similarly, East Indians were allowed entry only if they arrived non-stop from India (Buchignani, 1980). More recently, Chileans whose political orientation differed from that of the Canadian government were admitted with reluctance (Higgitt, 1992).

Currently, refugees are accepted if they fit into the Canadian quota system and have the "potential to settle successfully" (Adelman, LeBlanc and Therian, 1980:145). However, we really know very little about the process of resettlement or exactly what successful resettlement means. Furthermore, we tend to make assessments based on our expectations, without considering those of the refugees.

The point of my inquiry was to gain insight into the process of resettlement from the refugee's perspective. My specific objectives were to understand how refugees define successful resettlement and to develop a conceptual model of that process. I used an interpretive approach because of my conviction that it would broaden our current theoretical understanding.

Although many persons experience dislocation of one kind or another, the experience of refugees is perhaps more extreme than most. According to Tepper, "refugees are not immigrants, people who voluntarily depart from their homelands to seek a better life. They are emergencies: the homeless, the stateless, the dispossessed" (Tepper, 1980:5). Situations which give rise to refugee movements are generally precipitated by traumatic events such as political upheaval, ideological purges or physical deprivation. Departures are often abrupt and frequently difficult. Refugees seldom have the opportunity to select their final destination and are seldom cognizant of it when they depart. Many are unable to bring material resources with them and often arrive with only the clothes they are wearing. They are seldom able to return to their country of origin or have family and friends visit them. Most experience considerable family disruption, and communication with those left behind is often difficult or impossible. These problems are compounded because refugees, especially in recent times, usually come from countries significantly different from the countries of resettlement. Compared to immigrants, refugees are less prepared for the resettlement process. They maintain a greater commitment to their country of origin and often hope to return to it, no matter how unrealistic such hopes may be.

A CRITIQUE OF CURRENT RESETTLEMENT LITERATURE

We have considerable demographic information about refugees and their economic conditions (e.g., Neuwirth, 1987; Statistics Canada, 1988; White, 1990). Although these kinds of data have provided us with an empirical description, they have done little to promote an understanding of the process of resettlement and the variables involved in that process.

Attempts to go beyond the demographics of resettlement have been varied and often ambiguous. In the literature about immigrants for instance, Berry (1980) considered change on the part of immigrants in terms of conflict reduction. Szapocznik, Scopetta, Kurtinez and Aronalda (1975) determined how immigrants make personal and social changes to fit into their new environment. From a structural perspective, Gordon (1964) considered their entry into institutions of the dominant society. Others have focused specifically on the economic dimension.

In the refugee-related literature, some researchers have focused on cultural change. Hurh, Kim and Kim (1980), for instance, studied how refugees modify their attitudes and behaviour so as to resemble the dominant group, that is, how they acculturate. Others have emphasized structural change, especially economic integration. For example, Bach (1988) and Neuwirth (1987, 1988) studied economic and occupational adjustment. Only a few, such as Kunz (1973) and Scudder and Colson (1982), developed typologies relating specifically to the process of refugee resettlement.

Although these studies have contributed valuable insights about resettlement, serious gaps remain. For instance, it has been more than forty years since Jones (1954) identified a need to be informed about the aspirations of newcomers, the extent to which those aspirations are realized and the way in which the newcomers respond when their aspirations are frustrated. To date, few researchers have addressed these questions and no one, with the exception of Ferguson (1984), has explored resettlement from the refugee's perspective.

Several authors have addressed the need to examine these issues more closely. Bach and Bach (1980) identified a lack of information on the subjective dimensions of the resettlement process. Robinson (1990) argued for a research approach that would allow us to understand how refugees see themselves. He suggested grounding the research in the refugee experience. As Stein (1981) said, researchers need to consider the expectations refugees have for their own resettlement because expectations have a large impact on behaviour during resettlement. Finally, Baker (1990) suggested that, despite considerable research on the topic of refugees, we still do not know why some refugees resettle more successfully than others.

THE CASE FOR AN INTERPRETIVE APPROACH

Although there are many different ways to generate data about refugees, an interpretive approach was considered useful in trying to understand the resettlement process from the refugee's perspective. It is well-suited for research that seeks to uncover the nature of people's experiences and to develop a conceptual understanding of that experience (Strauss and Corbin, 1990). Researchers working in the field of refugee studies (for example, Haines, Rutherford and Thomas, 1981; Taft, 1986) have recommended an interpretive approach as being particularly useful with refugees who come from environments where language, values and lifestyles may differ considerably from those of the researcher.

Grounded theory was selected as the method to guide this study because of its emphasis on discovery and because "its systematic techniques and procedures of analysis enable the researcher to develop a substantive theory that meets the criteria for doing good science" (Strauss and Corbin, 1990:31). Developed by sociologists Glaser and

Strauss (1967), grounded theory is an advanced technique for the collection and analysis of data gathered in the everyday world and has the capacity to generate theory which is derived from or grounded in the data. Through theoretical sampling, constant comparative analysis and development of an increasingly abstract coding paradigm, grounded theory method can produce theory with the power to explain the phenomenon of interest (Chenitz and Swanson, 1986).

Research Strategy

In any field research it is important to develop trust and rapport between researchers and participants. When cross-cultural factors are involved, this requirement becomes not only important but imperative. According to Oakley (1981) and Thorogood (1987), this type of approach enables the researcher to act as an instrument through which the participants can make their personal experiences known. Making their perceptions and experiences central to data-gathering and interpretation helps to counter any imposition of assumptions and values by the researchers. According to Oakley (1981:58),

The mythology of hygienic research with its accompanying mystification of the researcher and the researched as objective instruments of data production [should] be replaced by the recognition that personal involvement ... is the condition under which people come to know each other and to admit others into their lives.

At the time of the study I had been associated with refugees and organizations providing services to them for nine years. I spent considerable time as a participant-observer at a recreational centre for refugee youths, volunteered in an organization through which former refugees provided programs to more recent newcomers, and assisted in developing and implementing an alternative form of supportive housing for refugees. While participating in such community activities I developed close friendships with several families who provided me with an intimate glimpse of their lives. These experiences were invaluable opportunities for becoming familiar with refugees and for developing an understanding of the issues involved in the resettlement process. Moreover, they served to build trust and credibility within the community and they allowed me access to that community for in-depth interviewing.

Over 12 months, I spent approximately 100 hours interviewing 24 men who were refugees from Vietnam. Refugees were defined as persons who had fled their homeland and sought refuge elsewhere because of perceived threats to their well-being (Rogge, 1987). Participants were selected through a snowball sampling technique. Initially, I worked with key informants who were known to me and they referred me to others. As my network expanded, the selection of participants was guided by the concept of theoretical sampling (Glaser and Strauss, 1967).

I selected participants who provided a mix of background variables, including ethnic affiliation, age, occupation and marital status. Most participants were interviewed only once, although about a third were interviewed more than once. In addition, I met frequently with three key informants. In all cases, written notes were taken during the interviews and expanded as soon as possible afterward. Initially, I had intended to interview both males and females, but limited resources prevented me from including women, who tended to be less accessible and to have more limited English skills than men.

Interviews were conducted in English using a topical guide. Examples of questions asked include: a) What does successful resettlement mean? b) Why are some newcomers more successful than others? c) How do you determine whether someone is successful? and d) Compared to others, how would you describe your resettlement? My interviewing style was to pose questions as broadly as possible within a given topic area and then to clarify responses through follow-up comments and probes. Most interviews took place in participants' homes, although some were conducted in coffee shops and offices.

Grounded theory guided the analysis. Constant comparative analysis was used to compare, contrast and verify information emerging from the data. Patterns identified in the data were coded. When new patterns emerged, previously coded material was re-examined for the new patterns. When new data only confirmed the information already collected and no new information was being generated the sample was considered saturated (Glaser and Strauss, 1967). Descriptive codes were collected and collapsed into more abstract codes. Gradually, categories were developed and relationships among categories were identified and worked out. As the analysis progressed a conceptual model of the resettlement process was constructed, based on participants' definitions of success, levels of adaptation identified by them and their expressed satisfaction with those levels. I also incorporated ideas from existing literature, particularly Dosman's (1972) work on aboriginal persons who move from reserves to cities. *The Ethnograph* (Seidel, Kjolseth and Seymour, 1988), a computer software program for qualitative research was used to assist with data management.

Biographical Profiles

The participants were ethnic Vietnamese (16) and ethnic Chinese (8) men who arrived in Winnipeg from Vietnam between 1975 and 1988. They fled Vietnam primarily to avoid communism and the effects of war. The majority came from Saigon or from small villages surrounding the city. They ranged in age from 22 to 50 years. Almost half (11) were married and living with their spouses, who were either ethnic Vietnamese or ethnic Chinese, except for one who was a Canadian-born Caucasian. One participant was waiting to be reunited with his spouse and another was cohabiting with a female partner. The others were single. Almost all had been separated involuntarily from extended family members. Escape experiences varied but most had suffered some degree of trauma and hardship. Very few participants knew any English on arrival.

Although it was common for participants to live in extended families in Vietnam, their households in Winnipeg were more varied. Three lived in extended family units. Nine lived in nuclear family units consisting of couples with or without children. Nine lived in survival units structured to facilitate the sharing of resources with nonfamily members and three lived in single units. Several participants resided in houses owned by them; however, the majority lived in modest apartments in the central area of the city. Most homes were modestly or sparsely furnished.

Nine participants were employed as blue collar workers and five had white collar jobs. Seven were students and three depended on social assistance. Annual household incomes ranged from $3,600 to more than $50,000. Two participants who owned businesses represented the highest economic levels. Interestingly, both had conducted businesses previously in Vietnam and both were ethnic Chinese. However, one came from a wealthy family and had not yet recovered his former status while the other came from a poor family and had surpassed his former status. Most of the others had not recovered their former socioeconomic status, although some enjoyed a higher standard of living than they had in Vietnam.

These participants considered successful resettlement as the continuation of life in a new environment. Definitions of success were interpreted through their traditional culture as well as in response to their immediate environment. For instance, participants frequently referred to aspects of Vietnamese culture to explain what success meant to them in Canada. Although the economic dimension was very important to them, they were also concerned with non-economic aspects of resettlement, including feelings of self-worth and satisfaction, a sense of belonging, family support, knowledge about Canadian society, acceptance by other Canadians and the opportunity for active participation in local and national institutions. In the words of one participant: "We need to be able to live with confidence."

CONCEPTUAL MODEL

By using an interpretive approach, I was able to explore dimensions not previously developed. For instance, rather than imposing any particular bias in defining successful resettlement, this approach allowed participants to define such resettlement as they perceived it. By comparing case to case and concept to concept, I became sensitive to differences and similarities in the experiences of different participants and to what accounted for those variations. This process facilitated the development of a conceptual model of successful resettlement that remained faithful to the participants, experiences, that is, the model was grounded in the data.

Findings from the study indicate that these refugee men defined successful resettlement holistically. In contrast to its definition in much of the literature, successful resettlement represented for them a state of general well-being consisting of economic, psychosocial and political dimensions. Although the economic dimension was very important to them, they were also much concerned with non-economic aspects of resettlement.

On the basis of these definitions, successful resettlement was equated with general well-being and a conceptual model was constructed, indicating the components of such resettlement and the relationship among the components. Prior to this, there was no indication in the literature and only a suspicion on my part that refugees would consider successful resettlement in such a holistic manner.

Components of Successful Resettlement

In the model, successful resettlement is equated with general well-being, consisting of three interrelated dimensions: these are economic, psychosocial and political (see Figure 6.1). Each dimension affects and is affected by the others. All are necessary and none is sufficient by itself. However, their influences are not equal. The economic dimension is considered to have the greatest influence, based on the logic that economic well-being is fundamental to both psychosocial and political well-being.

FIGURE 6.1

SCHEMATIC VIEW OF WELL-BEING
ACCORDING TO REFUGEE DEFINITIONS

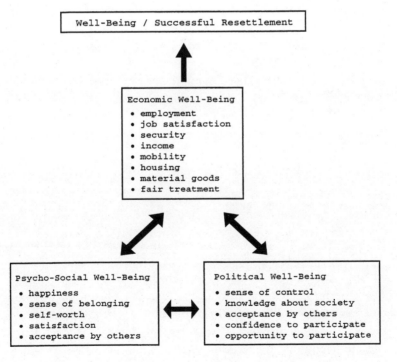

Source: Adapted from Canadian Council on Social Development, *Not Enough: The Meaning and Measurement of Poverty in Canada* (Ottawa: CCSD, 1984), 9.

Economic Dimension. Most refugees considered employment a basic requirement for success. However, they clearly indicated that the nature of the job was more important than the amount of income earned. It was important that their employment should be suitable and that they should be satisfied with it. According to participants: "Success is a good job, not lots of money but not work too hard. Work with head, not hands. Vietnamese are not strong. Many work too hard. To be successful, a person would have to have a job, be happy with that job and the job would have to fit with that person's qualifications."

Participants used several criteria to judge the suitability of employment. For instance, it should suit them physically, that is, it should not require great physical strength or endurance. This criterion relates to the fact that many Vietnamese men are relatively small in physical stature, compared to Canadian men of European ancestry. In some cases, their size actually made the work difficult, but in other cases, they experienced discrimination by Canadian employers who perceived their size negatively.

Income from employment should be adequate for their desired lifestyle. In this regard, most participants had modest expectations for material goods, for example, a small house, a car and quality audio-visual equipment. According to one young man: "I don't want to make too much money but enough to support wife and future children. Health is the main thing. I need to do something that I enjoy ... use my brain."

Another important aspect of employment was a sense of security. As most refugees had experienced considerable instability in the past, they were seeking stability in their new country, both in their work and in their lives. One participant expressed security this way: "three meals a day, a house, car, children have good education, some money in bank account, some money for old age." It was also important that their employment should offer opportunities for advancement. Although refugees were grateful for the freedom they enjoyed in Canada, they considered Canada a prosperous country and they wanted to be treated fairly and allowed to share in that prosperity.

Psycho-social Dimension. Participants considered happiness an important part of success. As one man said: "Happiness is the main thing for success. If you are happy with what you are doing. If you get married and are happy that is successful, even if minimum wage. If you feel happy, family feels happy, that is successful. Success is to be happy with yourself." Other important components were a sense of belonging to family and society, feelings of self-worth and satisfaction in the sense of being comfortable with oneself.

Participants also stressed the importance of getting along with others. A typical comment was: "Get along well with everybody. Make new friends and help each other. Able to help family in Vietnam. Not worried about money. Able to get along with everybody here. You like it here." However, being accepted by others was not easy. Participants indicated it was difficult to make friends with other Canadians and they feared not being accepted by them. For example, one participant who spoke of feeling isolated at school said: "I did not feel comfortable and others did not feel comfortable with me. We were scared of each other. What kind of joke should I tell them? I was afraid I would offend them so I said nothing."

Additionally, participants emphasized it was important to integrate past and present experiences to develop a sense of wholeness within themselves. As one participant said: "You need to integrate the two experiences. Enhance the past experience into the new one. It is hard. There are strong feelings of fear, of being lost, denied and rejected in new environment and former community."

Political Dimension. As part of the political component, participants referred to experiencing a sense of control, having knowledge about society, being accepted by others and having confidence to participate actively in society and the opportunity to do so. To these refugees, being successful meant knowing how the institutions in Canada operate and how to access those institutions to their advantage. For instance: "A person who is successful is one who understands how to function independently, knows exactly what they want and the process to get it." Additionally, success meant knowing where they fit into the system and feeling comfortable in that niche. According to participants, active participation in the political dimension was an important part of successful resettlement. This might take the form of voting or lobbying various levels of government for change or of participating in ethnic or non-ethnic organizations.

Levels of Adaptation

The second component of the model involved the development of categories to represent the varying levels of adaptation. Dosman's (1972) work was useful here. Just as he identified three distinct groups among aboriginal migrants, patterns were identified in this study which suggested that refugees can be sorted into three separate categories according to their levels of adaptation.

Categories were derived from participants' assessments of their resettlement progress. The data suggested that refugees base their assessments on the extent to which their achievements match their expectations for resettlement. Such expectations played an important role in determining whether refugees felt satisfied with their progress. Analysis of data from both the field work and the interviews suggested that expectations are derived from several factors, including: the level of remembered well-being in the country of origin; the amount and accuracy of information obtained about the country of resettlement and the process of resettlement; and, finally, the attitude toward resettlement, that is, whether it is considered a positive or negative opportunity.

My research suggests that refugees often use the level of well-being they remember in their country of origin as a measure for assessing their well-being in resettlement. As with any retrospective task, some memories are more accurate than others so that they are not necessarily comparing with what actually was but rather with how they remember what was.

Using data generated from the assessments by refugees along with the work of Dosman (1972) and others (e.g., Anderson, 1974; Model, 1988) three categories were constructed, based on the congruence between participants' expectations for resettlement and their achievements, their level of satisfaction with the resettlement progress, and the level of well-being experienced (see Figure 6.2). The categories of adaptation and their distinguishing characteristics are as follows. First, *the settled* achieve a good fit between their expectations and achievements, are satisfied with their resettlement status, and experience well-being in all three dimensions (economic, psycho-social and political). Second, *the marginals* experience tension between their expectations and achievements, are only somewhat satisfied with their resettlement status, and experience both positive and negative aspects of well-being. Finally, *the unsettled* are unable to reconcile their expectations and achievements, are not satisfied with, or are indifferent toward, their level of adaptation, and experience negative well-being.

Variables Influencing Levels of Adaptation

The third component of the model consists of variables that could affect the levels of adaptation achieved. Using the refugee literature in

FIGURE 6.2

CATEGORIES OF ADAPTATION DURING THE RESETTLEMENT
PROCESS AND DISTINGUISHING CHARACTERISTICS

Distinguishing Characteristics	Categories of Adaptation		
	Settled	Marginals	Unsettled
Fit Between Expectations and Achievements	Congruent	Marginally Congruent	Incongruent
Level of Satisfaction with Resettlement	Satisfied	Somewhat Satisfied	Not Satisfied
Level of Well-being:			
Economic	Good	Fair	Poor
Psychosocial	Positive	Mixed	Negative
Political	Positive	Mixed/ Ambivalent	Negative/ Absent

conjunction with the patterns identified in the data relevant variables
were identified (see Figure 6.3). These include conditions in the host
society; conditions of exodus; ethnicity; family characteristics such as
socioeconomic status and composition in the country or origin and
resettlement; and personal characteristics, including age, marital status,
personality and English language proficiency. Of particular concern in
this paper are conditions in the host society.

Conditions in the Host Society. According to Kallen (1982) conditions
in the host society are of paramount importance in providing an explanation for a lack of general well-being among minority populations. In
the case of the Vietnamese refugees under consideration here, government policies, the state of the economy and job transferability all play
a part in facilitating or inhibiting the adaptation process. Underlying
these three factors and equally important in its own right, is discrimination.

The attitudes of government and those of the general population
define the context in which resettlement occurs. Government policies

FIGURE 6.3

VARIABLES AFFECTING CATEGORIES OF ADAPTATION

Conditions in Host Society

	Government Policy
	Economic Conditions
	Job Transferability
	Discrimination

Conditions of Exodus

| | Flight |
| | Trauma |

Ethnicity

Family Characteristics

| | Socioeconomic Status |
| | Composition in Countries of Origin and Resettlement |

Personal Characteristics

	Age
	Marital Status
	Personality
	English Language Proficiency

and public support for cultural and racial diversity determine the extent to which refugees are permitted to participate in the larger society. Although Canada's Immigration Act recognizes the important role of refugees in Canada, not all Canadians hold a positive attitude toward newcomers, especially those who are visibly different from the dominant groups. Similarly, while Canada's multicultural policy should facilitate the participation of refugees in Canadian society, the attitudes and behaviours of many Canadians impede it. There is, for example, ample evidence that systemic racism exists in Canadian society and that it affects the well-being of newcomers (Canadian Task Force, 1988).

Government policy is reflected not only in the numbers and types of refugees accepted and the source countries from which they come but also in their integration into society. Policies relative to education, training, documentation and employment can help or hinder integration. The host society's reaction to refugees reflects to the existing economic environment, the employment situation and the provision of public services, as well as prevailing attitudes about newcomers. The ease or difficulty of resettlement depends on the interplay of all these factors.

The data from the present study indicate that government policy regarding programs is a critical factor in some resettlement differences. For example, some participants in the marginal category indicated that it was very difficult for them to get into government-sponsored training programs. A service-provider explained: "They become frustrated with the narrow criteria of available programs. They want to get into subsidized affirmative action programs because they provide an income and training is seen as a way to get out of low level jobs." Students, who belong to the marginal category, were particularly concerned about the lack of jobs available for them and considered this a government policy problem. As one student said: "Need to make sure students get a job after graduate. Otherwise, they can't repay student loan and live without a job. Where is a job? What happens to us?"

Professionals have particular difficulty gaining recognition in Canada. Their documents may not be available, their certification may be unacceptable or their experience may be discounted because it is not Canadian. As an example, medical doctors face enormous systemic barriers to resuming their careers. To do so, they are usually required to complete an internship in a recognized hospital. In most cases, however, they cannot gain acceptance to the required program because insufficient openings are available. Hence, many are trapped in the marginal category of resettlement.

Discrimination plays an important role in the process of resettlement. It might be supposed that communities which promote multiculturalism might be receptive to new ethnic groups, especially visible minorities such as the refugees from Vietnam (Burnet, 1980). For example, Winnipeg, with a strong multicultural heritage, might be expected to absorb this refugee population more readily than more homogeneous communities. There is, however, evidence of ambivalence and even negative opinion about accepting visible minorities. In a poll conducted by the *Winnipeg Free Press* in January 1986, more than half of 3,200 respondents wanted fewer immigrants admitted from Asia and Central America and indicated a preference for European immigrants who are less visible. Although the reliability and validity of a newspaper poll can be questioned, it does indicate resistance to a multicultural philosophy and has implications for the resettlement success of refugees such as those from Vietnam (Higgitt-Copeland, 1988).

Other more rigorous studies support this view. For instance, in a study of 2,500 high school students in Winnipeg, Driedger and Mezoff (1981) found considerable social distance in the form of stereotyping, prejudice and discrimination. Approximately one third of the sample, particularly persons who were Jewish, black or Asian, reported experiencing discrimination, ranging from ethnic jokes to vandalism. In a study of university students in the same city, Dhruvarajan (1985) found that Asian students perceived prejudice and discrimination, particularly from white students, but also from professors and administrators. Students reported feelings of being treated like strangers even when they wanted to integrate into society. Finally, Pankiw and Bienvenue (1990) found evidence of ethnic harassment among children attending elementary schools in the same city. The targets of this discrimination were children categorized as belonging to visible minority groups.

Although refugees participating in this study could not always articulate their problems in this regard, some mentioned discrimination as a factor in adaptation. According to one man, for instance: "Black hair makes it difficult to get job. Makes me worry." Another described his experience this way:

Discrimination makes it hard. I have felt this. You can tell if someone discriminates because of their eyes. You can feel it. You can see in their eyes what people think. I feel discriminated when I talk to people sometimes. [For example] My drivers are white and not dressed like I am [in a suit] and they tell me how they are able to get out of a parking ticket. But not me.

While collecting observational data, I witnessed examples of the discrimination to which some participants referred. On one occasion, for instance, while I was waiting to cross a downtown street with a small group of young, male refugees, passengers in a passing car shouted that the men should go back to where they came from.

The discrimination that participants have reported acts to reduce general well-being in the resettlement process. For instance, in terms of economic well-being, participants felt that they did not get jobs because of the colour of their hair or their physical size. During difficult economic times they reported experiencing more discrimination than in better times. In the psychosocial dimension, discrimination contributes to negative feelings of self, and in the political, it inhibits or prevents refugees from participating in community activities.

In this study, it was the more articulate participants who discussed systemic barriers to their resettlement. The topic was usually brought up by participants who understood both the existence and impact of such barriers. For instance, one particularly articulate man in the settled category spoke of the way in which refugee policy and programs frequently operate to maintain the status quo, that is, to maintain refugees as dependent persons. He was concerned that service-receivers are seldom consulted by policy-makers or service-providers. It is necessary, he said, to give newcomers the opportunity to develop their strengths, their self-confidence and self-image. Not only do they need knowledge of what Canadian society is all about; more importantly, they need the opportunity to participate. This can be given, he said, by allowing the newcomers to be partners in the resettlement process, rather than passive recipients. Others expressed similar ideas but in a much less articulate way. For instance, some mentioned how the clothes they receive on arrival are "funny, no mainstream person would wear them. It makes us stick out. We would rather have money to purchase what everyone else is wearing."

CONTRIBUTION TO UNDERSTANDING THE RESETTLEMENT PROCESS

The model developed here is significant for a number of reasons. Including the refugee's point of view made it possible to extend the definition of successful resettlement beyond what is proposed in the existing literature. The study indicated refugees have definite ideas about success that differ considerably from the objective measures used by others. Their definitions are based on a holistic understanding of resettlement that equates success with general well-being. In contrast, many definitions of success found in the literature have tended to focus exclusively on economic aspects (e.g., Bach, 1988; Finnan, 1981; Samuel, 1987). This tendency to focus on economic factors is also found in the more general migration literature, as noted by Currie and Halli (1989).

The well-being model provides a fundamental and dynamic means for distinguishing one level of resettlement from another. Specifically, the relationships among economic factors and the psychosocial and political dimensions facilitated the identification of characteristics pertaining to the settled, the marginals and the unsettled. The variables identified are useful in establishing the parameters of resettlement. These variables cover the life span of refugees, including their background in the country of origin, their flight experiences and factors associated with the receiving society. As the findings suggest, expectations for resettlement are important. This dimension was essential for probing refugees perspectives and for arriving at some understanding of what they consider to be satisfactory adaptation and how they justify their own assessments.

DISCUSSION OF POLICY IMPLICATIONS

From a practical point of view, the results of this study bear on the need to reexamine refugee policy and practice. For instance, in the case of some policy-makers, immigration officials and service-providers, self-sufficiency appears to be the primary indicator of success. As Johnson (1989) noted, self-sufficiency is defined in terms of earned income and independence from social welfare programs. Thus, questions frequently asked about refugees are: "Do they have jobs?" and "Are they still receiving assistance?" A comment by an employee of a non-governmental organization that assists refugees to Canada illustrates this approach: "Successful resettlement is being invisible, no problems heard or seen."

Although self-sufficiency may be an objective indicator of success, it is too simplistic to assume that it is the most important factor in successful resettlement or that economic success leads to success in other aspects of resettlement. To understand successful resettlement as refugees perceive it, it is necessary to consider resettlement holistically, that is, to consider their definitions of success along with the factors influencing their expectations for resettlement, the quality of well-being they achieve, the fit between their expectations and their achievements and their attitudes toward achievements.

Looking at the economic dimension of well-being, there is a need to reconsider policies regarding education, training and the documentation of both education and work experience, so that the skills and experience that refugees bring with them can be used. For instance, an effective mechanism is required to facilitate the recertification of professionals and to improve access to the retraining or upgrading required to meet Canadian standards. In addition, effective means are required to reduce the negative impact of prejudice and discrimination on visible minorities such as Vietnamese refugees. Despite affirmative action programs and human rights legislation there is ample evidence of the negative effect these attitudes and behaviours have on employment and self-esteem.

Within the psychosocial dimension, government policies on family reunification, for example, need to be reassessed with a view to facilitating the process by which family members are reunited. In many cases, the delays are long and the barriers great. It is very important for families to be reunited so that individual members receive the support and guidance they have been socialized to expect.

In the political dimension, it is apparent that refugees need more opportunities to learn about Canada. They need more information about the society, its institutions and its agencies of redress so that they are better able to partake in Canadian society productively and to their advantage. Although there are some provisions for this, in many cases the opportunities are limited or presented prematurely. For instance, refugees are provided with information about living in Canada within the first three weeks of their arrival; however, many refugees cannot deal effectively with this information at that time. In addition to these short orientation programs, progressive programs available over several years could be implemented.

CONCLUSION

This study contributes to a general understanding of the process of refugee resettlement that is useful for government, service-providers and other researchers. In terms of government policy, for instance, the findings suggest that under the present conditions working class refugees who are able to reunite with other family members may have the greatest potential for successful resettlement. Similarly, the study provides service-orientated agencies with an enhanced understanding of the resettlement process, and more particularly, the way in which refugees perceive that process.

The results constitute an addition to the sparse literature on successful resettlement. They contribute to the development of a definition of successful resettlement through the identification of significant variables associated with that process. Most importantly, they increase the limited information on the subjective dimensions of the process and address the need, identified by Stein (1981), to consider the expectations refugees have for their resettlement, in view of the fact that expectations have a large impact on behaviour during resettlement.

7

ECONOMIC ADAPTATION OF ASIAN IMMIGRANTS

RAVI B.P. VERMA AND KWOK BUN CHAN

AGAINST THE BACKGROUND of a historical reconstruction of the phases and patterns of Asian immigration to Canada, accompanied by an analysis of Canada's federal and provincial policy changes in regard to Asian immigrants, this paper attempts to examine the Asian immigrants' economic adaptation and performance. Basing ourselves on the 1991 Census data on total income from all sources, we have tried to answer two questions. On average, did Asian immigrants in Canada have lower or higher incomes than Canadian-born persons comparable in relevant characteristics such as age? Did they have lower or higher incomes than other immigrant groups? The paper concludes with an interpretation of the implications of our findings regarding a lack of economic adjustment of Canada's Asian immigrants to the host society that could result in their returning home. In addition, we also review some of the recent policy changes, including amendments to Canadian acts and regulations related to labour market and immigration, intended to ensure that the economic disparity between the Asian immigrant groups and the Canadian-born population will ultimately level off.

HISTORY OF ASIAN IMMIGRATION AND POLICY CHANGES

Massive numbers of immigrants from the European countries were encouraged to settle in Canada before World War I. At that time, Asian immigrants to Canada represented very small numbers and were primarily from China. Before World War II, the prevailing public policy toward immigrants from Asia was one of restriction — the Chinese, Japanese, and East Indians were seen as a threat to the financial stability and cultural identity of the Canadian province of British Columbia, where the bulk of the Asians first landed.

The number of immigrants entering Canada after World War II increased significantly from the low levels of the 1930s and the war years. Immigrant annual intake levels reached an all-time high of 282,164 in 1957; 222,876 in 1967; 218,465 in 1974; and 230,781 in 1991 (Kosinski, 1993).

Between 1951 and 1960, European countries were the largest sources of immigration to Canada, supplying 84.3 percent, compared to 5.6 percent from the U.S., 7.9 percent from Australia and New Zealand, and only 1.8 percent from Asia. Between 1971 and 1980, though Europe was still the largest single source of immigrants, with 36.2 percent, those from non-European countries became more numerous. In fact, as many as 30.1 percent were from Asia, an unprecedented high. By 1981-85, Asia had surpassed Europe as the top source of immigration to Canada, with 40.7 percent versus 30.6 percent. The Asian proportions in subsequent years increased further to 48.2 percent in 1986-90 and 52.1 percent in 1991-95 (Table 7.1). The corresponding proportions for the European immigrants were, respectively, 25.0 percent and 18.6 percent (Michalowski, 1996).

TABLE 7.1
IMMIGRATION FLOW TO CANADA BY COUNTRY OF LAST PERMANENT RESIDENCE, 1970-95

		PERCENTAGE DISTRIBUTION BY:					
		Country of last permanent residence			Immigration class		
Period	Total number of immigrants	Asia	Europe	Other	Family	Refugees(2)	Other(3)
1970-80	1,588,033	30.1	36.2	33.7	32.4	6.7	60.9
1981-85	511,225	40.7	30.6	28.7	43.1	17.9	39.0
1986-90	819,419	48.2	25.0	26.8	32.2	13.7	54.1
1991-95(1)	1,058,271	52.1	18.6	29.3	39.7	12.0	48.3

Note: 1) The 1994 data are preliminary for 1994: January to September data only; 2) Refugees class consists of persons who fled for political reasons; 3) Includes self-employed, entrepreneurs, investors, retired and others.
Source: Multiculturalism and Citizenship Canada (1990); Kosinski (1993), Tables 1 and 3; and Michalowski (1996), Table 2.

The immigration regulations of 1967 instituted a non-discriminatory but selective immigrant intake system, based on a point scheme that favours educational attainment, occupational skills and financial sources while minimizing personal, idiosyncratic biases in selection. Three classes of immigrants were thus created: family class, selected workers class, and refugees. In 1982 a restriction on selected workers was introduced in response to the employment difficulties resulting from the economic downturn. This restriction specified that selected workers must have arranged employment approved by a Canada Employment Centre in order to be eligible for admission to Canada. The term "selected workers" is defined as principal applicants destined for the labour force in the independent categories, excluding entrepreneurs, self-employed persons, retirees, and persons who are admitted under special humanitarian measures. Canadian immigration policy is fully oriented towards facilitating family reunions. The family class immigrants and retirees are admitted on the basis of good health and security check up only. Assisted relatives are not selected on the basis of knowledge of English and French, designated occupation and location of relatives. Canada's commitment to accept refugees on humanitarian grounds is also noteworthy. In 1973, Canada also had an amnesty program to provide legal status to those who were living in Canada illegally.

The 1976 Immigration Act and the Immigration Regulations of 1978 further entrenched the 1967 regulations. These measures have resulted in an immigration system that is universalist and compassionate toward the economically and politically disadvantaged on the one hand, and is at the same time targeted to meet the demographic and labour market needs of the country (Kubat, 1987:236). Becoming increasingly industrialized and urbanized, Canada deems it essential to continually upgrade the quality of its workforce. It is to make continued attempts to meet employers' needs for workers without either distorting the occupational structure (by channelling too many immigrants into a single occupation) or allowing occupations to become "ghettoized" by immigrants (Papademetriou, 1991:25).

The current natural increase of the Canadian population does not seem to guarantee its growth into the next century. In the late 1980s, projective indications were that, assuming the present 1.7 fertility rate and no increases in immigration, Canada's population would have declined as early as the second decade of the following century (Papademetriou, 1991: 24). Immigration is therefore the solution to the twin problems of quality labour force shortage and demographic decline. The postwar policy turnaround toward Asian immigrants must be understood and interpreted in this context.

Immigrants tend to congregate in three major urban metropolitan areas: Toronto, Montreal, and Vancouver. In 1986, the respective immigrant populations in these three census metropolitan areas were 1,233,095; 459,490; and 391,850; they accounted respectively for 36.3 percent, 15.9 percent, and 28.8 percent of the three total metropolitan area populations. In 1991, about 1.5 million lived in Toronto, accounting for 38 percent of its total population. Immigrants represented 17 percent of Montreal's and 30 percent of Vancouver's population. In 1991, more than half of Canada's immigrants (57 percent) lived in the three areas.

Numbering 129,420 in 1986 census, the Asians in Vancouver constituted the second largest immigrant group after the Europeans — 33.1 percent of the total population. Numbering 240,580 in Toronto and representing 19.5 percent of its population in 1986, they were the second largest immigrant group there, again behind the Europeans (totalling 736,745 or 59.7 percent).

In 1986, Asian immigrants (697,000) comprised 17.9 percent of all foreign-born persons enumerated in Canada (3,900,000). In the 1991 Census, Asian immigrants totalled 1,065,000 in Canada. They represented about 24.5 percent of all foreign-born persons enumerated in Canada (4,342,890). During the period of 1981-85, about 91,000 Asian immigrants were admitted under the family reunification plan of the 1976 Immigration Act. In addition, during this period, 37,100 Indochinese refugees were admitted into the country. These two categories represented 43.1 percent and 17.9 percent, respectively, of the total Asian immigrants (207,800) who arrived in Canada during the period 1981-85. During the next two periods, 1986-90 and 1991-95, more Asian immigrants were admitted into Canada under the family class, 127,000 and 241,000 respectively. However, their proportionate shares of the total of Asian immigrants were lower — 32.2 percent of total Asian immigrants (395,000) arriving in 1986-90; and 39.7 percent of total Asian immigrants (606,000) arriving in 1991-95. Similarly, the proportionate shares of refugees accepted from Asian countries declined to 13.7 percent in 1986-90 and 12 percent in 1991-95. Thus, the composition of the Asian immigrant group is quite unique. Currently, more independent and business class immigrants are admitted into Canada.

PAST RESEARCH ON INCOME OF IMMIGRANTS

Over the past two decades, a number of studies of immigrants' earnings in Canada have been undertaken (Kalbach, 1970; Richmond and

Kalbach, 1980; Basavarajappa and Verma, 1985; Verma, 1985; Beaujot, Basavarajappa and Verma, 1988; Beaujot and Rappak, 1988; and Verma and Basavarajappa, 1989). Taken as a whole, these studies suggest that age, education and length of stay in Canada are the most important variables in explaining the relative income status of different birthplace groups. However, other factors — changing immigration policies, labour market situation prevailing at the time of arrival of immigrants, cohort effect, discrimination, employment characteristics — cannot be ignored in explaining the earnings disparity between the immigrant groups and the Canadian-born (Miller, 1992; Swan et al., 1991; Boyd, 1992; and Bloom et al., 1995)

The analysis of the 1981 Census data (Beaujot, Basavarajappa and Verma, 1988) indicated that, at the Canada level, immigrant men earned an average of $21,830 in 1980, which was 4.9 percent above that earned by Canadian-born men, while immigrant women earned an average of $13,007, which was 1.8 percent below that earned by Canadian-born women. However, adjustments for differences in age and education brought the ratios to 3.1 percent (for males) and 4.5 percent (for females) below the respective incomes of the Canadian-born. The differences across birthplace groups were sizable. For males, the six groups from developing regions (Africa, South Asia, Southeast Asia, East Asia, Western Asia and Oceania, and Other) were all found in the lower half of the income distribution, with incomes 9 to 22 percent below those of Canadian-born males. The incomes of females were 5 to 14 percent below those of Canadian-born women. It was also found that immigrants who had been in Canada for less than 20 years had average employment incomes that were below their Canadian-born counterparts. Most immigrant groups improved their relative economic positions as length of residence in Canada increased.

Using the 1981 and 1986 Census data Miller (1992) compared the earnings of the Canadian-born group with those of selected groups of immigrants, including four major Asian groups. He found that the decline in earnings of the foreign-born workers relative to the earnings of the Canadian-born workers, observed over the period 1971-81 (Chiswick and Miller, 1988), continued over the period 1981-86. This decline characterized all major birthplace groups and particularly Asian groups. While earnings growth associated with Canadian experience increased for both native-born and immigrant groups, earnings growth associated with pre-immigration experience did not change for the foreign-born. Consequently, immigrants lost ground relative to the native-born. The increase in the admission of immigrant classes (e.g., family classes, refugee claimants), where the point system does not apply, has been offered as a possible explanation for the relative decline in the earnings of the foreign-born population by birthplace groups.

Our analysis of earnings data from the 1986 census has shown that Asian immigrant men and women respectively earned average annual incomes of $27,627 and $18,167 in 1985. These were 6 percent below those of the Canadian-born men and women ($29,443 and $19,420). Among immigrant groups, the Asians' incomes were higher than those of three other immigrant groups: Caribbean, South and Central American and Southern European. After controlling for age and education, the disparity between immigrant groups and the Canadian-born increased incredibly. Within the Asian region, the income status of the immigrants from Southeast Asian countries was the lowest. In comparison with the Canadian-born, the disparity was higher for Asian immigrants arriving in 1980-84 and residing in census metropolitan areas than for those who came in 1975-79. For both men and women the difference decreased over time, although Asian immigrants did not achieve parity with the average employment of the Canadian-born.

Among other immigrant groups, the time required to achieve parity in average employment income with the Canadian-born was greater in 1985 than in 1980, 23 years as opposed to 20 years. This may be due to the changing Canadian immigration policies in recent years, recession, general employment, and structural changes in the economy.

On the basis of the 1986 Census data, Swan et al. (1991) examined the effect of discrimination on earning differences among birthplace groups. They claimed that "there is no significant discrimination against immigrants in general or coloured immigrants in particular." However, there is an income disadvantage for immigrants who received all of their education and some of their labour market experience in their home countries, especially in the case of recent arrivals from the developing countries. Their observation on absence of discrimination was found to be limited by the question of statistical reliability (Reitz, 1993). The study had looked at immigrants arriving under the age of five and now in the labour force. But the numbers involved were very small, particularly among the Asian groups: 43 East Asians, 27 West Asians, 30 South Asians and 10 South East Asians.

Using multiple classification analysis based on the 1986 Census data, Boyd (1992) found that once adjustments are made for the socioeconomic differences, that is, "if all groups had the same socioeconomic profile, being foreign-born, a member of visible minority group, or female would be associated with lower earnings." She showed further that these disadvantages accumulate and that foreign-born visible minority women received the lowest wages and salaries.

In 1995, Bloom, Grenier and Gunderson used pooled 1971, 1981 and 1986 Census data to evaluate the extent to which (1) the earnings of immigrants at the time of immigration fell short of the earnings of comparable Canadian-born individuals; and (2) immigrants' earnings grew more rapidly over time than those of the Canadian-born. They found that, prior to 1965, complete labour market assimilation within 15 years was the norm for both men and women and for immigrants originating from different regions. Thereafter, assimilation took longer and longer, with full assimilation appearing completely out of reach for post-1970 immigrants. Assimilation has been particularly slow for immigrants from Asia, Africa, and Latin America, as compared with those from Europe and the United States. These authors suggested that three major factors — changing immigration policies, heightened discrimination as the number of visible minorities among the immigrants increased, and the prolonged recession of the 1980s — have contributed to the decline in immigrant income assimilation.

The non-recognition of qualifications obtained overseas remains a serious problem for all newly arrived immigrants, particularly those selected as "skilled" on the basis of a revised points system. The "segmented structural change" hypothesis (Richmond, 1991) led us to expect immigrants to enter at the lower end of the expanding service sector and to move up when they had requalified and the economy was booming. Prolonged recession plus structural change has made this more difficult (Richmond's letter to Ravi Verma, dated 6 December 1996).

Recently, two papers related to Asian immigrants in Canada have been published (Samuel, 1994 and Michalowski, 1996). Samuel's 1994 paper reviews several studies related to many aspects of Asian immigrants. He concluded: "Generally speaking, Asian immigrants have adapted and integrated well. Yet access to Canadian territory as permanent residents, or access to Canadian citizenship, does not necessarily mean access to equal opportunity in the economy and society, though to a certain extent, Canada may have succeeded more than Australia" (Samuel, 1994:465). The economic adaptation indicators for Asian immigrants were based on analytical information available from the 1986 Census data and previous censuses. Michalowski (1996) analyzed female immigrants from Asian regions, West Asia/Middle

East, East Asia, Southeast Asia and South Asia. Her analysis was based on flow data from Citizenship and Immigration Canada and stock data from the 1991 Census. In one of her analyses, she focused on the labour force characteristics of Asian immigrant groups, all immigrant groups and the non-immigrant group: "The 1991 census data reveal that females were concentrated in clerical occupations regardless of their national origins. In fact, one-third of the native-born females and 27 percent of females from Asia were found in these occupations" (Michalowski, 1996:72). For females, we notice that the values of the index of dissimilarity, showing differences in percentage distribution of occupation between each of four Asian groups and the total immigrant group, on the one hand, and Canadian-born women on the other, were found to be 13.4 percent (Asia), 10.2 percent (West Asia and Middle East), 11.9 percent (East Asia), 19.2 percent (Southeast Asia), 17.5 percent (South Asia); and 7.8 percent (total immigrant group). These indices indicate that the occupation structures of Asian female immigrant groups and the Canadian-born females were not similar. Comparisons of the two occupational structures show that "in general, Asian females experience a lower status in the labour force than native-born. The lower status of female Asian immigrant groups could be due to the fact that many of them had entered Canada as refugees or joined immediate family members and might lack relevant occupational skills or sufficient language proficiency. In the situation of economic stagnation and high labour force competitiveness experienced in Canada at the end of the 1990s, such disadvantages could prevent them from gaining employment" (Michalowski, 1996).

In contrast to female occupational differences, the values of the index of dissimilarity for males were observed to be larger: 16.6 percent (Asia), 17.8 percent (West Asia and Middle East), 37 percent (East Asia), 24.6 percent (Southeast Asia), 12.8 percent (South Asia), and 9.9 percent (total immigrant group). The higher values of the index of dissimilarity for males show once again that the occupational structures of Asian immigrant groups were relatively different from those of the Canadian-born. In 1991 more male immigrants from Asian countries were employed, as compared with the Canadian-born workers, in managerial, administrative and related, professional and related, and service occupations. Similarly, more female immigrants from Asian regions over the Canadian-born were employed in service occupations (Table 7.2). As the occupational structures of the Asian immigrant groups in 1991 were considerably different from those of the Canadian-born, their earning levels were expected to be lower.

TABLE 7.2

PERCENTAGE DISTRIBUTION OF OCCUPATIONS AND INDEX
OF DISSIMILARITY BETWEEN CANADIAN-BORN PERSONS
AND ASIAN IMMIGRANTS, MALES AND FEMALES, 1991

Gender/ Occupation	Canadian-born persons	All Immigrants	Asia	West Asia Middle East	East Asia	Southeast Asia	South Asia
MALES (Total)	6,756,140	1,572,065	394,190	57,385	129,700	108,555	98,550
Mgt./admin./rel.	13.2	14.6	13.4	16.0	18.0	7.1	12.6
Prof./rel.	13.1	16.4	17.5	15.7	21.5	14.7	16.4
Clerical/rel.	7.2	7.1	9.3	8.8	8.9	9.9	9.4
Sales	9.3	8.0	9.2	13.2	11.0	6.2	8.1
Service	10.3	11.8	16.2	14.7	21.1	16.4	10.3
Primary	7.7	3.2	1.7	0.8	1.1	1.6	3.2
Processing	6.7	8.2	8.4	4.8	4.0	12.2	12.2
Prod. fabr./ assembly	8.2	10.3	10.5	10.7	5.8	16.9	9.4
Construction	10.7	9.6	3.7	5.3	2.5	4.1	4.1
Other	13.6	10.7	10.0	10.0	6.1	10.9	14.3
Index of Dissimilarity		9.9	16.6	17.8	37.0	24.6	12.8
FEMALE (Total)	5,769,330	1,286,395	329,615	30,130	115,235	111,640	72,610
Mgt./admin./rel.	9.7	9.8	8.4	9.6	11.3	6.0	7.2
Prof./rel.	21.6	19.7	17.1	17.9	15.6	20.1	14.5
Clerical/rel.	32.2	27.7	26.8	28.9	28.6	24.0	27.4
Sales	9.9	9.0	8.4	14.7	10.0	5.7	7.4
Service	16.7	17.4	18.7	17.2	18.6	20.8	16.1
Primary	2.5	1.9	1.8	0.4	0.6	1.1	5.7
Processing	1.9	2.5	3.2	1.8	2.6	3.5	4.2
Prod. fabr./ assembly	2.2	7.5	10.8	7.0	9.7	13.8	9.6
Construction	0.4	0.3	0.2	0.2	0.2	0.3	0.3
Other	3.0	4.1	4.5	2.4	2.9	4.8	7.5
Index of Dissimilarity		7.8	13.4	10.2	11.9	19.2	17.5

Index of dissimilarity shows occupation group differences between the different Asian immigrant groups, all immigrants as a group, and Canadian-born persons.
Source: 1991 Census data, special tabulations.

Statistics Canada's Census monograph from the 1991 Census on "Immigrant Employment, Earnings and Expenditures" (Nakamura, Masso Nakamura, Christopher J. Nicol and W. Erwin Diewert), was published in 1997. Their study provides more insight into the economic adjustment of different immigrant groups while ascertaining whether the disparity in earnings between the Asian immigrants and other immigrant groups over the Canadian-born has been reduced or increased.

ANALYSIS OF INCOME DIFFERENTIALS

Recently, some profiles of immigrant groups (from Germany, Hong Kong, India, Italy, Lebanon, the Netherlands, People's Republic of China, the Philippines, Poland, Portugal, the United States, Vietnam, Total Immigrant Population), and the Canadian Population from the 1991 Census of Canada were published jointly by Statistics Canada and Citizenship and Immigration Canada (cat. no. Ci62-2/14-1996). In these country profiles figures on average income from all sources were published. These data are analysed in the following sections.

In the present paper, the term "immigrants" refers to those persons with a valid year of immigration who were born outside Canada and were not Canadian citizens at birth. In addition to persons who were part of the native-born population in 1991, Canadian-born included: (1) children born to Canadian diplomatic, military and other person-nel working outside Canada, and (2) persons in Canada who were not Canadian citizens at birth, but became legal immigrants at a later date.

Since the objective of this paper is to present an overall picture of the economic performance of Asian immigrants compared that of to the Canadian-born, we analyzed the total income of all individuals from all sources (Basavarajappa, 1996). In addition, past studies on earnings of Asian immigrants were made at the region level, West Asia/Middle East, Southeast, East and South Asia. Some variations in average incomes of immigrants from individual countries within each region were lost (Boyd, 1986). Hence, we confined our analyses to selected Asian countries: Lebanon, India, Vietnam, the Philippines, China, and Hong Kong.

The classificatory variables included are age and gender. With the exception of age and gender, the information on socioeconomic charac-teristics of the population was collected in the 1991 Census on the basis of a 20 percent sample of all households. The census data were subject to coverage, response, processing and sampling errors, and any errors introduced by random rounding. It was estimated that the 1991 Census had an overall undercoverage of about 3.21 percent. There was also an indication that the extent of undercoverage was higher in certain seg-ments of the population, e.g., young adults and recent immigrants.

If the cell frequencies are large, the net effect of the above errors may be negligible as errors (i.e., random errors) will be made in both directions. However, the error proportion or rate of net random errors increases as the population or cell size decreases. Thus, considerable caution must be exercised in interpreting small differences or differences based on small frequencies. In the 1991 Census of Canada immigrants arriving during the period 1990-91 were directed not to report their income acquired outside Canada during 1990. They were, therefore, excluded from this analysis. To make the comparisons valid, income of each birthplace group was adjusted for differences in age by using the technique of direct standardization. The distributions of Canadian-born males and Canadian-born females were used as standards for immigrant males and females respectively.

Table 7.3 shows the average total incomes from all sources in 1990 for Asian and other immigrant groups and for the Canadian-born. We see that the relative lower income status of West Asia (Lebanon), Southeast Asia (Vietnam, Philippines) and East Asia (China), as compared with the Canadian-born and other immigrant groups, which was observed in 1985, continued in 1990. The incomes of Asian immigrants from Vietnam were the lowest, at $20,204. In comparison with the average incomes of the Canadian-born, the index of average incomes of immigrants from Lebanon, Vietnam, the Philippines and China were 80, 74, 91, 85 percent, respectively. These differences remained when their average incomes were adjusted for age. Only two Asian immigrant groups, those from India and Hong Kong, had higher incomes in 1990 than those of the Canadian-born population. However, after controlling for age, all Asian immigrant groups had lower income than the Canadian-born population. Their relative incomes are expected to decrease further when we control for age and education. Such negative effects of adjustment for age and education on the comparison of average earnings between immigrant groups and the Canadian-born population had been noticed during the analyses of the 1981 and 1986 data.

In 1990, the gap between the incomes of immigrants from all Asian countries, except the Philippines and Hong Kong, and those of the Canadian-born population was more pronounced for males than females. The female immigrants from the Philippines and Hong Kong had higher incomes, when adjusted for age. The indexes of their average incomes, with incomes of the Canadian-born females used as base, were 104 percent and 106 percent respectively. The difference could be partly associated with higher proportions of immigrant females working full time and the full year, a higher proportion of employed immigrant females aged 15-64, a greater proportion of self-employed, and a greater proportion of these immigrant females employed in managerial and professional occupations.

TABLE 7.3

AVERAGE INCOME AND RELATIVE INDEX OF SELECTED IMMIGRANT AND CANADIAN-BORN GROUPS, 1990

Birthplace Groups	AVERAGE INCOME Both sexes Observed	Adjusted	Males Observed	Adjusted	Females Observed	Adjusted
Canadian-born	23,749	23,749	29,837	29,837	17,457	17,457
Immigrants (All)	25,318	23,904	32,089	29,647	18,266	17,647
ASIA						
Lebanon (West Asia)	19,041	18,932	22,490	22,613	13,169	13,048
India (South Asia)	25,174	23,263	31,923	29,153	17,195	16,279
Vietnam (Southeast Asia)	17,626	16,696	20,358	19,699	14,276	13,356
Philippines (Southeast Asia)	21,712	20,356	24,439	23,703	19,833	18,121
China (East Asia)	20,204	19,588	25,009	23,946	15,009	15,138
Hong Kong (East Asia)	25,385	23,278	30,394	28,161	20,380	18,556
U.S.	27,126	26,509	36,019	35,039	20,071	19,608
U.K.	28,697	27,931	38,772	36,520	19,603	19,620
Germany	28,258	26,309	36,748	33,785	19,471	18,678
Netherlands	27,836	26,085	36,407	33,469	17,513	17,165
Italy	26,027	25,360	32,957	31,655	16,924	17,476
Portugal	22,640	21,414	28,476	26,818	15,676	15,114
Poland	23,192	21,668	29,074	27,116	17,036	15,962
RELATIVE INDEX						
Canadian-born	100	100	100	100	100	100
Immigrants	107	101	108	99	105	101
ASIA						
Lebanon (West Asia)	80	80	95	76	75	75
India (South Asia)	106	98	107	98	98	93
Vietnam (Southeast Asia)	74	70	68	66	82	77
Philippines (Southeast Asia)	91	86	82	79	114	104
China (East Asia)	85	82	84	80	86	87
Hong Kong (East Asia)	107	98	102	94	117	106
U.S.	114	112	121	117	115	112
U.K.	121	118	130	122	112	112
Germany	119	111	123	113	112	107
Netherlands	117	110	122	112	100	98
Italy	110	107	110	106	97	100
Portugal	95	90	95	90	90	87
Poland	98	91	97	91	98	91

Note: Age standardized in respect to Canadian-born persons.
Source: Ci62-2/1-15-96, Immigrant Profiles.

TABLE 7.4

MEASURES OF ECONOMIC PERFORMANCE OF SELECTED
IMMIGRANT GROUPS AND CANADIAN-BORN PERSONS, 1991

Birthplace Goups	% aged 15-64 employed		% Self-employed		% Employed Full-time, Full Year		Unemploy-ment Rate	% of persons with income from gov't. transfers,	% of persons with low
	Men	Women	Men	Women	Men	Women	(%)	1990	income
Canadian-born	76.0	62.9	12.4	5.8	58.7	45.2	10.7	11.4	14.8
Immigrants (All)	75.5	62.1	15.6	7.7	62.9	49.6	10.8	11.6	24.4
ASIA									
Lebanon									
(West Asia)	67.4	42.2	21.9	9.6	50.6	37.4	18.5	12.9	45.8
India (South Asia)	76.9	58.5	12.0	5.3	60.2	43.9	17.0	8.5	17.3
Vietnam									
(Southeast Asia)	66.5	53.2	5.9	5.3	54.9	45.4	17.5	12.0	31.6
Philippines									
(Southeast Asia)	80.4	78.4	4.9	2.9	57.0	55.2	8.1	6.5	20.2
China (East Asia)	73.8	59.9	18.0	9.8	63.6	49.3	10.2	12.2	31.1
Hong Kong									
(East Asia)	71.4	59.2	14.8	7.0	62.4	52.1	9.1	3.9	28.2
U.S.	78.8	64.6	17.0	10.4	60.0	43.2	8.7	11.5	17.9
U.K.	82.7	71.4	13.7	7.3	69.9	51.1	7.3	12.3	12.2
Germany	81.0	67.0	20.6	11.9	69.0	51.7	11.9	10.3	17.0
Netherland	87.4	68.3	27.6	15.7	74.1	47.4	4.8	10.9	13.2
Italy	81.1	61.9	18.3	6.7	66.7	53.3	10.8	10.7	19.8
Portugal	78.5	62.6	7.9	3.4	57.4	52.4	13.8	19.7	29.6
Poland	68.8	55.4	16.2	7.5	54.7	43.8			

Note: Figures for the Immigrant population are age standardized to the Canadian-born population.
Source: Immigration Research Series by Statistics Canada and Citizenship and Immigration Canada, Cat. no.
Ci62-2/1-15, 1996.

In Table 4 we have compared some employment indicators from
the 1991 census for the Asian and other immigrant groups and the
Canadian-born population. These indicators also show the current economic adaptation of Asian immigrant groups to Canada. Immigrants
aged 15-64 who came from the Philippines were employed more than
the Canadian-born population. The percentage was much higher for
employed female workers (78.4 percent versus 62.9 percent) as compared with employed male workers (80.4 percent versus 76.0 percent).
The immigrant men from Lebanon and Vietnam were considerably
less employed (67.4 percent and 66.5 percent). The proportion of
employed female immigrants from these two countries was even lower
(42.2 percent and 53.2 percent). The proportion of self-employed
Asian male immigrants from Lebanon (21.9 percent), China (18.0 percent), and Hong Kong (14.8 percent) was higher than the comparable
proportion for the Canadian-born (12.4 percent). The proportion of

male immigrants from China (63.6 percent) and Hong Kong (62.4 percent) who were working full-time during the entire year was very similar to the comparable figure for the Canadian-born (62.9 percent). For females, the proportion of immigrants from the Philippines (55.2 percent), China (49.3 percent) and Hong Kong (52.1 percent) who were considerably employed full-time for the full year was considerably higher than the figure for Canadian-born female workers (45.2 percent).

In 1991 immigrants from three Asian countries (Lebanon, India and Vietnam) had much higher unemployment rates than did the Canadian-born or the immigrant population as a whole. After adjustment of the unemployment rates for age differences the rates for immigrants from Lebanon, India, and Vietnam remained higher (18.5 percent, 17.0 percent and 17.5 percent respectively). The rates for the Canadian-born and total immigrants were relatively lower (10.7 percent and 10.8 percent). We found that young adult immigrants from Lebanon, India and Vietnam were more unemployed. Consequently, the proportions of persons under the low income cut-off were considerably higher among Asian immigrant groups, ranging from 17.3 percent (India) to 45.8 percent (Lebanon). For the Canadian-born population the figure was 14.8 percent. A large proportion of persons with low incomes were younger adults and elderly persons aged 65 years and over. Young adult immigrants aged 15-24 from Lebanon included a higher proportion with lower incomes (45 percent) than did the elderly aged 65 years and over (33.9 percent). This situation was reversed when elderly immigrants from China were examined. Their primary source of income was from government transfers; a large number of these elderly persons were dependent on their families. However, only two Asian groups from Lebanon and China received a higher proportion of their incomes from government transfers compared to the Canadian-born (Statistics Canada, and Citizenship and Immigration Canada, cat. no. Ci62-2/14-1996).

In sum, on the basis of analysis of some economic indicators from the 1991 Census we can make some broad observations on the economic disparity between the Asian groups as a whole and the Canadian-born population. Asian immigrants from Lebanon (West Asia), China (East Asia) and Vietnam (Southeast Asia) had relatively lower economic achievement in Canada. In contrast, other Asian immigrant groups from India (South Asia), the Philippines (Southeast Asia) and Hong Kong (East) were relatively more integrated, economically speaking, into Canadian society. The economic success of immigrants from Hong Kong can be partially attributed to the presence among them of the business class immigrants.

It is still too early to attempt an overall assessment of the economic and social success of Asian business immigrants — the new Asian economic elite — on Canadian society. There have not been systematic analyses of the patterns and processes of their economic adaptation and performance. Longitudinal studies need to be made of cohorts of business immigrants to permit assessment of the extent to which they have been successful in becoming part of the Canadian economy.

Nevertheless, several problems that have already begun to surface among the Chinese business immigrants deserve attention. Internal competition among co-ethnics within an enclave economy happens when an inordinate number of immigrants launch similar types of business, cashing in on a particular ethnic niche (Waldinger et al., 1990). Competition is often structurally built into the very configuration of ethnic enterprise when immigrants follow in one another's "commercial footsteps" too closely, a process which, in turn, invariably leads to saturation and excessive competition. In Toronto, Montreal and Vancouver Chinatowns we have witnessesed in recent years a dramatic proliferation of Cantonese restaurants — one new restaurant springs up as soon as another closes down. Chan and Cheung (1985:147), in their study of Chinese business in Toronto, reported that 60 percent of their respondents admitted facing competition from other Chinese businesses: 64 percent found the internal competition "quite strong" or "very strong." Somewhat less competition from non-Chinese business was reported. The Chinese restaurateurs in Canada, like the Asian businessmen in the London borough of Wandsworth (Aldrich, 1977), cope with competition by putting in extra hard work, or by self-exploitation: opening on Sundays and holidays, working longer hours each day and more days a week, and lowering employees' wages. Internal competition among co-ethnics often develops into an unending vicious circle of cost-cutting and longer hours — it leads to still more competitive behaviour. Even the most energetic and vibrant enclave economy would eventually reach its saturation point if competition were to continue unabated.

So, quite ironically, one may argue that the more institutionally complete an ethnic community is — that is to say, the stronger the centripetal forces and the weaker the centrifugal forces — the stronger the propensity toward internal economic competition will be. While ethnic ties, informal family and kin networks as well as immigrant institutions are obviously enabling because of the myriad of resources embedded in them, they can also be limiting and circumscribing, possibly leading to "ghettoization" of ethnic businesses of a similar type and, worse still, business failures or bankruptcies.

RETURN MIGRATION

Some economic indicators from the 1991 Census of Canada show that the lower economic performance of some Asian immigrant groups from West Asia (Lebanon), Southeast Asia (Vietnam, the Philippines) and East Asia (China), as compared with that of the Canadian-born in 1985, continued in 1990. Only immigrants from South Asia (India) and East Asia (Hong Kong) had higher incomes than those of the Canadian-born in 1990. However, after controlling for their differences in age, all immigrants from Asian countries had lower incomes than the Canadian-born.

The findings of our analysis could be useful in understanding the out-migration of the immigrant population from Canada. It has been found that approximately 10 percent of immigrants admitted between 1981 and 1986 had emigrated from Canada by the end of this period (Michalowski, 1991). These returns of recent immigrants comprised 35 percent of the total return migration during the period 1981-86. By place of birth, immigrants from Asia dominated and represented 35 percent of the total number of return migrants. Moreover, 59 percent of them were of Indian origin. Their return could be partly due to lack of economic and social adjustment in Canada. One could hypothesize that such emigration is an event that is unplanned and occurs primarily among migrants whose expectations are not satisfied.

Failing to find a job or business niche in the opportunity structure of the Canadian economy, many Asian immigrants are taking paths back to the East, mostly to their own motherlands, including India, Hong Kong, Singapore, Malaysia and Taiwan. Many of these countries are at present experiencing unprecedented periods of economic growth. All of this is happening against a background of racial prejudice and discrimination against the Chinese (Chan and Helly, 1987; Chan, 1991; Bolaria and Li, 1985a), South Asians from India, Pakistan, Bangladesh and Sri Lanka (Bolaria and Li, 1985b; Buchignani et al., 1985), Japanese (Ujimoto, 1985), and Indochinese from Vietnam, Laos and Cambodia (Chan, 1987). Several past studies by Sharma

(1980; 1981a; 1981b) have confirmed social adjustment problems experienced by recent Third World immigrants, which have sometimes been aggravated by racism. When Asian immigrants have worked in the same sector for the same duration as other Canadians comparable in level of education, age, gender and social class but have not been remunerated at a level comparable to that of other Canadians one would suggest that there seems to be a price attached to being Asian in the Canadian labour market. Li (1988:120) calls this price "the cost of discrimination," suggesting that "race remains a salient factor in determining income inequality." Li concludes that, with respect to the Chinese in Canada, if they "have overcome the historical obstacles of racism, they have yet to cross the barriers of racial discrimination in the Canadian labour market."

Kubat (1987:242) argues that "deprivation is tolerated essentially under two conditions: a prospect of hope for oneself or a certainty of succour in one's community. Certainly the prospect of returning home has been a driving force in the minds of many immigrants." While he is largely correct in saying that "enduring poverty and discrimination for a purpose, then, taxes one's patience somewhat less than where there is no hope at all" (Kubat, 1987:242), what he did not anticipate at the time of writing is the renewed sense of hope in the East. For some Asian immigrants in Canada, hope is going home.

In recent years, some prospects of better economic performance among Asian immigrants are also emerging in Canada. For example, international trade between Canada and Asian countries is expanding. In 1995 the Canadian trade mission visited India and Southeast Asian countries to promote Canadian business. There are some Canadian companies which are operating — or planning to expand their business — in Asian countries. Some Asian immigrants can explore their job opportunities with them.

CONCLUSIONS

During the last ten years several preventive measures have been introduced by federal and provincial governments in Canada to promote equal job opportunity for four designated groups: women, aboriginal peoples, visible minorities and persons with a disability. In 1986 the federal government recognized the disadvantaged status of these groups and introduced the Employment Equity Act. The objective of this legislation was to establish equality in the workplace so that no person would be denied opportunities for reasons related to ability. It provided that workforce areas like recruitment, training and development, promotion, pay, retention, and separation would be identified for improvement by the employers. Several other measures have already been in operation: quotas, targets, understanding of diversity, career planning, mentoring, networking, counselling, leadership, accountability, best practices, rewards and recognition, measurement, policies and services (Treasury Board, 1993). The new Employment Equity Act, which received royal assent on December 15, 1995, strengthens the original Act of 1986. The new Act continues to cover private sector employees under federal jurisdiction and in federal crown corporations with one hundred employees or more, besides expanding coverage to the federal public service. It clarifies employer obligations and gives the Canadian Human Rights Commissions (CHRC) the mandate to monitor and verify compliance through employer audits (*Canada Gazette*, September 7, 1996).

In 1993, amendments (Bill C-86) were made to the Immigration Act of 1976. The purpose of Bill C-86 was to ensure that the number and categories of immigrants who come to Canada could be managed so as to more effectively meet Canada's economic, social and humanitarian goals (Citizenship and Immigration Canada, Annual Report, 1993). The new selection criteria include more emphasis on those factors that enable the immigrant to adapt and contribute to an economy, namely, higher levels of education, official language ability, decision-making skills, motivation and initiative. This shifts the focus away from specific occupations to the potential for long-term success in a changing labour market (see Citizenship and Immigration Canada, Annual Report, 1996).

Integration is a two-way process that requires adaptation on the part of newcomers as well as acceptance and accommodation by Canadians. A number of government programs run in partnership with nongovernmental organizations are now in place in Canada. These include: the adjustment assistance program, the immigrant settlement and adaptation program, the language instruction program for newcomers to Canada, the labour market language training program and others. It is hoped that newcomers, particularly those from Asian and other Third World countries, will benefit from these programs in the process of their adaptation to Canada.

8

EMPLOYMENT EQUITY FOR VISIBLE MINORITIES

T. JOHN SAMUEL AND ALY KARAM

CANADA'S POPULATION and its labour force have changed significantly as a result of immigration from Third World countries. By 1991, over nine percent of the labour force belonged to the visible minority group. This percentage is bound to increase further in the years to come in view of continuing immigration and natural increase among the visible minorities. The present paper looks at the progress of employment equity for visible minorities in the "federal work force" — the Public Service and the federally regulated private sector — in Canada.

AWARENESS OF INEQUITIES

The origins of the employment equity program for visible minorities in Canada go back to the 1970s. Primarily it reflects two influences: the impact of rising levels of immigration from the Third World and the affirmative action program in the United States started in the sixties.

Impact of Rising Levels of Immigration

The universalization of Canada's immigration policy in the sixties brought to the country a relatively large number of people from the Third World. About half of them settled in Ontario, particularly Toronto. The Canadian public was unprepared to cope with such large numbers of visible minority immigrants in their midst. Naturally social tensions arose. The year 1977 was an important year for race relations and employment equity for visible minorities. Two reports on the social tensions and the resulting violence against South Asians in Toronto in particular appeared in 1977. A report to the attorney general of Ontario by Bhausaheb Ubale (1977:145) on "Concerns of the South Asian Canadian Community Regarding Their Place in the Canadian Mosaic" included the observation that "the phenomenon of discrimination appears to be very active in employment, but cannot be pinpointed in precise statistical terms." A month later a Task Force on Human Relations, chaired by Walter Pitman, recommended, among other things, that Metro Toronto Council "adopt a policy of making appointments to boards and commissions from visible minorities until the representation of these visible minorities on the boards and committees has some relationship to the present mix of population in Metropolitan Toronto" (Pitman, 1977). The seeds of the employment equity principle were sown. These two reports appear to be the forerunners of the principle of "employment equity" (later coined by Rosalie Silberman Abella, 1984) for visible minorities in Canada.

At the same time the affirmative action program was gathering momentum in the U.S. The Civil Rights Act of 1964 covered both private employers and those in the public sector such as state and municipal governments, educational institutions and private firms with 15 or more employees. Between 1965 and 1981 the U.S. federal courts handled more than 5,000 cases appealing decisions related to affirmative action. The U.S. contract compliance program covered 41 million workers in 1981 (Jain, 1988:21). When evidence based on studies done in the U.S. showed that the affirmative action program was effective in increasing employment and earnings of minorities the thinking on a similar employment equity program in Canada received a boost.

CANADIAN ACTION

Another important report appeared in the same year, 1984, entitled *Equality Now!*, and produced by a special House of Commons Committee. It stated that visible minorities were being denied full participation in Canadian society and institutions. Comprehensive recommendations were made with regard to social integration, employment, education, Public Service appointments, legal and justice issues, media and government. Most of the recommendations have now been adopted by different levels of government.

The Abella Report

In 1983 the government of Canada established the Commission on Equality in Employment with Rosalie Abella as Chair. The Commission had a mandate to investigate the most effective ways of promoting equality of employment for women, aboriginals, people with disability and visible minorities. Its report examined the concept of equality and fairness in employment and the extent to which members of the target groups had experienced equitable treatment in the workplace (Abella, 1984). The Employment Equity Act of 1986 incorporated most of the recommendations made.

Several studies have reported that persons with origins in the Third World experienced higher rates of unemployment, earned less money, and were unable to find work in their chosen fields (Samuel, 1984; Billingsley and Musynski, 1985, Ginzberg and Henry, 1985; Reitz, 1985; Stasiulis, 1989; Burke, 1990; Kirschmeyer and McLellan, 1990; Samuel, 1991; Basavarajappa et al. 1993). Though Canada has come a long way in fighting racially discriminatory labour practices it was found, according to Statistics Canada's National Graduates Survey of 1992, that even with respect to graduates from Canadian universities and colleges, "the employment rates of visible minorities are substantially lower than those of other graduates: by almost eight percentage points for university graduates and about six percentage points for community college graduates. These differences, which are due to both lower participation rates and higher unemployment rates for visible minority graduates, appear for graduates of most fields of study in most regions (except British Columbia)" (Wannell and Caron, 1994:1).

Employment Equity Legislations, 1986 and 1995

The federal government has been playing a role, though an informal one, in employment equity with regard to race-related matters; its formal role started in 1986 with the Employment Equity Act. The purpose of this Act was to "achieve equality in the workplace, and to correct the conditions of disadvantage in employment experienced by designated groups — women, aboriginal peoples, persons with disabilities, and members of visible minorities in Canada" (Minister of Employment and Immigration, 1988). The Act applied to employers and crown corporations under federal jurisdiction with a hundred employees or more. It required that all federally regulated employers file an annual report with the Canada Employment and Immigration Commission (CEIC) from June 1988 onward. This report was to provide information on industrial sector location and employment status (representation of designated and occupational groups, salary levels, promotions and terminations). Penalties were to be imposed in case of failure to comply. The reports were to be available publicly and the Canadian Human Rights Commission (CHRC) was vested with the authority to investigate in suspected cases of systemic discrimination. The employers were also to prepare annual employment equity plans with goals and timetables for up to three years.

The federal Contractors Program, introduced in 1986, affects organizations with a hundred or more employees bidding for federal government contracts worth $200,000 or more. Such contractors are to sign a certificate of commitment to design and carry out an employment equity program for the purpose of identifying and removing barriers to the selection, hiring, promotion and training of designated group members. There were legal challenges to the employment equity program, particularly regarding the power of human rights tribunals. The Supreme Court of Canada held that such programs were legal (Jain, 1988: 2). A number of commissions, advisory committees, academics, ethnocultural organizations, labour unions and non-governmental organizations proposed amendments to the 1986 Employment Equity legislation to strengthen the federal contractors' program, to bring the public service, the RCMP and the armed forces under the employment equity program, to collect data on visible minorities by Statistics Canada, to set goals, timetables, sanctions and other remedies for dealing with problems of employment equity (Canada Employment and Immigration Advisory Council, 1992; Jain, 1988; Samuel, 1991; Canadian Ethnocultural Council, 1992)

The Employment Equity Act was revised in 1995 (Bill C-64) and was adopted, as revised, by the Canadian Parliament in December 1995, strengthening the legislation and bringing the public service, the RCMP and the military within the purview of the Act.

STUDIES AND REPORTS IN THE PUBLIC SECTOR

The Treasury Board took some initiatives to address the visible minority issue in the public service. In April 1985, a Treasury Board secretariat survey revealed that 3,791 persons (1.7 percent) in the public service identified themselves as belonging to visible minorities, compared to 4.3 percent in the Canadian labour force in 1981. The survey also showed that South Asians and Chinese were mostly in the Scientific and Professional category while the Blacks and Filipinos were in the Administrative Support category (Jain, 1988:8).

Minorities in the Public Service

The federal government introduced an employment equity program for visible minorities in the public service as of September 1985. Treasury Board Secretariat asked the Public Service Commission to implement a number of special measures that would facilitate the self-identification of visible minorities, monitoring of their recruitment, referral, appointment and training processes. A special employment program, with a staffing provision of up to 300 person-years for 1986-89, was also announced, along with the establishment of visible minority coordinators in regional offices (Jain, 1988:16-17).

By 1995 the federally regulated employers had produced the eighth of their set of annual reports on the representation of visible minorities, drawn from the four designated groups, in their workforce of nearly 600,000. The public service employed about 218,000. However, downsizing has been a major factor that has affected hirings in recent years, in both the private and the public sectors. As is stated in the 1995 Annual Report of the Canadian Human Rights Commission, "for the fifth year in a row terminations exceeded new hires. At the same time, with over 50,000 hires reported (and over half a million since the Act was adopted), ample scope remained for improvements in the representation of all four groups" (59).

As can be seen from Table 8.1, within the designated groups, the proportion of women in the public service rose from 42.9 percent in 1988 to 47.3 percent in 1995, which may be compared with the labour force availability rate of 47.3 percent in 1991. During the same period, Aboriginals in the public service increased from 1.7 percent to 2.2 percent (with census labour force availability of 2.6 percent in 1991). Persons with disabilities increased their percentage in the public service from 2.7 percent to 3.2 percent, while the labour force availability was 4.8 percent. As seen, above, none of those other than visible minorities had a representation rate in the public service so much lower than their labour force availability rate.

Representation by Occupation

As seen in Table 8.2, the Scientific and Professional category contained almost a quarter of the visible minority public servants. The 8.3 percent came close to the estimated 10 percent of the total population who constituted visible minorities.

TABLE 8.1

REPRESENTATION OF DESIGNATED GROUPS
IN THE PUBLIC SERVICE, 1988-95

	Census '86	1988	1989	1990	Census '91	1991	1993*	1994**	1995**
Women	43.4	42.9	43.7	44.5	47.3	45.3	46.1	47.0	47.4
Aboriginals	1.8	1.7	1.8	1.9	2.6	2.0	2.0	2.0	2.2
Persons with disabilities	4.5	2.7	2.8	3.1	4.8	3.0	3.1	2.9	3.2
Visible minorities	5.9	2.9	3.1	3.5	9.0	3.8	3.8	3.8	4.1

* Data in 1993 show numbers from the period from 1 January 1992 to 31 March 1993.
** Data are recorded for the months between 1 April to 31 April of the following year.
Sources: President of the Treasury Board, *Employment Equity in the Public Service: Annual Report, 1992-93*; President of the Treasury Board, *Employment Equity in the Public Service: Annual Report, 1994-95*.

In 1994, the 8,566 visible minority public servants still represented only 3.8 percent of the total 224,640 employed. Visible minorities were least represented in Operational Services (1.6 percent), followed by Technical (2.3 percent), Management/Executive (2.3 percent), Administrative Support (3.8 percent), and Administrative/Foreign (3.8 percent) Service. Among those who control, recruit and manage the public services, visible minorities presence was still very limited, with the great deal of work to do.

Progress Over Time, 1987-95

During the period 1987 to 1995, visible minorities in the public service have increased their proportion from 2.7 percent to 4.1 percent as seen in Table 8.3. These figures may be compared to the workforce availability rate of 5.9 in 1986 and 9.0 in 1991.

In defence of the low percentages for visible minorities reported in the public service it is said that a certain proportion of the members of such minorities chose not to identify themselves. "There are always a certain number of people who choose not to identify themselves as members of a designated group. It is currently not known how many of these individuals there are, where they are in the hierarchy, or to which occupational groups they belong. The only safe generalization is that the actual numbers reported here are probably on the low side" (Treasury Board Secretariat, 1989:2). On the other hand, anecdotal

TABLE 8.2

VISIBLE MINORITIES IN THE PUBLIC SERVICE BY OCCUPATIONAL
CATEGORY AND AGE, 1993-95

	Age	1993* All employees	VM	%	1994 All employees	VM	%	1995 All employees	VM	%
Management/	under 34	24	1	4.20	21	0	0.00	11	0	0.00
Executive	35 - 49	2,476	47	1.90	2,187	42	1.92	2,050	42	2.04
Group**	over 50	1655	50	3.02	1,670	46	2.75	1674	46	2.75
subtotal		**4,155**	**98**	**2.40**	**3,878**	**88**	**2.30**	**3,735**	**88**	**2.40**
Scientific and	under 34	5,701	303	5.31	5,515	315	5.71	5,068	317	6.25
Professional	35 - 49	13,795	998	7.23	14,181	1,001	7.06	14,194	1,025	7.22
	over 50	5604	778	13.88	5,902	815	13.81	6,155	842	13.68
subtotal		**25,100**	**2,079**	**8.30**	**25,598**	**2,131**	**8.30**	**25,417**	**2,184**	**8.60**
Administrative	under 34	18,349	881	4.80	17,747	878	4.95	16,298	907	5.57
and Foreign	35 - 49	42,944	1335	3.11	44,386	1,344	3.03	45,636	1,431	3.14
Service	over 50	11,105	520	4.68	11,940	585	4.90	12,791	653	5.11
subtotal		**72,398**	**2,736**	**3.80**	**74,073**	**2,807**	**3.80**	**75,001**	**2991**	**4.00**
Technical	under 34	6,462	133	2.17	6,320	137	2.17	5,680	132	2.32
	35 - 49	13,994	278	1.99	14,315	264	1.84	14,403	268	1.86
	over 50	5,438	193	3.55	5,640	201	3.56	5,535	215	3.88
subtotal		**25,894**	**604**	**2.3**	**26,275**	**602**	**2.30**	**25,618**	**615**	**2.40**
Administrative										
Support	under 34	21,058	707	3.36	20,614	681	3.30	17,055	646	3.79
	35 - 49	30,576	1255	4.10	32,534	1,247	3.83	31,823	1,300	4.09
	over 50	9,797	468	4.78	10,134	496	4.89	9,881	561	5.68
subtotal		**61,431**	**2,430**	**4.00**	**63,282**	**2,424**	**3.80**	**58,759**	**2,507**	**4.30**
Operational	under 34	7,349	128	1.74	6,733	114	1.69	5,570	123	2.21
	35 - 49	16,333	247	1.51	14,537	241	1.66	15,913	260	1.63
	over 50	8,454	140	1.66	8,305	148	1.78	7,771	146	1.88
subtotal		**32,136**	**515**	**1.60**	**31,534**	**514**	**1.60**	**29,254**	**529**	**1.80**
Total in Public	under 34	58,943	2,153	3.65	56,950	2,125	3.73	49,957	2,125	4.25
Service:	35 - 49	120,118	4,160	4.46	124,099	4150	3.34	124,019	4,326	3.49
	over 50	42,053	2,149	5.11	43,591	2,291	5.26	43,808	2,463	5.62
ALL PUBLIC SERVICE EMPLOYEES		**221,114**	**8,462**	**3.80**	**224,640**	**8,566**	**3.80**	**217,784**	**8,914**	**4.10**

* Data in 1993 show numbers from the period from 1 January 1992 to 31 March 1993.
** Starting in 1993, this category is called Executive Group.
Sources: Treasury Board Secretariat, *Employment Equity in the Public Service: Annual Report, 1992-1993*; Treasury Board Secretariat, *Employment Equity in the Public Service: Annual Report, 1993-1994*; Treasury Board Secretariat, *Employment Equity in the Public Service: Annual Report, 1994-1995*.

information indicates that some non-visible public servants who are opposed to the policy of employment equity for visible minorities report themselves as members of such minorities. While no one knows the extent of such underreporting or overreporting, it has been pointed out that "reluctance to self-identify would affect both employment

TABLE 8.3

VISIBLE MINORITIES IN THE PUBLIC SERVICE, 1987-95

Year	Members of Visible Minorities in the Public Service (%)
1987	2.7
1988	2.9
1989	3.1
1990	3.5
1991	3.6
1992	3.8
1993	3.8
1994	3.8
1995	4.1

Sources: Treasury Board Secretariat, *Status Report on the Representation of Women, Persons with Disabilities, Aboriginal Peoples and Members of Visible Minority Groups in the Federal Public Service, 1988-1990;* Treasury Board Secretariat, *Employment Equity in the Public Service, Annual Reports,* 1992-93, 1993-94 and 1995-96.

and availability data, and thus would likely amount to a 'zero-sum game'" (Canada Employment and Immigration Advisory Council, 1992:50). However, the fact that the comparable percentages are fairly high in the federally regulated private sector industries would justify the assertion that the public service ought to do better.

In 1990, the representation of visible minorities in the federal public service was only half that of their representation level among federally regulated employers (Canadian Ethnocultural Council, 1992:2). During the period 1988-91 their representation rate in the public service improved by one percent and, according to the Ethnocultural Council, "much of the gains by visible minorities can be solely attributed to a greater number of individuals self-identifying" (Canadian Ethnocultural Council, 1992:2). Some departments had two to three times the representation level of others. However, in only a few federal institutions was the representation equal to or more than the availability rate for visible minorities, though the private sector often had twice the rate of the public sector especially in management. For instance, while 2.1 percent of the total public service employees were designated management only 1.2 percent of visible minorities were in that category. The recruitment rate of visible minorities in the public service has been less than half that achieved by federally regulated employers in 1988-90 (Canadian Ethnocultural Council, 1992:2). At the same time the proportion of visible minorities was "released" in

1990 was higher than that for the entire public service. Visible minorities had the lowest percentage of individuals in the 20-29 age range in that year.

Some of the studies by interest groups have been very critical of the government of Canada and its efforts to bring about employment equity for visible minorities in the public service. In a report, appropriately titled *Employment Inequity* (1992), the Ethnocultural Council said that the public service has no leadership with regard to this issue and the Public Service Commission, which is in charge of recruitment, the Treasury Board Secretariat as the manager of the public service, Human Resources Development Canada, which implements employment equity and monitors the Federal Contractors Program, and the Privy Council Office, which sets priorities and is in overall control of the government, are "setting poor examples."

Appointment of Consultative Groups

Efforts have been made by the Treasury Board Secretariat to increase the representation of visible minorities in the public service. In this connection, a Visible Minority Consultation Group on Employment Equity was formed to advise the Secretariat on what could be done. The group produced two reports in 1992 and 1993, which examined the question of self-identification and the ambivalence of visible minorities with regard to labelling. While self-identification does not provide any direct benefits, it has been feared that it may be damaging. Other reasons cited for not self-identifying were that it had nothing to do with merit, it was distasteful and it was an invasion of privacy.

The Visible Minority Consultation Group pointed to the need to develop a "supportive culture that facilitates new visions and ways of working"; this would "be a fundamental prerequisite to any success that may be achieved in employment equity" for visible minorities (Visible Minority Consultation Group on Employment Equity, 1992:4). It held the view that the Scientific and Professional category "seems to have become a trap ... for visible minorities" and said that "to what extent this concentration (24.8 percent of the visible minorities were in this category, compared to 10.8 percent in the public service) in the Scientific and Professional category affects their ability and propensity to gain access to management is not clear but is certainly worthy of further investigation in terms of its role as one of the principal feeder categories to the management category" (Consultation Group, 1992:10).

Another point made was that about a fifth of the management rank was appointed from outside the public service, but few visible minorities are recruited this way.

The consultation group pointed out that time alone would not correct the situation of underrepresentation of visible minorities at the management level and "efforts similar in scope to those designed to increase the representation of francophones and women in the public service will be necessary" (Consultation Group, 1992:11). "The women's (Employment Equity) program is effective, especially for Anglo-Celtic women" (Training and Development Associates, 1992:19).

While larger departments and agencies had proportionately more visible minority employees, the report stated that the performance of central agencies — Treasury Board Secretariat, Finance and the Privy Council Office, which play a pivotal role in the formation and development of the managerial cadre — showed less than average representation and that the situation in Foreign Affairs and International Trade was similar (Consultation Group, 1992:13). The group found that visible minorities were well represented in Ontario (outside the National Capital Region), Alberta and British Columbia, especially on the front lines. The "double jeopardy" faced by visible minority women was particularly noted. The need for management training was considered to be at the core of the visible minority issue. The report drew attention to the corporate culture built on misconceptions, such as "employment equity is a 'leg-up' for the disadvantaged, and perhaps the unqualified ... or to compensate ... for past wrongs ... and it runs counter to the merit system" the program was not seen as enabling the public service "to fairly represent the diverse population it serves" (Consultation Group, 1992:19). While many visible minority public servants are cynical about employment equity some public service managers are guilty of stereotyping minorities. The consultation group argued for "a higher profile and priority" for employment equity and urged that there be a stronger "political will to pursue it vigorously" (Consultation Group, 1992:19).

The Consultation Group found that "employment practices are believed by most visible minority employees interviewed to be unfair, to lack integrity, and to be racially biased. These views were validated by a majority of those at the management and even senior management levels. Time and again we were asked whether the current interest in employment equity was real or whether it was 'just more window dressing.'" (Visible Minority Consultation Group, 1993:3). The 1993 report referred to the "abuse of acting appointments," the perception that selection boards for promotion "are 'mock boards,' are 'fixed' and are 'a farce'" (Consultation Group, 1993:3), the view that "too much weight is accorded to the 'personal suitability' factor," and complaints about "old boy" and "new girl" networks that work against visible minorities. A two-pronged strategy was proposed: 1) improving the culture of the public service for visible minorities through persistent, visible leadership by deputy ministers; and 2) preparing visible minorities for full participation at all levels, especially with respect to access to and promotion within management" (Consultation Group, 1993:7). Accountability was stressed as a means of improving the climate for employment equity.

A 1995 report by the Canadian Alliance for Visible Minorities discusses the barriers facing visible minorities in the public service. It characterizes the shrinking public service as a "bureaucratic institution in a state of demoralization," experiencing a "castration of bureaucratic power" (Canadian Alliance for Visible Minorities, 1995:17). The current situation was "summarized by three words — flux, uncertainty and fear." The report itemized a number of perceived problems and issues in the public service, such as excessive duration of management procedures, concentration of power at the level of senior managers, ineffectiveness of personnel departments and employment equity offices, absence of skills inventories, shrinking opportunities, lip service paid to visible minority issues, exclusion of visible minorities on grounds of personal suitability, poorly defined performance measurement criteria, lack of concern for and interest in visible minority issues, narrow scope of the appeal process, non-acceptance of visible minorities in the bureaucratic corporate culture, lack of mentors, and a tendency to stonewall about any wrongdoing on the part of managers. The report also referred to some other factors such as fear of reprisals felt by visible minorities, the unfamiliarity of these persons with the intricacies of the system, and their difficulty in dealing with corporate communication culture. The report observed that "because the concepts of performance and efficiency have very elastic meanings in the bureaucratic system, the merit principle becomes a noble fiction without any credibility" (Canadian Alliance for Visible Minorities, 1995:21). It concluded that the "documentation and advice available attempt to show that the system can accommodate them (visible minorities) provided they follow the marvellous path to nowhere. And in case they cannot reach their target it is simply their fault. This is an ideal case of blaming the victim" (Canadian Alliance for Visible Minorities, 1995:25).

It may be legitimately asked why such efforts made to make the Canadian public service more representative of the Canadian public have failed so far? In part, the answer can be found in the view that institutional change has been slow in the public service. Institutions serve a dual purpose, where they act as a collective memory carrying forward values, principles and traditions — an important purpose; they also provide the social structures through which those values, principles and traditions become operational in contemporary society. Frequently institutions are slow in responding to changes in their operating milieu." Unless pushed hard institutions do not change very rapidly.

In the area under discussion there is no evidence that such a push has been attempted so far. In a 1990 presentation to a conference a federal minister (Alan Redway) referred to the appointment of a visible minority person to the top ranks of the Public Service Commission and said that "the message ... was that one of his prime jobs was to make sure that affirmative action in the public service of Canada worked and got going in a hurry" (Redway, 1990:605). As statistics proved, this initiative did not have the anticipated effect.

PRIVATE SECTOR

The other (and stronger) leg of the Employment Equity Program is the private sector. However, the principles, policies and practices of the private sector are quite distinct from those of the public service. Whereas the latter performs a monopolistic service — the productivity and quality of which are not easily measured — the former "defines its own mandate, develops its markets, raises its funds, and rises or falls on the basis of performance." (Canadian Alliance for Visible Minorities, 1995:18).

Canadian employers who introduce employment equity programs are protected from the charge of reverse discrimination (Tarnopolsky, 1980). Section 15(1) of the Canadian Human Rights Act permits the implementation of special programs that will prevent or reduce disadvantages to designated groups or remedy the effects of past discrimination. Under section 41(2) of the Act, a Canadian human rights tribunal can order special programs where such an action is deemed necessary to prevent such practices in the future. For instance, in 1984, the Canadian National Railways was ordered by a tribunal, under the federal human rights legislation, to undertake a mandatory employment equity program for women (Jain, 1988:17). The Supreme Court affirmed this authority in a 1987 ruling (8-0). The following table shows the progress in the employment of visible minorities in the federally regulated private sector between 1989 and 1994. The base year chosen was 1989, in order to give the sector time to implement the program which was introduced in late 1986. Only parts of the private sector are covered by federal legislation.

TABLE 8.4

TOTAL AND VISIBLE MINORITY (VM) EMPLOYEES BY SECTOR
FOR FEDERALLY REGULATED INDUSTRIES, 1989-94

Sector	Total Employees		VM Employees		Percentage of Total	
	1989	1994	1989	1994	1989	1994
Banking	180,827	176,820	21,832	24,187	12.1	13.7
Communications	200,896	201,997	10,705	14,573	5.3	7.2
Transportation	205,875	158,098	7,785	6,729	3.8	4.3
Other	47,763	60,904	1,774	3,793	3.7	6.2

Sources: Human Resources Development Canada, *Annual Report: Employment Equity Act, 1995*, A 5-6; Employment and Immigration Canada, *1990 Annual Report: Tables*; Employment Equity Act, 32-33.

As observed by the Canadian Human Rights Commission, "it is ... clear that a broad spectrum of organizations are responding to the growing diversity of the Canadian population; and this can only be counted on the encouraging side of the ledger" (Canadian Human Rights Commission, 1986:62).

Banking Sector

The banking sector has led the others in the hiring of visible minorities at a time when the total numbers of employees have actually been declining — an indication that declining overall employment is not necessarily a reason to curtail the employment of visible minorities. The Canadian Human Rights Commission said in its 1988 Annual Report that "visible minorities were also not doing too badly in the banking industry, There was a higher representation of women in the banks. Though many were in the clerical worker category, both sexes increased their share of jobs in the middle managerial, professional and supervisory occupational categories compared to availability. The rankings were as follows: Toronto Dominion Bank (16.6 percent), Bank of Nova Scotia (15.7 percent), CIBC (14.8 percent), Bank of Montreal (12.4 percent), Royal Bank (11.0 percent) and National Bank (2.8 percent). (Canadian Human Rights Commission, 1989:31). In 1988 the Bank of Montreal ranked as the best overall in its employment practices for visible minorities, while the Banque Nationale was the worst with Toronto Dominion Bank as the second worst (Poole, 1989:43). In both 1989 and 1994 the banking sector had employed more than the labour force availability of visible minorities. The other three sectors have done better in 1994, as compared to 1989. Among the three the transport sector was lagging behind, "even in cities like Toronto and Vancouver where the visible minority population is well above the national average" (Canadian Human Rights Commission, 1989:31).

The biggest of the chartered banks, the Royal Bank, has been active in accessing and recruiting good quality candidates from visible minorities. The approaches used are: making employment equity a priority for senior management, sending a clear message to search firms, outreach initiatives, setting aside training or summer positions for visible minorities, encouraging the staff to take active roles in visible minority organizations, funding upgrading costs of employees, and cross-cultural awareness training programs for senior and line managers (White, Undated:5-6).

Another chartered bank, the Bank of Montreal, has linked its equity goals to its business needs by adopting measures to create a supportive environment for racial minorities, providing training and a "buddy system" for minority staff and implementing strategies to attract quality candidates. Many of these initiatives were headed by a very senior executive. As stated by a Vice-President, David McVay, "the concepts of equality and diversity are becoming part of the fabric of the organization. They are redefining who we are in the minds of the consumer and the communities we serve. The culture of the organization is changing, and the Bank is becoming more successful as a result" (Taylor, 1995:14).

Communications and Transportation

In 1989 representation of visible minorities among permanent employees in three of the six organizations in the communications sector was lower than the external, nongovernmental, labour force (Jain, 1990:25). It was highest for multilingual TV (18.3 percent) and low for

CHUM and CBC (2.2 percent and 2.9 percent respectively), while the others — Global (4.6 percent), Bell Canada (7.1 percent) and CTV (7.4 percent) — came in between.

Transportation Sector

The transportation sector was the worst performer. Visible minorities did not reach their labour force availability rate in six out of the seven major transportation companies. Visible minority women fared very poorly. Among permanent employees, in 1989 6.9 percent of VIA Inc. were visible minority members, while in Voyageur Inc. the percentage was only 0.6. Between these two extremes, Canadian Airlines International recorded 5.7 percent and Air Canada 4.2 percent for visible minorities. Lower levels were found in CNR (3.3 percent), CP Rail (2.4 percent) and Greyhound (2.7 percent).

Between 1989 and 1994, the percentage of visible minorities in the Other sector (such as metal and coal mines, crude petroleum and natural gas, grain elevators, industrial chemicals, etc.) increased from 3.7 to 6.2, an increase of 27.5 percent in absolute numbers.

OBSERVATIONS AND CONCLUSIONS

Canada as a country has received a high ranking in the human resources development index published annually by the UN. Generally speaking, Canada is also well known in the community of nations for the racially tolerant policies it follows. However, the public service is becoming less and less reflective of the population and the labour force it represents as far as visible minorities are concerned. The restructuring in the public service is partly blamed for this situation, though it cannot be claimed that the explanation is adequate since many federally regulated private sector industries have dramatically improved the representativeness of visible minorities while undergoing restructuring. In response to the low representation of visible minorities in the public service and the new function of auditing government departments recently established by the Employment Equity Act (1995), the Canadian Human Rights Commission has launched a study to examine the question of visible minorities and the public service. The study, involving data analysis, focus groups and questionnaires, was completed and released in February 1997. It concluded that "commitment at the highest level of authority is a must to herald change. Once that commitment is there, the process can begin in earnest to establish and accomplish diversity goals that fully reflect the spirit and the law of both the Public Service Employment Act and the Employment Equity Act.... What the public service needs is not quotas for visible minorities but a removal of barriers to make sure that real merit is recognized and rewarded.... Canada needs a public service that is dynamic, adaptive and productive. For this, the Canadian public service needs a new diversity strategy" (Samuel, Stanford and Tremblay, 1997:5).

In sum, according to studies and reports reviewed in this survey the public sector, despite its early start (1985) and bold words, did poorly in the hiring, retention and promotion of visible minorities. On the other hand, the federally regulated employers in the private sector did much better, with the banks leading the way. The fact that the private sector operates on the basis of a profit motive, in contrast to the service motive of the public sector, needs to be kept in mind when one is comparing them. Moreover, it seems that most success in the private sector was achieved by corporations in which senior management took an active interest in promoting employment equity for visible minorities because the policy was perceived to be advantageous to the bottom line.

Population projections indicate that visible minorities in the Canadian population are likely to increase from 9.4 percent in 1991 to about 14 percent by 2001. Visible minorities are already seriously under-represented in the public service and the current situation is likely to get worse in the years to come, unless barriers that prevent hiring of visible minority persons and their normal functioning in the public service are removed.

III

RACISM AND DISCRIMINATION

9

PUBLIC OPINION ON VISIBLE MINORITIES

LEO DRIEDGER AND ANGUS REID

THE VISIBLE MINORITY POPULATION in Canada is growing, so we need to sketch the reasons for the changes, and then survey changing attitudes that have occurred since the sixties. The recommendations of the Bilingualism and Biculturalism Commission and the introduction of a more just immigration policy in the sixties, combined with Pierre Trudeau's greater emphasis on multiculturalism in the seventies, has resulted in a shift from the largely European immigration of previous periods to a greater inflow of Asian immigrants during recent decades. Fortunately, we have a number of national surveys which plot attitudinal shifts, so we can report changes in general public opinion. Let us sketch these changes briefly, in order to better understand what is happening demographically and socially.

INCREASED VISIBILITY OF MINORITIES

The 1971 census reported that about 95 percent of the Canadian population was comprised of white persons of European origin, and it was hard to find more than five percent who could be considered to be members of non-white visible minorities. Only twenty years later, in 1991, the visible minority population had doubled to ten percent, and projections are that this will likely double again within a few more decades (Statistics Canada, 1991). Such a basic racial shift in population must surely affect attitudes of the largely white Canadian population.

Pre-Sixties Research on Race

While American research on race relations has been prolific for almost a century — twelve percent of the population of the United States being black and almost ten percent Hispanic — similar Canadian research was minimal before the 1960s. Howard Palmer (1988) briefly outlines how the colonial British and French contacts with Aboriginals were often prejudicial and discriminatory in the time of the fur trade, but these accounts were based on sketchy historical research. The same is true for the history of blacks in Canada and the early beginnings of slavery, although Wilson Head (1975; 1981) and Daniel Hill (1981) did some early work. In the days of colonialism and imperialism European powers were more interested in promoting their dominance than describing what happened to the peoples they subjugated. As Driedger and Halli suggest in Chapter 4 of this volume, Anglo- and Franco-conformity was assumed, and the aspirations of minorities were hardly considered.

Palmer (1988) and Richmond (1988) have also described how earlier immigration policy favored white European immigrants, where it was assumed that others would assimilate into north European charter group languages and cultures. Chinese workers were brought in to help build the railroad and the Japanese especially on the west coast were considered "inferior and unassimilable" (Palmer, 1988). Before and between the two world wars the west was opened up to Poles, Ukrainians, Mennonites, Doukhobors and Jews; these newcomers were white, but their cultures and religions were often considered to be different and suspect. During the two world wars Canadians of German heritage were pressured to give up their cultural distinctiveness, and the Japanese during World War II were interned and expelled from their west coast communities and sent farther inland. In those days there were few if any attitudinal surveys on prejudice, discrimination and stereotypes.

The Royal Commission on Bilingualism and Biculturalism

In 1965 John Porter published his classic *The Vertical Mosaic*, in which he classified the founding British and French as charter groups, all others who entered Canada later as belonging to the entrance group, and the Aboriginals as belonging to the treaty group. It was the two charter members who comprised more than 90 percent of the Canadian population in 1867 when they formed a confederation east of the Great Lakes. However, over time, their proportionate numbers declined, and those of the entrance group populations rose.

By 1963 the Quiet Revolution in French Quebec had escalated to the point that it was deemed necessary to appoint a Royal Commission on Bilingualism and Biculturalism, which published its preliminary report in 1965. This commission crisscrossed Canada, and its hearings resulted in seven published volumes, the first ones being devoted to the official languages, which the dominant charter groups were most concerned with. The recommendation to create two official languages in Canada, English and French, opened the way for the use of more than one language, thus modifying the colonial European unitary concept of a nationalist state. In addition, unexpectedly, a fourth volume on *The Contributions of Other Ethnic Groups* (1970) was also published by the commission, recognizing that there were more than the two official — British and French — cultures. The members of the commission soon found that the demographic, linguistic and cultural heterogeneity of Canada had greatly increased by the sixties. In 1971 Prime Minister Pierre Trudeau officially declared Canada a bilingual and multicultural nation. Race however, was not yet an issue — only five percent of the population was non-white.

Changes in Immigration Policy

The Royal Commission on Bilingualism and Biculturalism stirred up more than charter group concerns with official languages. Indeed, Quebecers who wanted equal status for French language and culture realized that opening up such issues would soon raise others, quite apart from questions of race which came into prominence later. Indeed, the ferment in the sixties raised many questions about an immigration policy which favoured European whites, and many also asked about the unfairness of screening out Third World persons who were more visible.

Between 1967 and 1977 new legislation was introduced by order-in-council which distinguished independent, sponsored and nominated immigrants (Richmond, 1988; 1994). Independent applicants could now apply from anywhere in the world, and the regulations of 1967 established nine criteria by which they were to be assessed. These changes opened up the immigration system, so that large numbers of young, educated, occupationally skilled applicants could compete for entrance into Canada. Immigration thus became possible for visible minorities and the major sources of immigrants had shifted from Europe to Asia by the nineties. It is for this reason that the visible minority proportion of the Canadian population has increased from five to ten percent in twenty years, and the trend will continue

(Statistics Canada, 1991). The category of refugees has increased inflows of visible minorities, and this too will likely continue. As white Europeans age they will not sponsor so many next of kin, and it will be interesting to see whether this category will be as useful to visible minorities in the future.

By the seventies Canadian researchers had become more aware of the need for research to find out whether new Third World immigrants were accepted. Thus research into visible minorities, prejudice, discrimination, stereotypes and racism has mushroomed recently, and to this we turn next.

Conceptualization of Prejudice and Discrimination

Allport (1954) suggests that prejudice refers to attitudes while discrimination refers to action. Both phenomena are subject to irrational emotions that often lead to attitudes and behaviours inconsistent with the values of freedom and equality legitimized by a democratic society. Francis (1976:268-70) defines prejudice as illegitimate categorization, and discrimination and differential treatment have recently preoccupied many scholars studying ethnic prejudice and discrimination (Francis, 1976; Berry et al., 1977, 1995, 1996; Hagan, 1977; Driedger 1982, 1996; Driedger et al., 1981, 1984; Ramcharan, 1982; Mackie, 1985; James, 1990, 1995; Henry et al., 1984, 1994, 1995). In democracies, where freedom and equality are highly valued, there are many discrepancies between ideal and real attitudes and behaviour.

But the problem is even more complex because actions and attitudes that are considered legitimate for all may be based on a society's expectations of what should happen to minorities or immigrants in that society. Assimilationists expect that all people should fuse in a cultural "melting pot," while pluralists deem differentiation and a multitude of subidentities to be the legitimate right of minorities. Questions arise about the rights of members of a society to extend their political and religious diversity to include ethnic and religious pluralism. In Canada such a legal right has been extended to the two founding people (the British and the French), and by 1982 the Charter of Rights extended more individual rights to all others as well (Kallen, 1995:292-98).

Hagan (1977:168) suggests that *differential treatment* can predispose members of a society to discrimination. All humans have to categorize their experiences, but some categories may promote the norms of a society more clearly than others. Canadians, for example, hold to the ideal of the right to equal treatment in a democratic society but, in reality, not all people are treated equally and differentation that does not provide equal distribution of opportunities or rewards can also be seen as discriminatory.

Francis (1976:269-70) adds the dimension of functional and dysfunctional differentation, which complicates the matter still further. "Foreigners are admitted on the, at least tacit, assumption that relations with their hosts will be governed by particularistic norms specified by the terms of their admission. Thus, participation in the host society is, on principle, contractual and valid until further notice" (Francis, 1976:269). The situation is different when a newcomer is expected to settle permanently in a modern state:

Although he is not a member upon arrival, he is a prospective member supposed to acquire, in due course, all the qualifications necessary for regular membership. Whereas the hosts expect him to comply with the conditions under which he has been admitted as a prospective member, the ethnic in turn expects that, upon assuming his obligations, he will be granted all the benefits the host society has to offer to its charter members in accordance with generally accepted "universalist" rules (Francis, 1976:269).

Prejudicial treatment is viewed by Hagan (1977:170) as a negative predisposition to behaviour that could lead to discrimination. Francis (1976:264) says, "Prejudice is a legal term referring to the anticipation of judicial decision without due process." Prejudice is a prejudgment insofar as preconceived opinions have been assumed to be true before being put to the test. What makes identifying prejudice difficult is that it is made of the same stuff as categorization (which we are all involved in) but is based on invalid negative attitudes.

Hagan (1977:170-71) suggests that *denial of desire* can be a form of discrimination if we assume that all persons should be allowed equal preference and the freedom to choose. "Restrictions on immigration and naturalization have been common, yet once immigrants have been admitted to potential regular membership, their differential treatment is relatively soon recognized as illegitimate" (Francis, 1976:272). Recently, it has been possible for these egalitarian democratic principles to be expanded to broader spheres of social life such as club membership or intermarriage. This raises the question of how open or closed a society or community may be with regard to access to its institutions and places of social, economic, and political life. Those who seek greater freedom and equality, however, are in any case presumed to be discriminated against if they are denied such opportunities as jobs, open housing, or access to leisure and institutional activities.

Hagan (1977:17) designates *disadvantageous treatment* as a clear form of discrimination. Such discrimination occurs when the object of prejudice is placed at some disadvantage not merited by his own misconduct and it may be defined as the effective injurious treatment of persons on grounds rationally irrelevant to the situation (Driedger, 1996:271-73).

The definition of disadvantage and the level of disadvantage induced is important. Freedom to compete for the rewards of society and equal opportunity to obtain these rewards have already been designated as "rights" in a democratic society. Those who are abused verbally may also be subject to more severe forms of action, such as receiving hate literature, being vandalized, or being attacked physically, and such experiences can undoubtedly be designated as discriminatory disadvantage. Thus we must examine a wide range of disadvantageous action.

The four characterizations of prejudice and discrimination (differential, prejudical, disadvantageous treatment, and denial of desire) form a useful continuum. The differentation end represents predisposition to prejudice, while the disadvantageous treatment end represents blatant forms of discrimination.

Driedger and Mezoff (1981:1-17) asked students in Winnipeg to report whether they had been discriminated against in various situations, and what types of discrimination were involved. Six types were found, ranging from ethnic jokes to vandalism. Wilson Head (1981) conducted a study of racial minorities in Toronto related to discrimination in housing, employment and community services, and found that 90 percent of Blacks and 72 percent of South Asians felt "some" or a "great deal" of discrimination, in contrast to only 35 percent of European respondents who reported discrimination. Henry and Ginzberg (1984) in their Toronto study *Who Gets the Work?* matched black and white jobseekers applying for jobs advertised in a major newspaper, and found that whites received three times as many job offers. They also found that telephone callers with accents, especially South Asian and Caribbean, were more often screened out when they inquired about job vacancies (Henry and Ginzberg, 1984). In a follow-up study of employers who advertised these jobs, Billingsley and Musynski (1985) found that 28 percent of the respondents felt that racial minorities did not have the ability to meet their performance criteria. Jain (1988) concluded in his study of visible minorities that they face pay and employment discrimination. Ponting and Wanner (1983:57-76) found that blacks in Calgary encountered similar discrimination in areas of employment and housing, and the same finding was reported by Christianson and Weinfeld (1993:26-44) and Henry (1989). Similar problems were found among black students in school by Dei (1993:45-65), and as a black teacher, Dei (1993:38-51) outlines challenges which teachers face in antiracist teaching (see also Tuzlak, 1989:103-19). Recent more qualitative research on blacks by James (1990, 1992) and Henry et al. (1994) illustrates well the complexity and diversity of the situation of these black immigrants who have come to Toronto.

Race and Racism

Ramcharan (1982:88) proposes that discriminatory behaviour in Canada can be analyzed from two perspectives: the colour-class and the strangers theses:

With regard to the colour-class thesis, the supposition is that the majority groups in the society identify nonwhites with the lowest social class mainly because of the historical relationships between whites and nonwhites. The strangers thesis sees the nonwhite immigrants as archetypal strangers both in appearance and behaviour, and react to them with distrust, antipathy, and a resultant negative attitude (Ramcharan, 1982:88).

Ramcharan suggests that both of these perspectives may be operating for many people. As a result, non-whites may be seen as both outsiders and strangers, marginal to society but also relegated to an inferior socioeconomic status. Whether such attitides have been institutionalized in Canada, and whether they can still be changed, then becomes an important topic for research.

Recently there has been a much larger influx of non-white immigrants so that colour and racial factors are creating larger visible minority sectors, especially in some of the larger cities such as Toronto, Montreal, and Vancouver. Studies by Frances Henry et al. (1984; 1994; 1995) show that the Black presence in Toronto is resulting in more racism. Research in that city reveals that there is discrimination against non-whites in regard to employment and access to housing four to eight times as often as against whites (James, 1995:135-46). Ramcharan's study of West Indians in Toronto (Ramcharan, 1982:89) shows that 58 percent reported discrimination in housing, 38 percent in access to housing, and 16 percent in hotels, bars, and relations with the police. The Ontario Human Rights Commission reports that in 1977 over half of their complaints were from visible minorities. Since then Toronto has commissioned the Task Force on Race Relations to look into the problem. A very large proportion of recent immigrants entering Canada come to Toronto; many of these are non-whites, so Toronto is changing considerably.

Frances Henry classifies racism in three categories: "Individual racism refers to conscious prejudice; institutional racism is that which is carried out by an individual because of others who are prejudiced; and structural racism has its base in the inequalities rooted in the operations of society at large" (Henry et al., 1994, 1995). Her team has found (Henry et al., 1995:92,93) that roughly half of their sample in Toronto expressed some degree of racism; approximately 16 percent were considered very racist, 35 percent somewhat racist, 30 percent somewhat liberal, and 19 percent very liberal. They also found that younger Torontonians were less racist, and that the more educated also were less racist, which confirms Bibby's (1987:160) national findings. Again we must ask, what affirmative action should be initiated? These studies have been conducted in only a few Canadian cities, so how typical are they of the nation as a whole?

ATTITUDES TOWARD VISIBLE MINORITIES

Fortunately, we have three sets of national research survey, taken in the seventies, eighties, and nineties, which have examined the attitudes of Canadians during the past twenty years, when the proportion of visible minorities doubled from five to ten percent. John Berry and colleagues (Berry et al., 1977) did a major national survey in 1976, Angus Reid (1991) conducted a national survey in 1991, and Reginald Bibby conducted five national surveys in 1975, 1980, 1985, 1990 and 1995. All these surveys included questions on Canadian attitudes toward minorities.

The 1976 Berry Report

In 1976, five years after Trudeau pronounced Canada a multicultural nation, John Berry, Rudolf Kalin and Donald Taylor (1977) published

Multiculturalism and Ethnic Attitudes in Canada, supported by the national Multiculturalism Programme. This three-year study was designed to survey the extent of support for multiculturalism in its early stages, when only one person in five had heard of it.

What is important here is that they ranked 26 ethnic and racial groups, by asking their randomly selected national sample of 1849 respondents to rate each of these groups, using ten criteria including the following: hard work being regarded as important, Canadian, clean, similar to me, likeable, sticking together, wealthy, interesting and well known to me (Berry et al., 1995:101). Six of these 26 groups (Japanese, West Indian, Chinese, Canadian Indian, Negro and East Indian) were visible minorities. The aim was to find out how Canadians in the mid-seventies rated these minorities and where they ranked in relation to Canadian whites.

In Table 9.1 we see that the Japanese ranked eighth, the only visible minority group located in the top half. The other five were located in the bottom half, including West Indians (16th), Chinese (21st), Canadian Indians (24th), Negroes (25th) and East Indians (26th). The last three were located at the very bottom. Clearly most visible minorities were held in relatively low esteem, and the English (1st), Scottish (2nd) and French (3rd), who together represent Porter's charter group category, ranked on top. Except for a few responses, charter groups ranked first, North Europeans second, East Europeans third and visible minorities last, as Porter (1965) had predicted.

The 1991 Reid Report

In 1991 Heritage Canada, under the multiculturalism and citizenship branch of the government of Canada, commissioned the Angus Reid organization to undertake a national poll on the extent to which Canadians favoured diversity in Canada, and to ask certain other questions. John Berry (1995a, 1995b) helped design this study too. Some of the results are presented in Table 9.2 (Angus Reid, 1991:4-5). We note that a large majority of Canadians favoured a federal government policy which would promote and ensure equality, eliminate racial discrimination in education, health care and justice systems, and help police to improve their services and new immigrants to acquire skills and integrate. Indeed over one half to three quarters of the respondents gave their strongest support (a seven on a seven-point scale), for the top eleven items.

TABLE 9.1

MEANS OF EVALUATIONS OF VARIOUS ETHNIC GROUPS

Standard List of Ethnic Groups	Mean	N	Rank	Respondent-Nominated Ethnic Groups	Mean	N
English	.52	1801	1			
			2	Scottish	.49	186
French	.47	1786	3			
			4	Dutch	.46	138
			5	Scandinavian	.39	94
			6	Irish	.37	142
			7	Belgian	.35	48
			8	Japanese	.13	111
			9	Hungarian	.10	93
			10	Polish	.08	230
Jewish	.04	1717	11			
German	.02	1716	12			
			13	Czech	.02	47
			14	Russian	-.07	79
			15	Yugoslavian	-.09	54
			16	West Indian	-.11	48
Immigrants in General	-.12	1736	17			
Ukrainian	-.13	1601	18			
Italian	-.20	1719	19			
			20	Portuguese	-.25	112
Chinese	-.26	1736	21			
			22	Spanish	-.31	39
			23	Greek	-.36	127
Canadian	-.46	1786	24			
			25	Negro	-.52	51
			26	East Indian	-.95	102

Source: J.W. Berry, R. Kalin, and D.M. Taylor, *Multiculturalism and Ethnic Attitudes in Canada* (Ottawa: Supply and Services Canada, 1977), 109.

Eight out of ten also favoured proactive behaviour such as developing helpful school materials, recognizing that diversity is acceptable and assisting organizations to reflect Canadian diversity. There was less enthusiasm for funding festivals and special events and helping minorities preserve their heritage, with roughly six out of ten favouring such action. The proportion of respondents expressing very strong support (7 on scale) dropped to below one third for items 12 and 13. The questions usually included both "ethnic" and "racial" designations, and a majority of the respondents seemed to favour support for both categories.

The Angus Reid survey also asked respondents how comfortable they would feel being around recent immigrants, drawn from 13

TABLE 9.2

CANADIAN ATTITUDES TOWARD IMMIGRATION, ETHNIC
AND RACIAL DIVERSITY, ANGUS REID, 1991

Canadian Federal Policy Should:	General Disagreement	Neither Agree nor Disagree	General Agreement
	1, 2	3, 4, 5	6, 7
		(percentages)	
1. Promote equality among all Canadians regardless of racial or ethnic origin	4	5	91
2. Ensure equal access to jobs regardless of ethnic or racial background	4	6	90
3. Eliminate racial discrimination through public education	5	7	88
4. Eliminate racism in health care, the justice and education systems	6	7	87
5. Help police to improve their ability to deal with different ethnic/racial groups.	6	7	87
6. Help citizens who are immigrants to acquire skills/knowledge to integrate	6	9	85
7. Have people from different ethnic/ racial groups live in the same country	5	11	84
8. Help everyone deal with ethnic, cultural and racial diversity	6	7	83
9. Develop school materials to teach children and teachers about other cultures/life	11	9	80
10. Recognize that cultural/racial diversity is fundamental to Canadian society	10	14	76
11. Ensure that organization reflect the cultural and racial diversity of Canadians	9	12	79
12. Fund festivals and special events celebrating different cultures	26	16	58
13. Help ethnic and racial minorities enhance their cultural heritages	25	17	58

Source: Angus Reid Group, "Multiculturalism and Canadians: National Attitude Study 1991."
(Ottawa: Multiculturalism and Citizenship Canada, Supply and Services Canada, 1991), 4-5.

groups they listed. They asked them to use a seven point scale on which zero meant not comfortable and seven very comfortable. We have plotted the responses in Table 9.3. Seven or eight out of ten respondents felt very comfortable with the six white European groups listed, and almost none felt uncomfortable around these groups. Two thirds still felt very comfortable with Chinese, Jewish and West Indian Blacks, but more placed themselves in the middle between comfort and discomfort, although few claimed they were very uncomfortable in the presence of these groups.

TABLE 9.3

DEGREE OF COMFORT CANADIANS FEEL AROUND
A VARIETY OF RECENT IMMIGRANTS, 1991

Feel Comfortable Around:	Not Comfortable 1, 2	3, 4, 5 (percentages)	Very Comfortable 6, 7
British	3	14	83
Italians	2	11	77
French	5	11	74
Ukrainians	3	14	73
Germans	4	14	72
Portuguese	3	17	70
Chinese	5	16	69
Jews	4	22	64
West Indian Blacks	8	31	61
Arabs	11	37	52
Muslims	11	40	50
Indo-Pakistanis	13	39	48
Sikhs	17	40	43

Source: Angus Reid Group, "Multiculturalism and Canadians: National Attitude Study 1991." (Ottawa: Multiculturalism and Citizenship Canada, Supply and Services Canada), 7-8.

Barely a majority felt comfortable around Arabs, Muslims, Indo-Pakistanis and Sikhs which would clearly be visible religious and ethnic minorities. Ten to twenty percent felt uncomfortable around these four groups, and more than one third checked the middle range of the scale (3,4,5), being uncertain about their feelings. These data show that discomfort clearly increased as respondents moved from feelings about white European Christian groups to visible minorities.

Psychographic Types and Attitudes

To sort the relationship between multicultural attitudes and tolerance toward others, Reid (1991:54-59) ran a battery of 16 psychographic items designed to identify psychological and lifestyle characteristics, support for and opinions on multiculturalism, perception of shared values, limits of tolerance for minorities, and frequency of interethnic contact. In the process six psychographic clusters or types emerged, two positive toward multiculturalism, two in the middle (moderately supportive and moderately opposed), and two opposed to multiculturalism (see Figure 9.1).

Enthusiasts (24 percent) and Individualists (21 percent), who represented almost half of the respondents, were positive respondents toward multiculturalism, and they were relatively open to the idea of Canadians working together for a united Canada (Enthusiasts), and opposed to blending groups in an assimilationist way (Individualists). On the other hand, roughly one third comprised Antagonists (9 percent), who were strongly opposed, and Assimilationists (17 percent), who were moderately opposed, to multiculturalism (Reid, 1991:58). Antagonists who were strongly opposed to multiculturalism were also strongly opposed to promotion of cultural diversity, viewed multiculturalism as threatening, were dissatisfied with life in Canada and

FIGURE 9.1

PSYCHOGRAPHIC SEGMENTS BASED ON ATTITUDES
TOWARD MULTICULTURALISM

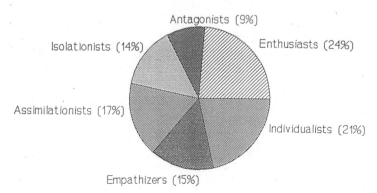

uncomfortable with people of different cultures, and were highly represented in Ontario. Isolationists, who were moderately opposed to multiculturalism, were more traditional, did not think Canadians shared common values, and were least likely to be proud of Canada, were highly represented in Quebec. Empathizers (15 percent) were the moderates willing to let all do their own thing, neither encouraging nor discouraging others much.

John Berry and Rudolf Kalin (1995, 1996) have also done more sophisticated analysis of the 1991 Reid survey, sorting ethnocentrism, consensual hierarchy and reciprocity. On ethnocentrism they found, first, that groups rated themselves more highly than they rated other groups. Second, there was a high degree of consensus among groups with regard to the relative comfort levels in the presence of various other groups, the British being rated highest and the Sikhs lowest, in a hierarchy similar to what Berry et al. (1977) had found in their 1976 national sample. Third, the mutual attitudes of pairs of groups were reciprocated (Kalin and Berry, 1996:253). Still more in-depth analysis of this kind, using national data, is required. Upward mobility factors such as increased education seem to enhance the multicultural attitudes, while a rise in income seems to dowse such tendencies. This finding needs to be analyzed further.

The 1975-95 Bibby Reports

Reginald Bibby (1987:161) asked his 1985 national sample of 1,630 Canadians whether they preferred the mosaic or the melting pot models. He found that well over one half (56 percent) preferred the mosaic and one quarter (27 percent) the melting pot. By 1995, however, the appeal of the mosaic had declined to 44 percent, and support for the melting pot (40 percent) was almost as high among his sample of 1,713 national respondents. Bibby (1995) reports that in these two sampling years younger Canadians, aged 18 to 34 (59 and 50 percent), supported the mosaic more than those over 55 (51 and 41 percent), while the reverse was true for the melting pot model. Not nearly as many young Canadians (22 and 34 percent) supported the melting pot model as older Canadians (33 and 44 percent). The more educated respondents with university degrees also favoured the mosaic more (69 and 50 percent), while relatively fewer (19 and 36 percent) favour the melting pot model.

TABLE 9.4

MOSAIC VERSUS MELTING POT PREFERENCES: 1985 AND 1995

	Melting Pot		Mosaic	
	1985	1995	1985	1995
	(percent)		(percent)	
National	27	40	56	44
British Columbia	38	39	50	43
Prairies	32	39	57	48
Ontario	31	44	56	46
Quebec	16	40	55	37
Atlantic	23	24	53	54
18-34	22	34	59	50
35-54	30	41	55	43
55+	33	44	51	41
Degree +	19	36	69	50
Post-Secondary	29	43	50	40
High School or Less	30	41	50	43

Source: Reginald Bibby, *The Bibby Report: Social Trends Canadian Style* (Toronto: Stoddart, 1995), 39.

To what extent do Canadians feel at ease with visible minorities and how have attitudes changed over time? Reginald Bibby (1995: 57,59) asked the "at ease" questions of Canadians in his five national samples in 1975, 1980, 1985, 1990, and 1995. He found that in 1975 a majority of Canadians (ranging from 84 to 91 percent) felt at ease with Jews, Canadian Indians, Orientals, and blacks. The proportion had increased slightly to 85-94 percent in 1995 (Bibby, 1995:57). There was some difference in attitudes toward the five visible minority groups: only 6 percent felt uneasy with Jews (visible religious group), while 15 percent were uneasy with East Indians and South Asians. The differences varied very little regionally, although in 1995 Quebecers (22 percent) and British Columbians (19 percent) felt the highest degree of uneasiness with Asians, and Quebec (14 percent) and Prairie (11 percent) residents were most uneasy with Aboriginals (Bibby, 1995:58). Once again, more educated respondents were more at ease with these minorities than were the less educated, but this attitude did not vary with gender or age. The percentages of respondents feeling "at ease" were so high that very few "ill at ease" respondents remained; however, there were roughly ten percent, depending on the visible minority group, and again, more analysis would be welcome.

TABLE 9.5

FEELINGS OF UNEASINESS: 1975 THROUGH 1995 (%)

	1975	1980	1985	1990	1995
East Indians/Pakistanis	**	22	18	16	15
Blacks	16	11	11	9	11
Asians (Orientals)	14	9	9	7	8
Natives	13	14	9	10	9
Jews	9	7	8	7	6

Source: Reginald Bibby, *The Bibby Report: Social Trends Canadian Style* (Toronto: Stoddart, 1995), 57.

TABLE 9.6

NATIONAL PERCEIVED DISCRIMINATION, 1980-95

		Do you feel that any racial or cultural groups in your community are discriminated against?	
		No (percent)	Yes (percent)
National	1995	33	67
	1990	41	59
	1985	46	54
	1980	45	55
British Columbia	1995	33	67
	1980	29	71
Prairies	1995	36	64
	1980	45	55
Ontario	1995	37	63
	1980	51	49
Quebec	1995	25	75
	1980	35	65
Atlantic	1995	42	58
	1980	68	32

Source: Reginald Bibby, *The Bibby Report: Social Trends Canadian Style* (Toronto: Stoddart, 1995), 52-54.

National Perceived Discrimination 1980-95

Reginald Bibby (1995), taking national samples every five years between 1980 and 1995, also asked, "Do you feel that racial and cultural groups in your community are discriminated against?" The results in Table 9.6 show that, while in 1980 about one half felt that some groups were discriminated against, by 1995 two thirds thought so. Since 1980, the percentage who think discrimination is getting worse has averaged about 15 percent; those who think it is better has risen from 15 to 20 percent, and those who think it is about the same has decreased from 45 to 33 percent (Bibby, 1995:52).

Quebecers (75 percent) are most likely to report discrimination in 1995, and residents of the Atlantic region (58 percent) least likely. Residents in all regions except British Columbia are reporting increases in discrimination since 1980 with exceptionally high increases in Ontario and the Atlantic region. One quarter of British Columbians think it is getting worse, while one quarter of Quebecers (the highest), think it is getting better now. Acknowledgement that discrimination exists varies little by ethnic group.

Approval of Intergroup Marriage

One measure of the acceptance of others is approval of intergroup marriage. There has been a gradual increase in the approval of marriage between different types of Canadians, ranging from a low of 57 percent in 1975 approving of marriage between whites and blacks, a figure which has increased to 81 percent in 1995 (Bibby, 1995:54). In 1975 three quarters approved of intermarriage between whites and Aboriginals, and that rose to 84 percent in 1995; two thirds approved of intermarriage between whites and Asians, and this figure too rose to 83 percent in 1995 (Table 9.7). Approval of marriage of whites with South Asians and with blacks was lower at 58 and 57 percent, but here too approval rates rose to eight out of ten. These are substantial increases in approval of intermarriage; is this further evidence of a shift from mosaic to melting pot attitudes? In such complex issues it is always difficult to know whether the indicators used are adequate, so that both reliability and comparability must be scrutinized and monitored continually.

Approval of religious intermarriage was higher in 1975, ranging from 78 to 86 percent, and the figures rose even higher, to roughly nine out of ten, for those who approved of intermarriage between Catholics, Protestants and Jews. Bibby (1995) did not ask for approval attitudes toward intermarriage between Judeo-Christians and persons of other faiths such as Buddhists, Hindus, Muslims and newer religions of more recent visible minority immigrants. It would be interesting to see

TABLE 9.7

APPROVAL OF INTERGROUP MARRIAGE: 1975 THROUGH 1995

Intermarriage between	1975	1980	1985	1990	1995
			(percentages)		
Whites and Natives	75	80	83	84	84
Whites and Asians (Orientals)	66	75	78	82	83
Whites and East Indians/Pakistanis	58	66	72	77	80
Whites and Blacks	57	64	72	79	81
Protestants and Roman Catholics	86	88	89	90	92
Protestants and Jews	80	84	84	86	90
Roman Catholics and Jews	78	81	82	85	89

Source: Reginald Bibby, *The Bibby Report: Social Trends Canadian Style* (Toronto: Stoddart, 1995), 54.

whether the various groups of Christians and Jews are banding together into a Judeo-Christian solidarity, or whether their tolerant attitudes also extend to a more inclusive diversity of faiths.

Relative Perception of Power

Numerically, socially, economically and politically European whites have dominated the development of Canada for the past century. As visible minorities have recently increased from five to ten percent of the Canadian population, what is the Canadian perception of access to power? In Table 9.8 we see that the national perception of too much white power has declined to nine percent, and all other visible minorities are perceived as having acquired more. Indeed, one third of the sample thought Aboriginals had too much power, and between 16 and 18 percent thought South Asians and Asians had too much. These Chinese and South Asians are the two largest new immigrant groups. Interestingly, while one quarter thought Jews had too much power in 1975, the proportion who thought so declined to 14 percent by 1995. Are more white Judeo-Christians now banding together to counteract the perceived rise of Asian visible minority power? These trends require more detailed study.

SUMMARY

With the growth of stratification and pluralism Canadians can expect a variety of attitudes and behaviour. The charter groups have received

TABLE 9.8

PERCEPTIONS THAT GROUPS HAVE "TOO MUCH POWER"
1975 THROUGH 1995

	1975	1980	1985	1990	1995
			(percentages)		
Natives	7%	6	13	18	33
East Indians/Pakistanis	NA	16	15	22	18
Jews	28	13	13	13	14
Whites	NA	NA	NA	17	9
Asians (Orientals)	NA	NA	7	14	16
Blacks	NA	NA	5	7	9

Source: Reginald Bibby, *The Bibby Report: Social Trends Canadian Style* (Toronto: Stoddart, 1995), 55.

special privileges in the Canadian Constitution to preserve their languages and culture. The British and French also reinforce their higher status and privilege by supporting their charter position and ranking other groups in lesser positions. The majority in Canada now supports bilingualism, although this support is greater in Quebec, where the French are a large majority, than in the West, where the ethnic mosaic is more diversified. Generally the linguistic heritage of the charter Canadians is established and is increasingly recognized.

Attitudes toward a culturally plural society are also developing, with a majority favouring the mosaic over the melting pot, although support for the melting pot seems to be on the rise recently. There is considerable recognition that such pluralism may not be easy to handle, with a sizeable minority who would rather dispense with greater freedoms in favour of multiculturalism. A huge majority claim that they feel relatively at ease with visible minorities, an openness which enhances hope for the future development of Canada's diversity, but there are always a minority of Antagonists and Isolationists who feel threatened.

It is clear that unfair treatment exists, based on ethnic origin, racial composition and religious affiliation. While the charter Canadians have achieved relatively high socioeconomic status and prestige, visible minorities continue to be on the periphery where opportunities and status are lower. In large cities there is considerable evidence of racism based on skin colour, especially as visible minorities try to compete for jobs and better housing. While many indicators suggest that Canada is becoming an increasingly pluralist society, more research on multiculturalism and diversity of colour, race, and beliefs is needed. Moreover, a sizeable minority neither accepts ethnic diversity nor complies with the ideals of minority rights and freedoms. It will not be easy to build a pluralist ethnic, racial and religious society. Attitudes and behaviour do not easily conform to ideals entrenched in legal rulings.

Linking all these studies and data to a larger conceptual frame, we are clearly faced with diverse populations, which are potentially in conflict, and which fit into Driedger and Halli's cells B, E, and D of their conformity-pluralist model in Chapter 4. The most dominant British (cell B), who have the best access to the economic and political "watering hole" in cell A, will be reluctant to give up their advantages. Inevitably some involuntary pluralists of other races — belonging to visible minorities — will see them as stonewallers, blocking opportunities and potentially causing conflict. The French charter Canadians, who also have historical and political advantages, will again be seen as having extra privileges, within their voluntary pluralism cell E, by visible minorities in cell D, who feel they are too much forced into an involuntary pluralist corner where they are marginalized. Visible minorities are very late in coming to the cell A trough, or the economic and political watering hole, so they will find it difficult to sort out the historical advantages which charter Canadians already have from factors which are in fact subtle prejudice and discrimination. Blatant racism will be easier to label but harder to admit to. Here too, there is much potential for conflict. The three chapters which follow explore further prejudice, discrimination and racism.

10

RACISM: EVIDENCE FROM NATIONAL SURVEYS

JOHN W. BERRY AND RUDOLF KALIN

RACISM: A SOCIAL PSYCHOLOGICAL PERSPECTIVE

WITHIN SOCIAL PSYCHOLOGY, *racism* is a specific form of the more general phenomenon of intergroup prejudice (Duckitt, 1992). As such, it is essentially a negative attitude held by individuals with respect to particular groups. For prejudice to qualify as racism, the target group must be defined in "racial" terms (rather than, for example, religious, linguistic or ethnic terms). "Race" is a conventional label for a group that is socially constructed on the basis of a few, rather superficial, biological features (such as skin colour, hair texture or facial structure). For most social psychologists, "races" have no biological validity, but have a social reality that can profoundly affect the way in which individuals and groups define and behave toward each other.

Racism involves both a negative evaluation (attitude) and negative behaviour (discrimination) toward individuals and groups defined in such racial terms. Ideally both the evaluations and the behaviours should be studied, since evidence shows that the correspondence between the two components is far from complete. There are some obvious reasons for this, the most important being that individual behaviour is controlled by factors other than one's own preferences: norms, roles, laws and situations can all limit the behavioural expressions of underlying attitudes.

Another important factor entering into the definition of racism is that of *power*: for some researchers, racism is a combination of prejudice plus the power to act on that prejudice; that is to say, prejudice held by a non-dominant group toward the dominant group would not qualify as racism. Since much of the research on racism has been conducted in societies where European-derived peoples have been dominant over non-European peoples, the phenomenon has often been considered specific to "whites." However, across history and cultures, other groups have been in dominant positions, and have exhibited "non-white" racism: Chinese and Indian peoples dominating the indigenous peoples of various countries in Southeast Asia, northern Indians exercising power over southern Indians in India, and Bantu-speaking peoples over Pygmy peoples in Central Africa.

In this chapter we take no position on the issue as to whether differential power is an inherent part of the definition of racism, but reject the view that it is purely a "white" phenomenon. However, in reality, in contemporary Canada persons of European origin are dominant in terms of numbers and economic and political power. Thus, in practice, racism in Canada is a form of prejudice that is held by peoples of European background toward those not of European background. But, as we shall see, these attitudes are sometimes shared by the latter category.

Of course, racism is not just a characteristic of individuals; it is also a feature of institutions and their conventional practices and structures. Such systemic or institutional racism is usually studied by sociologists and political scientists, rather than by social psychologists. However, it is almost certain that attitudinal racism is nurtured by systemic racism. Because of this, social psychologists usually do take such institutional practices into account when studying and interpreting racism in individuals; but it is rarely the focus of their attention, and will not be in this chapter.

Surveys of Ethnic and Multicultural Attitudes

In 1974 and 1991, national surveys were carried out to assess attitudes toward various aspects of cultural diversity in Canada. These surveys were both sponsored by the federal government ministry responsible for multiculturalism at the time. They included general measures of multicultural ideology (to be defined below), of prejudice and of attitudes toward some specific programs aimed at promoting diversity. In both surveys there were also measures of attitudes toward specific groups in Canadian society. Within these measures only some items referred to racial issues and to visible minorities. In this chapter, we present the overall picture obtained in each survey, and within this context, the specific orientations toward racial and visible minority groups.

Both the 1974 survey (Berry, Kalin and Taylor, 1977; Kalin and Berry, 1994), and the 1991 survey (Berry and Kalin, 1995; Kalin and Berry, 1996) obtained nationally representative samples (N = 1849 and

3325, respectively). In 1974, data were gathered by in-house interviews; in 1991 telephone interviews were used. In both, responses were obtained using 7-point scales, with 7 indicating the positive (acceptance) pole of each attitude dimension. For a variety of reasons, only a few of the scale items were used in both surveys; hence only limited tracking is possible over time. More problematic for this chapter is the fact that there was little explicit attention paid to racial issues in the 1974 survey, which further limits the potential for looking at trends over time.

The following measures were used:

1. *Multicultural Ideology* assesses the degree of support for having a culturally diverse society in Canada, in which ethnocultural groups maintain and share their cultures with others. There were 12 items used in 1974, and 10 in 1991, five of which were common to both surveys.

2. *Prejudice.* A six-item ethnocentrism scale was used in 1974, while a nine-item tolerance scale was employed in 1991. Both assessed a general rejection directed toward "others," including ethnic and racial groups, immigrants and foreigners. However, no items were common to the two scales.

3. *Program Attitudes.* This scale measured the relative degree of support for various concrete programs intended to implement federal multiculturalism policy. There were six items in the 1974 scale and nine items in the 1991 scale, with only one item in common.

4. *Attitudes Toward Specific Groups.* In 1974, nine groups were rated on six evaluative dimensions (e.g., hardworking, important, likeable) and a total evaluation score was calculated for each group. In 1991 a "comfort level" with respect to 14 groups was obtained by asking how comfortable the respondent would feel being around people of specific ethnic backgrounds. To the eight groups in the 1974 survey (English, French, Jewish, German, Ukrainian, Italian, Chinese, and Canadian Indians) were added six more in the 1991 survey (Portuguese, West Indian Blacks, Arabs, Muslims, Indo-Pakistanis and Sikhs). These additional groups were included in order to reflect the changing demographic composition of the Canadian population, and they obviously increase our attention to the presence of visible minority or racial groups.

Multicultural Ideology

Although concerns with diversity have been evolving in Canada (from concern with linguistic diversity to a focus on ethnocultural and racial diversity), there is a common underlying ideology: to what extent do individuals enjoy diversity, consider it to be a value rather than a source of problems, and wish to see it remain a feature of Canadian society? While the areas of specific concern have been changing (and hence the specific items used to assess this ideology), there is some use in examining the broad trends. In Table 10.1, the overall mean score and distributions are presented for the 1974 and 1991 surveys, followed by two items that specifically mention racial issues. With respect to the overall score it is evident that by a ratio of 2 to 1 in 1974 (63.9 percent vs. 32.2 percent) and a ratio of 2.5 to 1 in 1991 (69.3 percent vs. 27.3 percent) Canadians accept diversity in general. And on the two specific items mentioning racial issues in 1991, the ratios are 7 to 1 (77.7 percent vs. 10.4 percent) and more than 2 to 1 (58.0 percent vs. 25.3 percent) in support. One can interpret this profile as being rather positive (since the overall mean scores are on the positive side of the mid-point of 4.0, and the percentage distributions are clearly in favour); or one can view them as pointing to a problem (since between 10 percent and 27 percent of the population are on the negative side).

Prejudice

The objects of prejudice may have shifted in recent Canadian history, but the underlying principle is still that of rejecting others. So in Table 10.1 the two general measures of Ethnocentrism (1974) and Tolerance (1991) are presented. (Note that the ethnocentrism score is reversed in direction so that it becomes a measure of acceptance rather than rejection.) Overall, those on the tolerant side are twice as many as on the ethnocentric side of the distribution in 1974 (62.9 percent vs. 31.5 percent), and ten times as many in 1991 (88.9 percent vs. 8.8 percent). The ratio for the one 1974 item dealing with "colour" is 3.5 to 1 (69.2 percent vs. 19.1 percent) and for the two uniquely racial items in 1991 (numbers 5 and 6), the ratios are 5 to 1 (72.2 percent vs. 15.3 percent) and 3 to 1 (65.3 percent vs. 18.9 percent) in not rejecting racial others. For the two items that combine reference to ethnic and racial groups (item numbers 3 and 4), the ratios are even more accepting (over 20 to 1). These distributions, once again, can be interpreted positively (i.e., there is a high level of tolerance), or negatively (i.e., there is evidence that some Canadians are prejudiced).

TABLE 10.1

MEASURES OF ETHNOCENTRISM (1974) AND TOLERANCE (1991)

Scale / Item	Mean	Standard deviation	% Opposed Disagree	% Neutral	% Support/ Agree
MULTICULTURAL IDEOLOGY					
Total Score 1974	4.5	1.2	32.2	3.9	63.9
Total Score 1991	4.6	1.2	27.3	3.4	69.3
Items (1991)					
1. Recognizing that cultural and racial diversity is a fundamental characteristic of Canadian Society.	5.7	1.7	10.4	12.0	77.7
2. Helping ethnic and racial minorities preserve their cultural heritages in Canada.	4.7	2.1	25.3	16.8	58.0
PREJUDICE					
Total Ethnocentrism 1974	4.5	1.3	31.5	5.6	62.9
Total Tolerance 1991	5.4	1.0	8.8	2.3	88.9
Items (1974)					
1. It would be a mistake ever to have coloured people for foremen and leaders over whites. (R)	2.6	2.0	69.2	11.8	19.1
Items (1991)					
2. Shared values are more important than differences in skin colour in binding people together as a nation.	6.2	1.3	5.3	5.1	89.6
3. Having people from different ethnic and racial groups living in the same country.	6.1	1.4	4.9	10.4	84.8
4. Promoting equality among all Canadians regardless of racial or ethnic origin.	6.4	1.2	3.3	4.9	91.8
5. It is a bad idea for people of different races to marry one another. (R)	2.4	1.9	72.2	12.8	15.3
6. Non-whites living here should not push themselves where they are not wanted. (R)	2.7	2.0	65.3	15.8	18.9
PROGRAM ATTITUDES					
Total Score 1974	4.7	1.4	25.2	6.2	68.6
Total Score 1991	5.9	1.0	5.1	1.1	93.8
Items (1991)					
1. Eliminating racism in areas such as health care, the justice system and education.	6.3	1.5	6.7	5.4	87.9
2. Ensuring equal access to jobs regardless of ethnic or racial background.	6.4	1.3	4.7	4.7	90.7
3. Ensuring that organizations and institutions reflect and respect the cultural and racial diversity of Canada.	5.8	1.6	8.8	11.8	79.4
4. Eliminating racial discrimination through public education.	6.3	1.4	5.0	5.8	82.8
5. Helping everyone deal with ethnic, cultural and racial diversity.	6.0	1.5	7.1	8.6	84.3

Program Attitudes

As the needs of different cultural groups have changed, so too have the program emphases: initially the focus was on cultural maintenance, but it has shifted more toward participation and antiracism (Berry, 1984). Table 10.1 nevertheless shows a very high level of acceptance of multiculturalism programs in general in 1991 (93.8 percent on acceptance side), which is substantially higher than in 1974 (68.6 percent acceptance). This high level of support is consistent across specific programs; for the five items dealing with racial issues, acceptance is 80 percent or more in the 1991 sample.

Attitudes Toward Specific Groups

Affective reactions to people of different origins have been part of the social psychological study of ethnic relations for many decades. Early research employed a social distance measure (e.g., "would you be willing to have — as a co-worker"; as in Driedger and Peters, 1977); others have used "prestige" ratings of the "social standing" of specific groups (e.g., Pineo, 1977). In our 1974 survey we used six evaluative dimensions on which respondents rated nine ethnic groups (Berry et al., 1977). The 1991 survey asked "How comfortable would you feel being around individuals from the following groups?"; this question was asked with respect to people "born and raised outside Canada" (termed "immigrants"), and again with respect to people "born and raised in Canada" (termed "ethnics"). In both surveys, ratings are on a 7-point scale, with 7 indicating a positive attitude.

Figure 10.1 shows the overall evaluations of the eight groups in the 1974 study, while Figure 10.2 gives these according to the ethnic origin of respondents. For the 1991 survey, Figure 10.3 shows the mean "comfort levels" in the Total Sample with respect to the various "ethnic" and "immigrant" groups, while Figure 10.4 provides these for "ethnic" groups only, according to the ethnic origin of respondents (British, French or Other than British or French). Figure 10.5 presents findings from the three metropolitan areas (Montreal, Toronto, Vancouver) for "ethnic" groups only.

In both the 1974 and the 1991 data, there is a clear hierarchy of acceptance of groups: groups of European origin in Canada are rated more positively than those not of European origin. However, in 1991 both Chinese-Canadians and Native Canadian Indians are evaluated at

FIGURE 10.1

OVERALL EVALUATION OF NINE ETHNIC GROUPS
IN TOTAL SAMPLE, 1974

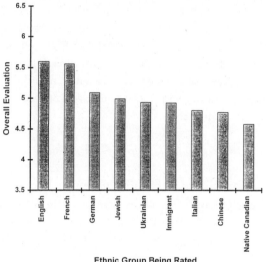

Ethnic Group Being Rated

FIGURE 10.2

OVERALL EVALUATION OF NINE ETHNIC GROUPS
BY ETHNIC ORIGIN OF RESPONDENT, 1974

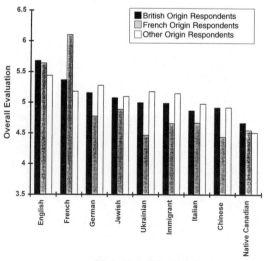

Ethnic Group Being Rated

Source: John W. Berry et al., *Multiculturalism and Ethnic Attitudes in Canada*
(Ottawa: Supply and Service, 1977).

FIGURE 10.3

COMFORT LEVELS FOR FOURTEEN ETHNIC AND IMMIGRANT GROUPS
IN TOTAL SAMPLE, 1991

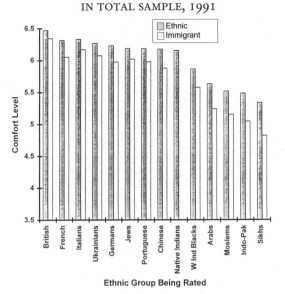

FIGURE 10.4

COMFORT LEVELS FOR FOURTEEN ETHNIC GROUPS, BY ETHNIC
ORIGIN OF RESPONDENT, 1991

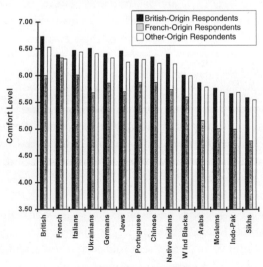

Source: John W. Berry and Rudolf Kalin, "Multiculturalism and Ethnic Attitudes
in Canada: An Overview of the 1991 National Survey," *Canadian Journal of
Behavioural Science* 27:310-20.

FIGURE IO.5

COMFORT LEVELS FOR FOURTEEN ETHNIC GROUPS,
IN MONTREAL, TORONTO AND VANCOUVER, 1991

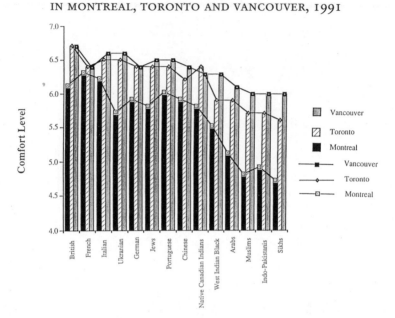

Source: Berry and Kalin, "Multicultural and Ethnic Attitudes."

much the same level (i.e., are on the same plateau) as the groups of
European origin. Thus, while "race" appears to be the main basis for
these differential ratings, the presence of these two groups at the same
level of acceptance suggests that other factors also have to be considered. One of these may be the length of time a group has been in
Canada in substantial numbers, providing an opportunity for famil-
iarization through intergroup contact. Obviously, Aboriginal Peoples
have the longest history of settlement; and among the other visible
minorities, Chinese also have a long history in Canada. Such an interpretation would also explain why Indo-Pakistani and Sikh Canadians
are relatively highly rated in Vancouver (Figure 10.5), where their settlement is long-standing.

The contact hypothesis has been explored for both surveys (Kalin
and Berry, 1982; Kalin, 1996). In these analyses the neighbourhood
was taken as a unit of analysis: the ethnic attitudes of respondents (who
were not members of a particular group) were plotted against the percentage of the particular group in the respondents' neighbourhoods. In

general, the higher the representation, the more favourable were the ethnic attitudes. However, in the 1974 study, this general pattern was not present for the one non-European group, namely, for Canadian Indians; there was essentially no relationship. In the 1991 study, the general pattern was for higher presence to be associated with more positive ethnic attitudes; this pattern held for Indo-Pakistanis, but not for Chinese, West Indian or Native Canadian Indians (where again there was essentially no relationship). Generally, then, for visible minorities, their percentage presence does not predict attitudes toward them in the same way as this variable does for other groups. One possible reason for the difference is that racism may counteract the familiarity effects that are found for groups of European origin. Another possibility is that demographic differences in settlement pattern for visible minorities may limit the likelihood of finding statistical regularities. Specifically, their percentage presence is lower than for other groups, and they may not be distributed equally across neighbourhoods.

In these Figures, there are clearly patterns of ethnic attitudes that differ according to the ethnic origin of respondents. In 1974 and 1991, those of French origin provide lower overall evaluations and comfort levels for all ethnic groups (other than French) than do those of British or other than British or French origin; and the comfort levels in Montreal are clearly lower than in Toronto or Vancouver. This difference is consistent with recent evidence from a study conducted for the government of Quebec (1996) in which "comfort levels" (the same measure used by Berry and Kalin, 1995) were lower for French-origin respondents with respect to a number of groups (English, Latin American, Asians, Indo-Pakistanis, Arabs, and "Minorities"); in contrast, comfort levels were higher with French, but no different with French-speaking blacks (Government of Quebec, 1996). This same study found similar differences between French-, and British- and Other-origin respondents, on a number of general measures of prejudice, parallelling findings from the 1991 National Survey (Berry and Kalin, 1995).

Individual Differences in Prejudice and Ethnic Attitudes

According to ethnocentrism theory, those individuals who are generally prejudiced will show a positive evaluation of their own group(s) and a negative evaluation of outgroups. This expectation was explored in the 1991 study by examining individuals' relative comfort levels with various groups in relation to their scores on the Tolerance scale.

FIGURE 10.6

POSITIVE OR NEGATIVE GROUP PREFERENCES

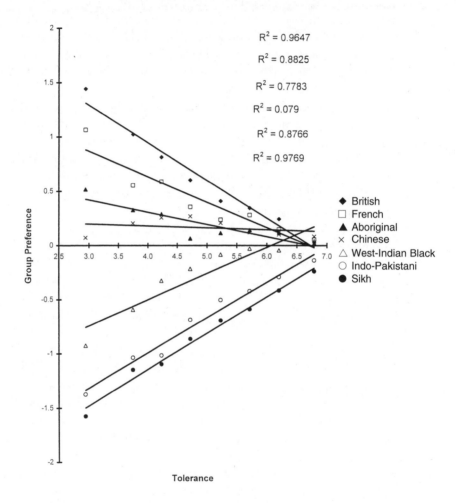

Source: Berry and Kalin, "Multicultural and Ethnic Attitudes."

Comfort levels are plotted against Tolerance in Figure 10.7, using "standardized" comfort levels (where a positive score indicates higher comfort relative to an individual's mean comfort with all groups, and a negative score indicates a lower relative comfort level).

The two "charter groups" (those most highly rated overall), and five "visible minority" groups (Chinese, Native Indian, West Indian

FIGURE 10.7

COMFORT LEVELS WITH FOUR VISIBLE MINORITY GROUPS, AS A
FUNCTION OF GROUP PRESENCE

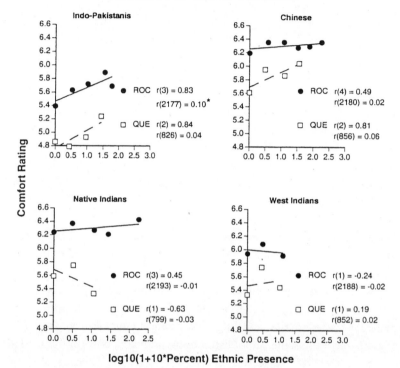

log10(1+10*Percent) Ethnic Presence

Source: Rudolf Kalin and J.W. Berry, "Interethnic Attitudes in Canada:
Ethnocentrism, Concensual Hierarchy and Reciprocity," *Canadian Journal of
Behavioural Science* 28:253-61.

Blacks, Indo-Pakistanis and Sikhs) are included in Figure 10.7. As
expected, the most Tolerant respondents make little differentiation in
their comfort level ratings of the various groups; the seven slope lines all
converge toward the neutral point of group preference at the right. Also
as expected, there is substantial variation in relative group preference
among the least Tolerant respondents: here, very positive ratings are
given to the British and French ethnic groups, while less positive ratings
are given to the various "visible minority" groups. This pattern clearly
evidences differential evaluations of ethnic groups along racial lines, but
predominantly among those who are the most generally prejudiced.

The pattern is a very complex one. Most clear is that for the two groups that are generally most preferred (British and French), where it is the least Tolerant who show the *most positive* ratings; in contrast, for the two groups that are generally least preferred (Indo-Pakistanis and Sikhs), it is the least Tolerant who show the *least positive* ratings. That is, the greatest differentiation in preference ratings are made by the least Tolerant individuals.

Less clear is the pattern for the three groups that are rated less extremely on the preference hierarchy. For the two groups that we previously noted were rated on the same plateau as groups of European background (Chinese and Aboriginal), there is a pattern that exhibits both relatively positive ratings (both slope lines are above the neutral point), but these ratings are not related to Tolerance (the preference ratings are at much the same level right across the Tolerance dimension). However, the pattern of preference ratings for West Indian Blacks resembles more those for Indo-Pakistanis and Sikhs: there is a slope that parallels the other two, but is less negative overall. Indeed, for the three highest categories of tolerance, the preference ratings are all close to the neutral point.

While racism may explain the general preference for European origin over non-European-origin groups, it is clear that Canadians are not generally racist in the sense that they rate all non-European origin Canadians in the same way. Distinctions are made, both in the *level* of group preference ratings (Figure 10.3), and in the *structure* of these ratings (Figures 10.6 and 10.7). In particular, the place of Aboriginal Canadians in this attitude pattern suggests that they are included as a positive reference group by respondents. This interpretation corresponds to an earlier finding (Berry et al. 1977:95) that Aboriginal Peoples (Indian, Inuit and Métis) are included in a cluster of groups around "Myself," along with "English," "French" and "Québécois" in a sorting task based on perceived similarity. It also corresponds to a conclusion (Berry and Wells, 1994) that Aboriginal Peoples have a "special status" in the attitudes of non-Aboriginal Canadians: they are admired for their durability as a people and for their role as environmental stewards, but are not completely accepted in affective terms ("comfort levels").

CONCLUSIONS

What can be said about the existence of racism in Canada on the basis of these social psychological data? First, Canadians clearly perceive and evaluate groups differently according to their origin (European vs. non-European), with non-European peoples generally lower in the preference hierarchy. However, it is also clear that not all non-European groups are evaluated in the same way: those of Chinese and Aboriginal origin are evaluated in ways that are similar to European-origin groups, both in terms of the level of acceptance and in the relationship of their acceptance to a measure of general Tolerance.

Second, Canadians are generally well-disposed toward the existence of ethnic and racial diversity in their society. Despite this generally positive conclusion, there is a significant proportion (varying from almost 20 percent to less than 5 percent) who respond negatively to attitude statements about inclusion or acceptance of racial others. This is clearly room for continued public education and anti-racism initiatives that are currently the focus of various governmental policies and programs.

11

DISCRIMINATION: AN INVISIBLE EVIL

DONALD W. TAYLOR, STEPHEN WRIGHT
AND KAREN RUGGIERO

WHENEVER WE LEAVE OUR IVORY TOWER to interact with real people — whether the occasion be a thanksgiving dinner with the family, a ride on the commuter train, pursuing our favourite sport, or walking the dog — the discovery that we study discrimination always provokes a heated debate. The feedback we get is captured in the following arguments: "What will immigrants find to complain about now!"; "Maybe there was discrimination in the past, but not now"; "Visible minorities are represented at the highest levels — look at Bill Cosby, wealthy black athletes, the mayors of many major American cities, the head of Canada's largest women's group"; "There are women in the boardrooms, and immigrants and refugees are treated better than native-born Canadians — face it, discrimination is dead, no group has any legitimate basis for complaint!"

This perception that prejudice and discrimination are, if not dead, at least fading quickly, is supported by surveys on racial attitudes. Beginning in the 1950s, there was a clear indication that overt racism was on the decline. For example, in recent surveys of ethnic attitudes and stereotypes, in both Canada and the United States, white respondents are not inclined to endorse negative beliefs about blacks, or to approve of discriminatory laws and policies (Gaertner and Dovidio, 1986; Elliott and Fleras, 1992; Schuman, Steed and Bobo, 1985).

This attitudinal trend, however, has not gone unquestioned. Theorists have argued that prejudice and discrimination have not really declined, they have merely gone underground. Thus, scholars have proposed such concepts as symbolic or modern racism (Kinder and Sears, 1981; McConahay, 1986), aversive racism (Gaertner and Dovidio, 1986), ambivalent racism (Katz and Haas, 1988), and democratic racism (Henry and Tator, 1994) to explain how traditional forms of prejudice and discrimination are being replaced with subtler expressions.

Much of the research on both traditional and modern forms of discrimination has focused on the holders of prejudice and the perpetrators of discrimination. Lost in the process has been the experience of discrimination from the point of view of potential victims. The aim of the present chapter is to redress this imbalance by describing two programs of research that explore the impact that discrimination has on its victims. The results are disquieting. They indicate why people of advantage might be led to conclude that disadvantaged groups no longer confront societal discrimination; they also help explain why victims of discrimination are required to bear the psychological brunt of the maltreatment they have suffered.

We begin our analysis with some observations on traditional social psychological approaches to the study of prejudice and discrimination and the ways in which they have tended to pose the wrong questions. In the following section we turn our attention to victims of discrimination and the practice of tokenism. In the final section, we explore how disadvantaged group members cope with discrimination.

ASKING THE WRONG QUESTIONS

Discrimination involves behaviour directed at a person on the basis of his or her category membership. At times people may want to be treated differently on the basis of their category membership, as when they wish to have their cultural or group identity acknowledged, or when affirmative action programs favour members of a particular category. For the most part, however, discrimination is a particularly bad experience, since it usually takes the form of behaviour toward others which is based exclusively on their category membership, is of a negative character, and is engaged in without the consent or desire of the group being discriminated against.

Discrimination, by definition, is an intergroup phenomenon, necessarily involving both a perpetrator and a victim. Social psychological theory and research has traditionally focused on the holders of prejudice and perpetrators of discrimination rather than on its victims. Thus, authoritarian, dogmatic, poor, uneducated, highly religious, and cognitively simple people with low self-esteem have been found to be prone to engage in acts of discrimination.

On the surface this approach would seem to be enlightened and socially responsible since it implies that the problem of prejudice and discrimination lies squarely with the advantaged or dominant group,

not with its victims. As most academic social psychologists have traditionally been mainstream white males, a focus on the perpetrators of
discrimination would seem to be particularly open-minded. But a closer inspection reveals a much less altruistic and less responsible orientation on the part of social psychologists.

The thrust of most research has been to adopt an individual differences approach, designed to reveal which few dominant group members are sufficiently psychologically deranged that they would engage in
irrational forms of discrimination toward disadvantaged groups. The
implication was, of course, that the vast majority of dominant group
members were psychologically healthy individuals who would never
engage in pathological behaviour such as overt discrimination. Once
the small number of "bigots" could be identified, the rest of the dominant group, including social scientists themselves, could be absolved of
any responsibility for social injustice. What better theoretical orientation could there be for an academic discipline dominated by middle-
class, Caucasian, male scientists?

Despite this traditional preoccupation with an individual difference
analysis of predispositions to discrimination among advantaged group
members, there has always been a small cadre of social scientists who
have pursued the topic of discrimination from the point of view of its
potential victims. The seminal work by the Clarks (Clark and Clark,
1947), the laboratory research of Dion and his colleagues begun in the
mid-seventies (Dion, 1975; Dion and Earn, 1975), the influential theory and research of Crocker and Major (1989), and a long-standing
tradition of research in sociology paved the way for current theory.
The research described in the present chapter builds on the perspectives
of these innovative social scientists.

TOKENISM: A SUBTLE FORM OF DISCRIMINATION

Tokenism is a structural reality that may be encountered by members
of virtually every disadvantaged group, including immigrants and
refugees, women, the disabled, and every racial, ethnic and language
minority. Tokenism is a strategy whereby a few capable members of a
disadvantaged group are accepted into positions usually reserved for
members of the advantaged group, while access is systematically denied
to the vast majority of qualified disadvantaged group members. Tokenism is a particularly subtle form of discrimination (see Laws, 1975;
Moreland, 1965), and to date there has been little research designed to

explore the reactions of those who fall victim to the exclusionary reality of this phenomenon.

Categorizing Disadvantaged Group Behaviour

In order for us to address the issue of tokenism it was first necessary to develop a framework for categorizing the multitude of behaviours that victims of discrimination might exhibit in response to their plight. The need for a behavioural framework arises because of limitations to research on intergroup relations. Research to date has tended to focus, not on behaviour per se, but rather on victims' perceptions and feelings. Prototypical of this emphasis is the legacy of research on relative deprivation theory (see Taylor and Moghaddam, 1994).

On those few occasions when behavioural responses are examined victims are presented with only two options: no action or choosing the one behaviour offered by the researcher. Clearly, it is possible that victims will not choose the single behavioural alternative available, because their preferred course of action was not even offered as a possibility. Thus, to assess disadvantaged group members' responses to inequality, it is necessary to present them with options that cover the entire array of behaviours actually available to them.

The problem is that the behavioural options for victims are wide ranging, varying from reluctant acceptance through to individual attempts at upward mobility to socially disruptive forms of collective action. In order to systematize reactions to discrimination, Wright, Taylor and Moghaddam (1990) proposed a behavioural framework that involves categorizing the possible behaviours that victims of discrimination might exhibit along two dimensions: the extent to which the behaviour is individual or collective, and the extent to which it is normative or antinormative, from the perspective of the advantaged group.

From these dimensions, five broad categories of behaviour arise. Victims of discrimination might 1) take no action, 2) attempt individual upward mobility through normative channels, 3) engage in individual actions that are contrary to the norms specified by the advantaged group, 4) instigate collective action that is consistent with prescribed norms, and 5) instigate collective action that is contrary to the norms. The behaviours described by these categories have dramatically different societal consequences and these are illustrated in the schematic diagram in Figure 11.1. For example, collective antinormative action (e.g., riots and illegal strikes) directly threaten the existing

FIGURE II.I

A FRAMEWORK FOR CATEGORIZING DISADVANTAGED GROUP
MEMBERS' RESPONSES TO INEQUALITY

		INDIVIDUAL ACTION	COLLECTIVE ACTION
NORMATIVE		Education Skill Training	Legal Strike **Ethnic Group Identity**
	NO ACTION		
ANTINORMATIVE		Income Tax Evasion Robbery	Terrorism Race Riot

social order, whereas no action and individual action (e.g., job training) serve to protect the status quo.

Research Paradigm

Having established a behavioural framework within which to examine systematically the responses of disadvantaged group members to "tokenism" we found it necessary to reproduce in the laboratory certain features of the "meritocracy" ideology that is central to Western democracy. This we have accomplished by informing participants in our laboratory experiments that "as in the real world" they must begin the experiment as a member of a low-status decision-making group, but again, as in the "real world," their performance on a decision-making task might earn them a promotion to a high-status decision-making group. Participants were also told that, as in real life organizations, it is members of the high-status group who set the decision-making test and decide on the performance criteria for promotion to the high-status group. Finally, it is explained that, because of their proven performance members of the high-status group participate in a $300 lottery, whereas member of the low-status group are relegated to a $30 lottery. (In fact, all participate in the $300 lottery.)

Following these instructions, participants complete a test of effective decision-making, a test, it is explained, that, while not favouring any group over another, measures a skill that is essential for anyone who aspires to a position of status and leadership. Participants are give 15 minutes to complete the test, ostensibly designed to assess their decision-making skills. Upon completion, their answers are taken by an assistant to another room where presumably a panel of high-status group members grade the participant's work.

After an appropriate delay, the assistant returns to the laboratory room with written feedback for each participant from the panel of judges. This written feedback is in fact prepared by the assistant and is the major mechanism by which "tokenism" is introduced. For example, through the written feedback, participants can be led to believe that they have succeeded or failed in their bid to be promoted to the high-status group. As well, the legitimacy of their fate can be manipulated, as can information about the fate of others from the low-status group who are aspiring to upward mobility. Thus, the paradigm mirrors the meritocratic structure of most real-world institutions, but allows for any number of experimental manipulations in order to examine the conditions under which participants will prefer one or more of the five categories of behaviour in response to their attempts at upward mobility.

Initial Findings

The experimental paradigm, coupled with the framework for behaviour, allowed for a test of how disadvantaged group members respond to "tokenism." Four experimental conditions were created (see Wright et al., 1990) by varying the written feedback that participants received as a result of their effort to gain entry to the high-status group. All participants were told that a grade of 8.5/10 was the mark required for success. In the "meritocracy" condition, participants failed in their quest because they achieved a score below the required 8.5. In the "100 percent discrimination" condition, participants received a grade above the required 8.5. But participants were told in writing by the panel of high-status group members that despite their good performance the panel had arbitrarily decided, after the fact, not to allow any member of the low-status group into the high-status group. In the "partial discrimination" condition, participants again received a grade above the 8.5 cut-off, but were told that access to the high-status group was denied because the panel of judges had instituted a 30 percent quota.

Of particular interest was the "tokenism" situation where a 2 percent quota was arbitrarily introduced by the high-status panel with the consequence that, from all low-status group members who received a grade above the 8.5 criteria, only 2 percent would be permitted entry to the high-status group.

Participants' behavioural responses to the four experimental conditions were particularly revealing. For the "meritocracy" condition, participants responded to their failure by either taking no action or by taking individual/normative action. Even those in the "partial discrimination" (30 percent) condition avoided any collective or antinormative actions. Despite the arbitrary introduction of the quota which lead to their failure, participants acted very much like those in the "meritocracy" condition.

The situation was very different for those in the "100 percent discrimination" condition. Here participants favoured collective/antinormative action, the most socially disruptive form of action from the point of view of the high-status group. Of particular interest were the responses of those in the "tokenism" (2 percent) condition, who confronted failure because of an imposed quota that made access to the high-status group almost impossible. Yet these participants did not respond as did those in the "100 percent discrimination" condition. Instead of opting for collective action, participants chose individual/antinormative action. This form of action, although in violation of established norms, is not particularly threatening to the status quo.

These findings, which have been subsequently replicated (see Lalonde and Silverman, 1994; Wright and Taylor, 1977), are both unexpected and disquieting. They are unexpected because the "tokenism (98 percent discrimination)" and "100 percent discrimination" conditions are virtually identical in terms of personal and collective outcomes. At the personal level, they are identical; despite performance that surpasses the stated criterion, the individual is robbed of a substantial personal gain because of his or her group membership. At the group level, both the "100 percent discrimination" and "tokenism" experiences are clearly discriminatory. In both conditions, many capable members of proven ability are being discriminated against. Yet when faced with tokenism, disadvantaged group members preferred individual action rather than the collective behaviours preferred by those confronted with an intergroup context involving total discrimination.

The results are disquieting because of their societal implications. If, indeed, advantaged group members engage in tokenism with the express purpose of discriminating against members of a disadvantaged group, then their strategy appears to be highly effective. Permitting a small token number of members of a disadvantaged group access to upward mobility appears to significantly increase the likelihood that other disadvantaged group members will limit their reaction to individual actions; a class of behaviours that are not especially disruptive of the status quo in general, and the privileged status of the advantaged group in particular.

Understanding Tokenism

In order to comprehend both the theoretical and societal implications of tokenism, the psychological processes of two subgroups within the disadvantaged group needs to be understood: 1) the disadvantaged group members who suffer the negative consequences of tokenism; and 2) those few disadvantaged group members who are the "tokens" and thus are permitted access to the high-status group.

For those who fail to become tokens, the theoretical challenge is to understand why they avoid the socially disruptive collective/antinormative actions taken by those who confront total discrimination. An hypothesis proposed by Wright (1995), which has received some initial support, is that tokenism is an unusually ambiguous social situation. It is this ambiguity that may lead unsuccessful low-status group members to behave in a unique way. That is, on the one hand, tokenism contains elements of complete segregation, in that access to the high-status group is almost impossible. On the other hand, there is an element of meritocracy, albeit a small one, in the sense that there are a token few among the low-status group who do achieve successful entry to a high-status group. Moreover, the success of the token few is based on extraordinary performance. Faced with such an ambiguous situation, low-status group members seem to prefer individual action because of the existence of vestiges of a meritocracy, but prefer antinormative behaviour because of the obvious discrimination inherent in tokenism.

Turning to successful tokens, Wright and Taylor (1992) have conducted an initial series of experiments in which two contrasting hypotheses were explored. On the one hand, advocates for the promotion of talented minority group members view such promotions as a breakthrough. The minority group member who has achieved high status is in a strategic position to facilitate the upward mobility of all minority group members. In direct contrast, according to a five-stage model of intergroup relations proposed by Taylor and McKirnan (1984), successful tokens are likely to shift the basis of their identity quickly to the high-status group and distance themselves from their prior group.

The result of the experiments consistently supported the five-stage model of Taylor and McKirnan (1984). Low-status group members, who were successful in gaining entrance to a high-status group despite a 2 percent quota, were asked to support various actions on the part of the low-status group. Successful tokens did not support collective and antinormative actions on the part of low-status group members, which might have prompted a real change in status for the low-status group. Instead, they appeared to immediately shift their allegiance from the low-status group to their new high-status group, and would only support low-status group members who took actions that would not threaten the status quo (no action; individual/normative action).

In the final analysis, tokenism emerges as a subtle but very powerful form of discrimination. Successful tokens quickly abandon their former disadvantaged group colleagues and shift the basis of their identity to the high-status group. Those who fail to become tokens, confronted with an ambiguous intergroup situation, consistently react in a manner that fails to threaten the status quo and thereby allows for the continuing advantages of the high-status group.

COPING WITH DISCRIMINATION

Crocker and Major (1989) have written a most provocative theoretical analysis of social stigma. They begin by noting that the major theme to emerge from much of the early research on prejudice and discrimination was that members of groups that are discriminated against suffer from low self-esteem. A variety of theoretical perspectives support this conclusion from symbolic interaction theorists (e.g., Cooley, 1956) and proponents of a self-fulfilling prophecy (e.g., Merton, 1948) to those interested in self-efficacy (e.g., Gecas and Schwalbe, 1983). The conclusion that members of groups exposed to discrimination would suffer from low self-esteem seems intuitively obvious. First, their objectively defined outcomes are relatively poor, and second, perpetrators of discrimination would have both the motivation and the power to promote a "victim-blame" explanation in order to rationalize discriminatory treatment toward, and poor outcomes for, disadvantaged group members.

Moreover, there was empirical evidence to support the notion that disadvantaged group members suffer low levels of self-esteem. The preference of black children and Maori native children for white dolls (Clark and Clark, 1947; Vaughan, 1972), the identification of some concentration camp prisoners with their aggressor (Bettelheim, 1947), and the positive reaction of French-speaking school children in Quebec to English-speaking voices (e.g., Lambert, Hodgson, Gardner and Fillenbaum, 1960) all were interpreted as evidence of low self-esteem among minority group members. So strong was the phenomenon that Allport (1954) was prompted to introduce the label "self-hate" to describe the low levels of self-esteem that so often accompanied membership in a disadvantaged minority group.

Attributional Ambiguity

Crocker and Major (1989) challenged the traditional wisdom that associated membership in a stigmatized group with low self-esteem. They reviewed the literature only to discover that for a variety of disadvantaged groups, including racial and ethnic minorities, women, the physically disabled, the learning disabled, homosexuals, the mentally ill and juvenile delinquents, there was no evidence of pervasive, low self-esteem. This prompted them (Crocker and Major, 1989:88) to conclude that "this research conducted over a time span of more than 20 years leads to the surprising conclusion that prejudice against members of stigmatized or oppressed groups generally does *not* result in lowered self-esteem for members of those groups."

In order to explain these unexpected findings, Crocker and Major (1989, 1993) theorized that members of disadvantaged groups face attribution ambiguities that are not faced by advantaged group members. The ambiguity arises because every time a disadvantaged group member receives negative, or indeed positive, feedback from an advantaged group member, there is the usual array of attributional judgements to make along with one important addition; the possibility that the feedback was due to discrimination.

While this ambiguity is itself stressful for disadvantaged group members, it does offer them the opportunity to engage in self-protection. Specifically, attributing negative feedback to discrimination, rather than to inadequate personal qualities, can protect self-esteem in the face of failure. Similarly, when experiencing success it would be highly ego-enhancing to have achieved the success despite having to face the hurdle of discrimination. In both instances, then, discrimination allows the disadvantaged group member to maintain high self-esteem, and thereby challenge the traditional notion that disadvantaged group members suffer from low self-esteem.

Evidence for this link between attribution to discrimination and maintenance of self-esteem was first obtained by Dion (1975) and Dion and Earn (1975), but has been tested most directly in a series of experiments by Crocker and Major, and their associates. For example, Crocker, Voelkl, Testa and Major (1991:study 1) found that women who received negative feedback from a male peer, who held negative attitudes toward women, were more likely to attribute the feedback to his prejudice, and were less depressed following the feedback, than were women who received the same feedback from a man who held positive attitudes toward women. In a conceptual replication of this study, Crocker et al. (1991:study 2) demonstrated that African-American students who received negative interpersonal feedback from a white student who could see them (and hence knew their race) were more likely to attribute the feedback to prejudice, and had higher self-esteem following the feedback, than African-American students who received the same negative feedback from a peer who could not see them.

The implications of Crocker and Major's theory and research (1989) are challenging. The suggestion is that at times members of groups who are potential targets for discrimination will be motivated to attribute their outcomes to discrimination in order to protect their self-esteem.

The Personal/Group Discrimination Discrepancy

Crocker and Major's innovative perspective on discrimination is especially interesting in light of another phenomenon associated with perceived discrimination that Taylor, Wright, Moghaddam and Lalonde (1990) have labelled the personal/group discrimination discrepancy. The phenomenon involves members of disadvantaged groups rating discrimination directed at their group as a whole substantially higher than their rating of discrimination aimed at themselves personally as members of that group.

The personal/group discrimination discrepancy is a particularly robust phenomenon. The tendency to rate discrimination higher at a group level, than at the personal level, was first documented by Crosby (1982) in her study of working women in the Boston area. Since then the discrepancy has arisen without exception among a wide array of disadvantaged groups, including: different samples of women, inner-city African-American men living in subsidized housing projects, visible minority immigrant women living in Montreal, and a sample of native people (see Taylor, Wright and Porter, 1993).

The notion that disadvantaged group members deny (Crosby, 1984), or at least minimize (Taylor et al., 1990), their personal experiences with discrimination is the explanation offered most frequently for the apparent low ratings of personal discrimination. Empirically testing the minimization hypothesis is, however, problematic. The difficulty is that minimization can only be demonstrated if perceptions of personal discrimination are systematically lower than *objective* levels of discrimination. Assessing objective levels of discrimination is extremely difficult both in a real-world context and in the confines of the laboratory.

In real-world contexts in which field research might be conducted, establishing with any certainty the actual amount of discrimination involved in a particular intergroup encounter is extremely difficult (Driedger and Mezoff, 1981). For example, in cases of potential wrongful dismissal, the employer will usually argue that the employee was terminated because of inadequate performance, whereas the disadvantaged group member will likely allege discrimination.

The laboratory, in contrast, does offer an environment where objective levels of discrimination can be created. The problem there is that if experimental conditions are created to produce discrimination that are completely unambiguous, then participants have no real opportunity to minimize their perception of the discrimination. Indeed, where experimental manipulation of discrimination is blatant, there is little room for psychological distortion in any form (Taylor, Wright and Ruggiero, 1992).

Ruggiero and Taylor (1995) introduced an experimental paradigm to address this dilemma, by adapting Kahneman and Tversky's method for exploring the representative heuristic (Kahneman and Tversky, 1973). The discrimination paradigm involves having disadvantaged group members receive negative feedback from an advantaged group member. Disadvantaged group members are given explicit information about the probability that the advantaged group member discriminates against members of their group. Recipients of the negative feedback are then asked to attribute the extent to which their negative feedback was the result of their own personal performance, or to what extent it was due to discrimination.

For example, in a typical experiment women would perform an achievement-oriented test and would receive a failing grade from a male evaluator. Women in different conditions would be told that their task was to be graded by one of eight males of whom either 100 percent, 75 percent, 50 percent, or 25 percent actively discriminated against women. An examination of women's attributions for failure either to the quality of their answers on the test or to discrimination in the different conditions allows for insights into the question whether, and the extent to which, women's attributions deviate from the probability information provided.

Minimizing Discrimination

Ruggiero and Taylor (1995) found in an initial experiment that women indeed appeared to minimize the discrimination that was directed at them in the experiment. As shown in Figure 11.2, when women were told that 100 percent of the judges discriminate against them, and hence when there was no ambiguity about discrimination, women judged that their failure was largely due to discrimination rather than to the quality of their answers. However, where there was

FIGURE 11.2

ATTRIBUTIONS TO QUALITY OF ANSWERS AND TO DISCRIMINATION, FOR DIFFERENT PROBABILITIES OF DISCRIMINATION

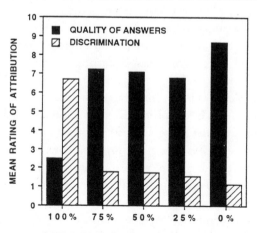

BASE-RATE PROBABILITY FOR DISCRIMINATION

any ambiguity, as was the case for the 75 percent, 50 percent, and 25 percent probability conditions, the women consistently judged their failure to be due to the quality of their work rather than to discrimination.

This tendency to minimize personal discrimination is puzzling in light of Crocker and Major's theoretical propositions about the links between perceived discrimination and self-esteem (1989). They argue that disadvantaged group members can protect self-esteem by attributing failure to discrimination. Thus, there would seem to be compelling reasons for disadvantaged group members *not* to minimize their perception of discrimination in the face of negative feedback. That women in the Ruggiero and Taylor experiment (1995) minimized their attribution to discrimination is striking, given that this evaluation required some distortion of base-rate information and the abandonment of at least one very important reason for making attributions to discrimination: protection of self-esteem.

In the light of these non-intuitive findings, Ruggiero and Taylor felt compelled to replicate the finding that women tend to minimize their personal experience with discrimination when confronted with failure (Ruggiero and Taylor, 1995, 1997). Moreover, it was important to extend the research to include other disadvantaged groups, especially since research has suggested that women may not be prototypic of a disadvantaged group when it comes to making attributions to discrimination (see Deaux, 1984).

Ruggiero and Taylor (1997), therefore, replicated the initial findings for gender discrimination and extended the experimental paradigm to include discrimination on the basis of race for samples of Asian and black students (Ruggiero and Taylor, 1995, 1997). The results provided striking confirmation of the minimization of discrimination effect. If participants in the experiment were responding to information about discrimination in a purely rational manner, then attributions to discrimination and to quality of answers on the test should have been extremely high in the 100 percent condition and then declined in a stepwise manner across the 75 percent, 50 percent and 25 percent conditions. Conversely, attributions to quality of answers should have risen in a mirror-like fashion from an initial low rating for the 100 percent condition to a high rating for the 25 percent condition.

The results produced a pattern that deviates from such a rational interpretation in a manner consistent with the minimization of personal discrimination. Where discrimination was made unambiguous, so that disadvantaged group members were informed that 100 percent of the advantaged group judges discriminated against their particular group, Asian and black participants all attributed their failure far more to discrimination than to the quality of their answers. However, when there was any ambiguity (75 percent, 50 percent, 25 percent conditions), Asian and black students consistently attributed their failure far more to the quality of their answers rather than to discrimination. Especially striking was the finding that for both groups, attributions to discrimination were as low for the 75 percent condition as they were for the 25 percent condition.

Why Minimize Discrimination?

If perceiving discrimination protects self-esteem, why would disadvantaged group members choose to minimize discrimination? While attributing negative feedback to discrimination may protect self-esteem, there may be psychological costs associated with perceiving discrimination.

Ruggiero and Taylor proposed that when disadvantaged group members confront failure in an achievement context two dimensions of self-esteem are relevant: performance self-esteem and social self-esteem (Ruggiero and Taylor, 1995, 1997). An attribution to discrimination may have very different consequences, depending on the dimensions emphasized. By attributing negative feedback to discrimination, participants are able to maintain a favourable evaluation of their performance. However, by claiming that they are victims of discrimination, these same participants must face the negative implications of being rejected socially on the basis of their category membership. Concomitantly, by minimizing discrimination as a reason for failure, participants admit to poor performance in exchange for social acceptance. Thus, in an achievement context then, attributing negative feedback to discrimination may protect self-esteem in the *performance* domain but be harmful to self-esteem in the *social* domain. In contrast, minimizing discrimination may protect self-esteem in the *social* domain but impair self-esteem in the *performance* domain.

Ruggiero and Taylor have pointed to a second potential cost of perceiving discrimination: the perception that one has no control over one's destiny (Ruggiero and Taylor, 1997). Specifically, as in the case of self-esteem, the minimization of discrimination has consequences for the perception of control in the *performance* and the *social* domains.

First, by minimizing discrimination as a reason for failure, disadvantaged group members are perceiving themselves as the cause of their poor performance. While this evaluation is perhaps threatening to performance self-esteem, the integrity of the individual's fundamental belief in control over personal outcomes in the performance domain is retained. The feeling of control arises from the knowledge that others' evaluations of their performance will be based on the quality of their work rather than on their category membership. Second, attributing negative feedback to discrimination implies that one's social acceptance is controlled by others, specifically, the out group. By minimizing discrimination, disadvantaged group members can maintain a sense of control over their social acceptability.

Thus, by perceiving discrimination disadvantaged group members protect their self-esteem in the performance domain. By minimizing discrimination, however, they protect their self-esteem in the social domain, and maintain the perception of control over outcomes in both the performance and the social domains.

The tendency for disadvantaged group members to minimize discrimination would seem, on balance, to be psychologically beneficial. For three of the four psychological consequences associated with interpreting discrimination minimization has a positive effect, whereas only for performance-based self-esteem is there a psychological cost.

CONCLUSIONS

The evidence suggests that traditional forms of overt discrimination are no longer pervasive, but may have been replaced by subtler, more disguised forms of unfair treatment. Our analysis of the experience of potential victims of discrimination underscores the hidden evil that characterizes the experience of discrimination. First, it would seem that subtle forms of structural discrimination, in the form of "tokenism," are highly effective from the point of view of the advantaged group. Victims of tokenism do not collectively challenge its discriminatory outcomes. It is difficult to mount a challenge when the discrimination is covert, when the advantaged group with all its resources has a vested interest in convincing everyone that no form of discrimination is being practised, and when the token presence of disadvantaged group members in high-status positions creates uncertainty among those who remain disadvantaged.

But even when victims are confronted with discrimination, their tendency is to minimize its occurrence. The psychological benefits for victims notwithstanding, the minimization of discrimination again serves the interests of the advantaged group. Minimization implies that there is more discrimination than is being acknowledged, but until it is made salient, there will be few calls for social change. The voices of people we encounter outside of academia, who are convinced that minority groups are well treated, will be clearly heard. Silent will be the victims whose coping requires that they minimize the discrimination they are forced to confront.

IV

MINORITIES COPING IN CITIES

12

REDEFINITION OF SOUTH ASIAN WOMEN[1]

HELEN RALSTON

THIS PAPER IS A FEMINIST QUALITATIVE STUDY of the interconnections of gender, race and class with settlement and multiculturalism policies and their impact on the lived experience of South Asian immigrant women in two regions of Canada: Atlantic Canada and British Columbia. In the study of migration and settlement experience it is necessary to consider where immigrants have settled as well as their origins. On the one hand, it has often been assumed that cultural origins account for the lived experience of immigrants, no matter where they settle. On the other hand, researchers who have adopted a Marxist or a political economy perspective have paid little attention to the differential experience of immigrant women or men in the centre, intermediate or peripheral regions of the international or the national political economy. Careless (1987) noted the significance of region in the construction of "limited identities" in Canada and observed that historians must pay attention to the interrelations of region — as well as class, gender, ethnicity and age — in any dynamic consideration of the past. Immigrants who establish themselves in the Atlantic region have different experiences from those encountered by persons who settle in highly industrialized regions of Canada. South Asian immigrant women who settle in the sparsely populated Atlantic region will be more geographically dispersed and more isolated, and they will not have the same level of informal networks and organized support services as those who move into Metro Toronto or into Metro Vancouver, two centres where over three percent of the population is South Asian. It is therefore important to consider *where the women have settled* as well as their origins. My study focuses on South Asian women as a particular case of post-World War II migration and settlement within the British Commonwealth.

SETTLEMENT AND MULTICULTURAL POLICIES,
PROGRAMS AND PRACTICES

In a previous paper (Ralston, 1994) I have examined gender, race and class interconnections and the impact of Canadian and Australian immigration policies with respect to South Asian *women's* lived experience. Post-World War II Canadian immigration policies shifted from being highly discriminatory in selection of immigrants to principles and ideals of non-discrimination on the basis of national origin, race, gender, ethnicity or religion.

After the explicit elimination of overt race and ethnic origin discrimination in 1967 gender discrimination still persisted. For example, prior to 1974, immigration regulations, discriminatory in terms of gender and marital status, defined the man as "head of household" and treated him as the principal applicant in a family, no matter what the woman's qualifications or work experience in the source country. Patriarchal ideologies have continuously constructed immigrant women as wives of immigrant husbands. The womanhood and the productive role of immigrant wives have been absent from rhetoric and reality.

The policies of the 1960s and early 1970s favoured the entering into Canada of South Asians, particularly South Asian men, who had professional and technical skills and who had been educated in English-language tertiary institutions. Some of these immigrant men were steered toward well-paid professional jobs and designated occupations in the less industrialized peripheral regions of the country, such as Atlantic Canada and interior British Columbia, where native-born Canadians did not wish to stay (if born there), or to go (if born elsewhere). Their immigrant wives accompanied (or often followed) them as dependants — to face a very different settlement experience from that of their husbands. Despite the change in immigration regulations in 1974, which permitted a married woman to be the principal applicant, most married women in fact still entered Canada as legal dependants. The legal assignment to wives of the status of "family class," "dependant," or "sponsored" not only implies a socially subordinate status, but has also created a legally subordinate status on entry which impacts on settlement experience.

As a result of changes in immigration and refugee policies in Canada over the past thirty years, there has been a significant change not only in the volume but also in the composition and settlement patterns of recent South Asian immigrant populations. According to the

1991 Canadian Census data (Statistics Canada, 1993), there were 420,295 self-identified people of South Asian origin in Canada, representing 1.6 percent of a total Canadian population of 26,994,045. They were unevenly distributed throughout Canada: Ontario, 55 percent; British Columbia, 25 percent; Alberta, 10 percent, Quebec, 7 percent; Manitoba, 2 percent; Atlantic provinces, 1 percent; with minuscule numbers in Saskatchewan and the Yukon and Northwest Territories. Although, numerically, South Asians were settled predominantly in Ontario, they represented only 1.6 percent of the Ontario population (the national average) as compared to 3.2 percent of the British Columbia population. Of all self-identified South Asians in Canada, 74 percent — that is, 311,018 persons — were first-generation immigrants. India moved into third place among the ten principal source countries for the period 1986 to 1990, with Great Britain having slipped to fifth place (Employment and Immigration Canada, 1986-1990). In addition, there has been an increase not only in numbers but also in ethnic diversity of immigrants from South Asian countries. Whereas the first South Asians who migrated to newly developing British Columbia a century ago were mainly male Sikh Punjabi farmers, the South Asian immigrants of recent decades have constituted a heterogeneous population in terms of regional, linguistic, religious and national origins. Furthermore, the emphasis on family reunification from the late 1970s until the early 1990s has resulted in a preponderance of female over male South Asian immigrants.

Settlement and multiculturalism policies and programs, and their redefinition over time, involve complex relations among federal, provincial, municipal and non-government community organizations which, in turn, influence the lived experience of immigrant women. Of particular import for immigrant women has been access to language programs, to job training and employment counselling programs, to training allowances, to social assistance, to employment equality and equity and to recognition of foreign qualifications. The policies and programs are closely related to ideological and political definitions and constructions of a nation's reality and identity.

As waves of migrants from diverse cultures entered Canada, settlement policies gradually shifted in their ideologies and programs away from (1) assumptions of cultural assimilation to the dominant Canadian (Anglo-Celtic or French) way of life; in the next stage (2) there were expectations of cultural integration with the assistance of language, bridging and welfare programs, and later (3) the recognition that plurality of language and culture was a reality of Canadian society, followed by the emergence of various philosophies and interpretations of multiculturalism.

In settlement policies, as in immigrant selection policies, there has been an implicit and explicit undervaluing of immigrant women's work, as expressed in the evaluation and recognition of their education, training and work experience in the source country; and in the access offered to language training and to job training and retraining in the settlement region. For example, in the mid-1960s, the Citizenship Branch of the Department of the Secretary of State worked with provincial governments and non-governmental organizations in offering language classes oriented toward citizenship and employment in the labour force. However, these settlement services, which were offered to the principal breadwinner in the family, for the most part bypassed immigrant women who entered Canada as dependent wives. It was not until 1992 that government-funded language training was made available to dependent or sponsored immigrants (Fincher et al., 1994: 167).

Philosophies, policies and ideologies of multiculturalism in Canada have reflected consciousness and recognition of the reality of cultural pluralism. Multiculturalism emerged as a policy in Canada in the context of a country that was already defined by the Act of 1867 establishing Confederation as constituted of two "founding" nations with two languages and two cultures. The Liberal policy of multiculturalism, which was proclaimed in 1972, enshrined the following principles: equality of status for all ethnic groups; ethnocultural pluralism as the essence of Canadian identity and unity; protection of civil and human rights for all citizens. In practical terms, the federal government, through the Department of the Secretary of State, funded Canadian ethnic studies, the writing of ethnic histories, the teaching of the English or French official language, and ethnic organizations for various social and cultural programs, like teaching ancestral languages (Burnet, 1978:107-13).

The federal government also assisted provincial governments with funds to establish multicultural programs (Christopher, 1987:335). Furthermore, section 27 of the 1982 Canadian Charter of Rights and Freedoms guaranteed "the preservation and enhancement of the multicultural heritage of Canada" (quoted in Christopher, 1987:331). With the passage of the Multiculturalism Act of 1988 came explicit recognition of "the cultural and racial diversity of Canadian society." The Act

(Canada, 1988) provided that all federal institutions should promote policies, programs and practices that would ensure that Canadians of all origins had an equal opportunity to obtain employment and advancement in those institutions. The New Democratic British Columbia government adopted a Multicultural Act of its own in 1993 (British Columbia, 1993).

The federal and provincial Acts served to ratify and support a number of federal and provincial (and, in addition, municipal and non-governmental) programs and services — many of them already in operation — which aimed to ensure racial and ethnic equality (Dorais et al., 1994:388, quoting Mitges, 1987). Gender equality and equity were assumed but not explicitly addressed by the legislative provisions. Various provincial and local multicultural and intercultural societies, such as the Multicultural Association of Nova Scotia (MANS), the (Halifax) Metropolitan Immigrant Settlement Association (MISA), the Intercultural Association of Greater Victoria, as well as other non-governmental organizations (NGOs), like the British Columbia and the Vancouver Immigrant and Visible Minority Women's Associations and the (British Columbia) India Mahila Association, addressed the concerns of women. At issue with respect to settlement services has been the desirability of providing them through mainstream agencies or through ethnospecific community organizations. Lanphier and Lukomskyj (1994:344-60) have outlined key elements in the historical development of intergovernmental relations with respect to settlement programs and services in both Canada and Australia.

The term "immigrant woman" refers not so much to legal status as to the processes of social construction in everyday life which describe some women who are visibly or audibly different in characteristics such as skin colour, language or accent, religion, dress, food customs and so on. Roxana Ng (1992), for example, has explored how minority women are constructed as "immigrant women" in the social relations between a community employment agency, the labour market and the Canadian state. On the one hand, in legal terms, "immigrant women" may be Canadian citizens who have been permanent Canadian residents for many years. On the other hand, the term "immigrant woman" is seldom applied to white anglophone Western women who have entered Canada from the United Kingdom, Ireland, Australia, New Zealand, Northern Europe or the United States. Some community agencies acknowledge distinctions between long-term residents and recent immigrants by socially designating the latter as "newcomers to Canada." As Jan Pettman (1992:43) has astutely observed, "Some overseas-born groups are presumed to be more migrant than others." There is now a burgeoning literature which documents and analyzes how state policies and practices have constructed gender relations and the legal and social dependent status of immigrant women (e.g., Dorais et al., 1994; Fincher et al., 1994). Himani Bannerji (1987:10) has argued that the colonial and imperialist economic, social and political practices of the past which constructed Canada are still operative today.

CONCEPTUAL AND METHODOLOGICAL CONSIDERATIONS

A feminist perspective and qualitative methodology puts women at the centre of the inquiry, enables them to articulate their experience, and is directed toward social change (cf. Olesen, 1994). For the conceptual framework, methodology and analysis of my research, I have drawn on Dorothy Smith's insights (1987, 1992). She has pointed out (Smith, 1987:2-4) that "(e)stablished sociology has objectified a consciousness of society and social relations that 'knows' them from the standpoint of ruling and from the standpoint of men who do that ruling." When society and social relations are known and understood solely from the perspective of men, then the "gender subtext" of relations of ruling is largely invisible. For Smith, lived experience is central to qualitative inquiry. The term "lived experience" refers to women's practical activities in all spheres of everyday life, be they so-called "private" or "public" sphere. In her conceptualization (Smith 1992: 88-90), the standpoint of women is the starting point for a method of inquiry "that situates inquiry in the actualities of people's living" (1992:90). Her sociological inquiry begins with a woman, "the knower who is actually located; she is active ... at work ... (at home); ... hook(ed) into extended social relations linking her activities to those of other people and in ways beyond her knowing" (1992:91). Smith's goal is to discover women's experience and to link it to "the politics and practice of progressive struggle" (Smith, 1992:88).

There is a considerable body of literature which explores the interconnected relations of race, ethnicity, class and gender and how these relations in a historical and social organization context have an impact on the lives of women, especially immigrant women (e.g., Anthias and Yuval-Davis, 1983; Bannerji, 1987; Stasiulis, 1990; Ng, 1993). Ethnicity, race, class, caste and gender are dynamically interconnected or "enmeshed in each other," as Anthias and Yuval-Davis (1983) have so graphically expressed the interrelationship. Using Dorothy Smith's conceptualization (1987:2-6), they are constructed in "relations of ruling" into "a complex of organized practices, including government, law, business and financial management, professional organization, and educational institutions as well as the discourses in texts that interpenetrate the multiple sites of power."

In my studies, I have started from the standpoint of the South Asian immigrant women who described their everyday lived experience. I have attempted to explore "*from that perspective* the generalizing and generalized relations in which each individual's everyday world is embedded" (Smith, 1987:185). I have used a case study approach, individual, face-to-face, semi-structured interviews with the women and some limited participant observation in organizational activities.

The term "South Asian" is sociologically problematic. It encompasses many distinctly different ethnocultural groups. Being South Asian refers not so much to the personal qualities of individuals who come directly to Canada from the Indian subcontinent (India, Pakistan, Sri Lanka, Bangladesh), or else indirectly, through their ancestors, from East Africa, the Caribbean or Fiji, but rather to social characteristics which have been constructed and reconstructed in historical and ongoing social relationships in specific social, economic and political contexts. How South Asian immigrant women construct their identity and represent themselves tends to vary in terms of whom they are addressing. In conversations, few "South Asians" identify themselves as such. Some women, particularly older women, have adopted the European designation of "East Indian." More commonly, particularly where there are large concentrations of regional cultural groups, women will identify themselves as Pakistani, Punjabi, Bengali, Indo-Canadian, and so on. Such self-definitions set limits and boundaries between "the community" and other South Asian groups, as well as other Canadians. When an interviewer such as myself is cognizant of regional, religious and linguistic distinctions among people of the Indian subcontinent and the diaspora, then South Asian women will be extremely specific about representing their identity. In my study "South Asian" refers to women who trace their ancestral origins to the Indian subcontinent.

I argue that policies and programs, by focusing on cultural differences rather than on inequalities among ethnic and racial categories of people, have constructed and reconstructed gender and race inequity and that multiculturalism has done little to combat ethnocentrism, racism or sexism in the lived experience of South Asian immigrant women. At the same time, the women have become sensitized to the racist and sexist organization of "relations of ruling" (Smith, 1987) in their lived experience, have resisted alienating activities through community organization, and have become active subjects in transforming their lived world.

Although much has been written about South Asian immigrants, it is the failure of previous research to take account of gender and race differences in their migration experience and of gender, race and regional differences in their settlement experience that has provided the major impetus for this comparative study. The field work was conducted in Atlantic Canada between 1988 and 1991, and in British Columbia between November 1993 and December 1994. Initially, I interviewed three women (not included in the sample) who told their personal stories of migration to and settlement in Canada. These interviews provided a guide for the formulation of a semi-structured interview schedule which was used in an exploratory study with 16 women in metropolitan Halifax (Ralston, 1988). It is important to understand the continuities and the breaks in the lives of South Asian migrant women attendant upon their entry into an advanced capitalist society such as Canada. The interview therefore covered such topics as place of birth, social background and early family history, the historical and social circumstances surrounding their emigration from the source country, educational training and work experience prior to migration and in Canada, and household and paid work experience in Canada. Since ethnic institutions (such as ethnic associations, temples, mosques, gurdwaras, churches, synagogues and other religious organizations, schools, language classes, community-oriented businesses, newspapers, other media, and the arts) play a significant part in the construction, maintenance and reproduction of ethnic difference and ethnic identity, the interview also examined religious, cultural, social and organizational activities of the women in Metro Halifax. General questions allowed for elaboration on more sensitive issues, such as isolation, loneliness and discrimination and for the introduction of any important topic not covered in the questionnaire. Finally, each woman was asked to describe in detail the activities of "a typical day" in her life — her response being categorized as "The Daily Round" in the analysis stage of the studies. As interviewer, I introduced myself as an immigrant woman from Australia who had no relatives in Canada and who had, at the time of the interviews, spent two years living, working and travelling throughout India and Sri Lanka. Each interview was of approximately one and a half to two hours duration and was conducted either at the immigrant woman's home or workplace at her preferred time; in rare instances, I interviewed women at my own home. This pilot or exploratory study provided guidelines for the major qualitative study in the four provinces of Atlantic Canada (Ralston, 1996). The interview provided a prospectus of the life each immigrant woman left behind in her source country and placed her in Canadian society at the time of the interview. It also revealed to me the heterogeneity of national, religious and linguistic backgrounds among South Asian women in the region.

In the 1986 census of Canada there were approximately 3,800 South Asians scattered throughout the four Atlantic provinces. About half the South Asian population resided in Nova Scotia, with nearly 40 percent in the Halifax Census Metropolitan Area (CMA). A directory prepared by the Indo-Canadian Association of Nova Scotia (INCA, 1988) proved to be a useful tool for drawing the sample in the three maritime provinces of Nova Scotia, New Brunswick and Prince Edward Island. In addition, at St. John's, Newfoundland, the Chinmaya Mission produced a directory of people in Newfoundland of South Asian cultural origin and of diverse religions (other than Islam, since Muslims did not wish to be included). These directories were considered by several informants to give a fairly comprehensive listing of the relatively small population of South Asians in the region, since the list was not based on membership in an association but rather on self-identification or identification by other South Asians.

Since I was interested in exploring how region of settlement influenced lived experience of South Asian women of diverse backgrounds, my Atlantic Canada sample was drawn randomly from these two directories, in proportion to the census distribution of South Asians in the four provinces. I purposely identified South Asian Muslim women in Newfoundland, so as to include three Muslim women of different national backgrounds in the sample and compare their experience with that of women of other community backgrounds. The total Atlantic Canada sample comprised 126 first-generation immigrant women aged 15 years and over, one tenth of the estimated total population of South Asian women of that age in the Atlantic region at the time. I conducted all the Atlantic Canada interviews myself.

In British Columbia, it was not possible to draw a similar sample. There was no list of eligible participants for the study. In metropolitan

Vancouver there was only a Business Directory available but it was inappropriate for the purposes of this project. As an alternative, a preliminary indication of the ethnic, linguistic, and religious composition of the South Asian category was obtained from 1991 Census data (Statistics Canada, 1993) and from lists of organization members and contact persons of the Vancouver Multicultural Society of British Columbia and other similar societies. With the help of key informants and resource persons in the heterogeneous South Asian community and in government and non-governmental organizations, a snowballing method was used, with a deliberate attempt to select women of diverse ages, class, community backgrounds, countries of origin and dates of entry into Canada and to locate women who were *not* organization members. Again, the total sample of one hundred women in British Columbia was drawn from first-generation immigrant women aged 15 years and over, in proportion to the distribution of South Asians in British Columbia. In the 1991 Census, the South Asian population in British Columbia had grown to 103,545 (from 69,250 in the 1986 Census). Of these, 75,430 (73 percent) resided in the Vancouver Census Metropolitan Area (CMA). Because the study included Indo-Fijians, who numbered 4,945 in British Columbia (with 4,640 of these in the Vancouver CMA), 74 of the total one hundred women were interviewed in the Vancouver CMA; 26 from other places in British Columbia. A research assistant, Emily Burton, conducted 45 interviews in Vancouver; I conducted the remaining interviews myself.

SUMMARY PROFILES OF THE SAMPLES OF WOMEN

The women were of very diverse national, linguistic and religious backgrounds — 14 birth countries, 15 mother tongues, 6 religious affiliations (with one British Columbia woman of no religious affiliation). Predominately, in both samples, they were Indian-born, with Punjabi or Hindi mother tongue, and of Hindu or Sikh religion.

Marital status and Migration

Almost all of the women (94 percent in Atlantic Canada; 82 percent in British Columbia) were married at the time of the interviews. In British Columbia, seven women were divorced or separated; in Atlantic Canada none were. In each sample, 6 percent were widowed. Except for one British Columbia woman, the sole single woman from Atlantic

Canada and the five British Columbia single women, were less than 32 years of age. Only 10 percent of the Atlantic Canada sample and 13 percent of the British Columbia sample were married in Canada. Among the married women, 75 percent of the Atlantic Canada sample and 69 percent of the British Columbia sample had entered into arranged (or what some chose to call "semi-arranged") marriages. By "semi-arranged" they meant that their parents had consulted relatives and members of their own caste and religious community or had placed advertisements in newspapers to find potential candidates for marriage with their daughter. A key person in an arranged marriage is the relative or friend who acts as "go-between" in bringing potential partners together. The woman might or might not have been previously acquainted with any one of the candidates. She was free to agree or disagree with the proposed marriage and she could express preference among the candidates. The man had similar freedom to accept or reject the proposed marriage. Marriage for the participants of the study generally implied a religious-legal union which determined gender relations in the family. India, for example, does not have a uniform civil code, despite ongoing efforts of the women's movement to obtain one. Marriage and family affairs of each religious community in India are governed by "personal law," that is, the law is based on the religion of the community. "Personal" marriage and family laws predominantly characterize the gender subordination of Indian women, particularly in the domestic sphere.

Age and Migration

In general terms, the Atlantic Canada sample had a higher proportion of women under 35 years of age than the latter sample. The later sample had a higher proportion (22 percent) of women over 55 years. In both samples 60 percent or more of the women were between the ages of 35 and 55 years, with Atlantic Canada having the higher percentage in that age bracket; in both, the majority of the women (60 percent in Atlantic Canada and 56 percent in British Columbia) had migrated between the ages of 20 and 30 years and about 80 percent in both samples were under 40 years. In other words, for the most part, they had come as young married women in their child-bearing years. Many had come through an arranged marriage contract.

Although immigration data have indicated that a handful of South Asian immigrants (five in total) gave one or other of the Maritime provinces as destination province from 1926 onward, there were no recorded South Asian residents in Atlantic Canada until the 1951 Census, and then only 26 in all 4 provinces (16 males and 10 females). In 1951 a special quota agreement was established between the Canadian state and the Asian members of the British Commonwealth. Its terms were that, commencing in 1951, there was to be an annual admission of 150 citizens of India; in addition, the wife, husband or the unmarried child under the age of 21 of a Canadian citizen of Indian origin was to be admitted. In 1952 the agreement was extended to permit one hundred nationals of Pakistan and fifty nationals of Ceylon to enter. In 1957 the quota for Indian nationals was raised to three hundred immigrants per year (Ralston, 1994).

In both research samples, the majority of the women entered Canada between 1965 and 1980 — 70 percent of the Atlantic Canada women; 65 percent of the British Columbia women. The 126 Atlantic Canada women had been in Canada an average of 17 years, the longest resident having immigrated in 1956 under the Indian quota system, the most recent in 1988. Only 13 women (10 percent) entered Canada prior to 1965; 74 women (59 percent) entered between 1965 and 1975, with the mode being 27 women (21 percent) between 1967 and 1969; and thereafter, 30 women (24 percent) arrived between 1975 and 1985.

The one hundred British Columbia women had been in Canada an average of 18 years, with the mode being 22 years of residence. The longest resident migrated in 1949, the most recent in 1994. Some women were spouses or offspring of Canadian-born Punjabi men who had arranged marriages in India. In fact, one woman's grandfather was a British Columbia settler in the early 1900s. Fifteen women arrived prior to 1965; 37 additional women between 1965 and 1975; and thereafter, 25 women between 1975 and 1985.

Education and Migration

The majority of women in both samples were highly educated at the time of their entry into Canada, with 82 percent in Atlantic Canada and 63 percent in British Columbia being educated beyond high school level. Only in the British Columbia sample was there a significant number of women with less than high school education.

Almost two-thirds of the women in each sample (63 percent in both Atlantic Canada and British Columbia) pursued further education after migration to Canada. The women in the Atlantic Canada sample reflected 1986 Census data, which gave 85 percent of South Asian women in Atlantic Canada as having university or other post-secondary highest levels of education (Statistics Canada, 1989). The 1986 census data for Atlantic Canada indicated that women of South Asian origin were much more highly educated than Atlantic Canadian women of all ethnic groups.

Lived Experience upon Settlement

As I have noted above, immigration policies and regulations of the late 1960s and 1970s favoured the entrance to Canada of men who could successfully integrate economically into the industrial development of Canada, particularly in areas where native-born Canadians did not wish to settle. One Atlantic Canada woman's story aptly described the migration experience of several others who entered Canada during that period.

That time [the early sixties] the Canadian government needed lots of doctors, they didn't have enough. So they [hospitals] organized all our visas and everything. We didn't have to go to the immigration offices or anything.... Whatever hospitals he applied to, they just looked for a house for us. And when we came, we had some place to get into. Of course the rent was our responsibility.

As Kalbach (1990:40) has pointed out, however, the facilitation of economic integration of male immigrants does not necessarily ensure successful social integration or moderate the ethnic and racial prejudice of other Canadian residents toward immigrant men or women. South Asian immigrant women, upon arrival in Canada, often experience alienation and discrimination. Their visible and audible differences in characteristics such as skin colour, language or accent, religion, dress, food customs and so on, identify them as "immigrant women."

The qualitative face-to-face interviews produced an abundance of empirical material which described the women's lived experience of migration and settlement in Canada. In exploring that lived experience, for analytic purposes, in this paper I consider five topics: 1) housing; 2) English language fluency and training; 3) getting an initial job outside the home; 4) lack of recognition for education, training and work experience gained before migration; and 5) ongoing work experience in the paid labour force. In particular, I examine the interconnections of eth-nocentrism, racism, class and gender with the woman's lived experience of settlement and of their daily activities outside the home in the work force and in the larger community. As in all qualitative analysis, the issue is not so much a quest for generalization "but rather an under-standing of the conditions under which a particular finding appears and operates." (Janesick, 1994:215). In Dorothy Smith's qualitative method of inquiry, the issue is to explore and map "actual organization and relations that are invisible but *active* [her emphasis] in the every-day/everynight sites where people take up resistance and struggle, (and to produce) a knowledge that extends and expands their and our grasp of how things are put together and hence their and our ability to orga-nize and act effectively" (1992:96).

Housing

Getting a suitable house on arrival in Canada was an issue for only eight of the Atlantic Canada women, and only thirteen of them had ever experienced difficulties in housing. In no case was the problem attributed to state policy. Ten women attributed the difficulty to a shortage of suitable housing. However, three women reported incidents in which they experienced racial discrimination. For example, one woman, a highly qualified professional who had migrated 18 years prior to the interview, had difficulties for five years in her interaction with neighbours. The immigrant woman's different style of dress became the object of verbal abuse prompted by racism. The size and kind of housing the family could afford because of their high family income also provoked verbal abuse based on race and class conflict.

When we built, the neighbour up back for the first five years gave us a hard time. He kept bugging us about not getting landscaping done. She didn't want to see my kind of clothing on the line. She hung hers out all the time, but she didn't want to see mine. It took me a while to understand what she meant. The first couple of years I didn't want to step out. I kept thinking, "she's watching me."... When we bought a second lot, the man next door to her complained, "You take our jobs and build big houses."... There were neighbours who wanted a fist fight. If people have a problem, if they have something on their mind, if they are provoked, that triggers them to say things.

We hear the woman trying for a time to understand the neighbour's racist behaviour, but later, with understanding, she resists and gets on with her own life.

Other Atlantic Canada women found that race made no difference to their getting suitable housing. One woman summed up her experience as follows, "When we came (in 1967), it was only a matter of money. If you paid the money, you got the house. That's the impression I got."

In the British Columbia sample, 23 women described difficulties about getting suitable housing. The nature of the difficulty varied considerably — most commonly, lack of money to pay rent, problems in renting an apartment because of having children or with landlords because of children's noise. For example: "With a kid, it's hard to find housing. The caretaker gave us notice that we can't stay with a kid. We went to several places. When they see you with a kid, they say no." Other difficulties were living with in-laws and extended families, "living in a basement apartment in a stranger's house," and being a divorced or separated mother supporting children.

For some British Columbia women, racism was an explicit factor in housing discrimination. For example, three women recounted the following stories of how race and class interacted in their experiences. The first stated,

We had all kinds [of housing problems].... We lived in a small place. It was too small when our daughters arrived. We looked for rental accommodations. We found a house we liked. We set up an appointment. Everything was fine. Next day, we went to give the deposit and the guy said he wouldn't rent to us. He gave excuses. The bottom line — because we're coloured. We were established, both members of Lions Club. We didn't think we would gain anything by pursuing the matter.... Eventually we got in a brand new building.

The second woman related,

We had three weeks at [a five-star] hotel for house hunting at government expense. We went looking for a house. We found one. The owner had to get permission from the neighbours (to sell it to us). They found out my husband was a scientist and a professor. We found out that he [the owner] was a carpenter who went to 7th grade.

And the third woman reported,

When we wanted to go to X Avenue, I phoned. I went to see a duplex,
to get the key from neighbours. I saw it, liked it. I went to sign the lease,
dressed in a sari. I was plump. The man saw me. "The situation's changed,"
he said; "the landlady wants to come and live there. She doesn't want to
rent." So I went to my husband's office and phoned three good friends —
a teacher, a Jewish lady, another (woman from my community). They all
phoned and asked for the place. They were told it was available, etc. I
phoned and asked for the general manager. I said I would write to the
attorney general.... [The manager] sent the key to my husband's office.
He became very friendly.

Two of these women consciously used superior class position
(based on the husband's occupation) as a powerful tool to resist racism.
It is also worth noting that the last woman threatened to resist race
discrimination by calling upon the powerfully placed attorney general,
who was in fact an Indo-Canadian.

English Language Fluency and Training

One interviewee summed up succinctly her optimism about the importance of English language for many immigrant women, when she stated, "Language (is the most important thing). Once you can speak, read,
write (English), you are home free." From the standpoint of an immigrant woman lack of fluency in the English language is one of the most
profoundly alienating experiences. As Schutz has noted, however, language as a scheme of interpretation and expression comprises more
than linguistic symbols and syntactical rules (Schutz, 1964:100-01). In
Schutz's terms, "Only members of the in-group have the scheme of
expression as a genuine one in hand and command it freely within their
thinking as usual" (101). The immigrant woman as outsider and newcomer is alienated by her lack of knowledge of the new linguistic cultural pattern and her inability to adopt it as her own mode of
expression. Once she has made it her own, she believes that she is free.
This assessment was confirmed by settlement workers, who made similar statements in different terms. Reality belies their belief.

Both the interviewee and the settlement workers have taken on
dominant ideologies as their own. Patricia Marchak has observed that
such observance is essential if the ruling class is to maintain its hege-
mony (Marchak, 1975:98, 115). Certainly, state programs indicate
that lack of fluency in the English language is assumed to be a funda-

mental cause of immigrants' "disadvantage." On the other hand, all the evidence has indicated that fluency in the English language may not necessarily lead to employment, and certainly not to employment commensurate with qualifications and experience in the source country. Unemployment or *under*employment is one of the greatest difficulties encountered by immigrant women in Canada, whether or not they have fluency in the English language.

In the two study samples, 63 percent of the Atlantic Canada women and 74 percent of the British Columbia women spoke English fluently, or at least functionally, on arrival in Canada. To a certain extent the Canadian linguistic cultural patterns were familiar to them, especially if they had been educated in a British colonial educational system. Nevertheless, some women who had considered themselves completely fluent in English before migration had difficulty in understanding variations in accent, pronunciation and vocabulary, especially colloquialisms and slang. They remained "outsiders" in everyday relationships with those for whom English was an integral part of their culture.

Among the women in each sample who had little or no English on arrival about half stated that English as a Second Language (ESL) classes had not been available to them, for reasons such as their cost, child care and other household responsibilities, and the need for paid work outside the home. The comments of these women supported the findings of the Law Union of Ontario that immigrant women tend to be more isolated than immigrant men from participation in the mainstreams of society (Law Union of Ontario, 1981:234). They carry disproportionate responsibility for household activities and child care; they have fewer opportunities for learning, or for improving their command of, the English language; they have more limited employment and job-training opportunities. The women were, in effect, more alienated from the institutions of society.

Women who immigrated in more recent years have had greater access to ESL classes through federally funded programs like the 1992 Language Instruction for Newcomers to Canada (LINC) and the Labour Market Language Training (LMLT), offered through intercultural or ethnospecific community organizations (EIC, 1992). For example, British Columbia women spoke of ESL language training and other settlement services provided by organizations such as the Immigrant Services Society (ISS), MOSAIC, a multicultural service agency, the Intercultural Association of Greater Victoria, the Vancouver Community College, with the help of federal, provincial and/or municipal funding, or through self-paid private classes for a small group of women of similar first language, such as Punjabi. Despite the numerous settlement agencies in British Columbia settlement workers stated that the needs of immigrant women far exceed the services and funds provided. In addition, some women argued for English language-training through community organizations that are culturally sensitive and in which a woman would feel comfortable and not feel embarrassed because of age, ignorance or other factors.

Being fluent in English or French is clearly a key element for all immigrants in getting paid work outside the home. Ramkhalawansingh (1981) stressed the importance of language training for integration of immigrant women. Research has shown that the lower labour force participation for women, higher unemployment, occupational and industrial concentration and lower wages are all associated with inability to converse in English or French (Rao, Richmond and Zubrzycki, 1984; Beaujot, Basavarajappa and Verma, 1988; Boyd, 1990).

Inability to converse in the language of the society can, however, create an even more profound experience of alienation. One British Columbia woman expressed this lived reality succinctly.

It's impossible to *live* without the language. If English is only for work, that's wrong. English is for survival. Otherwise you're insecure; not a human being; not considered valuable enough.... You have a right to know the language of the country you belong to.... You're ignored by family, by children, by neighbours, because you don't speak the language. Men have better education to begin with. They get on with their lives. English classes for women is a gender issue. Women being housebound is a disaster. They cannot pay for classes.

This woman highlighted the gender discrimination involved in linking free English-language training to work and the long-term social consequences for women if they cannot communicate in English in all areas of life, both within and outside the home. They become alienated from social relations with children, family, neighbours, as well as other institutions of the larger society. Anderson and Lynam (1987) examined the experiences of Indo-Canadian and Greek women employed in the lower echelons of the Canadian labour force, the majority of whom were unable to communicate fluently in English. They argued that the problems experienced by immigrant women should be understood not only in terms of their "cultural" differences, but also in the context of the larger social organization and ideological structures which generate particular types of experience. Giles (1988) has argued that linking women's access to government language courses with training allowances must be understood in the larger context of human rights.

Over ten years ago, Monica Boyd (1986) found that the treatment of immigrant women as "dependants" in the immigration admissions process had far-reaching consequences for their experiences in Canada. Initially, such a status could serve to disqualify them from government-sponsored language-training programs and from the training allowances associated with such programs. She concluded that stratification by language had three consequences: first, it contributed to the socioeconomic stratification of immigrant females; second, it intensified problems of isolation among those immigrant women who lacked familiarity with one or other of the two official languages; and finally, it reinforced female dependency on the male head of the household. My findings have confirmed these conclusions.

Getting an Initial Job Outside the Home

It was when the women entered (or tried to enter) the paid labour force that their experience of discrimination was most marked. In Atlantic Canada, 48 percent of the women had experienced difficulties in trying to get a job, and in British Columbia, 45 percent. Many of them found that they were socially defined as "different" because of educational qualifications, language, Third World origin, skin colour, work experience (or lack of Canadian work experience), and the like. Being "different" was all too often construed as inferior. Racism was an evident factor in alienating women from the work force. For example, a British Columbia woman reported,

[The most difficult thing] was discrimination. I would apply for a job. As soon as they'd see me, they'd say, "Sorry, the job has been filled." Once I called from a pay phone. I was told to come and apply. I went right away and was told the position was closed. Also, a friend from Australia went to see about a job. She was pushed on the ground by a man. He said, "You bitch niggers taking all our jobs."

Other women related similar stories of finding a job no longer available when they turned up in person after receiving a positive response to an application by a phone call.

A British Columbia woman, recounted her story of frustration in getting a job, as follows: "I want to work. I have gone to interviews but I didn't get the job. A fabric place. A chemical lab. I got called for an interview but never told why I am not hired. They do not like me. My English is not good. That's the main reason, I think. They ask, 'Have you experience in Canada?' No job."

This woman's story highlights her experience of alienation, her attempt to make sense of her experience and a recurrent theme, the catch-22 demand for "Canadian experience" and the complete discounting of experience gained in a foreign country. It is important to analyze the possible meaning of this lack of recognition of education, language and work experience that were obtained in the source country.

LACK OF RECOGNITION IN THE SOURCE COUNTRY

In Atlantic Canada, 41 percent and in British Columbia, 40 percent of the women in the respective samples stated that educational qualifications from their source country were not recognized or were downgraded or required recertification in Canada. Women found that they were treated differently in terms of their national background, with people from non-English-speaking countries and non-white, so-called Third World countries, experiencing more discrimination than others. In other words, national, ethnic or racial background was de facto a basis for discrimination. Moreover, the women had to jump over innumerable social and financial hurdles to get professional certification or recertification. It is impossible to assess from the data whether or not the fact that a woman had English-medium instruction in her home country made any difference to recognition of qualifications. The rule of thumb appeared to be that a baccalaureate degree counted for no more than university entrance; a postgraduate degree *might* give a woman a first-degree equivalency.

One very dissatisfied woman in Atlantic Canada (who had just completed specialized training in the health professions and actually held a highly paid job) found that "being an immigrant" was the salient constructed "difference" which influenced structural discrimination in the work force. She stated, "It is not essentially because you are South Asian, but being *not* Canadian (by birth)." In other words, though *legally* Canadian, she was *socially constructed* as alien.

Some women found that they were in a double-bind situation because of their qualifications. The superior class position they had held in their home country because of their educational qualifications was discounted in Canada. They found that they had to have a superior performance in exams or work just to be treated equally with other Canadians. As one woman put it, "You have to be first among the first to succeed as well as a (native-born) Canadian." Another stated, "It's hard to be a foreigner; I have to get 100 percent to get a job." On the other hand, they were too qualified for government training programs. One Atlantic Canada woman reported,

I think if you are *not* qualified you are fine, because you could do anything. You could start something. When you want to go to a program in Manpower and Immigration, if you have a degree they are not even going to look at you. They say you have a degree. But you take that degree and go for a job and they say, "Oh, we don't know this degree. We won't hire you." They won't say it in so many words, but that's the implication. So I think you lose out on both ends. You will not be taken for any of these Manpower programs because you are already too qualified.

Women in British Columbia spoke of the need for "help in evaluation of credentials; training to know the Canadian system; ways of transferring skills to the Canadian work place; labour market training; and job placement (to offset lack of Canadian experience)." As one woman remarked, "Sometimes you feel you have to work harder to be recognized here than in your own country.... There's resentment that immigrants are taking up all the jobs. My answer is that we are all immigrants except native people."

This woman's experience illustrated the inextricable linkage of race, gender and class, as well as the covert racism involved in imposing higher expectations of performance from an immigrant who belongs to a visible minority. It affirmed the anti-immigrant ideological stance on the costs of immigration to the Canadian-born members of the labour force. Her observation also indicated her conception of a multicultural Canada as a nation of immigrants — except for Aboriginal people.

Many researchers (e.g., Boyd, 1976, 1987; Satzewich and Li, 1987; Rajagopal, 1990) have noted the difficulty immigrants (both men and women) find in having their educational qualifications assessed. An (anonymous) reviewer of my paper has argued that "foreign qualifications are not equivalent [to Canadian] in critical ways, and that is the crux of the problem; [that] ... even Canadian trained physicians have trouble getting residencies of appropriate kinds."

I am not aware of any specific case of race discrimination against overseas trained doctors which has been submitted to a Canadian Human Rights Commission. I have, however, read the reasons for a decision delivered by the Human Rights and Equal Opportunity Commission of Australia under the Commonwealth Racial Discrimination Act 1975 (1995) in favour of an overseas trained complainant who was an Indian-born doctor. The complaint of racial discrimination was lodged against the Australian Medical Council (AMC). In their concluding remarks, the Commissioners (Sir Ronald Wilson, Elizabeth Hastings and Jenny Morgan) observed,

We find that the imposition of the quota, in the circumstances of its application, has impaired the enjoyment of that right [to work consistently with his/her qualifications and experience] on an equal footing with graduates of accredited medical schools by persons of a national origin other than Australia and New Zealand. *We find, further that a substantial number of persons of the same national origin as the complainant — that is, of Indian origin — has suffered the impairment* [my emphasis].... We believe the evidence in this case has exposed an intolerable situation which calls for urgent remedial action by the AMC and the relevant Governments. In its present form, the system governing the admission of OTDs (overseas trained doctors) is grossly unfair, resulting in unnecessary trauma, frustration and a deep sense of injustice in many doctors, their families and friends.... Furthermore, we regret to have to say that we were disappointed in the apparent inability of the respondents to appreciate the depth of the sense of injustice that the experience of the complainant has induced. We invited the parties to participate in a conciliation process in the hope that a spirit of compromise might enable some resolution of the difficulties confronting both the complainant and the respondents. But the respondents were unable to move beyond the bunker of their legal security and so any meaningful process of conciliation was doomed at the threshold. Frankly, we find it scandalous that Dr Siddiqui should have satisfied the minimum requirements of the MCQ (Multiple Choice Questionnaire) examination with a margin to spare on no less than three occasions but been prevented by (the manner of administering) the quota from proceeding to the clinical examination (33-35).

Certainly, one cannot argue from the Australian situation that a substantial number of overseas trained doctors of Indian origin has experienced racial discrimination in obtaining certification in Canada.

The point of including this decision in favour of a complainant in Australia is to demonstrate how powerful institutions like the Australian Medical Council and state health departments and their agents can and do impact on human rights and can be oppressive and unjust in the everyday lived experience of *foreign-trained* (as distinct from native-born, home-trained) professionals who try to work according to their qualifications and professional experience. In Dorothy Smith's framework, this case illustrates, explores and explicates the relations of ruling and organization pervading but largely invisible in the everyday world (Smith, 1992:91).

Liddle and Joshi have observed that South Asian professional women who have sought employment in Western countries have found that ideas of gender and race inferiority augmented the discrimination they encountered (Liddle and Joshi, 1986: 188-90). They have argued, moreover, that the notion of Indian women's inferiority to Western women is to be understood in the context of cultural imperialism and the power relations between the West and the Third World. Whereas the *class* position of South Asian professional women may be advantageous, within the context of cultural imperialism they are at a disadvantage compared with their Western counterparts.

According to women in both eastern and western regions of Canada, racism played an explicit role in their failure to get work.

You are looked upon as if you don't know anything or have a language problem, or will not do the job properly. They have these notions of Indian people. [They] won't even sit down and talk to me as soon as they see the colour of my skin. That really pains me. Why would they take it for granted that, okay, her colouring is brown, she must be from India, maybe she doesn't know anything, doesn't know English, doesn't have skills. [They] don't ask what you do know. Sometimes you apply for jobs and they do job interviews and close the file just to show, "We have interviewed so many ethnic women." They give the job to a mainstream person. It is very painful for us people not to utilize our skills. We are very hard working people and have a lot to give. If only someone would make an effort to take from us [what we do have to give]. Don't say, "You don't have B.C. experience." Or now, sometimes they say that I am *over*qualified.

This woman's statement is packed with many elements of racism — the assumption of ignorance because of skin colour; the assumption that her skills are useless, that the Indian woman has nothing to contribute or that whatever skills she has are valueless; the duplicity of tokenism in conducting the interview; the substitution of lack of "Canadian experience" as the overt reason for not hiring a person, when racism is the actual hidden reason.

Other women had similar stories to tell of race discrimination. For example: "[There's] quite a bit of racism. It won't show openly. You talk on the phone. They say they have the position available. You show up in person and they ask about your background. They're not so sure then. They ask for Canadian experience."

Such reports raise the serious question as to whether not having "Canadian experience" can be used as a form of racial discrimination that cannot be challenged by a Human Rights Commissioner. Rajagopal has raised questions about why Indo-Canadians in Ontario have been unable to obtain employment consonant with their qualifications (Rajagopal, 1990:98). He has suggested that the invisible glass ceiling may have its roots in their ethnicity. Today, in Melbourne, Australia, according to Joyce Rebeiro, Access and Equity Officer, City of Greater Dandenong, migrants refer to the *concrete* ceiling, because they cannot even see what is unavailable to them. South Asian immigrant women in Australia have similar stories to relate of race discrimination in terms of lack of recognition and downgrading of overseas qualifications and experience.

EXPERIENCE IN THE PAID LABOUR FORCE

Despite their relatively high educational and occupational qualifications, at the time of the interviews only 48 percent of the Atlantic Canada sample were working outside the home in the paid labor force. In contrast, in the British Columbia sample, 63 percent were working outside the home. It must be noted that, in general, Atlantic Canada has a relatively high unemployment rate compared to the rest of Canada, and certainly in comparison with British Columbia, with its fast-growing economy.

While the majority of immigrant women in Canada — especially if they are non-white — tend to be in the lower-paid, less skilled and less secure traditionally female occupations (Boyd, 1975, 1984, 1986; Ng and Ramirez, 1981), previous research has indicated that immigrant women are bimodally distributed in the occupational structure (Arnopoulos, 1979; Boyd, 1975, 1986; Stasiulis, 1986), a high percentage of them being concentrated in the more skilled and professional occupations. For some non-white immigrant women — including South Asians — the bimodal occupation distribution is replicated. Jabbra and Cosper found that South Asian women in Atlantic Canada were greatly over-represented in management, teaching, and medicine, and were above average in clerical positions and social sciences (Jabbra and Cosper, 1988:22-24). In British Columbia, there is a tendency toward bimodal distribution, with South Asian immigrant women working in unskilled occupations, like berry-picking and other farm work (Singh, 1987), in unskilled cleaning jobs, as well as in skilled business and professional occupations.

A high percentage of women in both research samples worked as medical or health care professionals, as social workers or counsellors, as teachers and librarians, as accountants (55 percent in Atlantic Canada; 38 percent in British Columbia); 3 percent in Atlantic Canada and 8 percent in British Columbia were semi-professionals, like lab assistants. Administrative personnel comprised 6 percent in Atlantic Canada and 6 percent in British Columbia. Only in British Columbia were there any self-employed large business owners (3 percent, representing just 2 women); 5 percent in Atlantic Canada were self-employed small business owners. Secretaries, book-keepers, cashiers, clerks and salespersons comprised 22 percent of the Atlantic Canada sample, 21 percent of the British Columbia sample. Skilled manual workers, technicians, and skilled machine operators comprised 3 percent in Atlantic Canada and 11 percent in British Columbia. Unskilled workers comprised 5 percent in Atlantic Canada and 13 percent in British Columbia.

Only 44 Atlantic Canada women (35 percent) and 39 British Columbia women (39 percent) had worked prior to migration as well as in Canada at the time of their interview. Case studies of many of these women revealed experiences of *under*employment. Many of the women in both samples were in jobs of low status and low pay which gave them few social benefits and little control over their lives. The experience of frustration in getting paid work outside the home in Atlantic Canada was greater for women with graduate degrees who had worked in their source country than for those women who were less highly qualified. For example, a medical doctor was an assistant health professional; some university and college teachers were research assistants, small business workers, or not working outside the home; public school teachers were in unskilled work or unemployed; nurses were working in unskilled health occupations or were unemployed.

Race, class, gender and region of settlement were inextricably interconnected in the women's lived experience of work discrimination. As one Atlantic Canada woman put it, "For women of colour it's difficult to find jobs, *particularly in a place where few jobs are available*" (my emphasis). Three women spoke of the complete lack of job opportunities in their geographical area for women with their advanced science qualifications. Not only could they find no research jobs, but they were also designated as "too qualified" for high school teaching or else were told that there was a surplus of teachers. Some women who had practised as medical doctors in the source country found it impossible to work as such in Atlantic Canada — either they could not get an internship or they were unable to take the necessary time for studying and writing certification exams. In several cases, the wife was unable to take accreditation exams because it was assumed that the husband had priority for similar studies and exams. Gender subordination and sexual division of labour operated materially by giving the woman responsibility for housework and child care and by placing the man in the paid work force.

There were some women in both Atlantic Canada and British Columbia who told of positive experiences in the paid-work world. In the first place, 19 of the Atlantic Canada women who had never worked in their source country were currently working in well-paid jobs in education, health professions and accountancy, or as book keepers and administrative secretaries; six women were in low-paid sales, cashier, secretarial and factory jobs; three women were self-employed in profitable small businesses. All of these women but one (a low-paid cashier) enjoyed their work. Work outside the home gave them some economic and social independence and a measure of control over their own lives. Similarly, in the British Columbia sample, some women related how they had worked hard and "made it" as immigrant women. For instance, women working in the health professions, as administrative secretaries or in their own successful businesses made comments such as the following,

I didn't say, "I am coloured, I am different, so I can't do things." I haven't experienced difficulties. I would defend Canada any time. This is my home now.... Canada is a wonderful country to live in. You can do anything, make money, get ahead.

Many things [have gone well for me here]. I have a good career, good health, good friends, financial security. It's a beautiful city to live in. The kids are settled with good jobs and health. I feel generally quite settled. I have time to do things that are close to my heart.

Both these women had migrated in the early 1970s when they were in their twenties. Both had a professional degree or diploma but had found difficulty in getting their first job because of lack of Canadian experience. Both overcame the difficulty of getting paid work by taking a first job for which they were overqualified. Then they moved ahead in their careers through superior performance in a job requiring fewer qualifications.

Community Organization. Elsewhere (Ralston, 1992, 1995b, 1997), I have documented and analyzed the part played by ethnoreligious and ethnocultural community organizations in the personal and social identity reconstruction of South Asian immigrant women and in their proactive resistance to race and gender discrimination. In both British Columbia and Atlantic Canada community organizations provided a context where people could meet and share their consciousness of common identity, language, tradition, and values and where they could foster the formation of an ethnic identity in their children. They also provided needed social, cultural, recreational and spiritual services. Organizations promoted group cohesion among the members and integration within the host society, especially for newcomers. At the same time, they served to establish boundaries not only between themselves, other immigrants and other Canadians, but also between South Asian immigrants of specific regional, cultural, linguistic and religious backgrounds. They helped create an ethnic South Asian Canadian identity which was specific and distinct.

One British Columbia woman summed up well the perspective of many interviewees. In bell hooks's terms, she claimed marginality or difference as "more than a site of deprivation" — as also a position of strength, "a site of radical possibility, a space of resistance" (hooks, 1990:149-50).

I know I'm different from other women. I think differently. I don't get discouraged soon. That keeps me going. This is my personal self evaluation. I set my priorities. I didn't realize these qualities in myself until I came here. You take a deep plunge and see the depth of the river.... Situations at work feel and are different. People are talking about you — the way you do things [or the way you] are dressed. If you can resist this, people start to respect you — if you are happy with who you are and your identity.

This immigrant woman was indeed empowered. She had resisted the consequences of the alienating experience of migration and reconstructed her own identity. She had become an agent in transforming her lived world.

In Metropolitan Vancouver many middle-class South Asian immigrant women were actively organized in advocacy-oriented groups to promote consciousness-raising, education, and change among men and among working-class grassroots women in areas of specific concern — violence against women, reproductive technology and amniocentesis clinics, racism, and recognition of foreign credentials and experience. For example, it was above all through advocacy organizations, like India Mahila Association (IMA), that British Columbia women, particularly in Metropolitan Vancouver, resisted violence in the family and struggled to create alternative new worlds. Organizations like the Vancouver Society of Immigrant and Visible Minority Women have targeted specific professions — teaching, accountancy and social work — and, with the cooperation of professional associations like the Teachers' Federation, have provided workshops and produced booklets which help to overcome the seemingly insurmountable hurdles immigrant women meet in trying to get a job in line with their qualifications and experience (Ralston, 1995; 1997).

In Atlantic Canada, advocacy goals and change in structures and relations were not the basis for organization, nor were critical gender issues the matter of discourse or action. I have speculated elsewhere about various demographic, historical and social factors that might account for the glaring difference in advocacy organization between British Columbia and Atlantic Canada (Ralston, 1995:140-42). Suffice it to note here that, first, the range of class among South Asians of British Columbia was broader than in Atlantic Canada, where most of the women were solidly middle-class in terms of their family background, their own and their husbands' education and occupation, and their family income. Second, in Metropolitan Vancouver, where there was a high level of proactive awareness of violence against women, networking and formal advocacy organizations became a reality among South Asian women. In Atlantic Canada, on the other hand, where the level of proactive awareness was lower at the time of the field work and where South Asians were relatively few in numbers, there was little or no support for advocacy goals.

CONCLUSION

The findings from the interviews have suggested that the women faced situations that were sometimes unique to them as *immigrant* women *of colour*; for example, the need for top performance in competition with native-born white Canadians to obtain scarce jobs. At other times, their experience was shared with other native-born Canadian *women*; for example, the need for top performance to get a typically "man's" job, such as financial comptroller.

The social and political construction of South Asian immigrant women as a visible minority immigrant category has a homogenizing effect which tends to ignore cultural and social differences among such migrants (Bai, 1992:23-26; Boyd, 1992:280; Das Gupta, 1994). The present research has indicated support for Stasiulis's contention that women and, I would add, visible minority women, cannot be treated as a homogeneous racial category (Stasiulis, 1990). Race interacts with gender and class in the historical and social organizational lived experience of these immigrant women of colour in Canada.

Moreover, one has to take into account the interconnectedness of race, class and gender in specific geographic contexts; for example, the location of the immigrant women (and men, for that matter) at the centre or the periphery of the Canadian political economy. The experience of visible minority women in the economically dependent region of Atlantic Canada, where few immigrants settle, was different from that of women in the burgeoning economy of British Columbia, the settlement place of many Asian immigrants.

Government policies, as they have applied to *settlement* of immigrants — whether assimilation, integration, or multiculturalism — have tended to focus on cultural and linguistic *differences* rather than on *inequalities* in economic and political structures and gender inequities within and among ethnic and racial categories of people. Although Canada has not encouraged immigrant people to forget their past and assimilate to the dominant society, many of the multicultural programs suggest a hidden agenda for assimilation, or at best integration, into the dominant society. As Gill Bottomley has noted, a focus on cultural activities can "distract attention away from the central problem of structural inequalities and access to resources" (Bottomley,

1988:5). The emphasis on *cultural* pluralism and cultural and linguistic *difference* masks race, class and gender inequalities and inequities.

Multiculturalism is a term used to describe the social reality of ethnic and racial diversity, as well as federal policy that informs settlement of immigrants. As Jean Burnet astutely noted in the early days of Canadian multiculturalism, one reason for the failure of multicultural policy to fulfil hopes even in the 1970s was the change in the kind of immigrants entering the country. The immigrants from the late 1960s onward were increasingly from Asian, African and West Indian regions. "The important issues for them ... because of the recency of arrival, their visibility, and their relatively high educational qualifications, have to do with human rights, especially in the job market, rather than cultural or linguistic rights" (Burnet, 1978:109).

Multiculturalism has been referred to and analyzed by social scientists as an ideology (Hawkins, 1982; Kallen, 1982; Moodley, 1983; Bolaria and Li, 1985; Elliott and Fleras, 1990; Roberts and Clifton, 1982, 1990; Abu-Laban and Stasiulis, 1992; Lewycky, 1992). Like ethnicity and race, multiculturalism is a dynamic concept, not static. Its ideology has been transformed and reconstructed in the context of changing historical, economic and political circumstances. In fact, Lewycky (1992) has analyzed multiculturalism as being, above all, "a site of ideological struggle" (381-95). Further, Dorothy Smith has argued that "those who occupy the positions from which ideologies are produced are almost exclusively men" (Smith, 1975:353-69).

Multiculturalism as federal policy is based on the premise that recognition of cultural pluralism can foster social cohesion, equality and equity in society. Some 25 years since the policy was espoused, the reality is otherwise. Despite policies, rhetoric, strategies and programs that have extolled and attempted to institutionalize "the equality of all Canadians in the economic, social and political life of Canada" (Canada, 1988:836), ethnic, racial and sex discrimination and inequities still persist; the class structure within Canadian society (and within so-called "ethnic communities"), and gender inequities within the class structure, remain intact. South Asian immigrant women *are* alienated from what Dorothy Smith (1987) has called the "ruling apparatus of society."

Sandra Harding (1995) has argued for redefinition of the theoretical construct of multiculturalism as a theory of social conflict, which focuses on the dimensions and causes of conflict and inequality rather than the conditions of social order, if it is to "shed any light upon the process by which an existing society may approach cultural and structural equality." A feminist perspective assumes that conflict is inherent in society and that conflict is rooted in class and power struggles for control of society's resources. Membership status of ethnic categories of people — be it visible minority status or ethnic minority status — is characterized in terms of unequal power relations with dominant groups and structures of society. These are accompanied by differential and discriminatory treatment, particularly in situations of competition for scarce resources, such as jobs in the paid labour force. A critical feminist conflict approach to multiculturalism is an alternative paradigm for analysis, policy and action aimed at creating a gender-just and equitable democratic society, where the voices of visible immigrant minority women are heard and heeded and where their experience and productive labour are valued.

In practice, many South Asian women who have made the passage from India to Canada have achieved a positive reconstruction of personal and social identity. Above all, they have used community organizational activities to adopt a proactive antiracist and antisexist position of resistance to alienation, discrimination and unequal relations of ruling in Canadian society.

NOTES

1. I gratefully acknowledge funding for this research from three sources: two Social Sciences and Humanities Research Council of Canada grants and a Saint Mary's University Senate Research Grant. I thank the women interviewees who gave me hours of unpaid personal time. I also thank research assistants Emily Burton, M.A. (who conducted 45 interviews in Vancouver), Catherine Chandler, Lina Samuel and Colleen McMahon. Raminder Dosanjh has been an invaluable British Columbia resource person.

13

ACCULTURATION AND CHINESE DELINQUENCY

SIU KWONG WONG

THE NUMBER OF IMMIGRANTS arriving in Canada from Southeast Asia, especially from Hong Kong, Taiwan, and China, has increased substantially in recent years. Immigrants from Hong Kong and the People's Republic of China represented 7.8 percent and 6.1 percent of all immigrants who came to Canada between 1981 and 1991 (Badets, 1993). The population of Chinese background in major Canadian metropolises has reached a significant proportion. For example, in Vancouver, people of Chinese background, both immigrants and the native-born, represented about one tenth of the population as of 1991 (Renaud and Badets, 1993). The corresponding proportion in Toronto was about 6 percent. However, there is relatively little research on immigrants and their children in Canada and still less effort has been devoted to the study of delinquency of Chinese immigrant children.

In this chapter studies of both Chinese and non-Chinese Asian Americans or Asian Canadians are reviewed due to the shortage of delinquency research concerned solely with the Chinese in North America. Although Chinese Americans and Canadians do not share an identical history, culture, and social and economic situation with Japanese and Korean Americans and Canadians (see, for example, Kwong, 1990; Lyman, 1977; Portes and Zhou, 1993) it is quite probable that Asian immigrant groups had lower rates of crime, delinquency, and other deviances than nonimmigrants due to similar correlational factors.

ARE IMMIGRANT CHILDREN MORE DELINQUENT?

Mental health of immigrants. There are a few studies of Chinese immigrant and native-born children in relation to mental health issues (Chang, Morrissey and Koplewicz, 1995; Hisama, 1980; Huang and

Ying, 1989; Kingsbury, 1994; Sue and Sue, 1973). These studies have listed problems and difficulties common to Chinese immigrant youth in North America such as racial discrimination, low language proficiency, ethnic identity problems, intergenerational gap and conflict exacerbated by culture conflict, the decreased authority of immigrant parents, confusion of roles within the family, reduced parental supervision as a result of both immigrant parents working to meet financial needs, and excessive psychological pressures due to the "model minority" stereotype. Therefore, psychological and psychiatric problems should be quite common among Chinese immigrants (Huang and Ying, 1989). The relatively low official rates of disorders and under-utilization of mental health services may be due to under-reporting.

The preceding observation emphasizes the aggravating effects of social and economic disadvantages, weakening of the family, and the lack of social support among immigrants (Aronowitz, 1984). Immigrant children are prone to psychological, emotional, and behaviour disorders because of the various disadvantages. Due to their dislocation experience and the sudden change in social environment, they are deprived of the resources and support they used to enjoy in their home country. Moreover, they are deprived, compared to native-born children, in terms of language, friendship ties, sense of belonging, ethnic identity, and family support. As a result, they are prone to develop problems in the host country.

Delinquency. The number of studies on Chinese delinquency in North America is limited and most do not distinguish between immigrant and native-born children. Moreover, much of the past research focused on gang activities or organized crime, which are quite different from common delinquency (for example, see, Bresler, 1981; Kelly, Chin and Fagan, 1993; Joe, 1994; Posner, 1988; President's Commission on Organized Crime, 1984). Nonetheless, existing studies have found that Chinese youth are less involved in delinquency and other behavioural deviances than the general youth population (Abbott and Abbott, 1973; Akutsu, Sue, Zane and Nakamura, 1989; Bachman, Wallace, O'Malley, Johnston, Kurth and Neighbors, 1991; Barnes and Welte, 1986; Chi, Kitano and Lubben, 1988; Elder, Molgaard and Gresham, 1988; Kallarackal and Herbert, 1976; Kitano, 1973; Li, Su, Townes and Varley, 1989; Li and Rosenblood, 1994; O'Hare, 1995; Pogrebin and Poole, 1989; Schwitters, Johnson, Wilson and McClearn, 1982; Sue, Zane and Ito, 1979; Touliatos and Lindholm, 1980; Wilson, McClearn and Johnson, 1978; Welte and Barnes, 1987).

Thus, the notion that Chinese immigrant children are prone to delinquency appears paradoxical. On the one hand, many Chinese immigrant children, like immigrant and minority children of other ethnic groups, are socially and economically disadvantaged. As a group, the Chinese in North America are underemployed, receive lower wages, and have higher rates of poverty and illiteracy (Huang and Ying, 1989). There has been a long history of discrimination, unfair treatment, exploitation, and oppression of the Chinese in North America (Li, 1988; Tan and Roy, 1985; Wong, 1985). This treatment is likely to be the source of mental and behavioural disorders. For example, studies of West Indian children of immigrant parentage in Britain found that they were more likely to display behavioural disorders than children of native parentage (Bagley, 1972; Cochrane, 1979; Rutter, Yule, Berger, Yule, Morton and Bagley, 1974). Thus, there is the expectation that Chinese immigrant children, like other immigrant children, will also be plagued by behaviour disorders or deviances.

On the other hand, the social and economic disadvantages do not necessarily translate into increased behavioural deviance. In an extensive review of research studies and theoretical perspectives Aronowitz (1984) noted that the prevalence of emotional and social disorders was not higher for immigrant children than for the native-born population. Although it has been suggested that behavioural deviance may manifest itself in school more often than at home (see also Huang and Ying, 1989) there is little evidence that immigrant children actually display more conduct disorders in school than the native-born. In fact, the rates of delinquency and other deviances tend to be higher for the native-born. For example, Sue et al. (1979) observed that Asian American students whose families had been in North America for multiple generations consumed more alcohol than the first or second generations. The native-born are also more likely to be involved in crime and delinquency than first-generation immigrants (Kendis and Kendis, 1976; Pogrebin and Poole, 1989; Sellin, 1938), and they are more likely to become marginalized or militant (Sue and Sue, 1973; Hisama, 1980). To that extent, the existing evidence does not support the notion that Chinese immigrant children in North America are more prone to behavioural deviance than native-born children.

However, none of the studies reviewed actually compared Chinese immigrant children with Chinese native-born children. Instead, they compared children of immigrant parents with those of native parents of various racial and ethnic backgrounds. For example, Touliatos and

Lindholm (1980) compared 2,991 native-born and 97 children of immigrant parents. The latter group of children might or might not have been born in the United States. In other words, a fair number of children of foreign descent in their sample were actually native-born American citizens. Thus, the results were confounded by racial and ethnic differences and it was difficult to distinguish the effects of immigrant status from those of race, ethnicity, and minority status.

In this study, I compare foreign-born and native-born (i.e., Canadian-born) children of Chinese descent with respect to their involvement in delinquency. The purpose is to determine whether the foreign-born have a different level of involvement in deviance from the native-born. In addition, culture-related factors are examined to determine the extent to which differences between the native- and the foreign-born are explained by acculturation.

Chinese Culture and Parental Control

Studies have shown that delinquency is positively related to acculturation. Those who detach from their ethnic culture are more likely to engage in delinquency. In a study of Japanese American delinquency, Kitano (1973) found that delinquent boys had fewer Japanese friends, fewer preferred ethnic activities and Japanese customs, and more of them preferred dating girls from other minority groups. Hisama (1980) contended that marginalized children, who had rejected their ethnic culture, were more likely to show antisocial behaviours. Marginality also explains the "street boy identity" of many native-born Chinese American boys who rejected part of their ethnic cultural heritage without being fully accepted by the host society (Kendis and Kendis, 1976). They involved themselves in unconventional and sometimes criminal behaviour to compensate for their shortcomings and to prove that they were in control and successful.

Cultural explanations have also been suggested in studies on alcohol use. Sue et al. (1979) concluded from their findings that alcohol consumption was positively related to the degree of assimilation into American society. Perhaps those who were less acculturated were less likely to drink because of stronger parental disapproval and traditional conforming attitudes. Using a similar cultural explanation, Chi et al. (1988) suggested that Chinese were lighter drinkers because their cultural values permitted moderate social drinking but caused disapproval of heavy consumption and drunkenness.

Perhaps differences between Chinese (or Asian) and North American cultures can be understood in race- or ethnicity-neutral terms, such as collective versus individual orientations (Akutsu et al., 1989). Cultures emphasizing the importance of the collectivity such as the family, the clan or the community are keen to demand conformity from their members. As a result, individuals are more likely to conform to the cultural norms. So, Chinese culture promotes strong social ties which, in turn, reinforce conformity. North American culture, on the other hand, encourages individual freedom and choice. Excessive individualism or weaker social ties, then, explain the higher rate of deviances in North American society.

The collectivity-individualism classification of Chinese and North American cultures may have depicted only one area of culture. It is an overgeneralization to claim that differences between the two cultures are only in terms of collectivity versus individualism. In fact, it is probably incorrect to say that Chinese culture considers the collectivity to be more important than the individual in *all* aspects of life. For example, strong territorial identity may hinder the development of national patriotism, and excessive devotion to the family may cause the neglect of civic duties and public welfare.

The cultural emphasis on the collectivity may be reflected in the strong commitment to the family which may, in turn, explain the low rates of deviance among Chinese and other Asian groups. As Lyman (1973) has noted, the family is of primary importance in traditional Chinese culture and the Chinese have stronger family, clanship, and territorial ties than European Canadians. Also, Chinese culture is keen on conformity, family solidarity, maintaining harmonious relationships, and respect for authority, particularly the unconditional respect for parents or filial piety (Fong, 1973).

Due to different cultural orientations, the parent-child relationship for the immigrant children may be quite different from that for the native-born. For example, Kelley and Tseng (1992) reported that traditional Chinese parents emphasized more physical control over their children and restrictive rearing practices than did American parents (also see Lin and Fu, 1990). Commitment to the traditional family enforces conformity whereas orientation to the North American standard has the opposite effect. Therefore, it is likely that for children of Chinese descent, the North American born are less subject to parental control than are the foreign-born. A lower level of parental control may, in turn, increase the likelihood of deviant and delinquent behaviours.

In general, findings from research support the preceding view. Kitano (1973) found that Japanese American delinquent boys were less subject to discipline by parents, less obedient, spent less time with parents, and had less communication with parents. Kendis and Kendis (1973) noted that street boys were detached from their parents and tended to be peer-oriented. They had difficulty mastering the Chinese language and found communication with their parents and other family members difficult and bothersome. Since their parents tended to be less proficient in English and too "Chinesey," the street boys had little or no respect for them. In a study of Chinese gangs, Joe and Robinson (1980) reported that the lack of parental supervision and the absence of the traditional Chinese extended kinship group were among the most probable explanations of ganging.

Similarly, Hisama (1980) has noted that the ethnically marginal person tends to be less respectful of his or her parents and less ready to give unquestioning obedience to them. Moreover, the parent-child relationship of the marginalist is further weakened by a feeling of guilt on the part of the child and a feeling of shame on the part of the parents. The child feels guilty about deserting his ethnic group and betraying his or her parents whereas the parents feel ashamed about their child's failure.

Strong parental control, therefore, may restrain delinquency. Akutsu et al. (1989) and Li and Rosenblood (1994) reported that perceived attitudes of parents toward use of alcohol had significant effects on consumption. Likewise, Chang et al. (1995) speculated that the lower prevalence of aggressive behaviour among Chinese American children was probably due to the strong intolerance of acting-out behaviour in the Chinese families.

In short, the foreign-born may have a stronger commitment to conformity than the native-born, due to their strong adherence to Chinese culture and the exercise of strong control by parents. Accordingly, in addition to comparing the relative delinquency involvement of the native- and the foreign-born, this study will also examine the relationship between acculturation and parental control and their effects on delinquency.

THE WINNIPEG CHINESE YOUTH STUDY

A survey of 315 adolescents and youth of Chinese descent in Winnipeg, Manitoba was conducted in 1995-96. The age of the respondents ranged from 10 to 20 years. The initial sampling involved identification of two thousand Chinese-sounding names from the Winnipeg telephone directory. Telephone interviews were used to determine whether the household had at least one person of Chinese ethnic background and to identify children between 10 and 20 years of age. From the two thousand households contacted 446 eligible subjects were identified. Then a mail survey was administered to the eligible subjects. After taking into account the number of responses, refusals, and nonresponses due to other reasons, the response rate was about 71 percent.

Comparing the Native- and Foreign-Born

In the questionnaire the respondents were asked whether they were born in Canada or in another country. About 48 percent (N = 152) of the respondents indicated that they were born in Canada. Regarding the immigrant status of the parents, over 90 percent of Canadian-born respondents in this sample were of immigrant parentage (93 percent immigrant fathers and 91 percent immigrant mothers). Among foreign-born respondents, all indicated that their parents were immigrants. Thus, an overwhelming majority of the native-born were brought up in families not unlike those of the foreign-born.

Comparisons between native- and foreign-born respondents reveal that the former were on the average younger than the latter (i.e., 14.9 years compared to 16.5 years, $t = -4.63$; see Table 13.1). On the other hand, there was a higher proportion of male members among the native-born (56 percent compared to 47 percent for the foreign-born). In terms of parents' education, the average for native-born respondents was about 13 years, compared to 11 years for foreign-born respondents (the means are 12.84 and 11.02, respectively, $t = 4.97$). In short, native-born respondents were younger with a higher proportion of male members and parents with a higher average level of education.

The Variables

Acculturation. The Behaviour Acculturation Scale (BAS) of Szapocznik, Scopetta, Kurtines and Aranalde (1978) is adapted to measure the extent to which the respondents were acculturated to Canadian culture or still adhered to Chinese culture. Lue and Malony (1983) applied the BAS to a sample of Caucasian Americans and first- and second-generation Chinese Americans and reported that it was able to discriminate

TABLE 13.1

THE WINNIPEG CHINESE YOUTH STUDY, 1995-96:
MEANS OF THE VARIABLES FOR NATIVE-BORN (N = 152)
AND FOREIGN-BORN (N = 163) RESPONDENTS

| | UNADJUSTED MEAN | | | ADJUSTED MEAN[a] | | |
	Native-born	Foreign-born	t[b]	Native-born	Foreign-born	t[b]
Age	14.90	16.53	-4.63	—	—	—
Sex (% male)	56%	47%	1.65	—	—	—
Parents' education	12.84	11.02	4.97	—	—	—
Total delinquency	10.82	8.71	1.74	11.35	8.25	2.67
Acculturation	4.07	3.42	10.56	4.04	3.44	9.52
Sensitivity to parents' opinion	4.81	4.75	.46	4.78	4.77	.25
Parental supervision	4.40	4.25	1.01	4.31	4.34	.46
Obedience to parents	4.93	5.04	-.63	4.86	5.12	-1.40

[a]The adjusted mean corresponds to the predicted value derived from the regression of the variable on age, sex, and immigrant status. In effect, it was adjusted for the average age and sex distribution for the sample.
[b]A t-value of 2.00 or greater indicates statistical significance at < .05

the subsamples. The BAS is based on 15 items of language use, customs, habits and lifestyle and nine items of cultural preferences.[1] Index scores are assigned to the items with 1 for "Chinese all of the time" or "Completely Chinese" and 5 for "Canadian (English) all of the time" or "Completely Canadian." Native-born respondents tended to have a higher level of acculturation than foreign-born respondents (the means are 4.07 and 3.42; see Table 13.1).

Parental control. Three indicators of parental control, that is, parental supervision, sensitivity to parents' opinion, and obedience to parents, are examined here. Parental supervision is measured as the mean average of the items related to the respondent's father and mother: "S/he knows where I am when I'm not at home." Sensitivity to parents' opinion is measured by the item "I care about what my father/mother thinks of me." Respondents were also asked if they agreed with the item "Disobeying my parents is a sin." On a scale of 1 to 6, the averages for native-born respondents were 4.81 and 4.40 for sensitivity and supervision, respectively. The corresponding averages for foreign-born respondents were 4.75 and 4.25. The differences between the subsamples are not statistically significant (see Table 13.1). Similarly, on a scale of 1 to 7, both native- and foreign-born respondents showed similar levels of obedience to parents (the means are 4.93 and 5.04, t = - .63).

Delinquency. Of a list of 19 delinquent acts, ranging from skipping classes and cheating to assault and robbery, respondents were asked to report the number of times they had committed the acts in the past 12 months. Most of the related items had been used in other delinquency research studies such as the Rochester Youth Development Study (Thornberry, Lizotte, Krohn, Farnworth and Jang, 1991), the National Youth Survey (Elliott, Huizinga and Ageton, 1985), or the Denver Youth Survey (Huizinga, Esbensen and Weiher, 1991). The sample as a whole had reportedly been responsible for an average of about ten incidents per person with a majority of minor offences (i.e., 10.82 and 8.71 incidents for native- and foreign-born respondents, respectively; see Table 13.1). About 85 percent of the respondents had committed at least one act in the past year, and 40 percent of the respondents were responsible for at least ten incidents of the acts listed. Indeed, the results are quite consistent with the notion that most people have the experience of breaking the law (Gabor, 1994).

FINDINGS FROM THE STUDY

As noted earlier, native-born respondents were considerably younger and had a slightly higher proportion of male members. Since age and sex may affect acculturation (Szapocznik et al., 1978) and delinquency, it seems necessary to control for their effects. In addition, parents' education is added to the model to control for the possible effects of family socioeconomic status.

Immigrant Status and Delinquency

The adjusted means for the variables, after controlling for the effects of age and sex, are reported in Table 13.1. The adjusted means show that native-born respondents reported a higher number of offences than foreign-born respondents. On the average native-born respondents reported 11.35 incidents of delinquent acts, compared to 8.25 incidents reported by foreign-born respondents. This finding supports the notion that immigrants are not necessarily prone to deviances despite their social and economic disadvantages (Aronowitz, 1984). In fact, the finding here has demonstrated that native-born Canadians are more prone to delinquency than immigrants. To that extent, it is consistent with the findings reported in previous studies (see, for example, Kendis and Kendis, 1976; Pogrebin and Poole, 1989; Sellin, 1938; Sue and Sue, 1973; Sue et al., 1979)

The preceding finding has to be interpreted with caution. The fact that immigrants do not show a higher level of involvement in delinquency than the native-born does not mean that their experiences with immigration-related stressful events and personal difficulties are less. As mentioned earlier, many Chinese immigrants are socially and economically disadvantaged (Huang and Ying, 1989; Li, 1988; Lyman, 1973, 1977; Tan and Roy, 1985; Wong, 1985). Perhaps a more appropriate interpretation is that whatever deprivations immigrants have experienced do not necessarily translate to behavioural deviances. Moreover, for the native-born, acculturation to Canadian society may in fact mean assimilation into the minority or lower-class segments of society (Portes and Zhou, 1993) which, in turn, explains their higher level of involvement in delinquency.

Immigrant Status and Other Factors of Acculturation

It has been suggested earlier that the native-born should be more acculturated to North American society than the foreign-born. Indeed, estimates from the regression of acculturation on immigrant status and other social and demographic factors provide much evidence to support the hypothesis (see Table 13.2). Native-born respondents were found to be significantly more acculturated than foreign-born respondents ($\hat{\beta} = -.24$, $p < .001$).

However, immigrant status is not the most important factor of acculturation. Length of residence in Canada has an even stronger effect on acculturation ($\hat{\beta} = .32$, $p < .001$). In fact, it is the strongest predictor of acculturation. Respondents who had been in Canada for a longer period of time were more acculturated. Acculturation of immigrants, then, is largely a function of time (see Rosenthal and Feldman, 1992; Szapocznik et al., 1978). Other important correlates are age and parents' education ($\hat{\beta}$ coefficients for the regressors are -.19 and .17, respectively). Older respondents had a lower level of acculturation than younger respondents. Parents' educational level has a positive effect on acculturation.

A closer examination of the correlates of acculturation for the subsamples reveals an interesting pattern (see Table 13.2). That is, contrary to the aforementioned observation, acculturation does not appear to be a function of time for the native-born. For the native-born, age

TABLE 13.2

THE WINNIPEG CHINESE YOUTH STUDY, 1995-96:
IMMIGRANT STATUS AND OTHER FACTORS OF ACCULTURATION

| | DEPENDENT VARIABLE: ACCULTURATION | | |
Regressor	Total sample	Native-born	Foreign-born
Age	-.19***	.04	-.30***
Sex (1 = male; 2 = female)	-.08	-.12	-.06
Parents' education	.17***	.18*	.18*
Immigrant status (1 = NB; 2 = FB)	-.24***	—	—
Length of residence	.32***	—	.40***
N	301	145	156
R^2	.39	.05	.29

All coefficients are standardized: $^*p < .05$; $^{**}p < .01$; $^{***}p < .001$.

does not have any significant effect on acculturation ($\hat{\beta}$ = .04).[2] Nonetheless, for the foreign-born, age has a negative effect on acculturation whereas length of residence has a positive effect as expected ($\hat{\beta}$s are -.30 and .40, respectively). Therefore, it is more accurate to say that acculturation is a function of time only for first-generation immigrants. For immigrants, acculturation is a somewhat "natural process" that progresses with the amount of time they have spent in the host country.

The Importance of Acculturation

In the hypotheses, it is suggested that acculturation may cause delinquency to increase and it may explain the difference in delinquency involvement between the native- and foreign-born. The findings presented in Table 13.3 lend support to the hypotheses. It is found that acculturation has a significant and positive effect on delinquency ($\hat{\beta}$ = .19, $p < .01$). The sign of the effect suggests that the higher the level of acculturation, the higher the level of involvement in delinquency. Conversely speaking, adherence to Chinese culture lowers the likelihood of involvement in delinquency.

Moreover, adding the acculturation variable to the regression model has reduced quite substantially the effect of immigrant status on delinquency, from a standardized effect of -.16 to -.08. To that extent, acculturation has mediated some of the effect of immigrant status on

TABLE 13.3

THE WINNIPEG CHINESE YOUTH STUDY, 1995-96:
EFFECTS OF ACCULTURATION ON DELINQUENCY

| | DEPENDENT VARIABLE: DELINQUENCY | | | |
Regressor	Total sample		Native-born	Foreign-born
Age	.24***	.27***	.24**	.29***
Sex (1 = male; 2 = female)	-.28***	-.26***	-.18*	-.37***
Parents' education	-.08	-.11*	-.13	-.11
Immigrant status (1 = NB; 2 = FB)	-.16**	-.08	—	—
Acculturation	—	.19**	.14	.19*
N	299	299	144	155
R^2	.17	.19	.14	.27

All coefficients are standardized: *p < .05; **p < .01; ***p < .001.

delinquency. In other words, a higher level of acculturation explains why native-born respondents were more involved in delinquency than the foreign-born.

Acculturation has more or less the same magnitude of effect on delinquency for native- and foreign-born respondents. For the native-born, the standardized effect of acculturation on delinquency is .19, compared to .14 for the foreign-born. This finding means that while the native-born are more acculturated than the foreign-born, acculturation increases delinquency involvement for both native- and foreign-born respondents alike. Those who are more acculturated to Canadian society are more likely to be involved in delinquency regardless of immigrant status.

The finding that acculturation has a positive effect on delinquency regardless of immigrant status implies that culture-related problems are not confined to the native-born (Sellin, 1938). The evidence suggests that the process of adopting the behaviour and cultural patterns of the host society is even more important than the individual's country of origin. Indeed, it has been shown in other studies that acculturation and participation in the host society, not just immigrant status per se, affect the individual's involvement in crime and delinquency (Ribordy, 1980).

Acculturation and Parental Control

The comparisons in Table 13.1 have revealed that native- and foreign-born respondents showed similar levels of sensitivity to parents' opinion, parental supervision, and obedience to parents. Essentially, the results suggest that the average amount of parental control is more or less the same whether the child was born in Canada or in other countries. As it has been mentioned earlier, over 90 percent of native-born respondents were of immigrant parentage. This may explain the lack of difference between native- and foreign-born respondents with respect to the amount of parental control.

In addition, an examination of the correlations among the variables reveals that the association between acculturation and parental control is rather weak (see Table 13.4). For example, the correlation between acculturation and sensitivity to parents' opinion is virtually zero ($r = -.02$). The correlation involving obedience to parents is also not significant ($r = -.06$). Therefore, it is quite obvious that those who adhered to Chinese culture were no more respectful or obedient to their parents than those who were well acculturated to Canadian society. This finding contradicts the notion that Westernized children are less respectful of their parents (see, for example, Fong, 1973; Sue and Sue, 1973; Hisama, 1980).

TABLE 13.4

THE WINNIPEG CHINESE YOUTH STUDY, 1995-96:
CORRELATIONS (PEARSON'S R) BETWEEN ACCULTURATION
AND THE VARIABLES OF PARENTAL CONTROL

| | Acculturation | | |
Parental Control	Total sample	Native-born	Foreign-born
Sensitivity to parents' opinion	-.02	.09	.01
Parental supervision	-.03	-.23**	.07
Obedience to parents	-.06	-.12	.01

All coefficients are standardized: $^*p < .05$; $^{**}p < .01$; $^{***}p < .001$.

While the correlation between acculturation and parental supervision is weak and nonsignificant for the total sample ($r = -.03$), it is reasonably strong and statistically significant for the subsample of native-born respondents ($r = -.23$). Also, the correlation is negative which means that weak parental supervision is attributed to a high level of acculturation. In other words, native-born respondents who were well acculturated to Canadian society were less subject to parental supervision. To that extent, the results provide some evidence that acculturation is associated with an individualist orientation in the shape of a higher degree of autonomy for the child.

On the surface, the observation that sensitivity to parents' opinion and obedience to parents are unrelated to acculturation whereas parental supervision is negatively related to it appears anomalous. Nonetheless, it is actually quite consistent with the findings in previous research studies. In their study of Vietnamese and American parents, Nguyen and Williams (1989) found that Vietnamese parents felt strongly about traditional values such as respect for the elderly and obedience to parents while nevertheless allowing their children a high degree of autonomy. Similarly, Lin and Fu (1990) reported that immigrant Chinese parents emphasized more independence for their children than did Caucasian American parents. In other words, although parents demanded obedience and respect, they were willing to grant their children autonomy. Perhaps a similar situation developed for this subsample of native-born respondents. On the one hand, parents demanded respect and obedience from their children regardless of how Canadianized or acculturated they were. On the other hand, they were willing to compromise and allow their children more autonomy.

The Importance of Parental Control

Despite the fact that parental control is only weakly associated with acculturation, it is important to examine its effect on delinquency. After all, parental control has been identified as one of the most important factors contributing to conformity (Hirschi, 1969). Research on the relationship between parental control and delinquency has found strong evidence of direct and indirect causal relationships (for reports of direct effect, see Agnew, 1985, 1991a; Cernkovich and Giordano, 1987; Hindelang, 1973; Larzelere and Patterson, 1990; Liska and Reed, 1985; Poole and Regoli, 1979; Rankin and Wells, 1990; for reports of indirect effects, see Hepburn, 1977; Massey and Krohn, 1986; Matsueda, 1982; Marcos, Bahr and Johnson, 1986; Wiatrowski, Griswold and Roberts, 1981; for reports of conditional effects, see Agnew, 1991b; Dembo, Grandon, LaVoie, Schmeidler and Burgos, 1986; Foshee and Bauman, 1992; Jensen and Brownfield, 1983).

Using multiple regression analysis, the effects of parental control on delinquency are estimated and the results are presented in Table 13.5. The results reveal that of the three parental control variables, only parental supervision has a significant effect on delinquency ($\hat{\beta}$ = -.35, *p*

TABLE 13.5

THE WINNIPEG CHINESE YOUTH STUDY, 1995-96:
EFFECTS OF PARENTAL CONTROL ON DELINQUENCY

Regressor	Dependent variable: Delinquency		
	Total sample	Native-born	Foreign-born
Age	.14*	.09	.20**
Sex (1 = male; 2 = female)	-.18***	-.13	-.24***
Parents' education	-.04	-.07	-.00
Immigrant status (1 = NB; 2 = FB)	-.08	—	—
Acculturation	.13*	.05	.19**
Sensitivity to parents	-.02	-.06	.03
Parental supervision	-.35***	-.34***	-.41***
Obedience to parents	-.10	-.07	-.11
N	289	141	147
R^2	.32	.26	.43

All coefficients are standardized: *$p < .05$; **$p < .01$; ***$p < .001$.

< .001) The sign of the effect is in the expected direction which suggests that parental supervision restrains the individual from engaging in delinquency. Moreover, it restrains delinquency involvement regardless of immigrant status. For native-born respondents, the standardized effect of parental supervision is -.34, compared to -.41 for the foreign-born.

More importantly, the results have shown that much of the effect of parental control on delinquency is independent of acculturation. In fact, parental control has a much stronger effect on delinquency than does acculturation. In this way, parental control may compensate for whatever aggravating effects acculturation has on behaviour. Parents play a key role in counteracting such effects. They are not exactly helpless when dealing with the acculturation-related problems of their children. The most direct and effective means of behaviour control is to maintain close supervision of their children regardless of the cultural orientation or immigrant status.

Selective assimilation as a process of parental control. Many immigrant parents are concerned about the negative impact of acculturation and some parents even employ a selective assimilation strategy for their children (Portes and Zhou, 1993); that is to say, to ensure the children's success in the future parents encourage them to do well in school and be proficient in English. On the other hand, parents discourage children from associating with American/Canadian friends and prevent them from adopting North American customs and lifestyle. Indeed, findings from this study support the idea that acculturation may increase the risk of involvement in delinquency. To that extent, parents may be justified in preventing their children from becoming too Americanized or Canadianized.

The argument for selective assimilation is even sounder if seen as a parental control process rather than as a mere a choice of cultural orientation. Selective assimilation is a form of control of the child by parents: that is, parents choose and select friends and social activities for their children and justify their control by cultural reasons. This particular parental control strategy is relevant not only for immigrant parents. It is also commonly used by parents in general. For example, middle-class parents, immigrant and native alike, may discourage their children from befriending children from the underclass. In a similar manner, parents with a certain religious affiliation may encourage their children to associate with those who go to the same church or religious group and minimize "pagan" influences on their children. Furthermore, regardless of class, religious affiliation, ethnicity, or immigrant status, most parents prefer their children to do well in school, learn the official language, and be successful in the future. Thus, selective assimilation is also practised by native parents, albeit in a more subtle manner.

Alternatives to Delinquency

Delinquency is just one of the many indicators of the social, emotional, and behavioural problems confronting immigrant children. Although such children are less involved in delinquency than the native-born it is inaccurate to conclude that they experience fewer problems in other areas. Similarly, the positive correlation between acculturation and delinquency may not represent the relationship between acculturation and other areas of a person's life, such as health problems, psychological and emotional disorders, language-related problems and social isolation. The results merely point to the facts that, first, immigrant children do not show more behavioural problems than native-born children, and, second, that there is a positive correlation between acculturation and delinquency.

As noted earlier, research studies have found that immigrant children tend to have psychological and psychiatric problems (Huang and Ying, 1989). Therefore, it appears that behavioural disorders, such as delinquency, may not be the best representation of problems confronting these children. One may speculate that whatever kinds of stress and frustration immigrant children may suffer, they are not expressed through the displays of delinquent behaviour. Instead, they may be shown through various emotional and psychological symptoms. Perhaps their unfamiliarity with the new social environment and thus small number of friends limit the involvement of immigrant children in delinquent activities, especially those that take place in a group context. On the other hand, adjustment and maladjustment to a new environment, and a relatively higher degree of social isolation, may contribute to the various emotional and psychological problems associated with immigration and acculturation. Thus, to obtain a more comprehensive view of the issue, future research on immigration and acculturation may examine the effects of these adaptation processes, using an array of social, psychological, health, and behavioural indicators.

A summary of the findings is presented in Figure 13.1. The results have revealed that the native-born are more prone to delinquency than are the foreign-born, although the difference diminishes once acculturation and other factors are taken into account. As expected, the native-born are found to be on average more acculturated to Canadian society than the foreign-born. Among first-generation immigrants, younger

FIGURE 13.1

SUMMARY OF FINDINGS

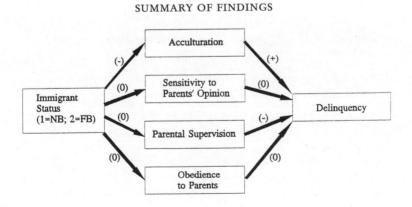

Note: "(0)"=weak or nonsignificant effect.

persons are more easily acculturated, and acculturation progresses with the length of residence in the host society. Thus, acculturation is more or less a "natural process" and basically a function of time. Also, it has been shown that acculturation increases the likelihood of delinquency involvement, and to a certain extent, it mediates the effect of immigrant status on delinquency.

However, the results have also shown that contrary to popular beliefs, individuals with a strong orientation in Chinese culture are not necessarily subject to stronger parental control. With the exception of the item of parental supervision for the native-born, parental control has been found to be quite independent of immigrant status and acculturation. Nonetheless, parental control has a strong restraining effect on delinquency which may serve to counteract the aggravating effects of acculturation. Parents, therefore, play a key role in the control of the child's behaviour in spite of the seemingly inevitable process of acculturation.

NOTES

1.   For the present study, two behaviour items, "way of relating to fiancée" and "dances," are modified and replaced by "way of relating to friends" and "games," respectively. The adjustments are necessary because Chinese dances are usually regarded as an art form rather than as personal recreation, and most respondents, at the age of 18 or younger, do not have a fiancée. The preference item "way of celebrating weddings" is replaced by "friends" and "school."

2.   For the native-born, age and length of residence in Canada should be the same, and so only the effect of age has been estimated.

14

CHINESE REFUGEES COPING WITH STRESS IN TORONTO

GUANG TIAN

ALTHOUGH MUCH IS KNOWN about the causes of stress and the subsequent coping reponses (Folkman and Lazarus, 1985; Lumsden, 1984), research on stress related to adaptation to Canada has increased considerably (Chataway and Berry, 1989; Sommers, 1993; Zheng and Berry, 1991). Adaptation, or changes resulting from first-hand contact with a new culture, can be very stressful (Berry and Kim, 1988; Sommers, 1993). This study examines the problems experienced by the mainland Chinese refugees (MCRs) in metro Toronto, it identifies the stress MCRs faced in their everyday lives, and it examines the resources which they can draw upon to cope. It also describes the social and economic achievements of specific MCRs to highlight the ways in which many of these people adapt. An outline of their ongoing process of adaptation to the host society is presented in this chapter.

The data used in this study were collected during a five-year period of field work. In addition to a questionnaire survey (N=116), a "snowball" sample of 56 MCRs were selected for open-ended interviews; the methods of participant observation from the beginning of the research were also used to collect the data. The target population of the study is comprised of mainland Chinese who claimed refugee status in Canada prior to February 1, 1993 (at which time Bill C-86 began to affect the inflow of MCRs and the refugee hearing process: see Tian, 1995). Due to Canadian prosperity, the perceived opportunity for a better life, and the well developed and organized Chinese communities, more and more MCRs chose Metro Toronto as their destination. According to the statistics released by the Immigration and Refugee Board of Canada (IRB), from January 1984 to February 1993, 8,992 mainland Chinese had made refugee claims in Canada. Based on the reports in local Chinese newspapers, it is estimated that about 2,500 MCRs live in Metro Toronto.

The arrival of increased numbers of MCRs in Canada is a recent phenomenon. The reforms and the "open door" policy in China in the 1980s exposes Chinese to the West more than ever before. The desire to emigrate was far greater than Canada's capacity to accept, resulting in large numbers of illegal emigrants and refugees. Once they left China, these illegal emigrants and refugees became members of the Chinese diaspora or overseas Chinese community, which now represents a total worldwide population of 50 million (Fu, 1994). Although some of them ultimately qualify as bona fide refugees, many who fail to meet Geneva convention criteria, are still permitted to stay permanently. Initially, they were allowed to stay in Canada temporarily under the special order made by the federal minister of employment and immigration in the summer of 1989 (Gilad, 1990:314).

INTERNATIONAL STRESS RESPONSE MODEL

Up to 1994 there were about 4,500 rejected MCR claims across Canada. Due to their uncertain legal status in Canada and other reasons the persons affected faced great stress in their daily lives. This phenomenon became the main concern of this study. The model for this study is a modified Lazarus and Folkman (1984) interactional model of stress response in the adaptation process (see Figure 14.1). Building on their cognitive appraisal model, Lazarus and Folkman (1984:35) define those in stress as coping with "changing cognitive and behavioural efforts to manage specific external and/or internal *demands that are appraised as taxing or exceeding the resources of the person.*" In their model the significance of "appraisal" includes cultural meaning. Following Lazarus and Folkman, coping refers in this study to attempts by MCRs to alter events or circumstances which they see as stress-producing. The forms of coping vary greatly, and may include attempts to: change the conditions that produce the stress; to redefine the meaning of stress as a way of de-emphasizing its significance; and manipulate the emotional consequences of stress-producing experience so as to contain them within manageable bounds (Pearlins and Schooler, 1978; Dressler, 1991).

The manner in which individuals cope is influenced both by personal resources available and by the constraints that limit the use of resources. Any individual's personal resources might include such factors as health and energy; social skills; social support; and wealth. Constraints are both personal and environmental in nature. Personal

FIGURE 14.1

CHINESE REFUGEES' COPING-ADAPTATION MODEL

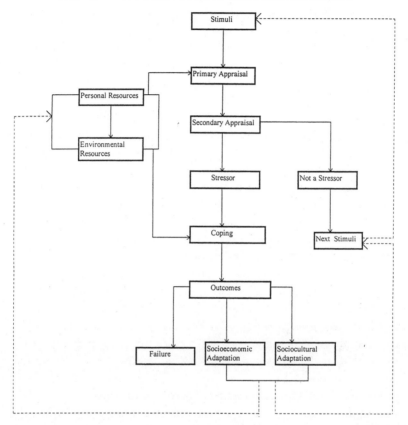

constraints include "internalized cultural values and beliefs that proscribe certain ways of behaving and psychological deficits." Environmental constraints include "demands that compete for the same resources and agencies or institutions that thwart coping efforts" (Lazarus and Folkman, 1984:179).

Resources which may facilitate coping by individuals include social networks, part of a relatively static component of the person's social environment. At the same time, to acknowledge that people maintain social relationships is not to state that they necessarily derive support from them, because these potential resources may create fluctuations in the quality of support provided by members of the network. Lazarus and Folkman (1984:250, 259) also identify three types of social support, including emotional support, tangible support, and informational support, and argue that "people will have better adaptational outcomes if they receive or believe that they will receive social support when it is needed."

Lazarus and Folkman see coping as a process (1984:142-43) which is often equated with adaptational success. Likewise, Berry (1991:27) points out that coping strategies are processual; they are drawn upon "until some satisfactory adaptation to the new situation is achieved." Similarly, Compas et al. (1992) consider coping as an effective process of adaptation, and for them "coping is frequently equated with successful adaptation." Lazarus and Folkman (1984:142) further state that coping is a shifting process in which "shifts may be the result of coping efforts directed at changing the environment, or coping directed inward that changes the meaning of the event or increases understanding." Following the Lazarus and Folkman model in this study, the link between the processes of coping and adaptation is determined in the context of the changed environment within which MCRs present and identify themselves. The MCRs' coping process is seen as part of the whole adaptation procedure; the more effective the coping strategies employed, the better the adaptive results, in terms of socioeconomic and personal achievements.

The general coping-adaptation model, outlined in Figure 14.1, shows that in the MCRs coping-adaptation process personal resources affect environmental resources. Personal and environmental resources provide bases on which cognitive evaluation of the various stresses take place. Since not all stimuli are stress-related, coping occurs when the appraisal process yields the conclusion that stimuli are stressful, with the form and effectiveness of this coping determined by the personal and environmental resources. Coping is part of effectively reducing stress, increasing available personal and environmental resources which help generate adaptive outcomes. Finally, the outcomes of coping lead to socioeconomic and sociocultural adaptation, which may in turn produce new stimuli. This includes another process of coping which may be part of a new set of strengthened resources based on new experience.

Seven types of sources of stress have been identified: 1) conflict between expectations and realities; 2) uncertainty of legal status; 3) separation from families; 4) nostalgia; 5) discrimination; 6) loss of achievements in China; and 7) deficiency of living skills. Although there are some other types of stress, such as unfamiliarity with the Canadian legal system (Chan and Hagan, 1982), these seven types are most salient in MCRs' adjustments, and thus are most commonly reported by our MCR respondents. Lazarus and Folkman have argued, "humans are meaning-oriented, meaning-building creatures who are constantly evaluating everything that happens" (1984:276-77).

While Lazarus and Folkman (1984:12-14) have presented a different taxonomy, in this study we classify types 2,3,6 as situational or external sources of stress; types 1 and 4 as emotional or internal sources of stress; and types 5 and 7 as situational-emotional or external-internal sources of stress. The situational or external sources of stress refer to the sources of stress that emerge objectively from the situations MCRs encountered which were hard to control, and which all MCRs faced. Emotional or internal sources of stress denote the stress resources that are produced by an individual's experiences and subjective feeling. This class is significant only for those MCRs who have the experiences and feelings which pertain to these sources of stress. The situational-emotional or external-internal sources of stress refer to the stress sources that exist objectively and may produce effects only when individual MCRs subjectively feel their presence (see below).

TABLE 14.1

TYPES OF STRESS AND RELATED FACTORS

Types	Type	Effective Range
Situational	2	All rejected MCRs
	3	All MCRs
	6	MCRs with high achievements in China
Emotional	1	MCRs with high expectations for migration
	4	MCRs with rural background
Emotional-Situational	5	Highly educated MCRs who interact with Canadians
	7	All MCRs, especially those interact with Canadians

Sources: Social Survey, interviews and participant observation.

Naturally, these three classes of sources of stress influence MCRs differentially, depending on personal experiences and feelings for issues, such as discrimination, inadequate use of English and lack of personal skills. In other words, different types of sources of stress have different effective ranges. For instance, uncertainty of legal status was encountered by all rejected MCRs prior to the DROC project (the Deferred Removal Orders Class, a classification under which most rejected MCRs are entitled to apply for permanent residence in Canada. See Tian and

Lu (1996) for a detailed discussion. Conflict between expectations and realities produced stress only for those MCRs who had high expectations of their migration. Situational-emotional stress from such a source as discrimination should have been encountered by all MCRs but in reality it was effective only for more highly educated MCRs who had more interaction with Canadians and were familiar with the issue of discrimination.

Clearly, different types of sources of stress generate stressful states for different MCRs; some sources of stress may be significant for all MCRs, and some may be significant only for a small number. Whether the different types of sources of stress are significant depends on the varied situations and how individuals appraise these situations, such as legal status and educational background. Resources used depend on the way in which individual MCRs pursue their coping process.

STRESS AND SHATTERED DREAMS

Conflict Between Expectations and Realities

As analysed elsewhere (Tian, 1995), the primary motives for most MCRs coming to this country are getting their personal freedoms and seeking better opportunities for personal development in Canada. Therefore, to make refugee claims is nothing more than a strategy for realizing their immigrant dream in Canada. Long interviews with MCRs show that the majority (43 out of 56 interviewed) realized that their lives would be different from what they were in China, but they were not prepared to deal with the difficulties they encountered in Canada. Their pre-migration perceptions depicted Canada as a highly developed country with absolute personal freedom and a very high standard of living. They imagined that once they arrived there would be few difficulties as long as they worked hard. As Zeng Jin, one of the rejected refugee claimants, said, "I imagined that life in Canada should be easier for me than in China."

Li Heping shared the same dream with Zeng Jin before his migration. He told the author that he never thought he would meet serious problems living in Canada before his migration because he could speak English much better than most of his fellow countrymen: "If they can make it, I am sure, I will make it much better in Canada, at least I do not need to worry about a language problem." "I expected to get my second master's degree in Canada quickly, and then find a job, and get my wife and my daughter to join me." "To be honest with you, before my arrival in Canada I had never expected the stress that I am experiencing now."

For Zeng Jin and Li Heping, as well as some other MCRs, the stress came when their expectations did not match social reality. More seriously, the stress became stronger and stronger due to expected and unexpected factors, such as uncertainty about their future and separation from close family members and friends. These factors contributed to the conflict between high expectations and Canadian realities. Lin Xi, a female rejected refugee claimant, was an engineer in China, who came to Canada as a visa student in 1991 and made a refugee claim later. Like Zeng Jin and Li Heping, Lin Xi was also full of expectations for her new life in Canada; in her premigration mind Canada was a place where she could realize all her beautiful dreams, provided she worked hard. She planned to take an English class for a half year and then get her language test passed so that she could go to the University of Toronto for her graduate studies. However, all her dreams vanished after she arrived in Toronto. She had only $2,000 U.S. at that time and that was only enough to pay her tuition fee for language class at the University of Toronto.

Facing this new situation, she decided not to go to the English as a Second Language (ESL) language class but to find a job first. Given the poor economy in Canada at that time it was not easy to find a job; she walked along streets and asked every possible employer if she could be hired. Unfortunately, for two weeks no one was willing to offer her the opportunity because she had no work permit, nor did she have Canadian experience. The cruel reality drove her to despair and she soon planned to go back. One day she read an advertisement in a Chinese newspaper that earthworm catchers were wanted, with no experience needed. She phoned the recruiter at once and got the job: "In China I would be sick even if I saw worms let alone to catch them, but here in Canada you are nobody, and you must do that to survive." Lin Xi suffered from serious stress which she had never expected and which almost drove her insane. She told the author that "I was very depressed after my arrival (in Canada). All the days you have to worry this and worry that, there are too many things for you to worry." "It was funny that when I was in the plane I was still reading a TOEFL book, but when I got landed I felt I was thrown off, nobody took care of you, you were forced to go your own ways. *Ni bixu miandui xianshi* (you must face reality). When I felt depressed I just kept myself busy, so that I would not have time to think, one way for me to get rid of stress."

Uncertainty of Legal Status

The uncertainty of legal status in Canada is the most crucial point of stress that most encounter after they make refugee claims. Such stress automatically disappears after refugees have been granted Convention Refugee status but it continues for those whose claims have been rejected. It makes all rejected claimants worry about their future in Canada and it also makes them feel that they are unwelcome here.

Moreover, the uncertainty of legal status makes their lives in Canada much more difficult than those of all the other Canadian residents who have legal status, because they are barred from many employment opportunities and are deprived of many social benefits. All these factors contributed to and reinforced the stress of MCRs, particularly the rejected claimants. Although the great majority of MCRs when facing such stress are able to bear it by patiently waiting for opportunities, a few of them, such as Han Yongjian and Han Shiqian, for example, experienced mental health difficulties.

These two brothers came to Toronto in October of 1990 with the hope that they could get resettled quickly in Canada. Unfortunately, their refugee claims were turned down in the summer of 1991, and their appeals were turned down in the following year. For them, making the refugee claim is the only effective stategy for accomplishing their immigration. Refusal of their claims for landed immigrant status meant that their road into Canada had been destroyed. The two brothers simply could not endure such stress and both became mentally ill; Han Yongjian even tried to commit suicide before he was taken to a mental hospital. Finally, the brothers were sent back to China under special arrangement, sorry that they came to Canada and having only two mental health certificates to show for their efforts (*The World Journal*, March 6, 1993:27).

Although the level of stress and mental health difficulties occasioned by uncertainty of legal status in Canada, such as the Han brothers experienced, does not occur very often, the degree of the stress should never be overlooked. It affects the mental health and adaptation process of all MCRs.

Separation from Families

Our research data support Chan's (1984) finding that separation from close family members and friends is among the most severe causes of stress among refugees. Of those interviewed, 87 percent (49 out of 56) claimed that they had suffered greatly from separation from their families and indicated such separation as the biggest loss for them. Of the valid cases in the survey, 92 percent reported that when they met with difficulties in Canada they would immediately want to see members of their family.

Still more seriously, for some married MCRs long separation from their spouses resulted in some broken marriages. We found that of 55 married MCRs whose spouses were still in China, 74.5 percent (41 cases) reported that long separations seriously affected their marriages, and 43.6 percent (24 cases) claimed that their families would be in danger of breaking up if the separation continued. In fact, a few of the MCRs who were interviewed had already been divorced from their spouses. Han Lu, a female, told the author that her husband simply did not believe her difficult situation in Canada, and conjectured that she had a boyfriend; otherwise she would bring him and her son to Canada quickly. Finally, in 1994, her husband divorced her and deprived her of access to her son. The divorce was so devastating that her health declined quickly and she had little energy left to take care of herself.

Nostalgia

Nostalgia is a kind of feeling for a return to, or a psychological reinstitution of, the personal past which affords optimal gratification (Zwingmann, 1973:23), and sometimes it results in a state of homesickness. As a social phenomenon, nostalgia is felt by MCRs after they experience the shock of transition. China and Canada are two countries which differ in many respects and these differences often drive MCRs into confusion. The interview data indicate that very few MCRs were informed about Canada before their arrival, but most of them were to feel and realize the differences between this country and their home country shortly after they arrived. At the very beginning, although aware of these differences, they had not located useful resources nor had they learned necessary skills to cope with the differences; they simply did not know how to adjust to these differences and therefore remained anxious, confused and sometimes in grief, longing for their "lost home" as Fried (1963) termed it. As a result, many turn to seek happiness in their memories, falling into a deep state of nostalgia.

Nostalgia may stimulate MCRs' stress reactions, based on their Chinese experience, which may result in neglect or violation of the expectations inherent in Canadian culture and social values. For example, one of the respondents who arrived in Toronto in early 1990 as a *minyun fenzi* (democratic movement activist), lived temporarily in a place arranged by a local Chinese *minyun tuanti* (democratic organization). Since he did not have good friends, and was not able to communicate in English, he became homesick and phoned his family and friends in China by using the telephone which belongs to the owner of the place where he lived. In a very short period, he made $8,000 worth of long distance calls. The bill was finally paid by the democratic organization which hosted him. He told the author that he was too homesick to control himself, and that, although he knew there was a charge for long distance calls, he did not know it would cost that much. Besides, in China telephone bills were always taken care of by *danwei* (sponsoring organization), and he thought he would not be asked to pay.

Similarly, another respondent became homesick after he had lived in Toronto for a few weeks. One day he wanted to go out to drive away his cares, so he borrowed a car and drove it on the highway aimlessly without a valid driver's licence. Finally he was stopped by police, fined $2,000, and deprived of the right to drive a car in Ontario for eight years. He stated that he did not realize that there was such a serious penalty for driving without a driver's licence in Canada because in China, when he was perturbed, he did the same thing but never encountered any problems.

The interview data indicate that nostalgia is in effect only for a short period of time, such as the first few months after the immigrants arrive in Metro Toronto. Access to Chinatown does help mediate stress and reactions caused by it (Lam, 1994:170). The interview data also indicate that nostalgia usually affects those who have came from rural areas in China, with a lower level of education than that attained by those who have come from the urban areas. Some of these incidents seem to have happened because of ignorance of urban life.

Perceived Discrimination

We also found that discrimination was not a significant factor. Only 7 percent of the 95 respondents indicated that they experienced discrimination from their non-Chinese neighbours. Of 77 respondents who had worked with Canadians, only 12 percent reported that they had been discriminated against by their Canadian working fellows. However, the interview data reveal that almost one third of the respondents (18 out of 56) reported that they had experienced discrimination. More highly educated respondents seemed to have had more opportunities to experience discrimination. For example, 15 of 31 (48 percent) respondents who had university education reported discrimination, while none of 14 respondents who had lower than high school education reported discrimination (see Table 14.2). This tends to show that highly educated MCRs have more interaction with Canadians in their everyday lives, in areas where discrimination can be experienced. It also shows that more highly educated MCRs are more sensitive to and aware of discrimination.

TABLE 14.2

MCRs' EXPERIENCE OF DISCRIMINATION BY EDUCATION

Reported Discrimination	N	Percentage	Did not Report Discrimination	N	Percentage
Graduate School	3	75	Graduate School	1	25
University	12	44.4	University	15	55.6
High School	3	27.3	High School	8	62.7
Middle School	0	0	Middle School	9	100
Primary School	0	0	Primary School	5	100
Total	18	32.1 *	Total	38	67.9 *

* Percentage of total 56 interviewed respondents

A female, whose claim to refugee status was rejected, had a university degree and planned to marry a Canadian after her claim had been turned down. She changed her mind later. She said that no matter how hard she presented herself as Westernized to her Canadian friends, they still treated her differently from their other Canadian girlfriends. She felt strongly that she was discriminated against by her Canadian friends, and this feeling became even stronger during her two-month period of job hunting. She mailed a total of 300 letters with her very well organized résumé to Canadian companies and she also advertised in the *Toronto Star* and other English newspapers during a two-month period, but no employer hired her. She attributed her unsuccessful job hunting to discrimination. She stated, "I think the difficulty is not that I do not want to learn nor that I am not diligent. I think discrimination is very strong, and better positions are all taken by the whites. Chinese are still looked down upon, particularly those who are refugees ... a third class citizen." She then decided that she would quit having white people in her circle of friends and get back to her Chinese network. She dreamed of having her own company where she would hire many white people who would have to obey her, otherwise she would fire them. Thus, she could teach them a lesson for their discriminatory actions against her. Although this is perhaps an extreme case, it illustrates stress reactions caused by MCR experience of discrimination.

Loss of Achievement in China

As indicated earlier, many MCRs came to Canada with the hope of having better opportunities for personal development. To obtain these better opportunities, they took the risk of losing their social and economic achievements gained in China. However, once they discovered that Canada might not provide better opportunities as quickly as they had expected, they began to worry about their losses in China. During the author's long interviews with MCRs, one particular question was designed to investigate what they lost by coming to Canada, and asked them, "What were your situations in China and how did you feel about yourself in China?" The answers to this question were similar to those given by Chinese refugees from Vietnam in Chan and Lam's research (1987:35-37). The crucial loss was separation from families, as discussed earlier, followed by loss in social and economic achievement such as social status, good jobs and higher positions, and loss of personal properties, such as savings or businesses.

The occupational categories of the respondents we interviewed included: government officials (11), managers (4), journalists (3), doctors (5), university and high school teachers (4), engineers (5), and agents of foreign corporations (3). All these occupations were valued as good jobs in mainland China, in a land where 80 percent of the total population are peasants. In China good jobs also mean higher pay and social status as well as access to more social resources for personal use. One particular loss often mentioned by the respondents was that of their well-established personal networks in China. Although several respondents planned to re-establish their networks here in Canada, they had to give up eventually, because they did not have the social resources to realize the plan. For them the loss of social achievements was a painful experience which hurt their feelings of self-pride and sense of achievement, resulting in considerable stress.

One interview sample also included seven private business owners who were among the richest in China. For example, one of these seven respondents had already accumulated over 500,000 yuan RMB by running a salon prior to her family's departure from China in 1990. Considering that an average annual income for an ordinary Chinese person at that time was only about 2,000 yuan RMB, she was very wealthy. However, in fear of the state changing its policy, she and her husband decided to seek better opportunities overseas. She gave almost all her money (500,000 HK dollars) to a *shetou* ("snake head," which means population smuggler) who in turn smuggled her and her husband to Canada. Although she was doing well after her arrival in Canada, at first she did not know whether the loss of all of their belongings had made it worthwhile to come here. The interview data indicate that for these rich *getihu* (higher status Chinese) the sudden loss of their wealth in China was a nightmare, although they knew that in coming to Canada by illegal means they must pay the high price. One of the respondents told the author that whenever he thought about the amount of money he had spent on coming to Canada and the fact that he might be driven out of the country for his illegal entrance, he would be in a cold sweat, because he might never be able to make that amount of money in China again in his lifetime.

However, loss of achievements in China was of little consequence to respondents with lower social status and lower income in China, such as peasants (5), factory workers (4), and the employees of the service sector (2). Since they were at the bottom of the social and economic structure, their achievements in China would not be enough for them to make a significant difference.

Deficiency in Living Skills

Lack of living skills in Canada was one of the most frequently reported problems. The interview and participant observation data show that the term "lack of living skills" refers mainly to two phenomena: 1) the inability of most MCRs to speak English; and 2) a lack of competency in the capitalism labour market system. These two problems seriously affected MCRs' social and economic lives in Metro Toronto, and made them feel socially inadequate and unskilled, thereby slowing their adaptation process.

Scholars consider ability to use one of the official languages to be the most powerful determinant of newcomers' ability to adapt and raise their level of adaptation in Canada. Newcomers often rank an inadequate capacity to use the official languages as the first difficulty to be overcome, in competing in work, education, health services, housing and the like (Dorais, 1987). Our research revealed that most MCRs in Toronto suffered from English language problems in their daily lives. According to the social survey conducted by MCRO (Mainland Chinese Refugees Organization) in the summer of 1993 (n=81), 31 respondents (38.3 percent) reported they could not speak English at all, 36 (44.4 percent) reported they could speak only in broken English while interacting with non-Chinese. Dorais (1987:52) has demonstrated that for newcomers in Canada "ignorance of the main Canadian languages greatly restricts what such a person can do." The findings of this study support Dorais' argument and demonstrate that poor language skills increased MCRs' stress in Canada because they were unable to participate fully in all the activities of daily life.

Poor competence in the Canadian labour market also showed up in the form of such problems as lack of required skills and Canadian experience, and unfamiliarity with the labour market mechanism and culture. While facing the strong competence of Canadians, the immigrants had to take any kind of low-paying job, even though many of them were professionals in China. Interviews showed that only one respondent, who was an engineer in China, claimed he was satisfied with the job currently held; all the other 14 respondents with professional backgrounds (4 engineers, 5 doctors and 4 teachers) reported they could not get jobs related to their professional training, and had to take labouring jobs which were not in line with their professional aspirations. Our survey revealed a similar situation, with only 17 respondents (14.7 percent) who currently held jobs in line with their Chinese work experience and education, 25 (21.6 percent) who reported their jobs were close to their experience and education in China, and 60 (51.7 percent) who stated their jobs did not at all match their experience and education in China.

In short, deficiency in living skills in Canada produced great obstacles to MCR adaptation and thus contributed to MCRs' stress. This affected most those who were more highly educated with professional backgrounds in China, because of their higher expectations and ambition to achieve occupational mobility in Canada. The less educated with no professional background tended to seek employment opportunities in existing Chinese communities and Chinese ethnic economies, although there, too, the market was competitive.

FACING STRESS AND COPING

Stress and Appraisal

As stated in this study earlier, coping is a behaviour that protects individual MCRs from stress (Dressler, 1991; White, 1974). Although Cawte (1968) developed a stress scale which has proved to be a reliable and valid measure of stress (Berry et al., 1988), the degree of stress caused by specific stress factors, as Hunter points out, is still difficult to quantify (Hunter, 1988:162). Accordingly, this study follows Scott and Scott's satisfaction model, applied in their study of immigrant adaptation, and using immigrants' subjective satisfaction with their material lives, jobs, social positions, social environment and cultural lives in Canada (Scott and Scott, 1989). People tend to be dissatisfied rather than satisfied in a stressful state, and the more stressful state the respondent is in, the less satisfication there tends to be.

The survey data reveal that 62 MCRs (53.4 percent) were satisfied with their material lives in Canada, whereas 21 (18.1 percent) were dissatisfied. Just under half (48.2 percent) of the respondents were satisfied with their jobs in Canada, while 27 (23.2 percent) were dissatisfied. Ninety (77.6 percent) respondents were satisfied with their social environment in Canada, while only 5 were dissatisfied; 15 (12.9 percent) were satisfied with their social status, while 70 (60.4 percent) were dissatisfied. A fourth (25 percent) of the respondents were satisfied with their cultural lives in Canada, and a third, 45 (38.8 percent) were dissatisfied (see Table 14.3).

TABLE 14.3

MCRs' SATISFACTION WITH SOCIAL LIFE IN CANADA

Content	Satisfied N	%	Neutral N	%	Not Satisfied N	%	No Answer N	%
Material Lives	62	53.4	31	26.7	21	18.1	2	1.7
Occupations	56	48.2	25	21.6	27	23.2	8	6.9
Social Environment	90	77.6	16	13.8	5	4.3	5	4.3
Social Status	15	12.9	27	23.3	70	60.4	4	3.4
Cultural Lives	29	25.0	39	33.6	45	38.8	3	2.6

Source: Survey data.

Clearly, the majority of our sample of MCRs (60.4 percent) who were dissatisfied were dissatisfied with their social status in Canada, which shows their stress was mainly connected with that factor. The sources of this dissatisfication or stress seemed to be mostly due to uncertainty of legal status, loss of achievements in China, and discrimination. The second largest group in our sample (38.8 percent) were dissatisfied with their cultural lives in Canada. Here stress seems to be related to the cultural differences between China and Canada. Nostalgia, separation from families, and deficiency of living (mainly cultural) skills seemed to be the sources of this kind of dissatisfaction or stress. Only 23.2 percent were dissatisfied with their jobs and 18.1 percent reported they were dissatisfied with their material lives. Finally, there were very few respondents (4.3 percent) who reported that they were dissatisfied with the Canadian social environment. Conflict between high expectations and what Canadian society offers could be the sources of this dissatisfaction.

A further analysis of the survey data reveals that the degree of MCRs' dissatisfaction or stress is closely connected to the individual's legal status in Canada and educational background in China. The respondents who had been granted landed status tended to report lower dissatisfaction and less stress. In terms of education, we found that more highly educated respondents reported a higher rate of dissatisfaction than less educated respondents (see Table 14.4).

TABLE 14.4

SATISFACTION BY FIVE FACTORS (%)

Respondent Range	Material Lives	Occupations	Social Status (%)	Social Environment	Cultural Lives
Satisfied					
Landed	60.0	25.0	40.0	80.0	60.0
Unlanded	54.2	52.9	12.1	81.2	24.0
Highly Educated	40.0	26.5	10.9	81.5	18.1
Less Educated	59.1	74.5	15.1	81.5	33.3
Neutral					
Landed	40.0	25.0	20.0	20.0	20.0
Unlanded	26.6	23.1	25.2	14.2	35.2
Highly Educated	27.3	28.6	25.5	13.0	34.5
Less Educated	27.3	18.2	22.6	14.8	33.3
Dissatisfied					
Landed	0	50.0	40.0	0	20.0
Unlanded	19.3	24.1	62.6	4.7	40.8
Highly Educated	32.5	44.9	63.7	5.6	45.4
Less Educated	3.6	7.3	62.3	3.7	33.3

Source: Survey data.

When asked "Are you satisfied now?," most of the rejected refugee claimants first answered that they were not satisfied because of their legal status. They mentioned feelings of stress more frequently than those who had achieved landed status. More highly educated respondents reported more stressful feelings, possibly because of higher expectations.

Lazarus and Folkman (1984), in their theoretical model, emphasize the role of cognitive appraisal processes as being also important. They suggest that by understanding the individual's internalized cultural and social norms we can begin to understand and predict what such individuals will perceive to be stressful, and how they react to, or cope with, stress.

Coping Resources and Strategies

The available coping resources for MCRs can be categorized as personal and environmental. The former are related to personal experiences and backgrounds, such as the amount of education, level of family support, and life experiences. The latter refer to the social supportive network, such as the existing Chinese communities and the government agencies and public facilities. In practice, as this study found, not only personal resources but also social resources mean different things to our respondents. In social interactions the way in which individuals present self to others is decided by personal resources, and this relationship in turn influences the quality and quantity of social support a person is able to get from social resources for coping. For example, many coping MCRs of the interview sample (66.1 percent) self-reported that they could not use English in their daily lives, and thus they assumed they would get less social support in dealing with stress. Inadequate command of English operates as a constraint that affects the use of social resources. We propose that personal resources are more decisive than social resources in coping strategies.

Both the interview and the participant observational data show that the coping process can be developed in both positive and negative directions. In keeping with Lazarus and Folkman (1984), coping requires effort. "Coping is frequently equated with successful adaptation" (Compas et al., 1992:49). Consequently, this study analyzes coping as a process requiring effort in adaptation (see Table 14.5).

Zheng and Berry (1991) report that Chinese sojourners (those who come and go) tend to use more positive ways of coping in their adap-

TABLE 14.5

MCRs' COPING RESOURCES AND BEHAVIOUR

Stress Types	Resources*	Coping Behaviour	Function**	Outcomes
1	Rationalities(P)	Lower Expectations	E-F	Facing Reality
	Chinese Media (S)	Pray God for the Future		Imaging Good Future
2	Optimism Sense(P)	Hopeful Thinking	E-F	Optimism Coping
	Experiences(P)	Building Positive Images	P-F	Achievements
	Chinese Community(S)	Social Interaction	P-F	Being Accepted
	Government Services(S)			
3	Families(P)	Emotional Contact		
	Public Services(S)	With Families	E-F	Friendships
	Friends(P)	Long Distance Call		
	Churches(S)	Writing Letters		Family Cares
		Making Friends		
4	Personalities(P)	Affiliation with Other		
	Chinese Media(S)	MCRs	E-F	Share Feelings
	Chinatown(S)	Keep Busy	P-F	Forget Past
5	Personalities(P)	Self Strengthen	E-F	Self-Respect
	Ethnicity(P)	Social Interaction	P-F	Self-Esteem
	Chinese Community(S)			
6	Abilities(P)	Emotional Balance	E-F	Satisfaction
	Personalities(P)	Hopeful Thinking	E-F	Enjoyment
	Chinese Community(S)			
7	Abilities(P)	Learning	P-F	To Be Skilled
	Chinese Community(S)	Taking Any Jobs	P-F	Well-Being
	Networks(S)	Seeking Jobs in		
	Government Service(S)	Ethnic Sector	P-F	Avoiding Demands
		Accepting Training	P-F	Gaining Skills

*(P) for personal resources, (S) for social resources.
**E-F for emotion-focused coping, P-F for problem-focused coping.
Sources: Interview data; participant observational data.

tation process; this study supports their finding. As shown in Table 14.5, both emotion-focused and problem-focused coping strategies were adopted by MCRs to counter different types of stress with the available resources. For example, uncertainty of legal status in Canada has been identified as the crucial form of stress for the great majority of MCRs (44 out of 56); most of them adopted positive coping behaviours to counter this stress, such as reducing the tension by positive thinking — taking the view that their problems would be solved sooner or later — and being willing to engage in hard work.

Passive coping occurred when individuals lost confidence in their ability to resolve the problems, a reflection of personal vulnerability rather than a rational reaction to stress. Withdrawal and complaint were the most frequently used passive ways of coping. Rather than working hard a few of them stayed on social welfare and complained that the Canadian government did not accept them as convention refugees.

A good example would be Li Heping; he came to Canada as a visa student but had never been to any educational institutions in Canada. In order to survive he made a refugee claim and got $599 welfare money per month. He constantly complained that he had made a wrong decision in coming to Canada, that Canadians looked down on him because he was not good at labour jobs, even though he spoke good English. He claimed his intelligence was overlooked because he was a university teacher in China, so that he almost became mentally ill. He solved the stress problem by abandoning his claim, and went back to China. Later he wrote that he had again got back his university position in China.

COPING AS EFFECTIVE ADAPTATION

In his study of refugee adaptation, Berry explored the relationship between adaptation, so that "through a process of coping some satisfactory adaptation to the new situation is achieved" (Berry, 1991:27). Compas et al. (1992) consider coping as an effective process of adaptation, and for them "coping is frequently equated with successful adaptation." In our analysis, the link between the processes of coping and adaptation are explored.

Socioeconomic Adaptation

Adaptation is a multidimensional social life phenomenon often influenced by many factors (Michalowski, 1987). Although in anthropology adaptation has often been treated as a group phenomenon (Kim, 1988), more recent research has explored it on the individual level (Chierici, 1989; Gold, 1992). We suggest that socioeconomic adaptation is crucial.

Having a good job is a practical necessity if there is to be progress beyond the level of mere subsistence or welfare. Employment is also perceived as an important means of establishing positive images and to presenting the self positively to the Canadians. Therefore, MCRs have shown a high degree of willingness to join the labour force, despite their uncertain futures in Canada and their lack of required skills.

Samuel (1987:66), in his study of economic adaptation of Indochinese refugees in Canada, argues that, "A central concern of a refugee on arrival in a new country is to quickly land a job." In our study a majority of MCRs started to work within one and a half years of arriving in Canada. Our survey data show that 81.9 percent of the respondents were employed, and 45.7 percent had been employed for more than 24 months. Less than 50 percent of the respondents whose legal status was uncertain reported they had been employed for more than 24 months. This again shows the significance of legal status for adaptation. More highly educated individuals had been employed longer and had started to work earlier.

In her study of Vietnamese socioeconomic adaptation in Victoria, Woo (1987) reported three sources were available to help refugees find jobs, namely government agencies, refugee sponsors and their acquaintances, and refugees themselves and their social networks. Our study shows that MCRs found jobs mainly by themselves (48.3 percent) or with the help of their relatives or friends (39.7 percent). Unfamiliarity with government agencies and lack of social networks makes access to government jobs difficult.

Most respondents felt that the length of time for which they had been employed represented the degree of successful adaptation to Canadian society. For example, one rejected female refugee claimant told the author, "I am very lucky, since I arrived in Canada I have been employed all the time. In my company many Canadians have been laid off but I have kept my job of which I am very proud. Although I am not satisfied with my job, it makes me feel comfortable and secure in Canada. I often think the Canadian government should give me the legal status since I have been paying tax all the time."

The North American immigration literature shows that when newcomers come to the postindustrial West there is initial downward mobility, unemployment is common, and upward mobility can be slow (Richmond, 1988; Samuel, 1987). The present study supports this conclusion. The survey data show that 58.8 percent of the respondents who were employed when the survey was conducted reported that their jobs did not match their educational and working experiences in China. The majority thought they were underemployed. The survey data also show that three out of four respondents believed that training in Canada was needed, so 69 percent of them had accepted educational or job training after they arrived in Canada.

As is the case with most refugees, MCRs initially had relatively low income levels, with a significant proportion living below the poverty line. However, MCR earning levels improved as the adaptation process continued (Samuel, 1987). One fourth (25.4 percent) reported that their annual incomes were below $10,000, almost half (43.3 percent) earned $10,000-15,000, one fourth (25.4 percent) earned $15,000-20,000, and a few (4.5 percent) $20,000-30,000. A significant difference exists between income levels and education levels (DF4,P<0.05). Richmond (1988:51) argues that education is one of the keys to immigrant adaptation, and that education is positively correlated with economic adaptation.

In spite of their lower incomes over half of the respondents reported that they were satisfied with their economic lives in Canada; only 18.1 percent were dissatisfied. An inverse relationship between education and subjective aspects of adaptation was found (Chi-Square test DF,P<0.001). Richmond (1974) made the same finding in Toronto.

The social welfare system is perceived by MCRs as a helpful support in their initial adaptation process. Most (88.8 percent) had collected welfare when they arrived in Canada, a majority (65.3 percent) collected welfare for less than one year. Over half (55.4 percent) reported that the social welfare system in Canada was too good to be believed.

Sociocultural Adaptation

Richmond sees sociocultural adaptation as the process of acculturation and social integration of immigrants (1988:49). In anthropological literature, acculturation refers to culture change that results from continuous, first-hand contact between two distinct cultural groups (Broom et al., 1967). According to Chimbos (1980:135), social integration "simply refers to a large degree of social and structural interaction between the ethnic minority and the rest of society." For him "social integration does not necessarily mean assimilation, the loss of the individual's ethnic identity or his language and culture."

Integration will be operationalized by measuring satisfaction with Canadian life, identification with the host nation, learning the host society's language, attending the larger society's activities, and engaging in friendship networks including intermarriage (Chimbos, 1980). Richmond (1974) notes that subjectively measured satisfaction is correlated with the degree of immigrant sociocultural adaptation. In immigrant literature, life satisfaction is often treated as an outcome rather than a predictor of adaptation (Scott and Scott, 1989:8).

The interview data indicate that, although MCRs have suffered from identity confusion, many of them tended to identify themselves as

Chinese Canadians. They simply loved this country and decided to stay at whatever cost (*The Toronto Star*, March 13, 1995:A1). When asked what they liked most in Canada, they answered immediately, without thinking: Canada's democratic system (freedom, environment, public facilities, social welfare, health care, education system); Canadians' politeness in social interactions; and human rights.

To learn and use the host country's language "constitutes the *sine qua non* condition of a successful adaptation" (Dorais, 1987:52). Our survey shows that two thirds had attended an ESL class. They saw learning and use of English as an effective and a necessary condition for finding more Canadian friends. One male respondent said, "Language is a big problem which prevents me from adapting to the mainstream society. If I had legal status and language skills, I would have a much better life in Canada."

Although most MCRs were eager to join the activities of the larger society and to have friendship networks with Canadians, only a few had such contacts. Our data show that only 30.2 percent of the respondents participated in mainstream society's activities, 7.8 percent interacted with their non-Chinese neighbours frequently, and 55.2 occasionally did so. Only four of the 56 interviewed claimed they had more than three Canadian friends. One was married to a Canadian, another was married to a Canadian-born Chinese.

SUMMARY

Based on Lazarus and Folkman's (1985) cognitive appraisal model, this study identifies seven forms of stress that MCRs face in their adaptation to Canadian society.

We found that the degree to which MCRs experienced stress was closely connected with their legal status in Canada, educational background in China, and the length of time for which they had been in Canada. The respondents who had been granted landed immigrant status tended to report lower dissatisfaction, and thus less stress and better adaptation. It was found that more highly educated respondents reported a higher rate of stress, partly due to the high expectations and the social realities in Canada. As was the case with Lazarus and Folkman's model, we found that when confronted with stressful circumstances, the coping strategies adapted varied according to the resources at their disposal. For Lazarus and Folkman's respondents coping "is typically equated with adaptational success" (Lazarus and Folkman, 1984:140).

In terms of socioeconomic adaptation we found that MCRs showed a high degree of willingness to join the labour force, despite their uncertain futures in Canada and their lack of required skills. The majority of MCRs started working within one and a half years after their arrival in Canada. It was found that more highly educated individuals had been employed longer and had started to work earlier. Unlike socioeconomic adaptation, sociocultural adaptation is a long-term process. We found that females were more adaptable than males; those who had received landed status tended to be more adapted than those who had not; and more highly educated persons seemed to be more adapted than the less educated.

REFERENCES

Abbot, B.G. and C.M. Beach. 1988. "Immigrant Earnings Differential and Cohort Effects in Canada." Unpublished manuscript.

Abbott, Kenneth A. and Elizabeth Lee Abbott. 1973. "Juvenile Delinquency in San Francisco's Chinese American Community: 1961-1966. In Stanley Sue and Nathaniel N. Wanger (eds.), *Asian-Americans: Psychological Perspectives*. Palo Alto, CA: Science and Behavior Books.

Abele, Francis and Daiva Stasiulis. 1989. "Canada as a 'White Settler Colony': What About Natives and Immigrants?" In W. Clement and G. Williams (eds.), *The New Political Economy*. Montreal: McGill-Queen's University Press.

Abella, Irving and Harold Tropper. 1982. *None Is Too Many*. Toronto: Lester, Orpen Dennys.

Abella, Rosalie Silberman. 1984. *Equality in Employment: A Royal Commission Report*. Ottawa: Supply and Services Canada.

Abu-Laban, Yasmeen and Daiva Stasiulis. 1992. "Ethnic-Pluralism Under Siege: Popular and Partisan Opposition to Multiculturalism." *Canadian Public Policy* 18:365-86.

Adelman, H., C. LeBlanc and J.P Therian. 1980. "Canadian Policy on Indochinese Refugees." In E. Tepper (ed.), *Southeast Asian Exodus: From Tradition to Resettlement. Understanding Refugees From Laos, Kampuchea and Vietnam in Canada*. Ottawa: The Canadian Asian Studies Association.

Agnew, Robert. 1985. "Social Control Theory and Delinquency: A Longitudinal Test." *Criminology* 23:47-61.

Agnew, Robert. 1991a. "A Longitudinal Test of Social Control Theory and Delinquency." *Journal of Research in Crime and Delinquency* 28:126-56.

————. 1991b. "The Interactive Effects of Peer Variables on Delinquency." *Criminology* 29:47-72.

Agocs, Carol and Monica Boyd. 1993. "The Canadian Ethnic Mosaic Recast for the 1990s." In James E. Curtis, Edward Grabb and Neil Guppy (eds.), *Social Stratification in Canada*. 3/e. Scarborough, ON: Prentice Hall.

Akbari, S.A. 1988. "Some Economic Impacts of the Immigrant Population in Canada." Ph.D. Dissertation, Department of Economics, Simon Fraser University, Burnaby, BC.

Akutsu, Phillip D., Stanley Sue, W.S. Zane and Charles Y. Nakamura. 1989. "Ethnic Differences in Alcohol Consumption among Asians and Caucasians in the United States: An Investigation of Cultural and Physiological Factors." *Journal of Studies on Alcohol* 50:261-67.

Aldrich, Howard et al. 1985. "Ethnic Residential Concentration and the Protected Market Hypothesis." *Social Forces* 63:996-1009.

Allport, Gordon. 1954. *The Nature of Prejudice*. New York: Doubleday.

Anderson, B. 1991. *Imagined Communities: Reflections on the Origin and Spread of Nationalism* (Revised Edition). London: Verso.

Anderson, G. 1974. *Networks of Contact: The Portuguese and Toronto*. Waterloo, ON: Wilfred Laurier University Press.

Anderson, Joan M. and M. Judith Lynam. 1987. "The Meaning of Work for Immigrant Women in the Lower Echelons of the Canadian Labour Force." *Canadian Ethnic Studies*. 19:67-90.

Anthias, Floya and Nira Yuval-Davis. 1983. "Contextualizing Feminism: Gender, Ethnic and Class Divisions." *Feminist Review* 15:62-75.

Arnopoulos, Sheila McLeod. 1979. *Problems of Immigrant Women in the Canadian Labour Force*. Ottawa: Canadian Advisory Council on the Status of Women, Supply and Services Canada.

Aronowitz, Michael. 1984. "The Social and Emotional Adjustment of Immigrant Children: A Review of the Literature. *International Migration Review* 18:237-57.

Bach, R.L. 1988. "State Intervention in Southeast Asian Refugee Resettlement in the United States." *Journal of Refugee Studies* 1:38-56.

————, and J.B. Bach. 1980. "Employment Patterns of Southeast Asian Refugees." *Monthly Labour Review* 103:31-38.

Bachman, Jerald G., John M. Wallace, Jr., Patrick M. O'Malley, Lloyd D. Johnston, Candace L. Kurth and Harold W. Neighbors. 1991. "Racial/Ethnic Differences in Smoking, Drinking, and Illicit Drug Use among American High School Seniors, 1976-89." *American Journal of Public Health* 81:372-77.

Badets, Jane. 1993. "Canada's Immigrants: Recent Trends." *Canadian Social Trends* 29:8-11.

Bagley, Christopher. 1972. "Deviant Behaviour in English and West Indian School Children." *Research in Education* 8:47-55.

Bai, David H. 1992. "Canadian Immigration Policy and the Voluntary Sector: The Case of the Edmonton Immigrant Services Association." *Human Organization* 51:23-34.

Baker, R. 1990. "The Refugee Experience: Communication and Stress, Recollections of a Refugee Survivor." *Journal of Refugee Studies* 3:64-71.

Balakrishnan, T.R. and Feng Hou. 1995. "The Changing Patterns of Spatial Concentration and Residential Segregation of Ethnic Groups in Canada's Major Metropolitan Areas, 1981-1991." Paper presented at the Population Association of America meetings in San Francisco, 6-10 April.

Barnes, Grace M. and John W. Welte. 1986. "Adolescent Alcohol Abuse: Subgroup Differences and Relationships to Other Problem Behaviors." *Journal of Adolescent Research* 1:79-94.

Basavarajappa, K.G. 1996. "Male-Female Differences in Income of the Elderly by Birthplace and Source of Income, Canada, 1990." Paper presented at the Population Association of America meetings in New Orleans, 9-11 May.

———. 1996. "Does Visible Minority Status Matter? An Analysis of Income Differences among Visible Minorities and Others." Paper presented at the Symposium on Immigrant Integration, Winnipeg, MB, 25-27 October.

———, and Ravi B.P. Verma. 1985. "Asian Immigrants in Canada: Some Findings from the 1981 Census." *International Migration* 23:97-121.

———. 1990. "Occupational Composition of Immigrant Women." In *Ethnic Demography*, S.S. Halli, F. Trovato and L. Driedger (eds.), Ottawa: Carleton University Press.

Basavarajappa, K.G., R.P. Beaujot and T.J. Samuel. 1993. *Impact of Immigration in the Receiving Countries*. Geneva: International Organization for Migration.

Beaud, J.P. and J.G. Prévost. 1993. "La Statistique des origines raciales au Canada, 1921-1941." Note de recherche no. 45. L'Université du Québec à Montréal.

———. 1994. "États et sociétés: la structuration des systemes nationaux, 1830-1945." Note de recherche no. 47. L'Université du Québec a Montréal.

Beaujot, Roderic P., K.G. Basavarajappa and Ravi B.P. Verma. 1988. *Income of Immigrants in Canada, 1980*. Ottawa: Statistics Canada, Supply and Services Canada.

Berger, Peter. 1967. *The Sacred Canopy: Elements of a Sociological Theory of Religion.* Garden City, NY: Doubleday.

Berry, John W. 1980. "Acculturation as Varieties of Adaptation." In A.M. Padilla (ed.), *Acculturation: Theory, Models and Some New Findings.* Boulder, CO: Westview Press.

————. 1984. "Multicultural Policy in Canada: A Social Psychological Analysis." *Canadian Journal of Behavioural Science* 16:353-70.

————. 1991. "Refugee Adaptation in Settlement Countries: An Overview with an Emphasis on Primary Prevention." In Ahearn and Athey (eds.), *Refugee Children.* Baltimore: The Johns Hopkins University Press.

————, Rudolf Kalin and D.M. Taylor. 1977. *Multiculturalism and Ethnic Attitudes in Canada.* Ottawa: Supply and Services Canada.

Berry, John W., U. Kim and P. Boski. 1988. "Psychological Acculturation of Immigrants." In Kim and Gudykunst (eds.), *Cross-Cultural Adaptation.* Newbury Park CA: Sage.

Berry, John W. and U. Kim. 1988. "Acculturation and Mental Health." In Dasen et al. (eds.), *Cross-Cultural Psychology and Health: Towards Applications.* London: Sage.

Berry, John W. and M. Wells. 1994. "Attitudes Towards Aboriginal Peoples and Aboriginal Self-Government in Canada." In J. Hylton (ed.), *Aboriginal Self-Government in Canada.* Saskatoon, SK: Purich Publishing.

Berry, John W. and J.A. Laponce. 1994. *Ethnicity and Culture in Canada: The Research Landscape.* Toronto: University of Toronto Press.

Berry, John W. and Rudolf Kalin. 1995. "Multicultural and Ethnic Attitudes in Canada: An Overview of the 1991 National Survey." *Canadian Journal of Behavioural Science* 27:310-20.

Bettelheim, B. 1943. "Individual and Mass Behavior in Extreme Situations." *Journal of Abnormal and Social Psychology* 38:417-52.

Bibby, Reginald. 1995. *The Bibby Report: Social Trends Canadian Style.* Toronto: Stoddart.

Billingsley, B. and L. Musynski. 1985. *No Discrimination Here.* Toronto: Social Planning Council of Metro Toronto and the Urban Alliance on Race Relations.

Blauner, Robert. 1991. "Racism, Race and Ethnicity: Some Reflections on the Language of Race." Paper presented at the Annual Meeting of the American Sociological Association, thematic session: Reexamining the Commonly Used Concepts in Race-Ethnic Relations. Cincinnati, OH, August.

Bloom, David E. and Morley Gunderson. 1989. "An Analysis of the Earnings of Canadian Immigrants." Department of Economics, Columbia University, New York.

Bloom, David E., Gilles Grenier and Morley Gunderson. 1995. "The Changing Labour Market Position of Canadian Immigrants." *Canadian Journal of Economics* 28:987-1005.

Bogdan, R. and S.K. Taylor. 1984. *Introduction to Qualitative Research Methods*, 2/e. New York: John Wiley.

Bogue, Donald. 1964. "A New Estimate of the Negro Population and Negro Vital Rates in the United States, 1930-1960." *Demography* 1:1-15.

Bolaria, B. 1985b. "East Indians." In B. Bolaria and Peter Li (eds.), *Racial Oppression in Canada*. Toronto: Garamond Press.

———, B. Singh and Peter S. Li. 1985. *Racial Oppression in Canada*. Toronto: Garamond Press.

———. 1985a. "Chinese." In B. Bolaria and Peter S. Li (eds.), *Racial Oppression in Canada*. Toronto: Garamond Press.

Bonacich, Edna. 1972. "A Therapy of Ethnic Antagonism: The Split Labour Market." *American Sociological Review* 37:547-59.

Borjas, G.J. 1985. "Assimilation Changes in Cohort Quality and the Earnings of Immigrants." *Journal of Labour Economics* 3:463-89.

Bottomley, Gill. 1988. "The Cultures, Multiculturalism and the Politics of Representation." *Australian Journal of Social Issues* 23:169-83.

Bowles, Roy. 1982. "Sociological Attempts to Understand Canadian Ethnicity: Two Examples." *Journal of Canadian Studies* 1:131-34.

Boxhill, Walton O. 1990. *Making Tough Choices in Using Census Data to Count Visible Minorities in Canada* (rev.). Statistics Canada: Employment Equity Data Program Report 4, 12, 1990. Ottawa: Supply and Services Canada.

Boyd, Monica. 1975. "The Status of Immigrant Women in Canada." *Canadian Review of Sociology and Anthropology* 12:406-16.

———. 1976. "Occupations of Female Immigrants and North American Immigrant Statistics." *International Migration Review* 10:73-80.

Boyd, Monica. 1984. "At a Disadvantage: The Occupational
    Attainments of Foreign-Born Women in Canada." *International
    Migration Review* 18:1091-119.

————. 1986. "Immigrant Women in Canada." In Rita J. Simon
    and Caroline B. Brettell (eds.), *International Migration: The
    Female Experience.* Totowa, NJ: Rowman and Allanheld.

————. 1987. *Migrant Women in Canada — Profiles and Policies.*
    Immigration Research Working Paper no. 2. Canada:
    Employment and Immigration Canada.

————. 1990. "Immigrant Women: Language, Socioeconomic
    Inequalities and Policy Issues." In Shiva S. Halli, Frank Trovato
    and Leo Driedger (eds.), *Ethnic Demography: Canadian
    Immigrant, Racial and Cultural Variations.* Ottawa: Carleton
    University Press.

————. 1992. "Gender, Visible Minority and Immigrant Earnings:
    Inequality, Reassessing an Employment Equity Promise." In Vic
    Satzewich (ed.), *Deconstructing a Nation: Multiculturalism and
    Racism in the 1990s in Canada.* Halifax, NS: Fernwood
    Publishing.

————. 1993a. "Measuring Ethnicity in the Future: Population,
    Policies, Politics and Social Science Research." In Gustave
    Goldmann and Nampeo McKenney (eds.), *Challenges of
    Measuring an Ethnic World: Science, Politics and Reality.* Ottawa
    and Washington, DC: Statistics Canada and the United States
    Bureau of the Census.

————. 1993b. "Measuring Ethnicity." Paper presented at the lec-
    ture series, Robert F. Harney Professorship and Program in
    Ethnic, Immigration and Pluralism Studies. Department of
    Sociology, University of Toronto, February.

————. 1996. "Constructing Ethnic Responses: Socioeconomic and
    Media Effects." Working Paper 96-133. Tallahassee, FL: Center
    for the Study of Population and Demography, Florida State
    University.

————, G. Goldmann and P. White. 1993. "A Rose By Any Other
    Name: Race in the Canadian Census." Paper presented at the
    Conference of the International Union for the Scientific Study
    of Population (IUSSP), Montreal.

Breedom Research Inc. 1988. "Report on Focus Groups to Study
    Reactions to Ethnicity/Race Questions for the 1991 Census."
    Report prepared for the Housing, Family and Social Statistics
    Division, Statistics Canada. Ottawa: Supply and Services.

Bresler, Fountain. 1981. *The Chinese Mafia.* New York: Stein and Day.

Breton, Raymond. 1984. "The Production and Allocation of Symbolic Resources: An Analysis of the Linguistic and Ethnocultural Fields in Canada." *Canadian Review of Sociology and Anthropology* 21:123-44.

————. 1986. *Employment Equity Act and Reporting Requirements.* Ottawa: Supply and Services Canada.

————. 1986. "Multiculturalism and Canadian Nation-Building." In A. Cairns and C. Williams (eds.), *The Politics of Gender, Ethnicity and Language in Canada.*

————. 1988. "From Ethnic to Civic Nationalism: English Canada and Quebec." *Ethnic and Racial Studies* 11:1-10.

British Columbia. 1993. *Bill 39-1993. Multiculturalism Act.* Minister of Education and Minister Responsible for Multiculturalism and Human Rights. Certified correct as passed Third Reading on the 29th Day of July, 1993.

Broadfoot, Barry. 1977. Years of Sorrow, Years of Shame: The Story of the Japanese in World War II. Toronto: Doubleday.

Broom, Leonard et al. 1967. "Acculturation: An Exploratory Formulation." In Bohannan and Plog (eds.), *Beyond the Frontier.* New York: The Natural History Press.

Bryce-Laporte, R. (ed.). 1980. *Sourcebook on the New Immigration,* vol. 1. New Jersey: Transaction Books.

Buchignani, Norman. 1980. "Accommodation, Adaptation and Policy: Dimensions of the Southeast Asian Experience in Canada." In K.V. Ujimoto and G. Hirabayashi (eds.), *Visible Minorities and Multiculturalism: Asians in Canada.* Toronto: Butterworths.

————. 1982. "Canadian Ethnic Research and Multiculturalism." *Journal of Canadian Studies/Revue d'études canadiennes* 1:16-34.

————, D.M. Indra, with Ram Srivastava. 1985. *Continuous Journey: A Social History of South Asians in Canada.* Toronto; McClelland and Stewart.

Burke, Ronald J. 1990. *Managing an Increasingly Diverse Workforce: Experience of Minority Managers and Professionals in Canada.* Toronto: York University.

Burnet, Jean. 1976. "Ethnic Relations and Ethnic Policies in Canadian Society." In F. Henry (ed.), *Ethnicity in the Americas.* The Hague: Mouton.

Burnet, Jean. 1978. "The Definition of Multiculturalism in a Bilingual Framework: An Interpretation." In A. Wolfgang (ed.), *Education of Immigrant Students.* Toronto: Ontario Institute of Studies in Education.

———. 1978. "The Policy of Multiculturalism within a Bilingual Framework: A Stocktaking." In A. Wolfgang (ed.), *Education of Immigrant Students.* Toronto: Ontario Institute of Studies in Education.

———. 1980. "The Policy of Multiculturalism and the Indochinese Refugees." In L. Driedger (ed.), *The Canadian Ethnic Mosaic.* Toronto: McClelland and Stewart.

Butz, W. and Gustave Goldmann. 1993. "Introduction." In *Challenges to Measuring an Ethnic World: Science Politics and Reality.* Proceedings of the Joint Canada-U.S. Conference on the Measurement of Ethnicity, 1-3 April 1992. Washington, DC: U.S. Bureau of the Census and Statistics Canada.

Callaghan, Barry. 1990. "French-English Translations not Popular in Canadian Publishing." *Globe and Mail* (Toronto): 27 January.

Canada. 1872, 1876. *Census of Canada,* volumes I and IV. 1871 *Census of Canada,* Department of Agriculture. Ottawa: King's Printer.

Canada. 1967. *The Official Languages,* volume I. Report of the Royal Commission on Bilingualism and Biculturalism. Ottawa: Queen's Printer.

———. 1988. An Act for the Preservation and Enhancement of Multiculturalism in Canada. *Acts of the Parliament of Canada* and Revised Statutes of Canada.Ottawa: Statistics Canada.

———. 1990. *General Review of the 1986 Census.* Catalogue 99-137E/F. Ottawa: Statistics Canada.

———. 1992. "Canadian Census Ethno-Cultural Questions, 1871-1991." Centre for Ethnic Measurement. Ottawa: Statistics Canada.

———. 1995. *Profile of Visible Minorities.* Reference Document. Ottawa: Statistics Canada.

———. 1996. Various 1996 Census documents: Questionnaires, Instructions, etc. Ottawa: Statistics Canada.

———. 1987. *Strengthening the Canadian Federation: The Constitution Amendments, 1987.* Ottawa: Government of Canada, Supply and Services Canada.

Canada. 1996. *Hansard.* Private members' business. Motion M-277. Deborah Grey, November 26. Ottawa: Supply and Services Canada.

———. 1997. *Hansard.* Private members' business. Motion M-277. Deborah Grey, November 26. Ottawa: Supply and Services Canada.

———. 1997. *Hansard.* Private members' business. Motion M-277. Deborah Grey, March 19. Ottawa: Supply and Services Canada.

Canada Employment and Immigration Advisory Council. 1992. *Last In, First Out: Racism in Employment.* Draft. Ottawa.

Canadian Alliance for Visible Minorities. 1995. *Employment Equity: A Cure or a Curse? A Study Commissioned by the Canadian Alliance for Visible Minorities.* Ottawa: Canadian Heritage, Supply and Services Canada.

Canadian Council on Social Development. 1984. *Not Enough: The Meaning and Measurement of Poverty in Canada.* Report of the CCSD Task Force on the Definition and Measurement of Poverty in Canada. Ottawa. Statistics Canada, Supply and Services Canada.

Canadian Ethnocultural Council. 1992. *Employment Inequity: The Representation of Visible Minorities in the Federal Government, 1988-1991.* Ottawa: Statistics Canada, Supply and Services Canada.

Canadian Human Rights Commission. 1989. *Annual Report, 1988.* Ottawa. Supply and Services Canada.

Canadian Task Force on Mental Health Issues Affecting Immigrants and Refugees. 1988. *After the Door Has Been Opened: Mental Health Issues Affecting Immigrants and Refugees in Canada.* Ottawa: Health and Welfare.

Cardozo, Arthur. 1996. *The Ottawa Citizen.* 14 May.

Cawte, J. 1968. "Personal Discomfort in Australian Aborigines." *Australian and New Zealand Journal of Psychiatry* 2:69-70.

———. 1972. *Cruel, Poor and Brutal Nations.* Honolulu: University of Hawaii.

Cernkovich, Stephen A. and Peggy C. Giordano. 1987. "Family Relationships and Delinquency." *Criminology* 25:295-321.

Chan, Janet and Cheung Yuet Wah. 1985. "Ethnic Resources and Business Enterprises: A Study of Chinese Business in Toronto." *Human Organization* 44:142-54.

Chan, Kwok Bun. 1984. "Mental Health Needs of Indochinese Refugees: Toward a National Refugee Resettlement Policy and Strategy in Canada." In D. Paul Lumsden, (ed.), *Community Mental Health Action*. Ottawa: Canadian Public Health Association.

———. 1987. "Perceived Racial Discrimination and Response: An Analysis of the Indochinese Experience in Montreal, Canada." *Canadian Ethnic Studies* 19:125-47.

———. 1991. *Smoke and Fire: The Chinese in Montreal.* Hong Kong: Chinese University Press.

———, and L. Lam. 1987. "Psychological Problems of Chinese Vietnamese Refugees Resettling in Quebec." In Chan and Indra (eds.), *Uprooting, Loss and Adaptation: The Resettlement of Indochinese Refugees in Canada*. Ottawa: Canadian Public Health Association.

Chan, Kwok Bun and Denise Helly. 1987. "Coping with Racism: A Century of the Chinese Experience in Canada." Special Issue, *Canadian Ethnic Studies* 19:1-14.

Chan, Kwok Bun and Ong Jin Hui. 1995. "The Many Faces of Chinese Entrepreneurship." In R. Cohen (ed.), *The Cambridge Survey of World Migration*. Cambridge: Cambridge University Press.

Chang, Luke, Richard F. Morrissey and Harold S. Koplewicz. 1995. "Prevalence of Psychiatric Symptoms and Their Relation to Adjustment among Chinese-American Youth." *Journal of American Academy of Child and Adolescent Psychiatry* 34:91-99.

Chapman, G. and H. Maclean. 1990. "Qualitative Research in Home Economics." *Canadian Home Economics Journal* 40:129-34.

Charles, Enid. 1948. *The Changing Role of the Family in Canada.* 1941 Census monograph. Ottawa: Dominion Bureau of Statistics.

———. 1956. *Report on a Visit to Burma.* Prepared for the World Health Organization.

Chenitz, W.C. and J.M. Swanson. 1986. *From Practice to Grounded Theory*. Don Mills, ON: Addison-Wesley.

Chi, Iris, Harry H.L. Kitano and James E. Lubben. 1988. "Male Chinese Drinking Behavior in Los Angeles." *Journal of Studies on Alcohol* 49:21-25.

Chi, Iris, James E. Lubben and Harry H.L. Kitano. 1989. "Differences in Drinking Behavior among Three Asian-American Groups." *Journal of Studies on Alcohol* 50:15-23.

Chierici, R.C. 1989. *Demele: "Making It," Migration and Adaptation Among Haitian Boat People in the United States.* New York: AMS Press.

Chimbos, P. 1980. *The Canadian Odyssey: The Greek Experience in Canada.* Toronto: McClelland and Stewart.

Chiswick, R.R. and P.W. Miller. 1986. "Earnings in Canada: The Roles of the Immigrant Generation." *Research in Population Economics* 6:52-70.

Christianson, Carole P. and Morton Weinfeld. 1993. "The Black Family in Canada: A Preliminary Exploration of Family Patterns and Inequality." *Canadian Ethnic Studies* 25:26-44.

Christopher, T.C. 1987. "The 1982 Canadian Charter of Rights and Freedoms and Multiculturalism." *Canadian Review of Studies in Nationalism/Revue Canadienne des études sur le nationalisme* 14:331-42.

Citizenship and Immigration Canada. 1995. *A Broader Vision: Immigration Plan.* 1996 Report to Parliament. Ottawa: Supply and Services Canada.

Clark, K.B. and M.P. Clark. 1947. "Racial Identification and Preferences in Negro Children." In T.M. Newcomb and E.L. Hartley (eds.), *Readings in Social Psychology.* New York: Holt.

Clark, S.D. 1968. *The Developing Canadian Community.* Toronto: University of Toronto Press.

Compas, Bruce E. et al. 1992. "Coping with Psychosocial Stress: A Developmental Perspective." In Bruce N. Carpenter (ed.), *Personal Coping: Theory, Research and Applications.* Westport, CN: Praeger.

Cooley, C.H. 1956. *Human Nature and the Social Order.* New York: Free Press.

Crocker, J. and B. Major. 1989. "Social Stigma and Self-Esteem: The Self-Protective Properties of Stigma." *Psychological Review* 96:608.

Crocker, J., K. Voelkl, M. Testa and B. Major. 1991. "Social Stigma: The Affective Consequences of Attributional Ambiguity." *Journal of Personality and Social Psychology* 60:218-28.

Crosby, F. 1982. *Relative Deprivation and Working Women.* New York: Oxford University Press.

———. 1984. "The Denial of Personal Discrimination." *American Behavioral Scientist* 27:371-86.

Currie, R.S. and S.S. Halli. 1989. Mixed Motivations for Migration in the Urban Prairies: A Comparative Approach. *Social Indicators Research* 21:481- 99.

Coser, Lewis. 1956. *The Functions of Social Conflict.* New York: Free Press.

Dabydeen, Cecil. 1994. "Citizenship is More Than a Birthright." *The Toronto Star.* 20 September.

Dahrendorf, Rolf. 1959. *Class and Class Conflict in Industrial Society.* Palo Alto, CA: Stanford University Press.

Daniels, Roger and Harry H.I. Kitano, *American Racism: Exploration of the Nature of Prejudice* Englewood Cliffs, NJ: Prentice-Hall, 1970.

Das Gupta, Tania. 1994. "Political Economy of Gender, Race and Class: Looking at South Asian Immigrant Women in Canada." *Canadian Ethnic Studies* 26:59-73.

Dashefsky, Arnold. 1975. "Theoretical Frameworks in the Study of Ethnic Identity." *Ethnicity* 2:1-15.

Davis, James F. 1991. *Who is Black: One Country's Definition.* University Park, PA: Pennsylvania State University Press.

Deaux, K. 1984. "From Individual Differences to Social Categories: Analysis of a Decade's Research on Gender." *American Psychologist* 39:105-16.

Dei, George J. Sefa. 1993. "Narrative Discourses of Black/African-Canadian Parents and the Canadian Public School System." *Canadian Ethnic Studies* 25:45-65.

de Lepervanche, Marie. 1984. *Indians in a White Australia: An Account of Race, Class and Indian Immigration to Eastern Australia.* Sydney: George Allen and Unwin.

Dembo, Richard, Gary Grandon, Lawrence La Voie, James Schmeidler and William Burgos. 1986. "Parents and Drugs Revisited: Some Further Evidence in Support of Social Learning Theory." *Criminology* 24:85-104.

Denzin, N. and Y. Lincoln. 1994. *Handbook of Qualitative Research.* Thousand Oaks, CA: Sage.

Dhruvarajan, V. 1991. "The Multiple Oppression of Women of Colour." *Briar Patch* 20:18-19.

Dion, K.L. 1975. "Women's Reactions to Discrimination From Members of the Same or Opposite Sex." *Journal of Research in Personality* 9:294-306.

Dion, K.L. and B.M. Earn. 1975. "The Phenomenology of Being a Target of Prejudice." *Journal of Personality and Social Psychology* 32:944-50.

Dirks, G.E. 1977. *Canada's Refugee Policy: Indifference or Opportunities?* Montreal: McGill-Queen's University Press.

Donnelly, Nancy D. 1989. "The Changing Lives of Refugee Hmong Women." Unpublished Ph.D. dissertation, University of Washington.

Donnelly, N. and M. Hopkins. 1993. "Introduction." In M. Hopkins and N. Donnelly (eds.), *Selected Papers on Refugee Issues: II.* Arlington, VA: American Anthropological Association.

Dorais, Louis-Jacques. 1987. "Language Use and Adaptation." In Chan and Indra, (eds.), *Uprooting, Loss and Adaptation: The Resettlement of Indochinese Refugees in Canada.* Ottawa: Canadian Public Health Association.

————, Lois Foster and David Stockley. 1994. "Multiculturalism and Integration." In Howard Adelman, Allan Borowski, Meyer Burstein and Lois Foster (eds.), *Immigration and Refugee Policy: Australia and Canada Compared,* vol. 2. Carlton, Victoria: Melbourne University Press.

Dosman, E.J. 1972. *Indians: The Urban Dilemma.* Toronto: McClelland and Stewart.

Dovidio, J.F. and S.L. Gaertner. *Prejudice, Discrimination and Racism: Theory and Research.* Orlando, FL: Academic Press.

Dressler, William W. 1991. *Stress and Adaptation in the Context of Culture.* Albany, NY: State University of New York Press.

Driedger, Leo. 1975. "In Search of Cultural Identity Factors: A Comparison of Ethnic Minority Students in Manitoba." *Canadian Review of Sociology and Anthropology* 12:150-62.

————. 1982. "Attitudes of Winnipeg University Students Towards Immigrants of European and Non- European Origin." *Prairie Forum* 7:213-25.

————. 1989. *The Ethnic Factor: Identity in Diversity.* Toronto: McGraw-Hill Ryerson.

————. 1993. "From Martyrs to Muppies: The Mennonite Urban Professional." *Mennonite Quarterly Review* 66:304-322.

————. 1996. *Multi-Ethnic Canada: Identities and Inequalities.* Toronto: Oxford University Press.

————, and Jacob Peters. 1977. "Identity and Social Distance: Towards Understanding Simmel's 'The Stranger.'" *Canadian Review of Sociology and Anthropology* 14:158-73.

Driedger, Leo and Richard Mezoff. 1981. "Ethnic Prejudice and Discrimination in Winnipeg High Schools." *Canadian Journal of Sociology* 6:1-17.

Driedger, Leo and Rodney Clifton. 1984. "Ethnic Stereotypes: Images of Ethnocentrism, Reciprocity or Dissimilarity?" *Canadian Review of Sociology and Anthropology* 21:287-301.

Dublin, Louis. 1926. *Population Problems in the United States and Canada.* Boston and New York: Houghton Mifflin.

Duchesne, Louis. 1993. *La Situation démographique au Québec.* Québec: Bureau de la Statistique.

Dunn, L.C. and T. Dobzhansky. 1944. *Heredity, Race and Society.* London: Penguin.

Duckitt, J. 1992. *The Social Psychology of Prejudice.* Westport, CN: Praeger.

Dworkin, Ronald. 1977. *Taking Rights Seriously.* Cambridge: Harvard University Press.

Editorial. 1995. *The Edmonton Journal*: 13 September.

Editorial. 1996. *Share*: 9 May.

Edmonston, B. and C. Schultze, eds. 1995. *Modernizing the U.S. Census. Summary.* Washington, DC: National Academy Press.

Elder, John P., Craig A. Molgaard and Louise Gresham. 1988. "Predictors of Chewing Tobacco and Cigarette Use in a Multiethnic Public School Population." *Adolescence* 23:688-702.

Elliott, Delbert, David Huizinga and Susan Ageton. 1985. *Explaining Delinquency and Drug Use.* Beverly Hills, CA: Sage.

Elliott, Jean Leonard and Augie Fleras. 1990. "Immigration and the Canadian Ethnic Mosaic." In Peter S. Li (ed.), *Race and Ethnic Relations in Canada.* Toronto: Oxford University Press.

Elliott, Jean Leonard and Augie Fleras. 1992. *Unequal Relations: An Introduction to Race and Ethnic Dynamics in Canada.* Scarborough, ON: Prentice-Hall.

Employment and Immigration Canada. 1986. *Technical Reference Paper No. 3.3.* Ottawa: Supply and Services Canada.

Employment and Immigration Canada (EIC). 1986-1990. *Immigration Statistics: Annual Reports.* Ottawa: Supply and Services Canada.

————. 1986. *Annual Report, Employment Equity Act.* Ottawa: Supply and Services Canada.

————. 1992. *Immigrant Language Training Policy Information Kits.* Ottawa: Supply and Services Canada.

Essed, Philomena. 1991. *Understanding Everyday Racism: An Interdisciplinary Theory.* Newbury Park, CA/London: Sage.

Featherstone, Michael. 1988. "In Pursuit of the Postmodern: An Introduction." In M. Featherstone (ed.), *Postmodernism: Theory, Culture and Society* 5:195-213.

Federation of Canadian Demographers. 1995. *Towards the 21st Century: Emerging Socio-Demographic Trends and Policy Issues in Canada.* Proceedings of the 1995 Symposium organized by the Federation of Canadian Demographers.

Ferguson, B.R. 1984. "Successful Refugee Resettlement: Vietnamese Values, Beliefs and Strategies." Unpublished doctoral dissertation, University of California, Berkeley.

Fincher, Ruth, Lois Foster, Wenona Giles and Valerie Preston. 1994. "Gender and Migration Policy." In Howard Adelman, Allan Borowski, Meyer Burstein and Lois Foster (eds.), *Immigration and Refugee Policy: Australia and Canada Compared,* vol. 1. Carlton, Victoria: Melbourne University Press.

Finnan, C.R. 1981. "Occupational Assimilation of Refugees, *International Migration Review,* 15:292-309.

Fiske, John. 1994. *Media Matters: Everyday Culture and Political Change.* Minneapolis: University of Minnesota.

Folkman, S. and R. Lazarus. 1985. "If It Changes It Must be a Process: Study of Emotions and Coping during Three Stages of a College Examination." *Journal of Personality and Social Psychology* 48:150-70.

Foner, Eric. 1983. "The New View of Reconstruction." *American Heritage* 34:10-15.

Fong, Stanley L.M. 1973. "Assimilation and Changing Social Roles of Chinese Americans." *Journal of Health and Social Behavior* 33:66-76.

Fontaine, Louise. 1993. *Un labyrinthe carré comme un cercle.* Montréal: L'Étincelle.

Foshee, Vangie and Karl E. Bauman. 1992. "Parental and Peer Characteristics as Modifiers of the Bond-Behavior Relationship: An Elaboration of Control Theory." *Journal of Health and Social Behavior* 33:66-76.

Fotheringham, Alan. 1993. "Fotheringham column." *The Toronto Sun*: 19 October.

Foucault, Michel. 1980. "Truth/Power." In C. Gordon (ed.) *Power/Knowledge.* New York: Pantheon.

Francis, E.K. 1976. *Interethnic Relations: An Essay in Sociology Theory.* New York: Elsevier.

Frankenberg, Ruth. 1993. *White Women, Race Matters: The Social Construction of Whiteness.* Minneapolis: University of Minnesota Press.

Franklin, John Hope. 1994. *Reconstruction after the Civil War,* 2/e. Chicago: Chicago University Press.

Frideres, James S. 1993. *Native People in Canada: Contemporary Conflicts,* 3/e. Scarborough, ON: Prentice-Hall.

Fried, Marc. 1963. "Grieving for a Lost Home." In L.J. Duhl (ed.), *The Urban Condition.* New York: Basic Books.

Gabor, Thomas. 1994. *Everybody Does It! Crime by the Public.* Toronto: University of Toronto Press.

Gaertner, S.L. and J.F. Dovidio. 1986. "The Aversive Form of Racism." In J.F. Dovidio and S.L. Gaertner (eds.), *Prejudice, Discrimination and Racism.* Orlando, FL: Academic Press.

Gagnon, Alain-G. 1993. *Quebec: State and Society,* 2/e. Scarborough, ON: Nelson.

Gardner, Daniel. 1995. *The Globe and Mail:* 21 October.

Gecas, V. and M.L. Schwalbe. 1983. "Beyond the Looking-Glass Self: Social Structure and Efficacy-Based Self-Esteem." *Social Psychology Quarterly* 46:77-88.

Gilad, Lisa. 1990. *The Northern Route: An Ethnography of Refugee Experiences.* St. John's, NF: Memorial University of Newfoundland.

Giles, Wenona. 1988. "Language Rights are Women's Rights: Discrimination against Immigrant Women in Canadian Language Training Policies." *Resources for Feminist Research* 17:129-32.

Gladney, Dru C. 1991. *Muslim Chinese: Ethnic Nationalism in the People's Republic.* Cambridge, MA: Harvard University Press.

Glaser, B. and A.L. Strauss. 1967. *The Discovery of Grounded Theory: Strategies for Qualitative Research.* New York: Aldine/Atherton.

Glazer, Nathan. 1995. "Black and White After Thirty Years." *The Public Interest* 121:35-41.

————, and Daniel P. Moynihan. 1963. *Beyond the Melting Pot.* Cambridge, MA: MIT Press.

Globe and Mail. 1996. Column by Donna LaFramboise. 24 August.

Gold, Steven J. 1992. *Refugee Communities: A Comparative Field Study.* London: Sage.

Goldberg, David Theo. 1993. *Racist Culture: Philosophy and the Politics of Meaning.* Oxford and Cambridge: Blackwell.

Goldmann, Gustave and Nampeo McKenney. 1993. *Challenges of Measuring an Ethnic World: Science, Politics and Reality.* Ottawa/Washington: Statistics Canada and the United States Bureau of the Census.

Goldscheider, C. 1993. "What Does Ethnic/Racial Differentiation Mean? Implications for Measurement and Analyses." *Challenges of Measuring An Ethnic World.* Washington, DC: United States Bureau of the Census.

Goldscheider, C. and P.R. Uhlenberg. 1969. "Minority Group Status and Fertility." *American Journal of Sociology* 74:361-72.

Gordon, Milton M. 1964. *Assimilation in American Life.* New York: Oxford University Press.

Gouvernement du Québec. 1996. *Rapport: Ministère des relations avec les citoyens et de l'immigration.* Québec.

Greenfield, Nathan. 1996. The *Ottawa Citizen.* 2 May.

Grossberg, Lawrence. 1993. "Cultural Studies and/in New Worlds." In Cameron McCarthy and Warren Critchlow (eds.), *Race, Identity and Representation in Education.* London and New York: Routledge.

Guindon, Hubert. 1988. *Quebec Society: Tradition, Modernity, and Nationhood.* Toronto: University of Toronto Press.

Gunter, Harold. 1996. *The Edmonton Journal.* 6 May.

Gwyn, Richard. 1996. *The Toronto Star.* 19 May.

Habermas, Jurgen. 1995. "Struggles for Recognition in the Democratic State." In Charles Taylor and Amy Gutman (eds.), *Multiculturalism: Examining the Politics of Recognition.* Princeton: Princeton University Press.

Hagan, John. 1977. "Finding 'Discrimination: A Question of Meaning." *Ethnicity* 4:167-76.

Haines, D. Rutherford, and P. Thomas. 1981. "Family and Community among Vietnamese Refugees," *International Migration Review* 15:310-19.

Hall, John and Mary Jo Neitz. 1993. *Culture: Sociological Perspectives.* Englewood Cliffs, NJ: Prentice Hall.

Hall, Stuart. 1990. "Cultural Identity and Diaspora." In Jonathan Ruderford (ed.), *Identity, Community, Culture and Difference.* London: Lawrence and Wishart.

Halli, Shiva S. 1987. *How Minority Status Affects Fertility: Asian Groups in Canada.* Westport, CN: Greenwood Press.

Halli, Shiva S., Frank Trovato and Leo Driedger. 1990. *Ethnic Demography: Canadian Immigrant, Racial and Cultural Variations.* Ottawa: Carleton University Press.

Harding, Sandra. 1995. "Multiculturalism in Australia: Moving Race/Ethnic Relations from Extermination to Celebration?" *Race, Gender and Class* 3:7-26.

Harney, Robert F.1988. "So Great A Heritage as Ours: Immigration and the Survival of the Canadian Polity." *Daedalus* 117:51-97.

Hawkes, David C. and Marina Devine. 1991. "Meech Lake and Elijah Harper: Native-State Relations in the 1990s." In Frances Abele (ed.), *How Ottawa Spends: The Politics of Fragmentation, 1991-92.* Ottawa: Carleton University Press.

Hawkins, Freda. 1982. "Multiculturalism in Two Countries: The Canadian and Australian Experience." *Journal of Canadian Studies* 17:64-80.

Head, Wilson. 1975. *The Black Presence in the Canadian Mosaic.* Toronto: Human Rights Commission.

———. 1981. *Adaptation of Immigrants: Perceptions of Ethnic and Racial Discrimination.* North York, ON: York University.

Hechter, Michael. 1978. "Group Formation and the Cultural Division of Labor." *American Journal of Sociology* 84: 293-318.

Henripin, Jacques. 1989. *Naître ou ne pas être.* Québec: Institut québécois de recherche sur la culture.

Henry, Frances. 1989. "Housing and Racial Discrimination in Canada: A Preliminary Assessment of Current Initiatives and Information." Ottawa: Policy and Research, Multiculturalism and Citizenship.

———. 1994. *The Caribbean Diaspora in Toronto: Learning to Live with Racism.* Toronto: University of Toronto Press.

——— and Effie Ginzberg. 1984. *Who Gets the Work? A Test of Racial Discrimination in Employment.* Toronto: University of Toronto Press.

Henry, Frances and Carol Tator. 1984. "The Ideology of Racism: Democratic Racism." *Canadian Ethnic Studies* 26:1-14.

——— and Carol Tator. 1985. "Racism in Canada: Social Myths and Strategies for Change." In Rita Bienvenue and J.E. Goldstein (eds.), *Ethnicity and Ethnic Relations in Canada,* 2/e. Toronto: Butterworths.

———, Winston Mattis and Tim Rees. 1995. *The Colour of Democracy: Racism in Canadian Society.* Toronto: Harcourt Brace.

Hepburn, John R. 1977. "Testing Alternative Models of Delinquency Causation." *Criminal Law and Criminology* 67:450-60.

Herberg, Will. 1955. *Protestant, Catholic, Jew.* New York: Doubleday.

Herrnstein, R.J. and C. Murray. 1994. *The Bell Curve: Intelligence and Class Structure in American Life.* Glencoe, IL: Free Press.

Higgitt, Nancy. 1992. "Toward a Conceptual Model of Resettlement: Vietnamese Refugee Men." Unpublished doctoral dissertation, University of Manitoba.

Higgitt-Copeland, Nancy. 1988. "The Southeast Asian Community in Winnipeg." In L.J. Dorais, K.B. Chan and D.M. Indra (eds.), *Ten Years Later: Indochinese Communities in Canada.* Montreal: Canadian Asian Studies Association.

Hill, Daniel G. 1981. *The Freedom Seekers: Blacks in Early Canada.* Agincourt, ON: Book Society of Canada.

Hindelang, Michael J. 1973. "Causes of Delinquency: A Partial Replication and Extension." *Social Problems* 20:471-87.

Hirschfeld, L.A. 1996. *Race in the Making: Cognition, Culture, and the Child's Construction of Human Kinds.* Cambridge, MA: MIT Press.

Hirschi, Travis. 1969. *Causes of Delinquency.* Berkeley, CA: University of California Press.

Hisama, Toshiaki. 1980. "Minority Group Children and Behavior Disorders: The Case of Asian-American Children." *Behavior Disorders* 5:186-96.

hooks, bell. 1990. *Yearning: Race, Gender and Cultural Politics and the Postmodern World.* Oxford/Cambridge, MA: Basil Blackwells.

Huang, Larke Nahme and Yu-Wen Ying. 1989. "Chinese American Children and Adolescents." In Jewelle Taylor Gibbs, Larke Nahme Huang and Associates (eds.), *Children of Color: Psychological Interventions with Minority Youth.* San Francisco, CA: Jossey-Bass.

Huizinga, David, Finn-Aage Esbensen and Anne Wylie Weiher. 1991. "Are There Multiple Paths to Delinquency?" *Journal of Criminal Law and Criminology* 82:83-118.

Hunter, Edna J. 1988. "The Psychological Effects of Being a Prisoner of War." In J.R. Wilson et al. (eds.), *Human Adaptation to Extreme Stress.* New York: Plenum Press.

Hurd, Burton. 1928. "Is There a Canadian Race?" *Queen's Quarterly* 35:615-27.

Hurd, Burton. 1929. *Origin, Birthplace, Nationality and Language of the Canadian People.* 1921 Census monograph. Dominion Bureau of Statistics. Ottawa: King's Printers.

———. 1937. *Racial Origins and Nationality of the Canadian People.* 1931 Census monograph. Dominion Bureau of Statistics. Ottawa: King's Printer.

———. 1965. *Ethnic Origin and Nativity of the Canadian People.* 1941 Census monograph. Dominion Bureau of Statistics. Ottawa: Queen's Printer.

Hurh, W.M., K.C. Kim and Y.C. Kim. 1980. "Cultural and Social Adjustment Patterns of Korean Immigrants in the Chicago Area." In R. Bryce-Laporte (ed.), *Sourcebook on the New Immigration,* vol. 1. New Jersey: Transaction Books.

Innis, H.R. 1973. *Bilingualism and Biculturalism.* An abridged version of the Royal Commission Report. McClelland and Stewart and the Secretary of State and Information Canada. Toronto: McClellant and Stewart.

Isajiw, Wsevolod W. 1978. "Olga in Wonderland: Ethnicity in Technological Society." In Leo Driedger (ed.), *The Canadian Ethnic Mosaic.* Toronto: McClelland and Stewart.

———. 1981. "Ethnic Identity Retention." *Research paper no. 125.* Toronto: Centre for Urban and Community Studies.

———, Aysan Sev'er and Leo Driedger. 1993. "Ethnic Identity and Social Mobility: A Test of the 'Drawback Model' and Resources." *Canadian Journal of Society* 18:177-96.

Jabbra, Nancy W. and Ronald L. Cosper. 1988. "Ethnicity in Atlantic Canada: A Survey." *Canadian Ethnic Studies* 20:6-27.

Jackson, John D. 1975. *Community and Conflict: A Study of French-English Relations in Ontario.* Montreal: Holt, Rinehart and Winston.

Jain, Harish C. 1988. "Employment Discrimination against Visible Minorities and Employment Equity." Hamilton: Faculty of Business, McMaster University.

———. 1990. *Employment Equity: Issues and Politics, Part 1.* Ottawa: Employment and Immigration Advisory Council.

James, Carl E. 1990. *Making It: Black Youth, Racism and Career Aspiration in a Big City.* Oakville, ON: Mosaic Press.

———. 1995. *Seeing Ourselves: Exploring Race, Ethnicity and Culture.* Toronto: Thompson Educational.

Jensen, Gary F. and David Brownfield. 1983. "Parents and Drugs: Specifying the Consequences of Attachment." *Criminology* 21:543-54.

Joe, Delbert and Norman Robinson. 1980. "Chinatown's Immigrant Gangs: The New Young Warrior Class." *Criminology* 18:337-45.

Joe, Karen A. 1994. "The New Criminal Conspiracy? Asian Gangs and Organized Crime in San Francisco." *Journal of Research in Crime and Delinquency* 31:390-415.

Johnson, P.J. 1989. "Changes in Financial Practices: Southeast Asian Refugees." *Home Economics Research Journal* 17:241-52.

Jones, F.E. 1954. "The Newcomers." *Food for Thought* 14:62-67.

Kahneman, D. and A. Tversky. 1973. "On the Psychology of Prediction." *Psychological Review* 80:237-51.

Kalbach, Warren E. 1970. *The Impact of Immigration on Canada's Population.* 1961 Census monograph. Dominion Bureau of Statistics. Ottawa: Queen's Printer.

———. 1980. "Historical and Generational Perspectives of Ethnic Residential Segregation in Toronto, Canada: 1851-1971." *Research paper no. 118.* Toronto: Centre for Urban and Community Studies.

Kalin, Rudolf. 1996. "Ethnic Attitudes as a Function of Ethnic Presence." *Canadian Journal of Behavioural Science* 28:253-61.

——— and J.W. Berry. 1982. "Social Ecology of Ethnic Attitudes in Canada." *Canadian Journal of Behavioural Science* 14:97-109.

———. 1994. "Ethnic and Multicultural Attitudes." In J.W. Berry and J. Laponce (eds.), *Ethnicity and Culture in Canada: The Research Landscape.* Toronto: University of Toronto Press.

———. 1995. "Ethnic and Civic Self-Identity in Canada: Analyses of 1974 and 1991 National Surveys." *Canadian Ethnic Studies* 2:1-15.

———. 1996. "Interethnic Attitudes in Canada: Ethnocentrism, Consensual Hierarchy and Reciprocity." *Canadian Journal of Behavioural Science* 28:253-61.

Kallarackal, A. and M. Herbert. 1976. "The Happiness of Indian Immigrant Children." *New Society* 34:24-34.

Kallen, Evelyn. 1982. "Multiculturalism: Ideology, Policy and Reality." *Journal of Canadian Studies* 17:51-63.

———. 1995. *Ethnicity and Human Rights in Canada,* 2/e. Toronto: Oxford University Press.

Kallen, Horace. 1924. *Culture and Democracy in the United States.* New York: Liverright.

Katz, I. and R.G. Haas. 1988. "Racial Ambivalence and American Value Conflict: Correlational and Priming Studies of Dual Cognitive Structures." *Journal of Personality and Social Psychology* 55:893-905.

Kelley, Michael L. and Hui-Mei Tseng. 1992. "Cultural Differences in Child Rearing: A Comparison of Immigrant Chinese and Caucasian American Mothers." *Journal of Cross-Cultural Psychology* 23:445-55.

Kelly, Karen. 1995. *Collecting Census Data on Canada's Visible Minority Population: A Historical Perspective.* Ottawa: Statistics Canada, Supply and Services Canada.

Kelly, Robert J., Ko-Lin Chin and Jeffrey A. Fagan. 1993. "The Dragon Breathes Fire: Chinese Organized Crime in New York City." *Crime, Law and Social Change* 19:245-69.

Kendis, Kaoru Oguri and Randall Jay Kendis. 1976. "The Street Boy Identity: An Alternate Strategy of Boston's Chinese-Americans." *Urban Anthropology* 5:1-17.

Kim, Young Yun. 1988. *Communication and Cross-Cultural Adaptation: An Integrative Theory.* Clevedon, PA: Multilingual Matters.

Kinder, D.R. and D.O. Sears. 1981. "Prejudice and Politics: Symbolic Racism versus Racial Threats to the Good Life." *Journal of Personality and Social Psychology* 40:414-31.

Kingsbury, Stephen. 1994. "The Psychological and Social Characteristics of Asian Adolescent Overdose." *Journal of Adolescence* 17:131-35.

Kirschmeyer, Catherine and Janet McLellan. 1990. "Managing Ethnic Diversity: Utilizing the Creative Potential of a Diverse Workforce to Meet the Challenges of the Future." Proceedings of the Administrative Science Association of Canada, June, Whistler, BC.

Kitano, Harry H.L. 1973. "Japanese-American Crime and Delinquency." In Stanley Sue and Nathaniel N. Wagner (eds.), *Asian-Americans: Psychological Perspectives.* Palo Alto, CA: Science and Behavior Books.

Kobayashi, Audrey. 1987. "From Tyranny to Justice: The Uprooting of the Japanese Canadians in 1941." *Tribune Juive* 5: 28-35.

Kosinski, L.A. 1993. *Impact of Migration in the Receiving Countries.* Geneva: International Organization for Migration.

Kralt, John. 1990. "Ethnic Origins in the Canadian Census, 1871-1986." In Shiva S. Halli, Frank Trovato and Leo Driedger (eds.) *Ethnic Demography: Canadian Immigrant, Racial and Cultural Variations.* Ottawa: Carleton University Press.

Kubat, Daniel. 1987. "Asian Immigrants to Canada." In J.T. Fawcett and B.V. Carino (eds.), *Pacific Bridges: The New Immigration From Asia and the Pacific Islands.* New York: Centre for Migration Studies.

Kumin, R. and C. Jones. 1995. "Business Immigration to Canada." In D.J. DeVoretz (ed.), *Diminishing Returns: The Economics of Canada's Recent Immigration Policy.* Toronto: C.D. Howe Institute.

Kunz, E.F. 1973. "The Refugee in Flight: Kinetic Models and Forms of Displacement." *International Migration Review* 7:125-46.

Kurian, George and Ram P. Srivastava, eds. 1983. *Overseas Indians: A Study in Adaptation.* Delhi: Vikas Publishing.

Kwong, Peter. 1990. "The Challenge of Understanding the Asian-American Experience." *Ethnic and Racial Studies* 13:584-90.

Kymlicka, Will. 1989. *Liberalism, Community and Culture.* Oxford: Clarendon Press.

———. 1995. *Multicultural Citizenship: A Liberal Theory of Minority Rights.* Oxford: Clarendon Press.

Lachapelle, Rejean. 1988. "Immigration and the Ethnolinguistic Character of Canada and Quebec." Research paper series, no 15. Analytical Studies Branch, Statistics Canada, Supply and Services Canada.

Laczko, Leslie. 1995. *Pluralism and Inequality in Quebec.* Toronto: University of Toronto Press.

Lalonde, R.N. and R.A. Silverman. 1994. "Behavioral Preferences in Response to Social Injustice: The Effects of Group Permeability and Social Identity Salience." *Journal of Personality and Social Psychology* 66:78-85.

Lam, Lawrence. 1994. "Searching for a Safe Haven: The Migration and Settlement of Hong Kong Chinese Immigrants in Toronto." In R. Skeldon (ed.), *Reluctant Exiles?* New York: M.E. Sharpe.

Lambert, W.E., R.C. Hodgson, R.C. Gardner and S. Fillenbaum. 1960. "Evaluational Reactions to Spoken Language." *Journal of Abnormal and Social Psychology* 60:44-51.

La Presse. 1987. "Interview with Jacques Henripin." 20 June.

La Presse. 1992. "Interview with Pierre Drouilly." 31 October.

Lanphier, Michael and Oleh Lukomskyj. 1994. "Settlement Policy in Australia and Canada." In Howard Adelman, Allan Borowski, Meyer Burstein and Lois Foster (eds.), *Immigration and Refugee Policy: Australia and Canada Compared,* vol. 2. Carlton, Victoria: Melbourne University Press.

Larzelere, Robert E. and Gerald R. Patterson. 1990. "Parental Management: Mediator of the Effect of Socioeconomic Status on Early Delinquency." *Criminology* 28:301-23.

Law Union of Ontario. 1981. *The Immigrant's Handbook: A Critical Guide.* Montreal: Black Rose.

Lawrence, Erroll. 1982. "Just Plain Common Sense: The Roots of Racism." In Centre for Contempory Studies (eds.), *The Empire Strikes Back.* London: Hutchinson.

Laws, J.L. 1975. "The Psychology of Tokenism: An Analysis." *Sex Roles* 1:51-67.

Lazarus, R.S. and S. Folkman. 1984. *Stress, Appraisal and Coping.* New York: Springer-Verlag.

Le Devoir. 1980. "Interview with Pierre Drouilly." 18 September.

———. 1993. "Interview with Henri Comte." 10 March.

Lewycky, Laverne M. 1992. "Multiculturalism in the 1990s and into the 21st Century: Beyond Ideology and Utopia." In Vic Satzewich (ed.), *Deconstructing a Nation: Immigration, Multiculturalism and Racism in 1990s Canada.* Halifax, NS: Fernwood.

Li, Han Z. and Lorne Rosenblood. 1994. "Exploring Factors Influencing Alcohol Consumption: Patterns Among Chinese and Caucasians." *Journal of Studies on Alcohol* 55:427-33.

Li, Peter S. 1982. "Chinese Immigrants on the Canadian Prairie, 1910-47." *Canadian Review of Sociology and Antrhopology* 19:527-40.

———. 1988. *The Chinese in Canada.* Toronto: Oxford University Press.

———. 1994. "A World Apart: The Multicultural World of Visible Minorities and the Art World in Canada." *Canadian Review of Sociology and Anthropology* 31:365-391.

Li, Xue-Rong, Lin-Yan Su, Brenda D. Townes and Christopher K. Varley. 1989. "Diagnosis of Attention Deficit Disorder with Hyperactivity in Chinese Boys." *Journal of American Academy of Child and Adolescent Psychiatry* 4:497-500.

Liddle, Joanna and Rama Joshi. 1986. *Daughters of Independence: Gender, Caste and Class in India.* London, UK: Zed Books.

Lieberson, S. 1993. "The Enumeration of Ethnic and Racial Groups in the Census: Some Devilish Principles." *Challenges of Measuring an Ethnic World.* Ottawa/Washington, DC: Statistics Canada and United States Bureau of the Census.

———— and M.C. Waters. 1988. *From Many Strands. Ethnic and Racial Groups in Contemporary America.* New York: Russell Sage Foundation.

Lin, Chin-Yau Cindy and Victoria R. Fu. 1990. "A Comparison of Child-Rearing Practices among Chinese, Immigrant Chinese, and Caucasian-American Parents." *Child Development* 61:429-33.

Liska, Allen E. and Mark D. Reed. 1985. "Ties to Conventional Institutions and Delinquency: Estimating Reciprocal Effects." *American Sociological Review* 50:547-60.

Loney, Martin. 1995. *The Toronto Star.* 16 November.

Lue, Lawrence J. and H. Newton Malony. 1983. "Validation of Two Measures of Acculturation for Chinese Americans." Paper presented at the Annual Convention of the Western Psychological Association, San Francisco, April.

Lumsden, David P., ed. 1981. "Is the Concept of 'Stress' of Any Use, Any More?" In D. Randall (ed.), *Contributions to Primary Prevention in Mental Health: Working Papers.* Toronto: Toronto National Office of the Canadian Mental Health Association.

————. 1984. *Community Mental Health Action: Primary Prevention Programming in Canada.* Ottawa: Canadian Public Health Association.

Lyman, Stanford M. 1973. *Chinese Americans.* New York: Random House.

————. 1977. *The Asian in North America.* Santa Barbara, CA: ABC-Clio.

Mackey, Eva. 1995. "Postmodernism and Cultural Politics in a Multicultural Nation: Contests Over Truth in the 'Into the Heart of Africa'" Controversy *Public Culture* 7:403-48.

————. 1996. "Managing and Imagining Diversity: Multiculturalism and the Construction of National Identity." Ph.D. Thesis in Social Anthropology, University of Sussex.

Mackie, Marlene. 1985. "Stereotypes, Prejudice, and Discrimination." In Rita Bienvenue and Jay Goldstein (eds.), *Ethnicity and Ethnic Relations in Canada.* Toronto: Butterworths.

MacIntyre, Alasdair. 1981. *After Virtue: A Study in Moral Philosophy.* London: Duckworth.

Major, B. and J. Crocker. 1993. "Social Stigma: The Consequences of Attributional Ambiguity." In D.M. Mackie and D.L. Hamilton (eds.), *Affect, Cognition, and Stereotyping: Interactive Processes in Group Perceptions.* Orlando, FL: Academic Press.

Malarek, V. 1988. *Haven's Gate: Canada's Immigration Fiasco.* Toronto: Macmillan.

Manpower and Immigration, Canada. 1974. *Three Years in Canada: First Report of the Longitudinal Survey on the Economic and Social Adaptation of Immigrants.* Ottawa: Information Canada.

Marchak, M. Patricia. 1975. *Ideological Perspectives on Canada.* Toronto: McGraw-Hill Ryerson.

Marcos, Anastasios C., Stephen J. Bahr and Richard E. Johnson. 1986. "Test of a Bonding/Association Theory of Adolescent Drug Use." *Social Forces* 65:135-61.

Marx, Karl and Friedrich Engels. 1848. *Communist Manifesto.* London: George Allen and Unwin.

Massey, D.S. 1995. "The New Immigration and Ethnicity in the United States." *Population and Development Review* 21:103-21.

Massey, James L. and Marvin D. Krohn. 1986. "A Longitudinal Examination of an Integrated Social Process Model of Deviant Behavior. *Social Forces* 65:106-34.

Matsueda, Ross L. 1982. "Testing Control Theory and Differential Associations: A Causal Modeling Approach." *American Sociological Review* 47:489-504.

McConahay, J.B. 1986. "Modern Racism, Ambivalence, and the Modern Racism Scale." In J.F. Dovidio and S.L. Gaertner (eds.), *Prejudice, Discrimination, and Racism: Theory and Research.* Orlando, FL: Academic Press.

McKenney, N. and A. Cresce. 1993. "Measurement of Ethnicity in the United States: Experiences of the U.S. Bureau of the Census." In *Challenges of Measuring an Ethnic World: Science, Politics and Reality.* Proceedings of the Joint Canada-U.S. Conference on the Measurement of Ethnicity, 1-3 April 1992. Washington, DC: U.S. Bureau of the Census/Statistics Canada.

McNeill, William H. 1986. *Poly-Ethnicity and National Unity in World History.* Toronto: University of Toronto Press.

Meng, R. 1987. "The Earnings of Canadian Immigrant and Native-Born Males." *Applied Economics* 19:1107-119.

Merton, R.K. 1948. "The Self-Fulfilling Prophesy." *Antioch Review* 8:193-210.

Michalowski, Margaret. 1987. "Adjustment of Immigrants in Canada: Methodological Possibilities and Their Implications." *International Migration* 25:21-35.

———. 1996. "A Contribution of the Asian Female Immigrants to the Canadian Population." *Asian and Pacific Migration Journal* 5:1-12.

———. 1991. "Foreign-Born Canadian Immigrants and Their Characteristics, 1981-1986." *International Migration Review* 25:112-30.

Miles, Robert. 1989. *Racism.* London: Routledge.

———. 1992. "Migration, Racism and the Nation State in Contemporary Europe." In Vic Satzewish (ed.), *Deconstructing a Nation: Immigration, Multiculturalism and Racism in 1990s Canada.* Halifax, NS: Fernwood.

Miller, Paul W. 1992. "The Earnings of Asian Immigrants in the Canadian Labour Market." *International Migration Review* 26:222-47.

Minister of Employment and Immigration. 1988. *Progress on Employment Equity.* Ottawa: Supply and Services Canada.

Ministère des communautés culturelles et de l'immigration du Québec. 1986. *La migration interprovinciale (1981-1986) des immigrants admis avant juin 1981: l'expérience du Québec.*

———. 1989. *Taux de présence de l'immigration au Québec: analyse et commentaires.*

Mitchell, Alana. 1995. *The Globe and Mail* (Toronto). 12 September.

Mitges, G. 1987. *Multiculturalism: Building the Canadian Mosaic.* Report of the Standing Committee on Multiculturalism, House of Commons. Ottawa: Supply and Services Canada.

Model, S. 1988. "The Economic Progress of European and East Asian Americans." *Annual Review of Sociology* 14:363-80.

Mol, Hans. 1985. *Faith and Fragility: Religion and Identity in Canada.* Burlington, ON: Trinity Press.

Montgomery, J. Randall. 1992. "Vietnamese Refugees in Alberta: Social, Cultural and Economic Adaptation." Ph.D. Thesis, University of Alberta, Edmonton.

Moodley, Kogila. 1983. "Canadian Multiculturalism as Ideology." *Ethnic and Racial Studies* 6:320-31.

Moreland, J.K. 1965. "Token Desegregation and Beyond." In A.M. Rose and C.B. Rose (eds.), *Minority Problems*. New York: Harper and Row.

Myrdal, Gunnar. 1944. *An American Dilemma: The Negro Problem and Modern Democracy*. New York and London: Harper and Brothers.

Nagel, Joane. 1984. "The Ethnic Revolution: Emergence of Ethnic Nationalism." *Sociology and Social Research* 69:417-34.

Nakamura, Mark. 1975. "The Japanese." In Norman Sheffe (ed.), *Many Cultures, Many Heritages*. Toronto: McGraw-Hill Ryerson.

Nash, Alan. 1987. *The Economic Impact of the Entrepreneur Immigrant Program*. Ottawa: Institute for Research on Public Policy.

———. 1993. "Hong Kong's Business Future: The Impact of Canadian and Australian Business Migration Programs." In Yenan Yeung (ed.), *Pacific Asians in the 21st Century: Geographical and Developmental Prospective*. Hong Kong: Chinese University Press.

Neuwirth, G. 1987. "Socioeconomic Adjustment of Southeast Asian Refugees in Canada." In J. Rogge (ed.), *Refugees: A Third World Dilemma*. Totowa, NJ: Rowman and Littlefield.

———. 1988. "Refugee Resettlement." *Current Sociology* 26:27-41.

Newman, William M. 1973. *American Pluralism: A Study of Minority Groups and Social Theory*. New York: Harper and Row.

Ng, Roxana. 1993. "Racism, Sexism and Nation Building in Canada." In Cameron McCarthy and Warren Critchlow (eds.), *Race, Identity and Representation in Education*. New York: Routledge.

——— and J. Ramirez. 1981. *Immigrant Housewives in Canada*. Toronto: The Women's Centre.

Nguyen, Nga Anh and Harold L. Williams. 1989. "Transition from East to West: Vietnamese Adolescents and Their Parents." *The American Academy of Child and Adolescent Psychiatry* 28:505-15.

Nozick, Robert. 1974. *Anarchy, State and Utopia*. New York: Basic Books.

Oakley, A. 1981. "Interviewing Women: A Contradiction in Terms." In H. Roberts (ed.), *Doing Feminist Research*. New York: Routledge and Kegan Paul.

O'Hare, Thomas. 1995. "Differences in Asian and White Drinking: Consumption Level, Drinking Contexts, and Expectancies." *Addictive Behaviors* 20:261-66.

Ornstein, M.D. and R.D. Sharma. 1983. "Adjustment and Economic Experience of Immigrants in Canada: An Analysis of the 1976 Longitudinal Survey of Immigrants." Toronto: Institute of Behavioural Research, York University.

Palmer, Howard. 1988. "Prejudice and Discrimination." *The Canadian Encyclopedia* 3:1740-43.

Pankiw, D. and Rita Bienvenue. 1990. "Parent Responses to Ethnic Name-Calling: A Sociological Inquiry." *Canadian Ethnic Studies* 22:78-98.

Papademetriou, Demetrios. 1991. "International Migration in North America: Issues, Policies and Implications." Paper presented in informal expert group meeting on International Migration in Geneva, organized by UN Population Fund with support of UN Economic Commissions for Europe, July.

Pendakur, Ravi. 1993. "Visible Minority as a Redefinition of Race." Proceedings of the Conference of the International Union for the Scientific Study of Population (IUSSP), Montreal, QC, vol. 3. Brussels: IUSSP.

Pendakur, Krishna and Ravi Pendakur. 1996. *Earnings Differentials among Ethnic Groups in Canada.* Strategic Research and Analysis, SRA-34b. Ottawa: Heritage Canada, Supply and Services Canada.

Persons, Stow. 1987. *Ethnic Studies at Chicago, 1905-1945.* Urbana: University of Illinois Press.

Peterson, William. 1987. "Politics and the Measurement of Ethnicity." In William Alonso and Paul Starr (eds.). *The Politics of Numbers.* New York: Russell Sage Foundation.

Petrie, Anne. 1982. *A Guidebook to Ethnic Vancouver.* Surrey, BC: Hancock House.

Petrie, D. Bruce. 1989. *Minutes of Proceedings and Evidence of the Standing Committee on Multiculturalism and Citizenship,* 19 December:37-42. Ottawa: Supply and Services Canada.

Philip, Nourbese M. 1992. *Frontiers: Essays and Writings on Racism and Culture.* Toronto: Mercury Press.

Pieterse, Jan. 1992. *White on Black: Images of Africa and Black in Western Popular Culture.* New Haven: Yale University Press.

Pineo, P. 1977. "The Social Standing of Ethnic and Racial Groupings in Canada." *Review of Sociology and Anthropology* 14:147-57.

Pitman, Walter. 1977. *Now is Not Too Late.* Toronto: The Municipality of Metropolitan Toronto.

Pogrebin, Mark P. and Eric D. Poole. 1989. "South Korean Immigrants and Crime: A Case Study." *The Journal of Ethnic Studies* 17:47-80.

Ponting, J. Rick and Richard A. Wanner. 1983. "Blacks in Calgary: A Social and Attitudinal Profile." *Canadian Ethnic Studies* 15:57-76.

Poole, Eric and Robert M. Regoli. 1979. "Parental Support, Delinquent Friends, and Delinquency: A Test of Interaction Effects." *Journal of Criminal Law and Criminology* 70:188-93.

Poole, Phebe-Jane. 1989. *Minorities in Banking.* Ottawa: The Canadian Centre for Policy Alternatives.

Porter, John. 1965. *The Vertical Mosaic: An Analysis of Social Class and Power in Canada.* Toronto: University of Toronto Press.

————. 1987. *The Measure of Canadian Society: Education, Equality and Opportunity,* 2/e. Ottawa: Carleton University Press.

Portes, Alejandro and Min Zhou. 1993. "The New Second Generation: Segmented Assimilation and its Variants." *Annals, American Academy of Political and Social Sciences* 530:74-96.

Posner, Gerald. 1988. *Warlords of Crime: Chinese Secret Societies — The New Mafia.* New York: McGraw-Hill.

President's Commission on Organized Crime. 1984. *Organized Crime of Asian Origin.* Washington, DC: U.S. Government Printing Office.

Priest, Gordon. 1990. "Ethnicity in the Canadian Census." Publications in Ethnicity, no. 1. Robert F. Harney Professorship and Program in Ethnic, Immigration and Pluralism Studies. Toronto: Department of Sociology, University of Toronto.

Pryor, Edward T. and Douglas Norris. 1983. "Canada in the Eighties." *American Demographics* 15:25-29.

Pryor, Edward T., Gustave Goldmann, Michael Sheridan and Pamela M. White. 1992. "Is 'Canadian' an Evolving Indigenous Ethnic Group?" *Ethnic and Racial Studies* 15:214-35.

Rajagopal, Indhu. 1990. "The Glass Ceiling in the Vertical Mosaic: Indian Immigrants in Canada." *Canadian Ethnic Studies* 22:96-105.

Ralston, Helen. 1992. "Religion in the Life of South Asian Immigrant Women in Atlantic Canada." *Research in the Social Scientific Study of Religion* 4:245-60.

————. 1994. "Immigration Policies and Practices: Their Impact on South Asian Women in Canada and Australia." *Australian-Canadian Studies* 12:1-47.

Ralston, Helen. 1995a. "Violence against Immigrant Women Knows No Religious Bounds: A Comparative Analysis of Canada, Australia and New Zealand." Paper presented at a session on "Religion, Feminism and Violence Against Women" at the annual meeting of the Society for the Scientific Study of Religion, St. Louis, MO, October.
———. 1995b. "Organizational Empowerment among South Asian Immigrant Women in Canada." *International Journal of Canadian Studies/Revue internationale d'études canadiennes, — Women in Canadian Society/Les femmes et la société canadienne* 1:121-46.
Ramcharan, Subhas. 1982. *Racism: Nonwhites in Canada.* Toronto: Butterworths.
Ramkhalawansingh, Geta. 1981. "Language and Employment Training for Immigrant Women." *Canadian Ethnic Studies* 13:91-96.
Rankin, Joseph and L. Edward Wells. 1990. "The Effects of Parental Attachments and Direct Controls on Delinquency." *Journal of Research in Crime and Delinquency* 27:140-65.
Rao, G. Lakshmana, Anthony Richmond and Jerzy Zubrzycki. 1984. *Immigrants in Canada and Australia,* vol. 1, Demographic Aspects and Education. Toronto: Ethnic Research Program, York University.
Rawls, John. 1971. *A Theory of Justice.* Cambridge: Harvard University Press.
Redway, Alan. 1990. "Racial Equality in the Workplace: Retrospect and Prospect." In Jain Harish et al. (eds.), *Equality for All.* Hamilton, ON: National Conference on Racial Equality in the Workplace: Retrospect and Prospect.
Reid, Angus. 1991. *Multiculturalism and Canadians: Attitude Study 1991, A National Survey Report.* Ottawa: Multiculturalism and Citizenship Canada, Supply and Services Canada.
———. 1993. "Tolerance and the Canadian Ethnocultural Mosaic." *Reid Report* 8:1-11.
Reinharz, Shulamit. 1992. *Feminist Methods in Social Research.* New York and Oxford: Oxford University Press.
Reitz, Jeffrey G. 1988. "Less Racial Discrimination in Canada, or Simply Less Racist Conflict? Implication of Comparisons with Britain." *Canadian Public Policy* 14:87-94.
———. 1993. "Statistics on Racial Discrimination in Canada." *Policy Options* 14:32-36.

Reitz, Jeffrey G. and Raymond Breton. 1994. *The Illusion of Difference: Realities of Ethnicity in Canada and the United States.* Toronto: C.D. Howe Institute.

Renaud, Viviane. 1994a. *Report No. 16. National Census Test: Ethnic Origin.* Ottawa: Statistics Canada, Supply and Services Canada.

————. 1994b. *Report No. 18. National Census Test: Population Groups.* Ottawa: Statistics Canada, Supply and Services Canada.

———— and Jane Badets. 1993. *Ethnic Diversity in the 1990s: Canadian Social Trends.* Ottawa: Statistics Canada, Supply and Services Canada.

Ribordy, François. 1980. "Culture Conflict and Crime among Italian Immigrants." In Robert A. Silverman and James J. Teevan, Jr. (eds.) *Crime in Canadian Society.* Toronto: Butterworths.

Richmond, Anthony. 1980. Environmental Conservation: A New Racist Ideology? In R.S. Bryce Laporte (ed.), *Source Book on the New Immigration.* Trenton, NJ: Transaction Books.

————. 1988. *Immigration and Ethnic Conflict.* London: Macmillan.

————. 1991. "Immigration and Structural Change: The Canadian Experience, 1971-1986." *International Migration Review* 26:1200-221.

————. 1993. "Reactive Migration: Sociological Perspectives on Refugee Movements." *Journal of Refugee Studies* 6:1-10.

————. 1994. *Global Apartheid: Refugees, Racism, and the New World Order.* Toronto: Oxford University Press.

———— and J. Goldlust. 1974. "Multivariate Analysis of Immigrant Adaptation." Downsview, ON: Institute for Behavioural Research, York University.

Richmond, Anthony and Warren Kalbach. 1980. *Factors in the Adjustment of Immigrants and Their Descendants.* Ottawa: Statistics Canada, Supply and Services Canada.

Roberts, Lance W. and Rodney A. Clifton. 1982. "Exploring the Ideology of Canadian Multiculturalism." *Canadian Public Policy* 8:88-94.

————. 1990. "Multiculturalism in Canada: A Sociological Perspective." In Peter S. Li (ed.), *Race and Ethnic Relations.* Toronto: Oxford University Press.

Robeson, Paul. 1958. *Here I Stand.* Boston: Beacon Press.

Robinson, V. 1990. "Into the Next Millenium: An Agenda for Refugee Studies." *Journal of Refugee Studies* 3:3-15.

Rocher, Guy. 1992. "Autour de la langue: crises et débats, espoirs et tremblements." In G. Daigle (ed.), *Le Québec en jeu: comprendre les grands défis*. Montréal: Les Presses de l'Université de Montréal.

Rogge, J.R. 1987. *Refugees: A Third World Dilemma*. Totowa, NJ: Rowman and Littlefield.

Roman, Leslie. 1993. "White is a Colour: White Defensiveness, Postmodernism and Anti-Racist Pedagogy." In Cameron McCarthy and Warren Critchlow (eds.), *Race, Identity and Representation in Education*. New York: Routledge.

Rose, Arnold. 1948. *The Negro in America*. Boston: Beacon Press.

Rosenthal, Doreen A. and S. Shirley Feldman. 1992. "The Nature and Stability of Ethnic Identity in Chinese Youth: Effects of Length of Residence in Two Cultural Contexts." *Journal of Cross-Cultural Psychology* 23:214-27.

Royal Commission on Bilingualism and Biculturalism. 1965. *A Preliminary Report*. Ottawa: Queen's Printer.

———. 1970. *The Cultural Contributions of Other Ethnic Groups*, vol. 4. Ottawa: Queen's Printer.

Ruderford, Jonathon, ed. 1990. *Identity: Community, Culture and Difference*. London: Lawrence and Wishart.

Ruggiero, K.M. and D.M. Taylor. 1995. "Coping with Discrimination: How Disadvantaged Group Members Perceive the Discrimination that Confronts Them." *Journal of Personality and Social Psychology* 68:826-38.

———. 1997. "Why Disadvantaged Group Members Perceive or Do Not Perceive the Discrimination that Confronts Them." *Journal of Personality and Social Psychology* 70:87-97.

Rushton, J.P. 1995. *Race, Evolution and Behaviour: A Life-History Perspective*. New Brunswick, NJ: Transaction Books.

Rutter, Michael, William Yule, Michael Berger, Bridget Yule, Janis Morton and Christopher Bagley. 1974. "Children of West Indian Immigrants and Rates of Behavioural Deviance and of Psychiatric Disorder." *Journal of Child Psychology and Psychiatry* 15:241-62.

Saha, Panchanan. 1970. *Emigration of Indian Labour (1834-1890)*. Delhi: People's Publishing House.

Samuel, T. John. 1984. "Economic Adaptation of Refugees in Canada: Experience of a Quarter Century." *International Migration* 22:101-21.

Samuel, T. John. 1987. "Economic Adaptation of Indochinese Refugees in Canada." In K.B. Chan and D.M. Indra (eds.), *Uprooting, Loss and Adaptation: The Resettlement of Indochinese Refugees in Canada.* Ottawa: Canadian Public Health Association.

―――. 1989. "Canada's Visible Minorities and the Labour Market: Vision 2000." In O.P. Dwivedi et al. (eds.), *Canada 2000: Race Relations and Public Policy.* Guelph, ON: University of Guelph.

―――. 1990. "Third World Immigration and Multiculturalism." In Shiva S. Halli, Frank Trovato and Leo Driedger (eds.), *Ethnic Demography: Canadian Immigrant, Racial and Cultural Variations.* Ottawa: Carleton University.

―――. 1991. "Racial Equality in the Canadian Work Force: The Federal Scene." *The Journal of Intergroup Relations* 18:32-45.

―――. 1994. "Asian and Pacific Migration: The Canadian Experience." *Asian and Pacific Migration Journal* 3:2-3.

――― and B. Woloski. 1985. "The Labour Market Experience of Canadian Immigrants." *International Migration* 23:225-50.

Samuel, T. John, Lloyd Stanford and Camille Tremblay. 1997. *Visible Minorities and the Public Service of Canada.* Ottawa: John Samuel and Associates.

Sandel, Michael. 1982. *Liberalism and the Limits of Justice.* Cambridge: Cambridge University Press.

Satzewich, Victor and Peter S. Li. 1987. "Immigrant Labour in Canada: The Cost and Benefit of Ethnic Origin in the Job Market." *The Canadian Journal of Sociology* 12:229-41.

Satzewich, Victor and Terry Wotherspoon. 1992. *First Nations: Race, Class and Gender Relations.* Toronto: Nelson.

Schulz, Alfred. 1964[1944]. "The Stranger." In Arvid Brodersen (ed.), *Collected Papers II.* The Hague: Martinus Nijhoff.

Schumann, H., C. Steed and L. Bobo. 1985. *Racial Attitudes in America.* Cambridge, MA: Harvard University Press.

Schwitters, Sylvia Y., Ronald C. Johnson, James R. Wilson and Gerald E. McClearn. 1982. "Ethnicity and Alcohol." *Hawaii Medical Journal* 41:60-63.

Scott, William A. and R. Scott. 1989. *Adaptation of Immigrants: Individual Differences and Determinants.* Oxford: Pergamon Press.

Scudder, T. and E. Colson. 1982. "From Welfare to Development: A Conceptual Framework for the Analysis of Dislocated People."

In A. Hansen and A. Oliver-Smith (eds.), *Involuntary Migration and Resettlement.* Boulder, CO: Westview Press.

Seidel, J.V., R. Kjolseth and E. Seymour. 1988. *The Ethnograph: A User Guide* (Version 3.0). Littleton, CO: Qualis Research Associates.

Sellin, Thorsten. 1938. *Culture Conflict and Crime.* New York: Social Science Research Council.

Sev'er, Aysan, W.W. Isajiw and Leo Driedger. 1993. "Anomie as Powerlessness: Sorting Ethnic Group Prestige, Class and Gender." *Canadian Ethnic Studies* 25:84-99.

Seward, S. and M. Tremblay. 1989. "Immigrants in the Canadian Labour Force: Their Role in Structural Change." Ottawa: Institute for Research in Public Policy.

———. 1990. "Immigration and the Changing Labour Market." Paper presented at Canadian Population Society, Victoria, BC.

Shaffir, William. 1993. "The Hasidic Community of Tash." In Robert Brym et al. (eds.), *The Jews in Canada.* Toronto: Oxford University Press.

Sharma, R.D. 1980. "Trends in the Demographic and Socio-Economic Characteristics of Metropolitan Toronto." Toronto: Institute for Behavioural Research.

———. 1981a. "Perceived Difficulties of Foreign-Born Populations and Services of Agencies." Unpublished Report. Toronto: Institute for Behavioural Research, York University.

———. 1981b. "A Multivariate Analysis of Difficulties Reported by Long Term Third World and Non-Anglophone Immigrants, in Toronto Three Years or More." Unpublished report. Toronto: Institute for Behavioural Research, York University.

Sheridan, William and Abdou Saouab. 1992. *Canadian Multiculturalism.* Current Issue Review. Ottawa: Library of Parliament, Research Branch. Catalogue no. 87-10E.

Shohat, Ella and Robert Stam. 1994. *Unthinking Eurocentrism: Multiculturalism and the Media.* London: Routledge.

Shore, Marlene. 1987. *The Science of Social Redemption: McGill, the Chicago School, and the Origins of Social Research in Canada.* Toronto: University of Toronto Press.

Simmel, Georg. 1955. *Conflict and the Web of Group Affilations.* Glencoe, IL: The Free Press.

Simmons, Alan. 1990. "'New Wave' Immigrants: Origins and Characteristics." In Shiva S. Halli, Frank Trovato and Leo

Driedger (eds.), *Ethnic Demography: Canadian Immigrant, Racial and Cultural Variations.* Ottawa: Carleton University Press.

Singh, Hira. 1987. "The Political Economy of Immigrant Farm Labour: A Study of East Indian Farm Workers in British Columbia." In Milton Israel (ed.), *The South Asian Diaspora in Canada: Six Essays.* Toronto: The Multicultural History Society of Ontario.

Smillie, Emmaline E. 1923. "An Historical Survey of Indian Migration within the Empire." *The Canadian Historical Review* 43:217-57.

Smith, David E. 1989. "Canadian Political Parties and National Integration." In Alain Gagnon and Brian Tanguay (eds.), *Canadian Parties in Transition: Discourse, Organization and Representation.* Scarborough, ON: Nelson.

Smith, Dorothy E. 1987. *The Everyday World as Problematic: A Feminist Sociology.* Toronto: The University of Toronto Press.

Sommers, Marc. 1993. "Coping with Fear: Burundi Refugees and the Urban Experience in Dar Es Salaam, Tanzania." In Hopkins and Donnelly (eds.), *Selected Papers on Refugee Issues: 2.* Arlington, VA: American Anthropological Association.

Spicer, Keith. 1991. *Citizens' Forum on Canada's Future.* Ottawa: Canadian Government Publishing Centre.

South Asian Women's Community Centre. 1992. "Regeneration of the Language Issue: What's Next?" In W. Dodge (ed.), *Boundaries of Identity: A Quebec Reader.* Toronto: Lester Publishing.

Stanley, F.G. 1960. *The Birth of Western Canada: A History of the Riel Rebellions.* Toronto: University of Toronto.

———. 1969. *Louis Riel: Rebel of the Western Frontier or Victim of Politics and Prejudice?* Toronto: Copp Clark.

Stasiulis, Daiva. 1986. "Anti-Racism and Black Feminism in the Canadian Context." Paper presented at the 10th annual meeting of the Canadian Research Institute for the Advancement of Women, Moncton, NB, 7-9 Nov.

———. 1989. "Affirmative Action for Visible Minorities and the New Politics of Race in Canada." In Dwivedi, O.P. et al. (eds.), *Canada 2000: Race Relations and Public Policy.* Guelph, ON: University of Guelph.

Stasiulis, Daiva. 1990. "The Symbolic Mosaic Reaffirmed: Multiculturalism Policy." In Katherine A. Graham (ed.), *How Ottawa Spends: 1988-1989.* Ottawa: Carleton University Press.

————. 1990. "Theorizing Connections: Gender, Race, Ethnicity and Class." In Peter S. Li (ed.), *Race and Ethnic Relations in Canada.* Toronto: Oxford University Press.

————. 1991. "Symbolic Representation and the Numbers Game: Tory Policies on 'Race' and Visible Minorities." In Katherine A. Graham (ed.), *How Ottawa Spends: 1988-1989.* Ottawa: Carleton University Press.

————. 1995. *Dimensions of Diversity in Canadian Business.* Ottawa: The Conference Board of Canada.

Statistics Canada. 1988. *1986 Census Highlights.* Ottawa: Supply and Services Canada.

————. 1989. *1986 Census: Special Tabulations, Population 15 Years and Over, Atlantic Provinces.* Ottawa: Supply and Services Canada.

————. 1991. *1991 Census Dictionary.* Catalogue no. 92-301E. Ottawa: Supply and Services Canada.

————. 1993. *Ethnic Origin: The Nation, 1991 Census of Canada.* Catalogue no. 93-315, Tables 1A and 1B, and Appendix 2. Ottawa: Industry, Science and Technology Canada, Supply and Services Canada

————. 1994. *Population Projections for Canada, Provinces and Territories, 1993-2016.* Ottawa: Supply and Services Canada.

————. 1994a. *1996 Census Consultation Report.* Ottawa.

————. 1994b. *Report of the November 1993 National Census Test Results.* Ottawa.

———— and Citizenship and Immigration Canada. 1996. *Profiles: Immigration Research Series.* Catalogue no. Ci62-2/14-1996. Ottawa: Supply and Services Canada.

Stein, B. 1981. "The Refugee Experience: Defining the Parameters of a Field of Study." *International Migration Review* 15:320-30.

Strauss, A. and J. Corbin. 1990. *Basics of Qualitative Research: Grounded Theory Procedures and Techniques.* Newbury Park, CA: Sage.

Sue, Stanley and Derald Wing Sue. 1973. "Chinese-American Personality and Mental Health." In Stanley Sue and Nathaniel N. Wagner (eds.), *Asian Americans: Psychological Perspectives.* Palo Alto, CA: Science and Behavior Books.

Sue, Stanley, Nolan Zane and Joanne Ito. 1979. "Alcohol Drinking Patterns among Asian and Caucasian Americans. *Journal of Cross-Cultural Psychology* 10:41-56.

Sugiman, Pamela and H.K. Nishio. 1993. "Socialization and Cultural Duality among Aging Japanese Canadians." *Canadian Ethnic Studies* 15:17-35.

Sunahara, M. Ann. 1980. "Federal Policy and the Japanese Canadians: The Decision to Evacuate, 1942." In K.V. Ujimoto and G. Hirabayashi (eds.), *Visible Minorities and Multi-Multiculturalism: Asians in Canada.* Toronto: Butterworths.

Swan, Neil et al. 1991. *Economic and Social Impacts of Immigration.* A Research Report by the Economic Council of Canada. Ottawa: Supply and Services Canada.

Szapocznik, José, Mercedes A. Scopetta, William Kurtinez and Maria Aronalda. 1975. *Acculturation: Theory, Measurement and Clinical Implication.* ERIC Document Reproduction Service no. ED 191958.

———. 1978. "Theory and Measurement of Acculturation." *Interamerican Journal of Psychology* 12:113-30.

Taft, J.V. 1986. "Methodological Considerations in the Study of Immigrant Adaptation in Australia." *Australian Journal of Psychology* 38:339-46.

Taft, Ronald. 1957. "A Psychological Model for the Study of Social Assimilation." *Human Relations* 10:141-56.

Tan, Jin and Patricia E. Roy. 1985. *The Chinese in Canada: Canada's Ethnic Groups.* Booklet no. 9. Ottawa: Canadian Historical Association and Multiculturalism Program, Government of Canada.

Tandon, B. 1978. "Earning Differentials Among Native-Born and Foreign-Born Residents of Toronto." *International Migration Review* 12:3-15.

Tator, Carol, Frances Henry and Winston Mattis. 1998. *Challenging Racism in Cultural Production in Canada: Six Case Studies.* Toronto: University of Toronto Press.

Taylor, Charles. 1979. *Hegel and Modern Society.* Cambridge: Cambridge University Press.

———. 1985. "Atomism." In *Philosophical Papers,* vol. 2. Cambridge: Cambridge University Press.

———. 1995. "The Politics of Recognition." In Charles Taylor and Amy Gutman (eds.), *Multiculturalism: Examining the Politics of Recognition.* Princeton: Princeton University Press.

Taylor, D.M. and D.J. McKirnan. 1984. "A Five Stage Model of
Intergroup Relations." *British Journal of Social Psychology*
23:291-300.

Taylor, D.M., S.C. Wright, F.M. Moghaddam and R.N. Lalonde.
1990. "The Personal/Group Discrimination Discrepancy:
Perceiving My Group but Not Myself to be a Target for
Discrimination." *Personality and Social Psychology Bulletin*
16:245-62.

Taylor, D.M., S.C. Wright and K. Ruggiero. 1992. "The
Personal/Group Discrimination Discrepancy: Responses to
Experimentally Induced Personal and Group Discrimination."
Journal of Social Psychology 131:847-58.

Taylor, D.M., S.C. Wright and L.E. Porter. 1993. "Dimensions of
Perceived Discrimination: The Personal/Group Discrimination
Discrepancy." In M.P. Zanna and J.M. Olson (eds.), *The
Psychology of Prejudice: The Ontario Symposium*, vol. 7.
Montreal: McGill-Queen's University Press.

Taylor, D.M. and F.M. Moghaddam, eds. 1994. *Theories of Intergroup Relations: International Social Psychological Perspectives,*
2/e. New York: Praeger.

Taylor, Kate. 1993. "The Single-Minded Approach." *The Globe and
Mail* (Toronto). 25 October.

Tepper, E. 1980. "The Need to Know." In E. Tepper (ed.), *Southeast
Asian Exodus: From Tradition to Resettlement. Understanding
Refugees from Laos, Kampuchea and Vietnam in Canada.* Ottawa:
The Canadian Asian Studies Association.

Thomas, William I. and Forian Znaniecki. 1918. *The Polish Peasant
in Europe and America,* vols. 1-4. Boston: The Gorham Press.

Thornberry, Terence P., Alan J. Lizotte, Marvin D. Krohn, Margaret
Farnworth and Sung Joon Jang. 1991. "Testing Interactional
Theory: An Examination of Reciprocal Causal Relationships
among Family, School, and Delinquency." *Journal of Criminal
Law and Criminology* 82:3-35.

Thorogood, N. 1987. "Race, Class and Gender: The Politics of
Housework." In J. Brannen and G. Wilson (eds.), *Give and
Take in Families.* London: Allen & Unwin.

Tian, G. 1988. *Zhonggou Xibu Minzu Diqu de Duiwai Kaifang yu
Jinji Fazhan.* Beijing: Zhonggou Zhanwang Chubanshe.

———. 1993. "The Canadian Society and the New Immigrants
from Mainland China." *The Spring of China,* no. 8.

Tian, G. 1995. "Presenting New Selves in Canadian Context: The Adaptation Processes of Mainland Chinese Refugees in Metro Toronto." Ph.D. Thesis, York University, Toronto.

—— et al. 1988. *Xuanze yu Fazhan: Zhongguo Bufada Diqu Jinzi Zhenxin Duanxiang.* Beijing: Shishi Chubanshe.

——, S. Li, X. Liu. 1994. *The Mainland Chinese Refugees in Toronto: A Research Report.* Presented to the Hon. Sergio Marchi, Minister of Citizenship and Immigration, Canada. Ottawa: Supply and Services Canada.

Tinker, Hugh. 1974. *A New System of Slavery: The Export of Indian Labour Overseas, 1830-1920.* London/New York/ Bombay: Oxford University Press.

——. 1976. *Separate and Unequal: India and the Indians in the British Commonwealth, 1920-1950.* Vancouver: University of British Columbia Press.

Touliatos, John and Byron W. Lindholm. 1980. "Behavioral Disturbance in Children of Native-Born and Immigrant Parents." *Journal of Community Psychology* 8:28-33.

Training and Development Associates. 1992. *Report on Executive Interviews Conducted for the Visible Minority Consultation Group on Employment Equity.* Ottawa: Supply and Services Canada.

Treasury Board Secretariat. 1988. *On Target: Progress in Employment Equity in the Federal Public Service, 1985-1988.* Ottawa: Supply and Services Canada.

——. 1993. *Distortions in the Mirror.* Ottawa: Supply and Services Canada.

——. 1994. *Employment Equity in the Public Service: Annual Report, 1992-93.* Ottawa: Supply and Services Canada.

——. 1995. *Employment Equity in the Public Service: Annual Report, 1993-94.* Ottawa: Supply and Services Canada.

——. 1996. *Employment Equity in the Public Service: Annual Report, 1994-95.* Ottawa. Supply and Services Canada.

——. 1996. *Employment Equity in the Public Service: Annual Report, 1995-96.* Ottawa: Supply and Services Canada.

Tuzlak, Aysan Sev'er. 1989. "Joint Effects of Race and Confidence on Perceptions and Influence: Implications for Blacks in Decision-Making Positions." *Canadian Ethnic Studies* 21:103-19.

Ubale, Bhausaheb. 1977. *Equal Opportunity and Public Policy.* Toronto: Attorney General of Ontario, Queen's Printer.

Ujimoto, Victor K. 1983. "Institutional Controls and Their Impact on Japanese Canadian Social Relations, 1877-1977." In Peter S. Li and B. Singh Bolaria (eds), *Racial Minorities in Multicultural Canada*, Toronto: Garamond Press.

———. 1985. "Japanese." In Bolaria and Li (eds.), *Racial Oppression in Canada*. Toronto: Garamond Press.

——— and Gordon Hirabayashi. 1980. *Visible Minorities and Multiculturalism: Asians in Canada*. Toronto: Butterworths.

United States/Canada. 1993. *Challenges of Measuring an Ethnic World: Science, Politics and Reality*. Proceedings of the Joint Canada-U.S. Conference on the Measurement of Ethnicity, 1-3 April 1992. Ottawa/Washington, DC: Statistics Canada and the United States Bureau of the Census.

Vallee, Frank and John deVries. 1978. "Trends in Bilingualism in Canada." In J. Fishman (ed.), *Advances in the Study of Societal Multilingualism*. The Hague: Mouton.

Van den Berghe, Pierre L. 1981. *The Ethnic Phenomenon*. New York: Elsevier.

Van Dijk, Teun A. 1987. *Communicating Racism: Ethnic Prejudice in Thought and Talk*. Newbury Park, CA: Sage.

Vaughan, G.M. 1972. "Ethnic Awareness and Attitudes in New Zealand Children." In G.M. Vaughan (ed.), *Racial Issues in New Zealand: Problems and Insights*. Auckland: Akarana Press.

Verma, R.B.P. 1985. "Income of Asian Indians in Canada." *Population Review* 29:1-2.

——— and K.G. Basavarajappa. 1989. "Employment Income of Immigrants in Metropolitan Areas of Canada, 1980." *International Migration* 27:441-65.

Vincent, Pierre. 1994. *Immigration: Phénomène souhaitable et inévitable*. Montréal: Éditions Québec-Amérique.

Visible Minority Consultation Group on Employment Equity. 1992. *Breaking Through the Visibility Ceiling*. Ottawa: Treasury Board Secretariat.

Wahlsten, D. 1995. Review of "Race, Evolution and Behaviour" by J.P. Rushton. *Canadian Journal of Sociology* 20:129-33.

Waldinger, Roger et al. 1987. *The Economic Impact of the Entrepreneur Immigrant Program*. Ottawa: Institute for Research on Public Policy.

———. 1990. *Ethnic Entrepreneurs: Immigrant Business in Industrial Societies*. Newbury Park, CA: Sage.

Walker, James W. St. G. 1985. *The Black Identity in Nova Scotia: Community and Institutions in Historical Perspectives.* Dartmouth: Black Cultural Centre for Nova Scotia.

Walker, James. 1992. "South Asians in Canadian Immigration Policy: An Historical Overview." In Ratna Ghosh and Rabindra Kanungo (eds.), *South Asian Canadians: Current Issues in the Politics of Culture.* New Delhi: Shastri Indo-Canadian Institute.

Walzer, Michael. 1983. *Spheres of Justice: A Defense of Pluralism and Equality.* New York: Basic Books.

Wannell, Ted and Nathalie Caron. 1994. "A Look at Employment Equity Groups among Recent Postsecondary Graduates: Visible Minorities." *Aboriginal Peoples and their Activity Limited.* Ottawa: Statistics Canada, Supply and Services Canada.

Wargon, Sylvia. 1995. "History of Demography in Canada." Draft manuscript. Ottawa.

Weedon, C. and G. Jordan. 1995. *Cultural Politics: Gender, Race and the Post-Modern World.* Padstow, UK: T.J. Press.

Welte, John W. and Grace M. Barnes. 1987. "Alcohol Use among Adolescent Minority Groups." *Journal of Studies on Alcohol* 48:329-36.

West, Cornel. 1990. "The Cultural Politics of Difference." In Russell Ferguson, Martha Gever, Trinh T. Minh-ha and Cornel West (eds.), *Out There: Marginalization and Contemporary Cultures.* New York: The New Museum of Contemporary Art and MIT.

Wetherell, Margaret and Jonathon Potter. 1992. *Mapping the Language of Racism: Discourse and the Legitimisation of Exploitation.* London: Harvester Wheatsheaf.

White, Linda. (Undated). "Employment Equity: A Background Paper." Toronto: The National Conference on Racial Equality in the Workplace: Retrospect and Prospect. Unpublished.

White, Pamela M. 1988. "Testing 1991 Ethnic Ancestry, Ethnic Identity and Race Questions." Paper presented at the annual meeting of the Canadian Population Society. Windsor, ON: Statistics Canada mimeo.

———. 1990. "The Indo-Chinese in Canada." *Canadian Social Trends.* Autumn:7-10.

———. 1992. "Challenges in Measuring Canada's Ethnic Diversity." In Stella Hryniuk (ed.), *Twenty Years of Multiculturalism: Successes and Failures.* Winnipeg: St. Johns College Press.

White, Pamela M. 1993. "Measuring Ethnicity in the Canadian Censuses." In Gustave Goldman and Nampeo McKenney (eds.), *Challenges of Measuring an Ethnic World: Science, Politics and Reality*. Ottawa/Washington, DC: Statistics Canada and the United States Bureau of the Census.

————, Jane Badets and Viviane Renaud. 1993. "Measuring Ethnicity in Canadian Censuses." *Challenges of Measuring an Ethnic World*. Ottawa/Washington, DC: Statistics Canada and the United States Bureau of the Census.

White, R.W. 1974. "Strategies of Adaptation." In Coehlo et al. (eds.), *Coping and Adaptation*. New York: Basic Books.

Wiatrowski, Michael D., David B. Griswold and Mary K. Roberts. 1981. "Social Control Theory and Delinquency." *American Sociological Review* 46:525-42.

Wiley, Norbert F. 1967. "The Ethnic Mobility Trap and Stratification Theory." *Social Problems* 15:147-59.

Wilson, James R., Gerald E. McClearn and Ronald C. Johnson. 1978. "Ethnic Variation in Use and Effects of Alcohol." *Drug Alcohol Dependency* 3:147-51.

Wirth, Louis. 1928. *The Ghetto*. Chicago: University of Chicago Press.

Wong, Eugene F. 1985. "Asian American Middleman Minority Theory: The Framework of an American Myth." *The Journal of Ethnic Studies* 13:51-88.

Wright, S.C. 1993. "Tokenism: The Responses of Victims." Unpublished manuscript, University of Santa Cruz.

————. 1995. "Responding to Restricted Group Boundaries: An Analysis of Tokenism." Paper presented at the 5th International Conference on Social Justice Research, Reno, NV.

————, D.M. Taylor, F.M. Moghaddam. 1990. "Responding to Membership in a Disadvantaged Group: From Acceptance to Collective Protest." *Journal of Personality and Social Psychology* 58:994-1003.

Wright, S.C. and D.M. Taylor. 1992. "Success under Tokenism: Tokens as Barriers to or Agents of Social Change." Paper presented at American Psychological Association Annual Meeting, San Diego, CA.

————. 1997. "Responding to Tokenism: Individual Action in the Face of Collective Injustice." Paper under editorial review.

Yeung, P., ed. 1993. *Pacific Asians in the 21st Century: Geographical and Developmental Prospects.* Hong Kong: Chinese University Press.

Zarbaugh, Harvey. 1928. *The Gold Coast and the Slum.* Chicago: University of Chicago Press.

Zeitlin, Irving M. 1990. *Ideology and the Development of Sociological Theory.* Englewood Cliffs, NJ: Prentice-Hall.

Zheng, X. and J.W. Berry. 1991. "Psychological Adaptation of Chinese Sojourners in Canada." *International Journal of Psychology* 26:451-70.

Zwingmann, Charles. 1973. "The Nostalgic Phenomenon and its Exploitation." In C. Zwingmann and M. Pfister-Ammende (eds.), *Uprooting and After ... .* New York: Springer-Verlag.

INDEX